The Invention of Ethnicity

THE INVENTION OF ETHNICITY

Edited by Werner Sollors

New York   Oxford
OXFORD UNIVERSITY PRESS

Oxford University Press

Oxford   New York   Toronto
Delhi   Bombay   Calcutta   Madras   Karachi
Petaling Jaya   Singapore   Hong Kong   Tokyo
Nairobi   Dar es Salaam   Cape Town
Melbourne   Auckland

and associated companies in
Berlin   Ibadan

First published in 1989 by Oxford University Press, Inc.,
200 Madison Avenue, New York, New York 10016

First issued as an Oxford University Press paperback, 1991

Oxford is a registered trademark of Oxford University Press

Library of Congress Cataloging-in-Publication Data

The Invention of ethnicity / edited by Werner Sollors.
p.   cm. Bibliography: p.   Includes index.
ISBN 0-19-504589-0.
ISBN 0-19-505047-9 (pbk)
1. American literature—Minority authors—History and criticism.
2. Ethnicity in literature.   3. Ethnic groups in literature.
4. Minorities in literature.   I. Sollors, Werner.
PS153.M56158   1988   810'.9'920692—dc19   88-5963

9 8 7 6 5 4 3 2
Printed in the United States of America

Contents

ISHMAEL REED

On the Fourth of July in Sitka, 1982

On the fourth of July in Sitka
Filipinos sold shish-ka-bob from their
booths in the park
On the fourth of July in Sitka, the children
dressed in deerskin jackets
and coonskin caps
On the fourth of July in Sitka, you
could buy fishpie in the basement of St. Michael's
Church, where the vodka-drunken Russians used to
pray
But the red white and blue cake was not for sale

On the fourth of July in Sitka the people
kicked off shoes and ran through the
streets, pushing beds
On the fourth of July in Sitka, tour buses
with yellow snouts and square heads
delivered tourists to the Shee Atika lodge
where they stared at floats designed by
Sheldon Jackson College and
the Alaska Women in Timber
On the fourth of July in Sitka the
Gajaa Heeen dancers performed, wearing their
Klan emblems of Beaver Wolf Killer Whale
Porpoise, and Dog Salmon

On the fourth of July in Sitka the Libertarian
Party announced the winners of its five dollar raffle
1st Prize, a Winchester .300 Magnum
2nd Prize, an Ithaca 12 gauge shotgun
3rd Prize, a Sportsman III knife

On the fourth of July in Sitka the
softball teams were honored at the American
Legion Club and the players drank champagne till dawn

On the fourth of July in Sitka, the night was
speckled with Japanese fireworks
sponsored by Alaska Lumber and Pulp

On the fifth of July in Sitka
a Canadian destroyer brought to Sitka
for the fourth of July in Sitka sailed
through Sitka Sound and out into the
Northern Pacific
All of the men on board stood at
attention, saluting their audience
three bald eagles, two ravens, and me
watching the whole show from Davidoff Hill
the fifth of July in Sitka

Introduction: The Invention
of Ethnicity

WERNER SOLLORS

". . . it's just as I feared, my invented island is really taking its
place in world geography. Why, this island sounds very much like
the old Dahlberg place on Jackfish Island up on Rainy Lake, people say, and I wonder: can it be happening? Someone tells me: I
understand somebody bought the place recently and plans to fix it
up, maybe put a resort there or something. On *my* island? Extraordinary!—and yet it seems possible. I look on a map: yes, there's
Rainy Lake, there's Jackfish Island. Who invented this map? Well,
I must have, surely. And the Dahlbergs, too, of course, and the
people who told me about them. Yes, and perhaps tomorrow I will
invent Chicago and Jesus Christ and the history of the moon. Just
as I have invented you, dear reader, while lying here in the after-
noon sun, bedded deeply in the bluegreen grass like an old iron
poker . . ."

—Robert Coover, *"The Magic Poker"*

"That wasn't a custom," said Bak Goong. "We made it up. We
can make up customs because we're the founding ancestors of this
place."

—Maxine Hong Kingston, *China Men*[1]

If the titles of some publications of the past two decades and the arguments made recently by scholars in various disciplines are at all representative of a larger trend, the word "invention" has become a central term for our understanding of the universe. "Invention" is no
longer reserved for accounts of technological advances such as the
telegraph, or limited to neo-Aristotelian discussions of the relationship
of poetry and history or of originality and plagiarism.[2] Even a casual

glance at publications since the 1960s and at recent critical interventions reveals that a variety of voices now use the word in order to describe, analyze, or criticize such diverse phenomena as the invention of culture; of literary history; of narrative; of childhood as well as the loss of childhood; of adolescence; of motherhood; of kinship; of the self; of America; of New England; of Billy the Kid and the West; of the Negro; of the Indian; of the Jew; of Jesus and Christianity; of Athens; of the modern hospital; of the museum of science; of the 1920s in Paris; of our ability to "see" photographic pictures; of the vision of the outlaw in America; or of the American way of death. In view of such evidence, Jacques Derrida's observation—made in 1986 in a memorial address honoring Paul de Man—that "invention" has become a rather popular category in intellectual discourse seems, if anything, an understatement.[3]

The term "invention" is, however, not just part of a fad; and we would not be better off without this buzzword, which, after all, offers an adequate description of a profound change in modes of perception. The interpretation of previously "essentialist" categories (childhood, generations, romantic love, mental health, gender, region, history, biography, and so on) as "inventions" has resulted in the recognition of the general cultural constructedness of the modern world. What were the givens in intellectual pursuits until very recently have now become the problematic issues. At this juncture the category of "invention" has been stressed in order to emphasize not so much originality and innovation as the importance of *language* in the social construction of reality. Some postmodern discourse has gone so far as to let "reality" disappear behind an inventive language that dissembles it. Michel Foucault's attack upon the faith in value-neutral language for the human sciences has intensified the perception among humanists that, as Hayden White put it, "the very constitution of their field of study [is] a *poetic* act, a genuine 'making' or 'invention' of a domain of inquiry."[4] Whereas the Renaissance Aristotelians used "invention" to clarify and define the dividing line between history and literature and to assert individual ingenuity, postmodernists speak of "invention" in order to lay bare the textual strategies in the construction of the "individual" and to show the dependence of historiography upon the rhetorical devices of literature; they thus portray biography and historiography as forms of "fiction-making."[5] To use an example from another discipline, in *Writing Culture* the anthropologist James Clifford invokes Michel Foucault, Michel de Certeau, Gerard Genette, Hayden White, and Terry Eagleton, reminds ethnographers of the rhetorical

tradition of viewing texts as "composed of inventions rather than observed facts," and stresses the meaning of "inventing" as "making up
. . . things not actually real."[6] Clifford places his enterprise into a
"post-anthropological" and "post-literary" context, in which he may
regard ethnographies, too, as fictions.

What is one to do after such knowledge? In some disciplines reactions have set in that resemble Monsieur Jourdain's sudden recognition
in Molière's *Le Bourgeois Gentilhomme* (II,iv) that he had been speaking *prose* all along, without knowing it. If language and rhetoric become productive forces that constitute the ideological terms which
then appear to be the "natural" signposts in our universe, this results
in a strengthened emphasis on linguistics in all disciplines. Instead of
old-style "factual" studies, self-conscious exercises in describing all
the world as a text and everything in it as "signs" are on the rise.
Similarly, "authors" and "individuals" are, at times, replaced by neo-
essentialist battles between rhetorical categories such as metaphor and
metonymy. Is it possible to take the postmodern assault seriously and
yet to adhere to some notion of history and of individual and collective
life in the modern world? Can one speak of invention in such contexts?

The forces of modern life embodied by such terms as "ethnicity,"
"nationalism," or "race" can indeed by meaningfully discussed as "inventions." Of course, this usage is meant not to evoke a conspiratorial
interpretation of a manipulative inventor who single-handedly makes
ethnics out of unsuspecting subjects, but to suggest widely shared,
though intensely debated, collective fictions that are continually reinvented. The anthropologist Michael Fischer recently argued in his contribution to *Writing Culture*: "What the newer works [of American ethnic literature] bring home forcefully is . . . the paradoxical sense that
ethnicity is something reinvented and reinterpreted in each generation
by each individual and that it is often something quite puzzling to the
individual, something over which he or she lacks control."[7] Even more
suggestively, the political scientist Benedict Anderson has, in *Imagined Communities,* reflected upon the conditions under which modern
national and ethnic groups have been invented (or "imagined").[8]

Anderson invokes Ernest Gellner's memorable argument: "Nationalism is not the awakening of nations to self-consciousness; it *invents*
nations where they do not exist." It is this understanding of nationalism that could be helpful toward an interpretation of ethnicity, too. The
invention of nationalisms and ethnicities must have been peaking in the
eighteenth and nineteenth centuries, in a period of very dramatic
changes. Technological inventions such as the steamboat, the railroad,

the Gatling gun, and, especially, the advances in printing techniques had a direct bearing on ethnic migrations and confrontations. As Anderson argues, the European aristocratic order, based on directly related families, was challenged by the American and French revolutions and increasingly replaced by various national bourgeois systems, which relied on the more *imaginary* ways of connectedness that the new technologies provided. In the wake of this development the idea that nation, nationality, or ethnic belonging mattered a great deal for people became more and more widespread. Though the revolutionary ideals of *egalité* or the Declaration of Independence provided the popular slogans for the termination of aristocratic systems, new hierarchies immediately emerged, often in the name of ethnicity. The nation-state was viewed as an ideal, and ethnic homogeneity or racial purity was advocated by thinkers like Louis Agassiz and Arthur Gobineau. In the era of these new hierarchies, however, communities needed to create a sense of cohesion by what Benedict Anderson has termed "reverberation." The immediate connectedness of the aristocracy was replaced by a mediated form of cohesion that depended, among other things, on literacy and "national" (and ethnic) literatures. Communities by reverberation relied, as Anderson stresses, on texts and on words; and in this sense, they were "invented" communities. Nationalism needed a literature to be spread. With Anderson, who mentions Benjamin Franklin as the crucial founding father *and* printer, one might speak of a double quest for literacy and nationalism in the modern world. One may also say that nationalism and ethnicity may be the most successfully exported items from Revolutionary America and from Napoleonic and post-Napoleonic Europe—as, indeed, ethnocentrism may ironically have become one of the universals around the globe.

    The book that may be seen as a model collection for applying the concept of "invention" to a critical, yet eminently historical, study of nationalisms is Eric Hobsbawm and Terence Ranger's volume *The Invention of Tradition,* which focuses on the invention and diffusion of modern cultural symbols—not just such texts as "folk" ballads and anthems but also such nonverbal symbols as flags and imperial pageantry—in the name of supposedly ancient national and ethnic traditions. The various contributors to *The Invention of Tradition* emphasize the very recent (and highly inauthentic) emergence of such cultural features as the Scottish tartan and kilt or the Welsh love for music.[9] Many traditions turn out to be "neo-traditions" that are made up in order to make more palatable breaks with actual traditions or to substantiate politically motivated feelings of peoplehood. Eric Hobsbawm develops the central argument at the end of his introduction:

> modern nations and all their impedimenta generally claim to be the opposite of novel, namely rooted in the remotest antiquity, and the opposite of constructed, namely human communities so "natural" as to require no definition other than self-assertion. Whatever the historic or other continuities embedded in the modern concept of "France" and "the French"—and which nobody would seek to deny—these very concepts themselves must include a constructed or "invented" component. And just because so much of what subjectively makes up the modern "nation" consists of such constructs and is associated with appropriate and, in general, fairly recent symbols or suitably tailored discourse (such as "national history"), the national phenomenon cannot be adequately investigated without careful attention to the "invention of tradition."[10]

The implications of this approach to the concept of "invention" for studies of nationalism are both devastating and fruitful. Obviously, a change is required in the old approaches that take the language of the nation's quasi-eternity at face value and search, in each national and ethnic grouping, for the typical features that romanticism dictated a nation ought to have: folk and fairy tales, costumes, the vernacular, people's superstitions, an epic tradition, and so on—all of this as the "nourishing ground" for both high art and peoplehood. With the help of "invention" (in the Hobsbawmian sense) such investigations do not have to give way to vague discussions of ahistorical rhetorical patterns, but can now be historicized.

By calling ethnicity—that is, belonging and being perceived by others as belonging to an ethnic group—an "invention," one signals an interpretation in a modern and postmodern context. There is a certain, previously unrecognized, semantic legitimacy in insisting on this context. After all, (as far as I know,) the word "postmodern" first appeared in print in 1916 as part of Randolph Bourne's *ethnic* reflections on "Trans-National America"; and, tellingly, the word "ethnicity" first saw print in 1941, in a book by W. Lloyd Warner that had the adjective "modern" in its title.[11] Ethnicity would thus seem to make a perfect subject for a modern approach that utilizes the decoding techniques familiar from the scholarship of "invention." Yet by and large, studies tend less to set out to explore its construction than to take it for granted as a relatively fixed or, at least, a known and self-evident category. The traditional way of looking at ethnicity therefore still dominates. It rests on certain premises:

Ethnic groups are typically imagined as if they were natural, real,

[handwritten margin note: naturalization + reification of ethnicity]

eternal, stable, and static units. They seem to be always already in existence. As a subject of study, each group yields an essential continuum of certain myths and traits, or of human capital. The focus is on the group's preservation and survival, which appear threatened. Conflicts generally seem to emerge from the world outside of the particular ethnic group investigated. Assimilation is the foe of ethnicity; hence there are numerous polemics against the blandness of melting pot, mainstream, and majority culture (even though these polemics themselves surely must have cultural dominance at this moment in history). The studies that result from such premises typically lead to an isolationist, group-by-group approach that emphasizes "authenticity" and cultural heritage within the individual, somewhat idealized group—at the expense of more widely shared historical conditions and cultural features, of dynamic interaction and syncretism. Some challenges to this view may be expressed in the following set of questions:

Is not the ability of ethnicity to present (or invent) itself as a "natural" and timeless category the problem to be tackled? Are not ethnic groups part of the historical process, tied to the history of modern nationalism? Though they may pretend to be eternal and essential, are they not of rather recent origin and eminently pliable and unstable? Is not modernism an important *source* of ethnicity? Do not new ethnic groups continually emerge? Even where they exist over long time spans, do not ethnic groups constantly change and redefine themselves? What is the active contribution literature makes, as a productive force, to the emergence and maintenance of communities by reverberation and of ethnic distinctions? Are not the formulas of "originality" and "authenticity" in ethnic discourse a palpable legacy of European romanticism? How is the illusion of ethnic "authenticity" stylistically created in a text? Despite all the diatribes, is not the opposition between "pluralism" and "assimilation" a false one? Does not any "ethnic" system rely on an opposition to something "non-ethnic," and is not this very antithesis more important than the interchangeable content (of flags, anthems, and the applicable vernacular)?

Such questions are inspired by some newer anthropological, sociological, and historical thinking, according to which ethnicity is not so much an ancient and deep-seated force surviving from the historical past, but rather the modern and modernizing feature of a contrasting strategy that may be shared far beyond the boundaries within which it is claimed.[12] It marks an acquired modern sense of belonging that replaces visible, concrete communities whose kinship symbolism ethnicity may yet mobilize in order to appear more natural. The trick that it passes itself off as blood, as "thicker than water," should not mislead interpreters to take it at face value. It is not a thing but a process—and it requires constant detective work from readers, not a settling on a fixed encyclopedia of supposed cultural essentials.

Looking at ethnicity as modern does not imply that ethnic conflicts thereby appear less "real" simply because they may be based on an "invention," a cultural construction. It also does not suggest that ethnic consciousness is weak because there is much interaction and syncretistic borrowing at its core. The awareness of its modernity and transethnic interchangeability, however, may enrich our understanding of the ethnic phenomenon as well as of specific texts. After all, texts are not mere reflections of existing differences but also, among many other things, productive forces in nation-building enterprises. Of course, it must be possible to acknowledge and describe concrete ethnic differences without necessarily reifying the concept of ethnicity. However, focusing on the differences out of the historical context of their emergence and at the expense of transethnic similarities—even when this effort stems from an act of self-defense or from an understandable grudge against those who, out of bias or ignorance, would deny the validity of any ethnic enterprise or misinterpret it persistently—may be exactly what sets off the ethnic mechanism that George Devereux has termed "dissociation," of dividing the x's and y's (and finding the core essence of x-ness in "not being a y"). It may also do a disservice to the texts or ignore their dynamic potential.

Since the "vernacular" (a category that, of course, goes back to the replacement of Latin by local modern languages in European literature) has recently been placed in the foreground of some approaches to American ethnicity, let me offer an Afro-American illustration here. Zora Neale Hurston uses the beautiful phrase "percolate on down the avenue" in a short story that has both a precise sense of the idiom and an openness toward the modern context within which any vernacular articulates itself: "'But baby!' Jelly gasped. 'Dat shape you got on you! I bet the Coca Cola Company is paying you good money for the patent!'"[13] Hurston, who accompanies her text with a six-page glossary, undoubtedly manages to suggest a unique and very specific cultural timbre, and the title "Story in Harlem Slang" (first published in 1942) is fully justified. Yet it deserves notice that her effect of "authenticity" is achieved not by some purist, archival, or preservationist attitude toward a fixed past but by a remarkable openness toward the ability of a specific idiom to interact with "outside" signals and to incorporate them. In that way elements of a widely shared everyday life, like a humanized soft drink bottle, or a verbalized "percolator" (not exactly a traditional cultural staple, many past "coffee" associations and Bessie Smith's "brand new coffee grinder" notwithstanding), become "natural" and even central elements in the vernacular. It is the ethnic text's ability to generate the sense of difference out of a shared cultural context of coffeemakers and Coca Cola bottles that makes this example representative.

It is not any a priori cultural *difference* that makes ethnicity. "The Chinese laundryman does not learn his trade in China; there are no laundries in China." This the Chinese immigrant Lee Chew asserts in Hamilton Holt's *Life Stories of Undistinguished Americans* (1906).[14] One can hardly explain the prevalence of Chinese-American laundries by going back to Chinese history proper. It is always the specificity of power relations at a given historical moment and in a particular place that triggers off a strategy of pseudo-historical explanations that camouflage the inventive act itself.

This is true not only for mild forms of symbolic ethnic identification, but also for those virulent types of ethnocentrism which manifested themselves as racism. For example, when Henry W. Grady mapped out the essentials of the white Southerners' creed in 1885, he invoked a supposed two-thousand-year-old "race instinct" that militates against social mingling across racial boundaries—an instinct that he felt was "deeper than prejudice or pride, and bred in the bone and the blood." Yet since his political purpose lay in the justification of the modern legalization of racial segregation as the defeated white Southerners' self-defense against Northerners, Grady paradoxically also had to grant that he was speaking of this supposedly permanent "race instinct" as a modern political scheme invented to prevent "amalgamation." He tellingly defined the "race instinct" with the following anecdote:

> [Milhaud], in voting in the French Convention for the beheading of Louis XVI, said: "If death did not exist, it would be necessary to-day to invent it." So of this instinct. It is the pledge of the integrity of each race, and of peace between the races. Without it, there might be a breaking down of all lines of division and a thorough intermingling of whites and blacks.[15]

This line of reasoning—modeled upon an attempt at passing off an execution as a natural part of the life cycle—reveals that what is advocated in the name of immutable instincts belongs not to the realm of biology but to that of political history, especially of the period since the French Revolution.

Afro-American writers have been particularly astute in detecting the sinister implications of the invention of ethnic purity, passed off as natural. For example, Charles W. Chesnutt, the highly acclaimed author of such books as *The Conjure Woman* and *The Wife of His Youth* observed in 1905: "We are told that we must glory in our color and zealously guard it as a priceless heritage." Yet he did not endorse this admonition, and his comment deserves to be quoted at length:

> Frankly, I take no stock in this doctrine. It seems to me a modern invention of the white people to perpetuate the color line. It is they who preach it, and it is their racial integrity which they wish to preserve: they have never been unduly careful of the purity of the black race. . . . Why should a man be proud any more than he should be ashamed of a thing for which he is not at all responsible? . . . Are we to help the white people to build up walls between themselves and us to fence in a gloomy back yard for our descendents to play in?[16]

The subject of this volume is the investigation of some aspects of "ethnicity" as an "invention," with a strong focus on the United States, yet with larger implications. It is a collection of new essays and interpretations, all of which pursue the subject of ethnicity in a historical and dynamic context or, to put it differently, in a somewhat revisionistic fashion, whether the authors are inspired by postmodern debates or by Eric Hobsbawm's emphasis on "invention." In general, contributors here do not use ethnicity as a category that explains other phenomena but rather take it as that which needs to be understood and explained.

In his thoughtful personal account, "An American Writer," Richard Rodriguez provocatively emphasizes his polyethnic Spanish-Indian-African background. His version of Chicano identity, far from claiming any racial "purity" or any immediate access to "Mexican" identity, may yet be seen as the vanguard of a future American melting-pot identity. His statement was recently echoed by Virgil Elizondo, the Catholic priest of San Antonio Cathedral (Texas), who, in a book published in France with a preface by Léopold Sédar Senghor, proclaimed, "*L'avenir est au métissage*" (The future belongs to the mixture).[17]

In "A Plea for Fictional Histories and Old-Time Jewesses," the literary critic Alide Cagidemetrio pursues the Rebecca-Rowena motif from Sir Walter Scott's *Ivanhoe* across national and racial boundaries and shows how the historical pressures that led to the emergence (or invention) of the historical novel were translated into works of British as well as white, black, and women's literature in the United States, all of which tended to support divergent (yet structurally similar) myths of national births. In "Ethnicity as Festive Culture: Nineteenth-Century German America on Parade," the historian Kathleen Neils Conzen takes her rich materials on German festivals as an occasion to interpret German-Americans as participants in the invention of tradition, though the festive culture they invented assisted Americanization and thus precipitated their own obsolescence.

The historian Judith Stein focuses on the political construction of Afro-American peoplehood by leaders such as Edward Blyden, W. E. B. Du Bois, and, most centrally, Marcus Garvey. She shows in "Defining the Race, 1890–1930" that the concept of Afro-American "identity," even when its definers invoke history, may reflect *current* ideas from the larger culture more than the black past and its specific traditions. The scholar Mary Dearborn delineates the growth of a Jewish immigrant woman's identity as the result of interactions. "Anzia Yezierska and the Making of an Ethnic American Self" investigates the emergence of the writer's voice out of struggles with her father, with John Dewey, or with Hollywood, and against the expectation of a Cinderella story—which collapsed on the very terms upon which it had been constructed. Yezierska's case illustrates how an ethnic self-made woman may negotiate her identity by contrast, by public relations, and by inventing an appropriate age (in the way Zora Neale Hurston and Nella Larsen, too, imagined themselves publicly into different age groups). In "Deviant Girls and Dissatisfied Women: A Sociologist's Tale," the Americanist Carla Cappetti reads a work by the Chicago sociologist W. I. Thomas as an ambivalently allegorical representation of deviance. For Thomas—whose own academic career collapsed in the wake of a sexual scandal—the deviant revealed the constructed nature of moral rules and suggested a utopian freedom, yet it also symbolized degeneration and the need for social work.

The literary critic William Boelhower analyzes, in "Ethnic Trilogies: A Genealogical and Generational Poetics," the importance of a literary form—the trilogy—that came into great prominence in the Western world in the 1920s and 1930s (when Knut Hamsun, Sigrid Undset, Thomas Mann, and John Galsworthy were among the Nobel Prize winners). The trilogy particularly helped ethnic writers to incorporate the modern experiences of crisis and rupture into a genealogical framework that suggested continuity through what Boelhower terms the three master topics of construction, deconstruction, and reconstruction. The literary critic Thomas Ferraro reviews, in "Blood in the Marketplace: The Business of Family in the *Godfather* Narratives," the relationship of family life and criminal enterprise in contemporary books and films on the popular Mafia topic from *The Godfather* to *Prizzi's Honor.* He arrives at the conclusion that Mario Puzo, often maligned as a popular hack writer, has overcome the cliché of the supposed antithesis between "blood" and "marketplace" and shown their functional compatibility, a thesis Ferraro finds paralleled in Francis Ianni's work on organized crime.

The writer Albert Murray gives an account of his own role in the writing of an "as-told-to" autobiography. In "Comping for Count Basie," Murray gives a multilayered interpretation of Basie, as well as of his own cultural expectations. The essay is thus located in a framework of musical, artistic, and literary questions that provide an unusually rich historical context for an understanding of Basie's idiom and of the task of modern biographical writing. The collection ends with expanded statements of positions which initially emerged in a discussion at the First Annual Alaska Native Publishing Conference on the topic "Is Ethnicity Obsolete?" The postmodern writer Ishmael Reed sets the tone with his longer remarks on "America's 'Black-Only' Ethnicity," which stresses the voracious nature and dangerous ability of the American categories of "Black" and "White"—despite their blatant inadequacy to describe a highly miscegenated polyethnic culture—to devour all other ethnic differentiations. Reed's observations are followed by the comments of the Chinese-American novelist Shawn Wong, the Irish-American poet Bob Callahan, and the Tlingit poet Andrew Hope. A selective index listing the names of those discussed in the text was prepared by Sally Wyner who also proofread the galleys.

The contributions reflect a variety of styles and approaches, but they are held together by a common concern for the modernity of ethnicity. Although the contributors come from diverse age groups and national, cultural, and ethnic backgrounds, nobody claims to speak from a privileged "in-group" vantage point. Noteworthy is the effort of many contributors to place their subjects in larger historical (and that is also to say, transethnic, polyethnic, and international) contexts. In keeping with George Devereux' insight into the dissociative nature of ethnicity, the essays call attention to the larger systems within which ethnic distinctions emerge and obtain virulence: be they black-Indian-white encounters, Jewish-Gentile self-definitions, or male-female oppositions. Countervailing the folk beliefs (shared by some academics) in ethnic purity, "ethnicity" here typically emerges not as a thing (let alone a static, permanent or "pure" thing) but as the result of interactions.

Ethnicity does not serve as a totalizing metaphor but simply as a perspective onto psychological, historical, social, and cultural forces. The volume attempts no coverage, no ethnic or thematic comprehensiveness, but the presentation of new work and new ideas in a loosely chronological arrangement from *Ivanhoe* to *Prizzi's Honor,* and from nineteenth-century German ethnicity to a continuing American ethnic debate. All essays were completed in 1986.

While most contributors are literary critics and historians, the study of "the invention of ethnicity" is an interdisciplinary field; and it is hoped that the essays will also be useful to others. The inclusion of self-reflexive writers in this collection shows the ongoing process of inventing ethnicity. In this world of self-made ethnics and constructed births of nations it is important to keep remembering that rhetoric, texts, and literature are needed to naturalize these processes. Yet while linguistic elements play a central role in the construction of the social universe and while the old ethnic ontologies of "authentic cultures" are examined critically, language does not here emerge as the new *Ersatz* essence that would substitute for history, the individual, or the social realm. Finally, the essays collected in *The Invention of Ethnicity* promote neither ethnic consciousness nor assimilation but attempt to understand the processes that continue to give ethnic debates such a virulent centrality in the modern world—while appearing to stem from time immemorial.

The Invention of Ethnicity

An American Writer

RICHARD RODRIGUEZ

When I left California it was warm. The plane headed east, against the grain of America, into the dark. Nevada. Utah. Long shadows over Utah. Deep purple wells in the Rockies which seemed inverted afternoons.

The Asian businessman on the airplane borrowed my newspaper for a time. The stewardess, a black woman, brought us dinner. In Hartford, Connecticut, the blond lady at the Avis counter looked at me through green eyes. From where? Poland? Scotland? "Patty"—the label on her costume.

I end up here after a long journey talking about ethnicity and the American writer. Which is to say my ethnicity and the way it figures in my work as a writer.

Utah. Colorado. Nebraska. . . . The country slipping into darkness as I rode the jet stream east. Looking at the clouds far below, I remembered the Dutch sailors at the close of *The Great Gatsby,* staring west, their whispered surprise.

Shall I use this American voice of mine to speak of my difference from you? A few years ago, I published an autobiography, called *Hunger of Memory,* describing what happened to me when I was a boy; how I grew up Spanish-speaking (the son of Mexican immigrants); how Spanish remained my primary language until I was seven years old; how I rarely ventured among the gringos, feared their voices; and how, when the time came for school, I was terrified to find myself in a classroom, to hear my name pronounced in American for the very first time. *Rich-heard*.

I have written about my initial fear of English; how I clung to the skirts of Spanish. For six months the problem student, unresponsive, watching the clock on the wall. High-strung. Downcast. ("Stand up," the Irish nun said. "Speak up and don't just talk to me; say it to all the boys and girls.") I remained silent. Midway in my second year, my teachers and my parents conspired. My mother and father began to use English at home. At school the nuns insisted I use public English, language addressed to an audience of "boys and girls."

I have written about the slow, consequent change; my emergence as a brat. I determined to learn English, initially, as a way of hurting my parents, and I have written about how that determination led me out of my own house and over to yours. We lay on the floor, watching television together. I watched you. I sang your songs. I laughed at your jokes. I learned your games. I lingered until your mom invited me to stay for dinner. One day I lost my accent.

In certain ways, mine is a conventional American story. For generations, this has been the pattern: immigrants have arrived in the city, and the children of immigrant parents have gone off to school and come home speaking an American English.

Colorado. Iowa. Illinois.

Americans end up sounding like one another. Americans end up acting like one another. We do not, however, easily recognize our common identity. Partly because America is still young to itself, still forming, we are uncertain of our collaboration. We easily forget—what the rest of the world knows about us—that America exists as a culture. Americans look different from other people. (An arrogance, a naïveté.) If you were to stand with me on the Paseo de la Reforma in Mexico City, I could point out to you which persons passing were Mexicans and which were Mexican-Americans.

The relatives of immigrant children expect those children to remain as unchanged by America as they suppose themselves to be. Adults remember another place out loud. They remember persecutions and dead patriots from their oval frames. At large family picnics in summer, relatives laugh at familiar jokes, rekindle political fervor, reconstruct from memory a world where the very stones were as fragrant, as yielding, as the crusts of cakes. *"Cuando yo era niño . . ."* But the child sighs; his eye wanders away to the distance where some kids are playing baseball.

America is the country where one stops being German, stops being

Chinese. Where grandmothers stand at windows, mistrusting, deploring, partaking.

Against some guilty knowledge of loss, we celebrate our "ethnic diversity." We speak of this country as a place where we become Americans, yes, but Americans still tied to our separate pasts. America is constructed upon a paradox: individuality is the basis of our union. Diversity was a fierce conviction of America's founding fathers. Our national virtue is the Puritan virtue of tolerance. Americans have come to prize individuality, but without celebrating the other fact about ourselves, which is that we form a community.

I have come to this lecture room, to face a room full of strangers, to say that I am an American like you. Thomas Jefferson is my cultural forefather, not Benito Juárez. I claim Martin Luther King. And Walt Disney. And Lucille Ball. And Elvis Presley. And Benjamin Franklin. And Sister Mary Regis.

A simple claim to be an American can be regarded with suspicion. (Surely I am trying to deny something.) Since the 1960s, since the heroic black-civil-rights movement, a middle-class romance has flourished in America. We think we reclaim some stature due us insofar as we style ourselves outsiders. *"¡Viva la raza!"* It is, after all, a very old American reaction, this Protestant defiance of the melting pot.

The drama of my life was not an ethnic drama, but one of social class. Once upon a time the language I used at home was a rural Mexican Spanish, a working-class Spanish of limited vocabulary, which was playful, colloquial, richly emotional. Mine, I must stress, was an intensely private Spanish. It was a language rarely used in public by my family. Never a language of power. Spanish was a warm, an invisible fortress, an implacable feather held against you, you and your public English.

But then school, the sickening clock. When my first-grade teacher told me to speak out in a loud voice, and to speak to an audience of "boys and girls," I was not only unwilling to do so; I did not believe that I could use language publicly, that I could address an impersonal audience. The Spanish I had gathered at home was as different from conventional standard Spanish as Appalachian white English is different from the English used in the University of Virginia.

The writers who teach me best about the drama of my life are not American. They are British. (Perhaps in a society less racially diverse than ours, the British better realize that the greatest social division is economic.) I think of Raymond Williams. I think of Richard Hoggart (his wonderful book *The Uses of Literacy*). I think of D. H. Lawrence, especially Lawrence—the boy, the son of a coal miner; his mother a schoolteacher. I cannot imagine writing my own story without the example of Lawrence.

I recently heard Carlos Fuentes, the celebrated Mexican novelist, say in a television interview that he had been a bilingual child. Fuentes is the son of a Mexican diplomat. He grew up in Washington, the embassy city, a world of private schools. He may indeed have known something of the trauma of bilingualism, but his bilingualism was of a different order from that of a working-class child.

A friend of mine, a black woman who went to college in the fifties, tells me of her first summer vacation from college. School was Bryn Mawr; home was rural North Carolina. She remembers getting off the Greyhound. She remembers the weight of her pink valise. She remembers the waiting shadow of her mother beyond the screen door. As the screen door opened to claim her, she remembers her mother's voice: "I don't want you talkin' white in here."

I think of D. H. Lawrence. His mother spoke the clipped petit bourgeois English of a schoolmarm, which she had been; his father sounded a long, broad Derbyshire. The child was torn between the two sounds, which represented not just two ways of speaking but two versions of self, two societies.

It was a division Lawrence tried romantically to bridge in *Lady Chatterley's Lover*. In that novel, Mellors, the hero, wields a kind of social bilingualism. On the one hand, Mellors is capable of using the language of power, an upper-class British accent. He can therefore speak to Lady Chatterley as an equal. But at various places in the novel, Mellors defiantly reverts to a Derbyshire accent. It becomes his way of evading the world of upper-class English, of remaining different, superior.

There is an important American story to be told in the silence of summer vacations. The scholarship boy home for three months. But Americans are a busy, optimistic people. We are anxious for social mobility (we want to make more money than our parents; that is what our parents want for us too). We are a pragmatic people. At a time when so many children of working-class parents have gone off to college, at a time when so many of us are schooled to become different from our parents, when parents and children no longer share the hope of a future in common, I think it is no coincidence that there has been a middle-class chase for ethnic roots. Such a celebration of continuity becomes a denial of loss.

A graduate student tells me she intends next summer to interview various members of her Indian tribe in northern California. She says she wants to "preserve" the ancient stories that have passed through generations. I do not mock her intention. There is every humane and academic reason to encourage the project. But, I think, in its deepest ambition, such a project is doomed. The graduate student who lures an old woman's voice onto a sheet of paper or alchemizes that voice to a circle of magnetic tape has already altered the "story" she had intended to save. The tribal legend belongs to an oral-aural culture. It is, after all, a tribal story. It means something to the tribal daughter to whom it is directly addressed, something else to the scholar or to the anonymous reader who comes upon it in a university library. The point is simple. As the old woman's voice is passed in a little plastic box from one culture to another, the voice—the story it transmits—is changed, made curious for an impersonal public. The story has been saved only insofar as it has been withdrawn from life.

Consider the voice, this voice passing through a copper wire, an electrified pulse, that awakens a drum within a box, that in turn amplifies what is small and mortal to the proportion of a paid speech. I assume my place in your society. There was a time when things were very different for me. There was a time when I held on to my family's Spanish so as not to have to attend to you. A long time ago I was a child of the working class, a "minority" child, born into the culture of poverty. And I must not let you romanticize that child and his predicament. Listen to this voice and attend to the change.

At the same time that I stress the social change in my life, I admit to a continuity. Yes, my life was changed by education, but in some mysterious way, I am whole.

When I turned, a few years ago, to write an autobiography, I felt estranged from my past. Here I was, a man nearing midlife, so obviously different from the boy I had been. My life seemed rent in two. When I needed to understand why, I turned to autobiography.

Judged in one way, it was an audacious choice for someone like me. In the classical tradition, autobiography belongs solely to the heroic life, to the man of great deeds. Conventionally, too, we associate autobiography with the accomplished life. It is the genre of retirement—an old man or an old woman, turning to reflect on the whole of a life as, somewhere outside a chilly window, leaves fall down.

But autobiography seems to me appropriate to anyone who has suffered some startling change, a two-life lifetime; to anyone who is able to marvel at the sharp change in his life: I was there once, and now, my God, I am here! (. . . was blind but now I see.) Here is the reason so many modern writers of autobiography are newly of the middle class and the first in the family to graduate from college. Many of us are nonwhite adults in white America, once ghetto or barrio children. The autobiography becomes our first book, our first expression, our new voice in the new world.

Autobiography is the genre of the discontinuous life. Think of Augustine; the greatest example, the *Confessions*. The youthful sinner; the redeemed adult. The adult's voice remarking with irony. (The Pauline formulation so crucial to Protestant autobiographies of the seventeenth century, to Bunyan, to the novels of eighteenth-century England: "When I was a child, I spoke as a child, I understood as a child, I thought as a child; but when I became a man, I put away childish things. . . .")

Augustine remembers his past to divorce himself from it yet again, to strengthen resolve, reinforce new habit. This, surely, is one of the functions of autobiography; one remembers the past in order to relegate it. But there seems to me an opposite function of autobiography. One can remember the past as a means of finding connection, healing the break in the discontinuous life.

When I wrote my autobiography I was driven by both of these impulses. Initially I wanted to face the painful past, to confront the moment of fracture, in order to understand better the change in my life. I wrote my book, I should tell you, against my parents' wishes; against their wishes I had the book published. I did not forget in all those months of writing, writing in public English, that I was committing a new sin against my past. But if writing an autobiography forced me to confront the divorce between the Spanish-speaking boy and the English-speaking man, something else happened too. I sensed a continuity in my life. And now I have come to believe it; perhaps I need to believe it: the past survives in my life, though in mysterious ways, deeper than choosing.

Someone who has read *Hunger of Memory* and who knows my family well remarked to me one day, "When you write in English, you sound like your father speaking in Spanish." I laughed at the suggestion, though privately I wanted to believe it. Then, rereading my words, it seemed to me true. When I write in English, the hesitation, the syntax, the tone, does echo my father speaking in Spanish. My words are bathed with resignation, as are the words of my father.

Thus far I believe in the influence of ethnicity in my work as a writer, if such as I have mentioned can be what is meant by the term "ethnicity": memory, response, attitude, mood, coded into the soul, transmitted through generations. Defined this broadly, I suspect, ethnicity is only a public metaphor, like sexuality or age, for a knowledge that bewilders us.

The mystery of inheritance: the father looks into his son's eyes and sees his own grandfather. It would be interesting to think that I respond to color in ways that have to do with the landscape of my ancestors. Unconsciously, I suppose, I gesture with my hands in imitation of relatives who lie with hands folded under the ground. There may be a legacy in my speech. Linguists have told me that I will always be wedded to the lustrous Spanish-speaking world because Spanish was my milk tongue. My English will be forever influenced by a prescient Spanish.

I am preoccupied by the distinction between public and private society, a distinction introduced to me by the Spanish pronouns I grasped as a child, the difference between *tu* (the familiar "you") and *usted* (the formal address). The American "you" certainly held no such batonlike distinctions for me as a boy. The American "you" I was issued by my teachers, a pointer, seemed only as informal and as royally democratic as the people who used it. "You" became my teacher. "You" was my best friend. "You" could be my parents or the Catholic priest, or "you" could be the person I hated most at school. "You" was everybody.

I have recently visited Mexico and I have been thinking about Spanish pronouns, the way they seem to have structured the very dwellings of Mexico, hence the lives. Mexicans live behind walls; Mexicans are a people obsessed by privacy though Mexicans retire from dinner to walk the great public squares. A fountain plashes behind a wall. The gate becomes as much a lure as an obscuration. Cool passageways connect sun-filled patios. Formalities are protected by doors. Doors lie beyond doors. Different doors open for different visitors; relationships are developed in steps. Fragments of amber or of green glass are cemented onto the concrete wall along the back of the house to deter the intruder.

I was not conscious of it at the time, but the opening chapter of *Hunger of Memory*, the chapter about growing up bilingual, might have been written in imitation of Mexican architecture. There is everywhere in that chapter mention of windows and glass and screens and hallways and doors.

I might surprise, even offend, you by how inconveniently Mexican I can be. I am, for example, still very much influenced by Mexican Catholicism. But do not worry. I learned long ago to shield this particular inheritance from public view. At the dinner party in San Francisco or Berkeley—you know the sort—where opinion is as uniform as it is liberal, I politely keep my silence, hide my stern Mexican face, when the conversation turns to a subject like abortion.

And yet the people at those same parties would be the first to tell me that I should maintain my culture—whatever that means. I get the feeling that what people refer to as culture is something very simple. A tolerance for chili. A humor. Or an eye for the insistent color. When I was teaching at Berkeley a few years ago, an undergraduate approached me, cautiously, as if I were a stone totem, to say with no discernible trace of irony, "God, it must be cool to be related to Aztecs."

What can I tell you? My grandmother, the oldest relative I knew as a boy, was no sweet old lady. She wouldn't have liked most of you in this room. She was fierce. She didn't live in that enchanted chamber of Latin-American fiction, a room full of butterflies or refracting crystals. And she didn't float over the bed. She knew no secrets of the Mexican *bruja*. Her bureau was crowded with the statues of Christian saints. ("Don't lose your culture, whatever you do.") In fact, I worship at the altar where my grandmother worshipped.

As someone whose blood springs from Mexico, I am created by an assimilationist culture. Mexico, not the United States, is the true assimilationist example. Most Mexicans do not belong to a single race. Most are of mixed race, mestizo, Indian and Spanish both. Look at me! Look at this Indian face! Remember, however, that I carry a Spanish surname. My father is light-skinned. On my father's side of the family there is a bewildering attic tangle of French-speaking aunts; red-haired Jews forced out of Spain. Look at me! I have Indian eyes. But my mother's surname is Moran, which could be Irish, or it might be a variant from the Spanish word for dark, *moreno,* a hint of Africa in my blood.

Insofar as I am of Mexico, a man of several races, I am the product of a melting-pot culture. Say what you must about the Spanish colonial era; there was this extraordinary catholic achievement: races were mixed, first in rape, then in conversion and marriage, now in memory. Today 90 percent of Mexico is mestizo. By contrast, consider Puritan America: the Indian and the Pilgrim drew apart and have regarded each other with suspicion over centuries. It was in Puritan America that "diversity" became a national virtue, and miscegenation became a sin and a crime. Paradoxically, I remain truest to Mexico, least the American, when I accept the inevitability of assimilation in my life. I am most Mexican when I refuse to use the past as a shield against my new American influence.

I am of Mexico. I mean I retain aspects of culture, the deepest faiths and moods of my ancestors, an inheritance deeper sometimes than I dare reveal to you, formal you. Finally, however, I must return to my earlier admission. While Mexico survives in me, the air I breathe is America. I am one of you.

The immigrant child has the advantage or the burden of knowing what other children may more easily forget: a child, any child, necessarily lives in his own time, his own room. The child cannot have a life identical with that of his mother or his father. For the immigrant child this knowledge is inescapable. And often very, very sad. ("Speak to us in Spanish," the chorus of aunts used to say, "in Spanish." I was afraid to turn back.)

In this immigrant country, the differences among us will, I trust, always be apparent. But the most interesting thing about our separateness is that, finally, it has the possibility of being shared. We talk somberly about some threatening "bicultural" possibility, but the comic reality is that America is wildly, if reluctantly, multicultural. And what it means to be of America is that one shares in the riotous variety of memory.

I remember the Clunie Library in Sacramento. When I was a boy, a fellow with old men, on summer afternoons I'd read book after book, willing to make myself educated in alphabetical order. I remember one July reading William Saroyan, pleasing myself with the discovery that I understood Saroyan's life and his fictional universe. I was an Armenian from Fresno that day. I was a Negro reading James Baldwin. It came as no surprise, then, to learn that I was a New York Jew reading Alfred Kazin's *Walker in the City*. I stood in the railroad station in winter with Willa Cather's immigrants in *My Antonía*. and one day, late in summer, I came to Hannibal, Missouri. I trailed Huck Finn through a dense thicket of American dialect—it was too hard for me— until at some clearing of comprehension, I looked up and saw the great American river whole.

We say it so easily, so often it is pinned up on the library wall, that I wonder if we really believe it: Books open doors.

When I was a teenager in the 1960s, I began to notice the declarations of nonwhite writers and critics, their claim to a private ethnic genius: only a black person can write about black experience. Therefore only a black can evaluate another black writer. Soon, the assertion was enlarged. Only a Hispanic can write about matters Hispanic. Only a woman. . . . There are newspapers in this country, and magazines, whose editors automatically assign a book written by a black writer to a black writer for review. There is a bookstore in San Francisco that has sexually divided the literature of the world. There is a freestanding male-literature section on one aisle, which runs headlong into a sort of Virginia Woolf lady chapel at the rear.

Richard Rodriguez (Hispanic, male) gets shelved in that section of the bookstore reserved for miscellaneous boogaloo—ethnic literature. Richard Rodriguez gets reviewed by Hispanic-American literary critics. Richard Rodriguez, I must add, gets published and reviewed. I am accorded attention as a writer for reasons that have more to do with the chic of ethnicity than with literary skill.

It was front-page news in the *New York Times* two years ago when Danny Santiago, the author of *Famous All Over Town,* a comic novel of Mexican Los Angeles, turned out to be Daniel James. Mr. James is not of Mexican descent; he is a man in his seventies, who lives in a grand house in Carmel, California. It should not have been news that Daniel James writes so well about life in East LA. The writer, any true writer, is gifted with an imagination larger than can be contained by any one neighborhood.

Within any one neighborhood, moreover, the reader must feel he has lived a lifetime or the writer will have failed. It is disappointing for me to find that some of my readers take me for a kind of sociologist. From letters I get and from reviews, I gather that some readers suppose I am trying to describe "the Mexican-American experience." In fact, I abhor the notion of a typical life. The sociologist may seek to build an average Mexican-American from statistical data. As a writer, I am after something more humble. Something large. When I rehearse my life, I describe one life only, my own. Richard Rodriguez, not even his brother, not his sisters. One childhood: that summer in 1955. August. One street in Sacramento, California, Thirty-ninth Street near "J". One yellow house. One solitude.

The magnifying power of literature is exactitude. In Jane Austen. Proust. In Dickens. The characters one remembers best are not typical; just the opposite—they are specific, they are unforgettable. The writer describes the special past of a character, the singular experience. Paris, a window, not a big window, a hanging lamp, a lamp of brass, a green baize table, a string of pearls, pinkish pearls, a hand, a spotted hand. The more specific a writer becomes, the more a text resonates. By always rejecting the notion of typicality, the writer may achieve universality.

Those letters which please me most express a reader's surprise that he can respond to my life. "You won't believe this—I am a fifth-generation American, I've spoken English all my life—but I think I understand what you went through as a bilingual child."

The reason that we respond to an individualized life in literature is that we all feel so alone. (Which is the reason that Puritans were such good novelists.) We are moved by the spectacle of a character bounded by absolute particularity. "Not even a sparrow falls. . . . " Oh, what hope to believe that; and in literature we draw near to consolation.

I was a boy. Short. Fat. I kept to myself. Coveted. I did not go to the junior prom. I was dark and thought myself ugly in a world that rewarded blondness. There were times when I desperately wanted to look like my brother (who, we all thought, looked like Mario Lanza). I kept company with books. I was camouflaged—I did not know it—and the active life passed over me.

Many years afterward, I became a writer because I hungered for communal assurance. Applause. The good review. It was your understanding that I desired. Some way out of the single life. So I wrote of my Mexican house, but in the words of the city.

I end up here. I end up speaking your language, not the language of my early childhood. I end up telling you things I don't tell my own relatives. You—strangers—hold my polished secrets in your silent stare.

Illinois. Ohio. Pennsylvania. I am moved by the landscape of the American soul. I look at your faces, so varied, so different, many of them, from mine. Where are you from? And how long has it taken for you to get here? How many generations are you away from a rural past or a ghetto?

I am an American only one generation from small Mexican towns that I can scarcely imagine. (I imagine church bells; I imagine footfalls on dust.) The tangle of desire with nostalgia and regret that my mother and father express to me in their old age—these attentions connect me to my Mexican past. But slowly that past recedes into silence. Until there is only their son speaking American English through his microphone. In a room full of strangers.

This is the American city.

A Plea for Fictional Histories and Old-Time "Jewesses"

ALIDE CAGIDEMETRIO

Was the Face of the Earth vacant of other Plants, it might be gradually sowed and overspread with one kind only; as, for Instance
with Fennel; and were it empty of other Inhabitants, it might in a
few Ages be replenish'd from one Nation only; as, for Instance,
with *Englishmen*.
—BENJAMIN FRANKLIN

Like the feudal princes of the old world, they fought among themselves, and exercised most of the other privileges of sovereignty.
Still they admitted the claims of a common origin, a similar language, and of that moral interest, which was so faithfully and so
wonderfully transmitted through their traditions.
—JAMES FENIMORE COOPER

In his influential book *The Rise of the Novel* (1957), Ian Watt invents
the modern novel tradition as the result of the eighteenth-century "realistic" interchange between society and its description, as a discourse
of class shaped through a recognizable contemporary, objectual, and
psychological depiction. Georg Lukács's *Historical Novel* (1937)
moves the birth of the modern novel, within a stricter class perspective, on to Walter Scott's prototypical historical novel. Lukács's focus
on history suggests that no contemporaneity can be written about or
understood without the recognition of the process that formed it in the
past and is still active in the present.

Both Watt's and Lukács's are pleas for the invention of a tradition

14

of the "modern." Watt's title implies a beginning, genetically oriented criticism in the make-it-new line of interpretation prevalent in modernism. Lukács consistently explores the genesis of the bourgeois discourse, the building up of its hegemony. Unlike Watt, he recognizes modernity not in the perception of contemporaneity alone but in the interchange between contemporaneity and history. Lukács's meaningful past, his modern novel tradition, couples "realism" with the representation of peoples and nations, as representative conflictual subjects of the modern novel. Ultimately he points to a field of investigation for a diachronical perspective of the invention of ethnicity. The centrality of the lesson of the past and a plausible beginning for a novelistic tradition of ethnic representation seem to coincide in historical fictions.

If modernity and modern issues arise from the so-called revolutionary era, from the time of the American and French revolutions, the "classic" historical novel opens up the world of modern representation; and as such it explores, works through, affirms and denies, and finally forges our "archetypal" discourse of national identity and national culture.

If modernity is already a tradition for us postmodern inventors of ethnicity, why not recognize that modernity for our recent modern ancestors, Marx and Freud, meant to build it up on the past itself, be it socioeconomical or psychological?

What follows is an attempt at reconstructing through a limited number of novels, published within a short span of time—the 1820s—the workings of historical fictions as nation-building discourses. The underlying analytical principle is that any discourse is the outcome of a compromise between opposite or contradictory drives, like amalgamation and rejection, acceptance and denial, or attraction and repulsion.

The main focus is on James Fenimore Cooper and the "Indian problem," historically the earliest instance of the "alien" as the fit subject for those fictions that proudly presented themselves as "American tales" and that were written by proud, sometimes anonymous, American ladies and gentlemen.

The generative archetype of archetypes is identified in Walter Scott's *Ivanhoe*. Because it is both an obvious choice and a much condemned novel, *Ivanhoe* is rarely taken seriously, at least in an American literary context. Its influence was downplayed to the point that Cooper reports he used only its *size* as a model for the total number of pages of his first novel.

Anglo-American Rebeccas

In the introduction to *Ivanhoe* (1819) for his edition of the Waverley Novels, Walter Scott pointed out two issues that were then, and have been since, the object of much debate. One is the choice of an English setting and a remote time; the other, the final casting aside of Rebecca, the beautiful Jewess, as a suitable match for the Christian hero Ivanhoe.[1] To the first, Scott replied to the effect that the historical novel was not of Scotland but of every nation; to the second, with reasons that apply to the concept of verisimilitude—the mésalliance was clear in itself, common sense. Yet *Ivanhoe* provides an interesting insight into the not altogether clear relation between nation, race, and the actual making of historical consciousness. "It seemed to the author," Scott writes, "that the existence of the two races in the same country . . . might, intermixed with other characters belonging to the same time and country, interest the reader by the contrast. . . . "[2] Race here is a concept of descent, as Diderot's *Encyclopédie* would have it: *"Extraction, lignée, lignage, ce qui se dit des ascendans que des descendans d'une même famille: quand elle est noble, ce mot est synonyme à naissance."* In *Ivanhoe* the two races are represented by the noble descendants of the Saxons and Normans, while the others "belonging to the same time and country" are mainly the Jew Isaac, his daughter Rebecca, and a few Saracens in the retinue of Brian de Bois Guilbert, the Templar, who, by becoming such has renounced his family and homeland. The avoided contrast of the novel is between Normans and Saxons, the latter well suited to meet Georg Lukács's idea of a decayed gentility overrun by a more powerful and of "necessity" victorious historical force.[3] King Richard will unify his kingdom and defeat his brother John's schemes; the Saxons will consent to honor a sovereign of another race. Cedric, the Saxon loyalist par excellence, pledges himself a faithful subject and restores both family name and fiancée to his son Ivanhoe, whom he had formerly disinherited because of his alliance to the Norman king. Often the plot of the historical novel devises an original complication in the lovers' separation because of their families' siding with opposite historical parties at the moment of their collision. The Romeo-and-Juliet pattern was intensified by the actual conflict that has taken place in the reader's recorded past. The happy ending thus sanctions the solution of a historical crisis. Scott, however, considered it an allowance to the fictional expectations of his neurotic female audience rather than a fit answer to the novel's ambitious discourse on history. The patched-up conclusion of *Old Mortality* (1816), soon to be followed by the gloomy ending of *The Bride of Lammermoor* (1819), is denounced by Scott and ironically redeemed through the staging of a dialogue between the narrator and the reader, as represented by Miss Martha Buskbody, whose experience ranges "through the whole stock of three circulating libraries." "You may be as harrowing to our nerves as you will in the course of your story," but, the worthy lady advises, "never let the end be altogether over-clouded."[4] In his Scottish novels English heroes do usually marry Scottish heroines. Race as descent, as purity of lineage, is finally defeated by their "mixed" marriage, and a new nation of polyethnic descent is to be expected. The future of their progeny is already the past for the reader; their birth dates lie somewhere between the past of the narration and the present of author and readers. The British baronet Walter Scott suggests that the real crisis that is past is the one that led to the acceptance of a new concept of nation, of the compromise between genealogical, aristocratic, exceptionalist community values and a consent-based society. The Glorious Revolution had imposed a pact, a covenant, upon the laws of descent: the final point that, neurotically or ideally, the novel can make is a good wedding, implying consent,[5] even if at the price of violence, war, and bloody strifes, which nonetheless have to be staged and not repressed if old-party nationalistic oppositions are to be cleared out of the reader's way. Those proud British subjects could project themselves, in and out of the fictional world, as the direct consenting descendants of a Waverley marriage in a unified nation coming out victorious from the Napoleonic Wars and sailing toward the prosperous waters of the Victorian era.

D. W. Griffith's silent film *Birth of a Nation* (1915) clearly uses a self-reflexive title, looking back to a well-established tradition, to a demand that arose in the postrevolutionary years of the early nineteenth century. It was then, as Alexander Welsh has pointed out, that the need was felt for the novel to project "an affirmative and permanent ideal of society," or, as John C. Dunlop put it in his *History of Fiction,* published in the same year as *Waverley* (1814), the novel is superior to both poetry and history because it allows a deeper insight into any people's "prevalent mode of thinking," into "their feelings and tastes and habits"—fiction thus becoming an indispensable means to describe the workings of individual and society and the formation of national cultures.[6] Those who cried for a "national" literature in the newly born United States of America were the same persons who praised these "modern" tales. Following Dunlop's argument, W. H. Gardiner maintained, in the influential *North American Review,* that "the characters of fiction should be descriptive of classes, and not of individuals," and that American society would certainly fit modern demands because of its unprecedented variety of races.[7] Interestingly enough, the American critics mainly discussed Scott as the author of the Waverley type of romance, while *Ivanhoe*—the novel that, in addition to Saxons and Normans, includes Jews, Saracens, and Brian de Bois Guilbert, a man without a nation—was less frequently invoked. *Ivanhoe*'s American reviewers, echoing their British colleagues, sentimentally complained about Rebecca's fate and overlooked the switching of the novel's conflict from Saxons and Normans to Jews and Gentiles.[8]

Yet the conflict between Jews and Gentiles, unresolved as it is by the ending, proves to be the more powerful shaping force in the novel. No real obstacle hinders the birth of the nation as the fusion of Saxons and Normans. Cedric, Ivanhoe's loyalist father, is not a true opponent, because of his unrelieved stubbornness and his inability to see the ludicrous anachronism of Athelstane, the Saxon pretender. On the other hand, Richard is consistently portrayed as a legitimate king. From the beginning, Ivanhoe, in contrast to the Waverley heroes, is on the king's side, making it clear that, though Saxon by birth, he is English at heart, thus embodying the very idea of the nation's birth. What is tested in the novel, then, is the applicability of this idea to characters of a different "race," to types whose racial traits are semantically linked not only to concepts of *lignage* but also to cultural and, one suspects, biological differences.

In the novel, Rebecca plays the role of the healer for the hero; she is in turn rescued by him when a champion is needed to clear her of a witchcraft charge. In "the judgement of God," Ivanhoe defeats Brian, whose sinful lust for the dark heroine makes the Saxon hero's purity even more compatible with Rebecca's. But in vain: notwithstanding the plot's logic, they still end up going their separate ways. Moreover, it is Rebecca who speaks of herself as English. "I am of England," she says to Ivanhoe, "and speak the English tongue, although my dress and lineage belong to another climate" (267). She posits herself as the conscious double of Ivanhoe, but hers is a very successful compromise between "dress and lineage" on the one hand and tongue and Englishness on the other. She identifies herself with a geographical entity (England) and its national expression (the English tongue). Both geography and language play an essential role in the representation of nation building. Historical detail matches geographical detail, and geographical descriptions function as the setting of the national past that can be verified in the reader's present. To build up a national geography was as necessary as to give distinct national features to the distant or recent past. The "authentic" English landscape is such because the aura of a recognizable past shapes it, and, conversely, national history fixes its space and boundaries in an actual physical reality.[9] Rebecca's Englishness makes her part of national history and geography, that is, of the "authentic" or "authenticating" strategies of the novel. And authentic she must have sounded to contemporary readers, since they too sided with her and expected her to marry the hero, and so recognized their national community identity in the beautiful Jewess. Yet, according to historical verisimilitude, Rebecca and Ivanhoe, the Jewess and the Christian Crusader, "ought never to have met," as Edgar Rosenberg has written.[10] Paradoxically, what is not historically true or plausible is perceived to be true and plausible in the nineteenth-century reader's response. In the dialectic between past and present values, Rebecca consistently embodies contemporary England much more than does the novel's canonic mediator, Ivanhoe. The hero, not to speak of the other characters in the novel, is hopelessly bound to past ideals of self-inflated heroism, based upon a misplaced antiquarian feeling of obsolete chivalry:

> "What remains?" cried Ivanhoe; "Glory, maiden, glory! which gilds our sepulchre and embalms our name."
> "Glory?" continued Rebecca; "alas, is the rusted mail which hangs as a hatchment over the champion's dim and mouldering tomb—is the defaced sculpture of the inscription which the ignorant monk can hardly read to the inquiring pilgrim—are these sufficient rewards for the sacrifice of every kindly affection, for a life spent miserably that ye may make the others miserable? Or is there such virtue in the rude rhymes of a wandering bard, that domestic love, kindly affection, peace and happiness, are so wildly bartered, to become the hero of those ballads which vagabond minstrels sing to drunken churls over their evening ale?" (283)

The Jewess challenges Ivanhoe by suggesting how ludicrous chivalry can be compared with the happiness of domesticity. Her argument parallels many of Scott's polemical declarations against antiquarianism in his own time. Certainly, the "ignorant monk" and the "inquiring pilgrim" are modern rather than medieval figures, and family happiness could hardly be proved a much-discussed topic in Ivanhoe's time. Scott's readers undoubtedly would have agreed on leaving behind unproductive idealism in the name of their own, bourgeois standards of loyalties and affections. As for Ivanhoe, he resembles one of those very ruins of the past, the "mouldering tomb," which had formed the

delight of Gothic novels. Rebecca's fate is to become a virtuous spin-
ster dedicated to good deeds, the "medieval" counterpart of many
nineteenth-century sisters. A contemporary reviewer noted indeed
that, in remote medieval times, "no Rebecca could either have acquired her delicacy, or preserved her honour." The author may therefore "be allowed to have had some scope for his inventions" beyond
the principles of historical verisimilitude.[11] With Rebecca, Scott does
expose the fake representation of the past and clearly establishes the
supremacy of the present in the texture of the historical-novel discourse: discourse of ambiguity that both makes a Jewess representative of nineteenth-century national values and denies that representative quality when resorting to the otherwise forgotten principle of
historical verisimilitude. Ivanhoe goes back to his blood by marrying
the fine Rowena, and Rebecca in the same mechanical way chooses to
return to the laws of her fathers. The plot simply could not sanction
the discourse of the present with the promise of a fused Jewish-English
identity. In making a Jewess his heroine, Scott ultimately unveils what
is kept hidden in the contemporary progressive and magnificent story
of a national fusion.

Every birth of a nation has its imperfect workings, as is further confirmed by the real life and deeds of Rebecca's own prototype, who, as
Scottian lore has it, was an American Jewess, Rebecca Gratz. Born in
Philadelphia, from a well-to-do family of truly American "merchant
venturers,"[12] she was a close friend of Mathilda Hoffman, Washington
Irving's lost love. Apparently it was Irving who described her character to the Scottish novelist. Sending him *Ivanhoe*'s first edition, Scott
wrote, "How do you like your Rebecca? Does the Rebecca I have pic-
tured compare well with the pattern given?"[13] And Miss Gratz, an ardent admirer of the Great Unknown, commented on reading the novel,

> [S]he is just such a representation of a good girl as I think human nature
> can reach—Ivanhoe's insensibility to her, you must recollect, may be
> accounted to his previous attachment—his prejudice was a characteristic
> of the age he lived in—he fought for Rebecca, tho' he despised her race—
> the veil that is drawn over her feelings was necessary to the fable, and
> the beautiful sensibility of hers, so regulated, yet so intense, might show
> the triumph of faith over human affections. I have dwelt on this character
> as we sometimes do on an exquisite painting until the canvass seems to
> breathe and we believe it is life.[14]

Rebecca Gratz, herself a good girl, had, prior to *Ivanhoe*'s Rebecca,
nourished a "noble affection" for one of her innumerable American

suitors but renounced him out of loyalty to her ancestral faith and "wedded herself to the most varied acts of philanthropy, and the rest of her career became one long chain of golden deeds."[15] Even long after the publication of *Ivanhoe*, Miss Gratz stuck to the Rebecca pattern and provided a wonderful example of racial heroism. All-American as she proved to be, she still confirmed the ban on sexual mixing with the Other. In a recent fictional biography addressed to young Jewish girls and tellingly entitled *Pattern for a Heroine* (1967), Miss Gratz, when confronted with the possibility of marrying the attractive American Gentile, is made to say, "Would my Jewish children regard their father as an outsider? Or would your Christian children have reason to be ashamed of their mother's alien faith?"[16]

Old-time beautiful Jewesses do indeed upset a discourse of fusion and amalgamation: Scott's Rebecca and her possible American prototype suggest a curious adaptation of the Wandering Jew type. Its transgressive potentiality is grounded in a historical discourse, thus making the type a figure of the alien within a national community. The alien both belongs to it and perceives himself as doomed to be different. National identity is both confirmed and challenged within its own accepted and codified principles of equality, without which no difference could arise. The Wandering Jew thus shows the failure of any project of unified identity when it suppresses either sameness or difference. The rhetoric of the historical novel does indeed attempt to naturalize both sameness and difference as a family compromise, a final wedding. Taking the past as its subject matter, it stages—as Lukács suggested—the time of a crisis whose outcome has already been sanctioned by history: the fusion of Saxons and Normans, as well as the unification of the British kingdom and, in the New World, the egalitarian birth of a new nation. Yet, paradigmatically, the crisis is *not* overcome; it is instead projected onto the present—happy endings notwithstanding—because of the structural recognition of the dialectic past/present, sameness/difference. English and Scottish peoples (like the immigrants of America) are represented as both nationally rooted in past national difference and in present British (or American) equality. The tension between past and present is ultimately the tension between alien and equal. It is that same tension that shapes Rebecca's character and role in *Ivanhoe*. She is not the result of an unfortunate character treatment, of a faulty, inartistic handling of plot; rather, she is the meaningful representation of the postrevolutionary, post-Napoleonic dilemma of national identity, the very embodiment of the historical novel's paradigm.

Rebecca's difference, her Jewishness, is presented as a cultural and religious tradition and as exoticism. But the exotic is conveniently transposed from distant lands to southern England and made to coexist with the indigenous. Her ravishing beauty, exotic as it is, stands out as the mysterious and seductive component of the Other, and Scott suggests that the recollection of it might have recurred in Ivanhoe's mind "more frequently than the fair descendant of Alfred might altogether have approved." The Wandering Jew, turned female and British, haunts man's dreams. Sexual attraction is introduced as the personal side of the national-historical alien/equal theme. Desired and forbidden, Rebecca is also the prototype of the American Other, or of the Other Americans, as Charles W. Chesnutt openly recognized in his historical novel *The House behind the Cedars* (1900). At the turn of the twentieth century, Chesnutt acknowledged the import of Scott's American tradition and paid his debt to *Ivanhoe*. The novel opens with a tournament scene that, though a much condemned southern, Scott-ridden, post—Civil War reality,[17] proves to be an essential frame of reference for the novel's main theme: the "passing" for white of the mulatto heroine and her brother. "Adapted to a different age and civilization," Rebecca is transformed into a white-black girl whose name is, for those telling symmetries of intertextuality, Miss Rowena Warwick.[18] As Rowena, and like Rowena, she is crowned Queen of Love and Beauty by George Tryon, a real southern gentleman, and a fit descendant of Ivanhoe. Chesnutt ironically stresses the girl's misplacement with direct allusions to Scott's Rebecca. In *Ivanhoe*'s tournament scene, Scott has Rebecca sit in the lower section of the gallery and Rowena in the higher and more dignified section. Similarly, Chesnutt has his Rowena sitting among "the best people" in the "grand stand," while "the poorer white and colored folks found seats outside." When it comes to the appreciation of the ladies' beauty, object of Prince John's sneering tirade in *Ivanhoe,* a young spectator in Chesnutt's novel comments, "[T]here are six Rebeccas and eight Rowenas . . . in the grand stand." And to end it all, John Warwick names the gallant knight to his sister, adding, "[I]f George were but masked and you veiled we should have a romantic situation—you the mysterious damsel in distress, he the unknown champion. The parallel, my dear, might be not so hard to draw, even as things are."[19]

"She should have been named Rebecca instead of Rowena," an Anglo-Saxon southern belle tells George Tryon, in anticipation of his discovery, only a chapter later, of Rowena's black blood and of his consequent refusal of her as his prospective bride and his children's mother. "No Southerner who loved his poor downtrodden country, or his race, the proud Anglo-Saxon race which traced the clear stream of its blood to the cavaliers of England, could tolerate the idea that even in distant generations that unsullied current could be polluted by the blood of slaves" (130–31). Chesnutt's intertextual irony goes as far as recalling England's cavaliers as the foundation of the southern miscegenation horror. "I shall never marry any man. . . . God is against it; I'll stay with my own people" (162): in the ravagingly beautiful octoroon's drama, Miss Rowena Warwick cannot but resort to race pride and wed herself to philanthropy, teaching little black urchins in a country school. And die shortly thereafter of a brain fever.[20]

Translation and Amalgamation

The birth of a nation of mixed descent was a threatening issue and still seems to be so now that the nation has come of age. Alternating modes of homogenization and rejection characterize the representation of racial relationships in the American historical novel. Amalgamation becomes a conflictual fictional issue when the novel opens up the province of representation to ethnicities and is at the same time bound to differentiate between ethnics as people of European descent and others—namely, Jews, blacks, and natives.

W. H. Gardiner's pride in America as the land of possibility for the modern heterogeneous homogenizable representation of the historical novel finds an obvious answer in James Fenimore Cooper: his "strange mixture of men of all countries" sounded distinctly American to a reviewer of *The Pioneers*,[21] as it still recently sounded to Kay Seymour House in her study *Cooper's Americans* (1965). Tellingly, Cooper's characters can be indifferently called by their proper names or by their nationality in descent. Their language, according to the craving for authenticity brought about by the "modern" novel, is diversified. It presents both descent languages, such as French or German, and their naturalization into English in terms of translation, or language mimicry, like that of blacks, whose distortions are often pushed to the extreme of comic nonsense. This is a feature they tend to share with the Irish, who in *The Spy* take the shape of Betty Flanagan, a fit counterpart of the Scottish-speaking low types in the Waverley Novels. As for the Indians, their dialect, unknown to large audiences, is constantly being referred to and is translated into either a highly figurative or an ungrammatical English. The power of Indian rhetoric—whose passionate defense was undertaken by John Heckewelder in his *Historical Ac-*

count of the Indian Nations (1819), with the evidence of Indian meta-
phors and sayings and their relative translation—is also mimetically
rendered in the speech of some Indian chiefs, heroes and villains alike,
from Chingachgook and Hard Heart to Magua and Mahtoree.[22] Cooper
was not the only mimetically language-oriented writer: a French immigrant, N. M. Hentz, wrote in English an Indian historical novel, *Tadeuskund, the Last King of the Lenape* (1825), with long monologues in
French, faithfully translated in the footnotes, while a Prussian soldier
consistently intermingles straight German with parodic English. An
Austrian refugee, Carl Postl (Charles Sealsfield), in his *The Indian
Chief; or, Tokeah and the White Rose* (1829), has his French-American
characters speak in their descent language; he also undertakes the
translation from one language to another of such idiomatic expressions
as *"Il faut faire bon mien à mauvais jeu,"* which becomes the Americanized "We won't hang ourselves because the buffalo has run
away."[23]

"[T]he actors in these works have not only a human, but a national,
and often provincial character. This, especially as exemplified in
modes of speech, may be either an advantage or a disadvantage,
though it is commonly the former," comments Jared Sparks in the
North American Review.[24] Such linguistic differentiations and their
common need of "translation" or "naturalization" point out, even
prior to plot or descriptive strategies, the novel's structural intent of
exposing a sort of melting-pot process, which is matched by the "anthropological" interest in ethnic signs and their exchange, from dresses
and behaviors, to songs, beliefs, and mythologies. In the anonymous
The Christian Indian; or, Times of the First Settlers (1825), several
translations of Indian songs are given, with authenticating footnotes,
such as "Yo-ke-wa, the Indian song of triumph. It is also chanted over
the fallen enemy."[25] On the other hand, the Indian cabin exhibits signs
of "communication with the European traders of the day," and the
protagonist, a Briton, as defined by the narrator, becomes commonly
referred to as "Yeango," one popular etymology of "Yankee" ascribed
to the Indians.[26] Firewater is to be found whenever an Indian is introduced on the novel's scene, and the aboriginal war implements are set
side by side with American or even European guns, as in Tokeah's
cabin, on whose walls "hung a rifle of American manufacture, next to
it a fowling piece, and a beautiful double-barrelled gun from Versailles.
On the opposite side were arrayed the implements of Indian warfare;
quivers of deer and alligator's skin, bows, scalping-knives, and toma-
hawks."[27]

Though partial on the side of "white" culture, the novel shows a translative process from native to immigrant cultures and vice versa. As early as 1799, Charles Brockden Brown could suggest, in *Edgar Huntly*, the presence of the Other by simply mentioning a "moccasoon," thus arousing the protagonist's and the reader's Gothic fears. Cooper, instead, as a historical novelist, stages both a white superficial implied reader and the correct reader of the Other's signs:

> "One moccasin is so much like another . . ."
> "One moccasin like another! you may as well say that one foot is like another; . . . One moccasin is no more like another than one book is like another; though they who can read in one, are seldom able to tell the marks of the other."[28]

Now the novel will get things straight and tell its readers the truth about moccasins and Indian dresses and customs. Accurate descriptions provide "authentic" Indian outfits, interiors, and behaviors, but also instances of fusion like Natty Bumppo's celebrated way of dressing. In *The Pioneers*: "A kind of coat, made of dressed deerskin with the hair on, . . . belted close to his lank body by a girdle of colored worsted. On his feet were deerskin moccasins, ornamented with porcupines' quills after the manner of the Indians. . . ."[29] In *The Last of the Mohicans*: "a hunting shirt of forest green, fringed with faded yellow, and a summer cap of skins which had been shorn of their fur. He also bore a knife in a girdle of wampum, like that which confined the scanty garments of the Indian. . . . " (29). In an 1831 footnote Cooper adds, "Many corps of the American riflemen have been thus attired; and the dress is one of the most striking of modern times. . . . " It is true, as Henry Nash Smith noted, that Natty Bumppo's prototypes filled the American frontier and that their type was snubbed in superior circles for its anarchy and marginality.[30] Yet Cooper's novels make the backwoodsman a "modern" instance, give him a new nobility, mainly because of Natty's function of mediation between society and wilderness, between monocultural and polycultural ideas of society, between past and future.[31] Natty is the sententious speaker who boasts of his ability to read in both "books." White and Indian cultures alike are his share, the former a "natural" acquisition, the latter a willing acquisition of a "natural" culture. Natty Bumppo becomes the Sign of Signs, the perfect hermaphrodite, born both "of savage state and of civilization," as Balzac suggested; "a hybrid offspring of civilization and barbarism," Francis Parkman echoed.[32] "A man without a cross," Natty can also stand for the Other ("the hunter like the savage whose place

he filled"), inhabit the wilderness ("whoever comes into the woods to
deal with the natives has to use Indian fashions"), and become the
unique translator ("he made such a communication . . . as he deemed
most suitable to the capacity of his listeners").

As a translator, Natty alone can understand the meaning of the maidens' song at Uncas's and Cora's funeral at the end of *The Last of the
Mohicans*. It is the Indian postmortem celebration of their marriage,
the future happiness of a pair who could not be united on earth but
would certainly be in heaven. On this occasion Natty does not translate
the Indian song's import for Heyward and Colonel Munro. The white
characters in the novel are denied a cultural translation, which is, however, dispensed to the reader in the authenticating narrative code of
relating the funeral customs of the Delaware tribe:

> Though rendered less connected by many and general interruptions and
> outbreakings, a translation of their language would have contained a reg-
> ular descant, which, in substance, might have proved to possess a train
> of consecutive ideas.
>
> A girl, selected for the task by her rank and qualifications, commenced
> . . . embellishing her expressions with those oriental images, that the
> Indians have probably brought with them from the extremes of the other
> continent, and which form, of themselves, a link to connect the ancient
> histories of the two worlds. (342)

Translation makes the Other's language a "regular descant" in the historical novel code. The narrator's task is to regularize the irregular, to
render it part of a shared knowledge. According to the *Oxford English
Dictionary*, to translate is "to change into another language retaining
the sense." Cooper moves beyond a mere translation when he proves
that the sense has always been the same in both languages. The maid-
en's song can be translated *and* naturalized for the Western reader because ideally those "oriental images" speak of the common mythical
origin of both Indians and whites.[33] *The Last of the Mohicans* moves
beyond its contemporary fictions such as *The Christian Indian, Tadeuskund*, or Lydia Maria Child's *Hobomok* (1824) and Catharine Sedgwick's *Hope Leslie* (1827), in radicalizing the translation process from
one culture to another. It moves a step beyond *Ivanhoe* with the insertion of a mythical universalizing strategy that gives form to Scott's unresolved dialectic between alien and same. Cooper seems to imply that
there can be no telling of a national historical conflict without a regu-
larizing translation, a rhetoric that successfully stresses the homoge-
nizing process of one language and its claim to universality.

The Last of the Mohicans does indeed acquire its deep structure in the very process of "translating" Indian myths into an American national myth. The mythical quality of Cooper's novel relies not only on the elementary functions of his heroes, hunters and warriors, and on their moving in the wilderness of space and time, but also on the "historical" quality of the discourse of Indian assimilation. To relate faithfully the customs and manners of peoples of different descents at a point of history was a programmatic tenet of the novel: Cooper's Indians were both a personal memory and a quotation from different published sources, most notably Heckewelder's *Historical Account of the Indian Nations*.[34] Personal and written validations make the Indians' representation as historically correct as possible and therefore verifiable. Moreover, as Scott himself had suggested in the dedicatory epistle to *Ivanhoe,* "our good allies the Mohawks and Iroquois" still retained in contemporary time the same "simple" and "patriarchal" customs of yore. To represent them was to stage the very anachronism necessary to the updating strategy of the novel. "It is necessary," Scott continues, "for exciting interest of any kind, that the subject assumed should be, as it were, translated into the manners, as well as the language, of the age we live in" (17). Cooper dealt in the present with the reality of the American nation-building process and the "last" actual presence of a mythical discourse of history, the Indians'. At the very beginning of *The Last of the Mohicans,* Natty's and Chingachgook's versions of the history of the red and white man's coming to the American continent are set side by side. They both speak, the author writes, "the tongue which was known to all the natives who formerly inhabited the country between the Hudson and the Potomack, and of which we shall give a free translation for the benefit of the reader; endeavoring, at the same time, to preserve some of the peculiarities, both of the individual and of the language" (30). The peculiarity is that Natty's historical "white" speech, delivered in English to the reader, is framed in the historically "mythical" register of the Indian. It is not only a dialogue between old friends but also the presupposition of the novel's narrative method: since the Indian mythical discourse is contemporary with the white man's progressively rational concept of history, the fictional discourse can be "realistically" framed within it. This allows the translation of myth into national history or permits the novel to embody the mythical foundation of a polyethnic nation: "Even your traditions make the case in my favour, Chingachgook," Natty says.

Once the Indian myth is spoken, the novel carries on a structural similarity that relies on the exchange of mythical and historical time.

The time of nature and the time of history meet in the representation of the wilderness as the locus of origin and eternity, of cycles, births, and rebirths,[35] but also a space marked with signs of a recognizable historical past, the ruins of forts, the remainders of previous strifes. The novel does not endorse Hesiod's cyclical time of successive eras, each unconnected with the other, or its Indian version as presented by Tamenund in *The Last of the Mohicans,* but makes it the universalizing descant of historical facts, a tale of origins, of all births of nations. In this way there will always be beginnings and endings, and for any new nation or any new man there will always be a last one. The lesson of the past becomes, then, the ahistorical sanction of sameness, which in its turn legitimizes the American nation's historical right to be different: the Indian as alien is turned into Native American, where native stands for the land, a geographical entity, but also for the new nation, as its symbolic natural ancestor. The last of the Mohicans can die: as the last representative of a concept of nation as *lignage,* he has indeed to disappear, but only after bequeathing land and culture for the realization of a better nation, where *lignage* is made to go back to God, the same "Nature's God" who recently gave Americans "a separate and equal station."

The Indian is both the figure of a culture of nature and a historical presence. Cooper's interest for Indian culture and his penchant for "translation" in fiction permit him to use Indian lore as an exchangeable, historically founded culture of mythical interpretation of facts. He thus fuses red and white in an American book of nature. He also introduces in the western novel the Indian method of reading "reality." His plot is indeed modified by the Indian's decoding ability. The law of chance, which usually rules over sequences in adventure-story lines, gives in to the cultural control of the "savage," whose system of reading traces—his step-by-step reconstruction of the movements of the pursued Magua, Alice, and Cora—provides rational order in the otherwise irrational chain of events. Uncas is the best of all, but Natty can do his share. The wilderness is thus transformed into a reconstructable space. No wonder that from Balzac to Sue, to his American epigones, it became common to identify Cooper's forest with the city and its retrievable mysteries. In Cooper, Balzac admiringly noted, the reader is made to play the detective: "[D]etecting Indians behind the trees, in the water, under the rocks . . . you think that you are bending beneath those giant trees to follow the trail of a moccasin. The dangers are so allied to the lay of the land that you examine attentively the rocks, the trees, the rapids, the bark canoe, the bushes. . . . "[36] Mark

Twain, in "Fenimore Cooper's Literary Offenses," is right in pointing out the ludicrous excesses in Cooper's adventure plots. His Chingachgook (turned "Chicago"), for example, finds a moccasin track in the bed of a running stream. Yet the Leatherstocking Novels still represent the first convincing literary mapping of a distinctly American wilderness. The romanticism of nature in the New World, as Chateaubriand had proved, could not be represented without the presence of or the identification with its inhabitant. In Cooper the "romantic" is mixed with the "authentic," and the forest is naturalized, made both an object of sublime contemplation and a universe of signs whose decoding is mainly dependent on the acquisition of the Other's culture. Cooper's wilderness as legitimate "Americana" does indeed open the way for black Jim and white Huck.

One could also be reminded of such distant historical Indian/white exchanges when, at the height of the frontier thesis, Buffalo Bill, touring America and Europe with his "Wild West Show," would announce in the program, "Buffalo Bill and Indians. The Last of the only known Native Herd,"[37] and present himself to the public dressed as a gaudy replica of Natty Bumppo. In his autobiography, which was sold at the circus entrance as a self-advertising foretaste of what would be shown onstage, he describes the adoption of his costume in the following way: "I determined to put on a little style myself. So I dressed in a new suit of light buckskin, trimmed along the seams with fringes of the same material; and I put on a crimson shirt handsomely ornamented on the bosom, while on my head I wore a broad sombrero."[38] The sombrero stands for Spanish America as a reminder that the compromise is structural and not unique. In 1902 Frank Norris, commenting on Americana, on that "peculiar picturesqueness of our lives," could find in William Cody and his crew what he termed "the real thing."[39]

The Father's Name, the Father's Blood, or Adoption in the New World

The Indians' own naming of white people is a recorded practice. Natty's multiple names in the Leatherstocking Novels show a progressive validation of the hero.[40] His given name, Nathaniel Bumppo, inscribes itself within a comic synthesis: a bumpy awkwardness is contrasted with the high-sounding Nathaniel, the biblical Nathanael, "an Israelite indeed, in whom is no guile," who "shall see heaven open, and the angels of God ascending and descending upon the Son of man" (John

1:47, 51). As for Natty, Shelley's 1812 usage was "As natty a beau as Bond Street ever saw." In *The Pioneers*, he was "Natty" because of his leggings, which were "of the same material as the moccasins, which, gartering over the knees of his tarnished buck-skin breeches, had obtained for him, among the settlers, the nickname of Leather-stocking" (23). As for the comic use of natty garters, "cross-garter'd" Malvolio is a case in point. Natty's white naming fits the pattern of a character of low origin whose "pretensions" can be made the object of laughter. Yet when Cooper published the Leatherstocking Novels as a series, those very leggings had acquired the status of a national epic symbol. The metamorphosis is already accounted for by Natty himself in *The Last of the Mohicans*:

> I am an admirer of names, though the Christian fashions fall far below savage customs in this particular. The biggest coward I ever knew was called Lyon; and his wife, Patience, would scold you out of hearing in less time than a hunted deer would run a rod. With an Indian 'tis a matter of conscience; what he calls himself he generally is. . . . (57)

It is man's essence that is recognized in Indian names, which are true to the man and not to his family denomination. The discrepancy between names and man's acts is abolished, and the comic gives way to the ideal celebration of pragmatic *Bildung*.

Benjamin Franklin, not casually quoted by Judge Temple in *The Pioneers* as the exemplary man, made a name for himself. Natty does the same when he becomes Hawkeye in *The Deerslayer*. Yet Natty gains his name in spilling blood, as has been stressed by various readers, from D. H. Lawrence to Richard Slotkin and Philip Fisher. It is nonetheless true that the killing, besides being presented as a necessity, is made to obey the Other's system of values. Primitive *and* mythical as such bloody and feudal-like "Indian" ritual is, it is made to coexist with Franklinian benevolence. Cooper stages Indian killing as *the* initiation, or the timeless structure of man's first step in value construction. Once again, Indian culture as universal myth is integrated into white culture, with Natty's adoption of an Indian name through the "noble" killing of his enemy. This act, if anything, bestows universal and natural meaning on the very concept of a nature-based theory of laissez-faire.

As Yuri Lotman has shown, myth-oriented cultures develop a strategy of meaning through a chain of naming acts—each separate from the other and consciously meaningful—which build up the mythological canon. In the interplay between mythical and historical thought, the latter is said to acquire in large measure the previous mythical arrangement of real facts and people; that is, it will retain the sense of the naming itself.[41] As a historical novelist, Cooper bequeaths to the American discourse a fiction that transforms American historical facts in the name of Indian mythological thought. The vanishing-Indian syndrome is contemporary with its cure; and one could not be known or effective without the other. Killing the Indian and adopting an Indian name are the signs that generate the discourse of the nation-building urge. When the generic "hunter" or "trapper' overlaps with Hawkeye, Leatherstocking is no longer marginal and anarchic; he is then the potential American father.

Mythic naming as a cultural strategy of historical interpretation can rely on epithets drawn from kinship. Figurative mothers and fathers certainly abound in historical discourses; "Father" Washington was indeed as frequent in Indian-white exchanges as "Uncle" Sam has been in more recent ones. Cooper makes Natty a father in *The Prairie* (1827). He is at first called Father after the Indian fashion, as the prominent aged figure of his own tribe or race. He is thus confronted with his Indian equivalent, an old man of the Dahcotahs, with a French name, Le Balafré. Appealing to a recognized custom of his people, Le Balafré claims the adoption of Hard Heart, the young and heroic Pawnee captive, in order to rescue him from sure death. Hard Heart, though respectful and grateful for such an honor, does not accept the old chief's offer, because if "he ever has another father it shall be that just warrior."[42] And truly enough, Natty's adoption had already been accomplished earlier in the novel, at the old man's request:

> "Young warrior, . . . I have never been a father or brother. The Wacondah made me to live alone. He never tied my heart to house and field, by the cords with which men of my race are bound to their lodges; if he had, I should not have journeyed so far, and seen so much. But I have tarried long among a people who lived in those woods you mention, and much reason did I find to imitate their courage and love their honesty. The Master of Life has made us all, Pawnee, with a feeling for our kind. I never was a father, but well do I know what is the love of one. You are like a lad I valued, and I had even begun to fancy that some of his blood might be in your veins. But what matters that? You are a true man. . . ." (322–23)

Adoptive kinship proves to be purer than natural kinship. It is not Uncas's blood that makes Hard Heart dear to the old man's fatherly heart but his structural similarity to the last of the Mohicans, whose potential postmortem adoption makes Natty's grief become one with Chingach-gook's, beyond the call of the blood.

Natty's isolation and his unmarried status fit the pattern of "ideal" male friendship described by Leslie Fiedler in *Love and Death in the American Novel* (1960) but also turn Leatherstocking into a mythically adopted father. Neither family blood nor race blood, as the refusal of Le Balafré's offer proves, can surpass the American Ideal Fatherhood. In preferring Natty to Le Balafré as a father, Hard Heart gives up his chance to be rescued and to live according to the principles of his people, thus exchanging legitimation with life itself. And Natty can comment, "I made him my son, that he may know that one is left behind him" (367). The descendant of the vanishing Indian is a father, the same father who at the end of the novel dies surrounded by offspring of both races, the young Pawnee and the American Middleton. The Native American as symbolic ancestor is made the son of an American man without a cross. Significantly, the action of *The Prairie* is set in the early nineteenth century, in a postrevolutionary time, post–Lewis and Clark expedition, when Father Washington had long since become a cult figure.

There are no ideal fathers in Walter Scott's fictional world, and the end of *Ivanhoe* witnesses Rebecca's refusal to be "adopted" within the white hero's family. In the Indian historical novels there are both characters who claim fatherhood and adopted children. Adoption is a constant motif, an American structure of compromise between blood and symbolic parenthood. Cooper's *The Pioneers, The Deerslayer,* and *The Wept of Wish-Ton-Wish* present forms of Indian adoption of white characters whose fate, to a greater or lesser degree, is determined by their consent to be adopted. Natty learns his Indian ways, while remaining a "man without a cross," is initiated into the wilderness, forms his friendship with Chingachgook, and prepares himself for ideal fatherhood in *The Deerslayer.* Edwards, alias Young Eagle, in *The Pioneers* has been adopted into the Delaware tribe and is known as a half-breed by the all-white characters of Templeton. Like Natty, he has both Indian and white ways and names. What makes them different is that the weight of "unpure" blood has to be lifted from him, in order to make him eligible as the husband of Judge Temple's daughter, Elizabeth. Young Eagle takes upon himself the function of the character of obscure origins, which the plot will uncover only at the end in a recognition scene. In the best *Tom Jones* tradition, he will be restored to his name, family, and property and will renew a social pact by marrying a compatible heroine. Cooper simply substitutes a fake blood impediment for the fake class impediment of many eighteenth-century nov-els.[43] In both cases adoption works as the necessary means through which the hero can learn how the other half lives, and become much the wiser once his unquestioned blood ties restore him to his rightful place. When Young Eagle visits the Reverend Grant's house, his eyes are attracted by such domestic decorations as specimens of needle-works, one of which represents a tomb and on which "there were names, with the dates of births and deaths, of several individuals, all of whom bore the name of Grant" (134). His dream of blood descent is there, and it will be fulfilled within the aristocratic lineage of the Effinghams. Notwithstanding Grant's generous illuministic mediation ("it is not color, nor lineage that constitutes merit"), he refuses, in a fit of passion, to accept his Indian rights to the land. As a presumed half-breed, he does not want to, or cannot, identify himself with one-half of his heredity. Only as a legitimate white—with Indian ways—can he own it.

In *Tadeuskund* the Indian chief has adopted a white child and given her the "Indian" name of Elluwia. Her white identity is kept a secret, *the* secret of the novel's plot. She behaves like a dutiful daughter to Tadeuskund and even refuses, because of blood barriers, to marry the white hero whose love she reciprocates. Adoption has been symboli-cally turned into regular blood descent. When finally her father's name and blood are discovered, notwithstanding her lover's relief at her being white, she refuses to abandon her adopted father and dies soon after him. Adoption and consent to it make marriage impossible. For opposite reasons, both novels prove the same thing. Adoption can be a blood substitute within cultural consent and even become irreversi-ble, as Elluwia's fate proves, but the "secret" that adoption hides is the superior right of the father's blood, both when it chokes its off-spring to death and when it restores it to land and property. Neither Edwards's nor Elluwia's blood is tainted, and both of them can be rein-tegrated into the founding of the nation—Edwards with his marriage, Elluwia with her death.

Adoption of white characters is proved to be desirable among Indi-ans, who, unlike the whites, are also willing to intermarry. In *The Christian Indian* an old Indian woman rescues a white captive in order to make him her son and the husband of her legitimate son's supposed widow. Her daughter-in-law falls in love with him, and the specter of consenting adultery haunts the novel once her husband turns out to be alive and Christianized. In Catharine Sedgwick's *Hope Leslie*, Faith Leslie—abducted when a child and adopted by Mononotto—eventually marries her childhood playmate and the chief's son, Oneco. Her sister, Hope, strives to win her back to her white family, out of both horror and pity: "God forbid!" exclaims Hope, shuddering as if a knife had been plunged in her bosom. "My sister married to an Indian!"[44] But Faith and Oneco, though childless, are too strongly tied to each other to be separated, and walk away from Boston to live forever in the mysterious woods. The novel stages also the opposite case, of the Indian maiden in love with the white hero, and her melancholy but firm rejection of even the thought of intermarriage. Magawisca is deliberately shaped as a descendant of Scott's Rebecca.[45] Like her—and like Pocahontas—she rescues the white hero, Everell Fletcher; she has to stand a trial for witchcraft in which Everell acts as her champion and disappears after having blessed his union with the white heroine, Hope. Beyond the literally intertextual character-and-situation identities between the Jewess and the Indian maiden, *Hope Leslie* turns into a triangle the opposition Rebecca/Rowena. Rebecca's traits are given both to Magawisca and to Hope; both speak for the "new woman," the republican female citizen of the postrevolutionary nation; they are both bold and independent, open-minded and generous. Magawisca's blessing of Hope and Everell is anticipated in the novel by Hope, who renounces Everell in favor of her bosom friend Esther, a true daughter of the Puritans, a saintly fair and rigorous maiden, as pale as her literary ancestor, Rowena. She would provide Everell with a clean Puritan record since his enlightened, and therefore objectionable, behavior has endangered him in the old-time community. But Everell is better off than Ivanhoe: both Hope and Esther come from illustrious families of pure English stock, and he can discard Esther and yet marry within his blood. With *Hope Leslie,* Sedgwick makes up for Scott's "awkward treatment"; her heroine establishes the supremacy of the present national self-invention and brings it back to genealogical purity. Magawisca remains a symbol of proud race consciousness and disappears in the wilderness in abeyance of the laws of her fathers. She, too, refuses to be "adopted": adoption becomes impossible when it is linked with a love affair that projects the shadow of mixed descent onto the future of the white race.

The ideal American father can adopt children of both races, provided that their nation as *lignage* is untainted, that they are born from a soon-to-be-called "unmiscegenated" ancestry, and that they will not deviate from their respective purity. In the American Indian historical novel the Romeo and Juliet pattern works only as a sentimental device, devoid of historical tension. As in Scott's *Ivanhoe,* it confirms the inevitability of the fusion—there of Saxons and Normans, here of opposite religious or ideological factions or of people of different European descent. In Cooper's *The Prairie,* Middleton, a citizen of the new Republic, becomes the Anglo-Saxon husband of a refined Spanish lady from the newly acquired territories of Louisiana. The historical rationale for their union is the American "melting pot":

> In such a novel intermixture, however, of men born and nurtured in freedom, and the compliant minions of absolute power, the catholic and the protestant, the active and the indolent, some little time was necessary to blend the discrepant elements of society. In attaining so desirable an end, woman was made to perform her accustomed and grateful office. The barriers of prejudice and religion were broken through the irresistible powers of the master-passion; and family unions, ere long, began to cement the political tie which had made a forced conjunction between people so opposite in their habits, their educations, and their opinions. (178)

Good weddings that show consent to the "melting pot" are weak endings in fictions built upon racial confrontations. The conflict still lies in the unresolved tension between nation as *lignage* and nation as consent-and-descent-based cultural ideals. The obsession with purity, the overstressing of the Other as belonging to a nation defined by *lignage,* noble and Roman-like as it is always presented, speaks for a resilience to accept the same category of fusion that is avowedly the sacred principle of the new nation. The useless marriage or the impossible intermarriage is replaced by an ideal compromise, a pure universal category of fatherhood. Cooper's Leatherstocking Tales stand out from contemporary historical fictions for their invention of a symbolic figure based on the historical paradox of cultural and ideological acceptance and denial of "democratic" fusion. Father seems to be the name of the melting-pot God, the supreme national self-invention. A sterile father who, in the name of the Indian who names him, can deny him progeny and make him his adopted son.

Hide-and-Seek or the Shining Veil

In *Hope Leslie* Sedgwick either forgets to mention or denies the existence of offspring in Faith and Coneco's marriage. In *The Wept of Wish-Ton-Wish* (1829) the offspring of the young chief Conanchet and of Ruth, his white Indian adopted wife, causes repulsion in her mother. Cooper must have thought that miscegenation caused repulsion in his readers, too. In the final, crucial scene when Narra-Mattah, the adopted and Indianized Ruth, throws herself at the feet of her dead husband, before the astonished eyes of all her white family, the child is simply laid aside and utterly and consistently forgotten through the rest of the novel. In recognizing his wife's blood ties and bringing her back to her family, Conanchet had hoped to make blood and adoption compatible. Not so: even Narra-Mattah is denied the sign of her blood right, and on her tomb there will not be her father's name but the sentimental anonymous epithet of "The Wept of Wish-Ton-Wish."

Yet early in the novel, Ruth's mother had trusted the young Indian captive Conanchet with her little daughter, thereby overcoming her child's terror of the red skin. True enough that it was during a most ferocious Indian attack, but the woman's confidence in the Other had been consistently proved up to that point. Mother and daughter bear the same name, Ruth: one the wife of the righteous Puritan, the other of the noble Indian warrior. Both are representative of the biblical wife's words: "Intreat me not to leave thee, or to return from following after thee: for whither thou goest, I will go; and where thou lodgest, I will lodge: thy people *shall* be my people, and thy God my God. . . ." (Ruth 1:16). Both are overcome by an unquenchable sorrow—the first for the loss of her child, the second for that of her husband. Symbolically, the mother is guilty of the loss of her child's desired object, Conanchet. Her repulsion for the offspring of their love is subdued only through a projection of little Ruth, as she used to be, on him. And Narra-Mattah herself can deny her Indian love only in a fit of madness that takes the shape of the affectionate prating of a little child. Childhood's innocence, as an edenic dream of integrity, can deny the Indian, while a wife's madness suggests its persistent disturbing quality.[46]

The Wept of Wish-Ton-Wish is a tale of the Puritans, the nation's Founding Fathers. To acquire the "Name-of-the-Father" means to recognize his laws, through the repression of any sexual desire opposed to them, including the unlawful desire for the other race. As Simone Vauthier has argued, there is a symmetry between incest and miscegenation.[47] The desire for the father is interchangeable with the desire for the Indian. The tale of the nation's Founding Fathers is turned into a childhood drama of repression and desire. The offspring of such desire cannot but be monstrous and nameless, because it is lawless. It cannot be adopted.

White adoption recoils in madness from the half-breed; yet in Lydia Maria Child's *Hobomok,* a half-breed is indeed adopted by a white father. "There can be, we believe, but one opinion respecting this story; it is in very bad taste, to say the least, and leaves upon the mind a disagreeable impression."[48] In "bad taste" and "disagreeable," *Hobomok* still good-naturedly exposes the hide-and-seek game, the game at once of purity and mixing, of amalgamation and rejection, of acceptance and denial, in the Indian historical novel. Mary Conant, the tale's heroine, marries Hobomok and begets his child. Her marriage to the Indian is the result of her stern and righteous-to-a-fault father's opposition to her marrying her Anglo-Saxon beloved, Charles Brown. The young man is consequently banned from New England because of religious differences and is reported to have died in a shipwreck. Mary Conant is opposing her father's law and opposes it even with supernatural means. In a novel where the love theme is punctuated with references to sin, and particularly to Adam's sin, where it is even disputed whether love is a matter of free will, Mary draws in the forest at night a devilish "mystic circle," while uttering the words "Whoever's to claim a husband's power,/Come to me in the moonlight hour . . . Whoe'er my bridegroom is to be/step in the circle after me."[49] With a shriek of terror, she beholds stepping into the circle not her Episcopalian beloved but what she thinks is the ghost of an Indian, who turns out, however, to be her good and living acquaintance Hobomok. "There is no telling what may come in asking the Devil's assistance," comments her friend Sally. Superstition is devilish, proves disobedience to the clarity of the father's law, but tells also of the return of what is repressed by the same law.[50] Mary's innocent desire for a husband, barred by the father's interdiction, becomes Mary's vision of an Indian. Her marriage will be of *routine* justified by her distress and represented as the result of a painful mental illness. Nonetheless, she ends up with loving Hobomok and their little son. He is a child that can be adopted, because he is symbolically only the result of a playful, temporary, "superstitious" return of what is repressed to an unjust extent by such "Un-Natty" father figures as the old Puritan Conant. In *The First Settlers of New England* (1829), Child opposes the humane law of the New Testament to the ferocious one of the law-abiding people of the Old. As a woman and a crusader for emancipation, she recognizes that the Founding Fathers' culture generalizes and radicalizes repression and that "superstition" is its outcome: the savage is not the Indian, a historically identifiable individual, but the American sexual projection of the Other. The new man, the quasi-contemporary enlightened American, Charles Brown—who has widely traveled—discards an old world for a new, defies superstition, and willingly adopts his betrothed's half-red offspring. The son of the Indian was named by his mother Charles Hobomok Conant; Hobomok's name is, since his son's birth, enclosed between Charles's and father Conant's. Once grown, Charles Hobomok Conant will deservedly go to Harvard.

Not so with Cooper's *Wept of Wish-Ton-Wish*. Little Ruth is from the beginning on the righteous father's side:

> "Thou hast knelt, my Ruth, and hast remembered to think of thy father and brother in your prayers."
>
> "I will do so again, mother, whispered the child, bending to her knees, and wrapping her young features in the garments of the matron."
>
> "Why hide thy countenance? One young and innocent as you, may lift thine eyes to Heaven with confidence."
>
> "Mother, I see the Indian unless my face be hid. . . ."[51]

Ruth prays for father and brother and has to hide her face. Earthly and heavenly fathers alike forbid looking upon the Indian, and the fervent acceptance of their laws begets guilt and fear. Mary has shown that the religious condemnation of her right to love hides a deeper taboo, that of mixing with the savage. In constructing the dialectic between repression and desire, fiction shows that the effort to deny one of the two terms can lead only to the recognition of the other. The stronger the denial, as in Cooper's case, the stronger the thing denied, and the supreme denial is death itself.[52] Hobomok's body will simply "vanish" in the forest, to leave Mary free to marry her alleged lost love, while Narra-Mattah barely survives the slaughtered Conanchet, and only because she is touchingly made to relapse into childhood's innocence. "Better dead (or mad) than married to an Indian," many fictional parents repeatedly say.

Race and sex have been traditionally associated; fear of sex is also fear of anarchy in a constituted social code that legalizes sex in marriage and progeny. Cooper's birth of a nation makes use of mythical forms explicitly drawn from otherness to regularize a polyethnic future nation, thus exorcising the possibility of the return of what is repressed. Yet perversion, or the letter of sexual desire, surfaces in the text, proving that there can be no regularization without the presence of its hidden content. The Other as historical entity, legitimized by the "authentic" of its customs and traditions, only imperfectly conceals the savage as the complex cultural sign of perversion.[53]

Not all the readers of *The Last of the Mohicans* recognize Cora's taint as a major element in the plot. The polarization white/red, the last-of-one's-race syndrome, does not account for Cooper's treatment of the mulatto, of the black drop that comes to symbolize what melodramatically ends in death in Indian historical novels. Yet early reviewers of *The Last of the Mohicans* dwelt on it, and in a resentful tone, speaking either of an unnecessary "frequent, inartificial, painful allusion," or complaining about Cooper's unhappy ending, the sacrifice "of two of them in whom he felt the chief interest," when their union would have been "natural." The anonymous reviewer of the *United States Literary Gazette* ends by saying, "Uncas would provide a good match for Cora, particularly as she had little of the darker race in her veins—and still more, as this sort of arrangement is coming into fashion in real life, as well as in fiction."[54] Cora's taint makes her both a statement of a universal "natural" law and a red-black feature of its historical anarchy. Her mixed blood originates in her father's past, and in a distant land; she is a tainted immigrant, taking her pollution to America, an American-settled Wandering Jew or disturbing mulatto.[55] Her liaison with Uncas would confirm the taint in the national future. And her possible liaison with Magua tells how dreadful its motivations can be.[56] Natural and universal as sex is, referring to it in history-making becomes "in-artificial." In a tainted birth of the nation, the novel is presumed to redeem nature, by using an artificial structure of concealment, excising the pain that is "coming into fashion in real life."

Two textual strategies are employed in the treatment of Cora's taint: the first is historically informative and is shown in the dialogue between Colonel Munro and Major Heyward. Munro's stay in the West Indies historically justifies mixed blood. Heyward's southernness justifies his "prejudice" against it. Otherwise, both Munro and Heyward recognize Cora's superior qualities. The second is symbolical and links Cora to the semantic field of the Indian as the complex imaginary figure resulting from the tension between the two opposites of the *bon sauvage* and the gothic villain. She shares with Uncas nobility, order, loyalty, respect for the elders; with Magua, a fiery and passionate nature, the lashing of contempt, a "sublime" wilderness. Like a Poe heroine, Cora is associated with the "plumage of the raven"; she belongs to the appalling mystery of the forest whose "shadows . . . seemed to draw an impenetrable veil before [its] bosom."[57] The dark side of nature, of the Indian, of the woman, coalesces in Cora's taint, which is, of course, her drop of black blood. Such a drop turns out to be a sort of litmus paper in the novel's design: no nobility of character, no good "Indian" qualities, can redeem its menace.

There remains something that has to be brought back to secrecy, hidden away. Cora, like the forest, is veiled. A veil does not erase; it imperfectly conceals. The two textual strategies come to a collision at the end of the novel. In one of the frequently disparaged, but nonetheless interesting, discrepancies in Cooper's fictions, old Tamenund, who has not been "informed" within the narration, almost instinctively "knows" Cora's taint:

> "I know that the pale-faces are a proud and hungry race. I know that they claim, not only to have the earth, but that the meanest of their colour is better than the Sachems of the red man. The dogs and crows of their tribes," continued the earnest old chieftain, without heeding the wounded spirit of his listener, whose head was nearly crushed to the earth, in shame, as he proceeded, "would bark and caw, before they would take a woman to their wigwams, whose blood was not of the colour of snow. But let them not boast before the face of the Manitto too loud. They entered the land at the rising, and may yet go off at the setting sun! I have often seen the locust strip the leaves from the trees, but the season of blossoms has always come again!"
>
> "It is so," said Cora, drawing a long breath, as if reviving from a trance, raising her face, and shaking back her shining veil, with a kindling eye, that contradicted the death-like paleness of her countenance "but why—it is not permitted us to inquire! . . ." (305)

Tamenund is a sacred prophet for his tribe. Cora, like Rebecca, a "woman . . . of the hated race . . . —A Yengee"—kneels down before him, "with a species of holy reverence." What he represents is the wisdom of the myth teller, one sacred because foreordained to know. In a mythical frame Cora's mixed blood can be spoken about as "natural" and opposed to the shame that has made the veil necessary. What sociohistorically has to be concealed is paradoxically discovered within that same structure of mythical discourse, which has successfully hidden the fear of red-white sexual mixing. As a result of the old man's words, Cora's veil is cast away. It shines as much as her eyes are enkindled in defiance of death itself. And her final remark, if applicable to Tamenund's "authentic" cyclical view of man's history, is also a reminder of the disappearance of Narra-Mattah's child from the narration, of the mysterious role the half-breed is made to play.

The veil is a romantic symbol generated by the dialectic between the sublime emotion of the mysterious natural state and the ideal aspiration for order and purity. Its semantic potential controls and stresses both mythic time, wilderness, sex, and difference *and* historical time, civilization, laws, and sameness. As such, Cooper's "veil" becomes a meaningful structure in the rhetoric of the American discourse of self-invention. In *The Pioneers,* when Chingachgook is turned into Christian Indian John and wears a dress that is "a mixture of his native and

European fashions," he shows a profusion of black hair concealing his features "as a willing veil, to hide the shame of a noble soul, mourning for glory once known" (86). A silver medallion of Washington hangs from his neck. The symbolic veil, a feature of mourning and shame, is contiguous to the acceptance of Washington's ideal fatherhood. "Society cannot exist without wholesome restraints. . . . The laws alone remove us from the condition of the savages," Father Temple states (382–83).

In a generative romantic treatise such as Edmund Burke's *A Philosophical Enquiry into the Origin of Our Ideas of the Sublime and Beautiful* (1754), a compromise is sought between natural emotions and social integration. Man's leading passions, Burke remarked, are self-preservation and society; man's delight results from the former, provided that the "danger and pain" associated with it do not "press too nearly"—are conveniently veiled—so as to enhance our curiosity, sympathy, or imitation. In such a way can the emotional quality of self-preservation compromise with society, go back to it with accrued moral value. What links self-preservation to social integration is the acknowledgment of desires and their voluntary repression through the perception of contradictory emotions—danger and safety, pain and relief. Chingachgook's veil stands for a restraint to the "emotion" sublimely linked with the savage state, his Washington medallion the equally sought-for price/prize for such restraint. A shredded piece of Cora's veil is found on the track of Magua's abduction. And the description of Uncas triumphantly discovering it is styled in the unrestrained savage code:

> Uncas, without making any reply, bounded away from the spot, and in the next instant he was seen tearing from a bush, and waving, in triumph, a fragment of the green riding veil of Cora. The movement, the exhibition and the cry, . . . again burst from the lips of the young Mohican. . . . (184)

An anticipation of Cora's own casting aside of the veil, Uncas's fragment is, according to the virgin-in-distress code, a sign of her danger, of Magua's feared infamous action. Cora will wear an astonishingly white dress in front of Tamenund and the assembled tribe. Both dress and veil will be replaced by Indian robes after her death. The "savage sounds" that Natty Bumppo "veils" for Heyward and Colonel Munro, the prospective American husband and the guilty immigrant father, celebrate Cora and Uncas's union both within and beyond the historical code. Within, because it is style from the reader as an authenticating translation of Indian costumes; beyond, because their heavenly union transforms and redeems savage desires into the mythical tale of happy hunting grounds. Within, because Heyward and Munro, as plausible historical characters, ought not to know; beyond, because symbolically Cora's veil and her white dress have been changed into Indian robes. Once again, the casting aside of the veil is made meaningful through an Indian sign, and the funeral scene unveils both fear and attraction, emotion and restraint, acceptance and denial. This is the hide-and-seek game of the newly born national identity.

In *Notions of the Americans* (1828) Cooper writes, "As there is little reluctance to mingle the white and red blood . . . I think an amalgamation of the two races would in time occur. Those families in America who are thought to have any of the Indian blood, are rather proud of their descent; and it is a matter of boast among many of the most considerable persons of Virginia, that they are descended from the renowned Pocahontas."[58] A mythic mother, Pocahontas, stands in Cooper's "objective" report of a fact, that there is a "little reluctance to mingle" among his contemporaries. The myth of the Indian, his own translation of Indian myths, has provided the new nation with a historically founded rhetoric for ideal amalgamation, yet *The Wept of Wish-Ton-Wish,* written in 1828 and published a year later, stages the tragic and horrifying outcome of an intermarriage. Cora's veil is finally the symbol of the mythic strategy that both hides and exposes mixing as a fact in American reality. Both an Indian and a black reality. Black blood was not culturally perceived, like Indian blood, to be potentially noble and redeemable.[59] If the "veil" is generated by the black drop in the heroine's veins, Cooper prophetically establishes the mulatto as the literary type of the drama of national identity, the racially mixed and sexually obsessive counterpart of Natty Bumppo, the chaste man without a cross and the ideal father of all races.

Cora's black taint makes her the American counterpart of the English Rebecca. When Scott's heroine takes leave from the newly wed Rowena, England, and Ivanhoe, she is shrouded in a "long white veil." As Rebecca Gratz wrote, "The veil drawn over her feelings was necessary to the fable." The Jewess's parting words have a family resemblance to Tamenund's:

> [T]he people of England are a fierce race, quarelling even with their neighbours or among themselves, and ready to plunge the sword into the bowels of each other. Such is no safe abode for the children of my people. . . . Not in a land of war and blood, surrounded by hostile neigh-

bours and distracted by internal factions, can Israel hope to rest during her wanderings." (447)[60]

In a nation that aims at representing itself as safe, pacified, and unified in the name of marriage and citizenship, there is no place for the Wandering Jewess, while there is a place in heaven for its mulatto counterpart.[61] As Rowena says to Rebecca, there is nothing to flee from or to fear in the new England. "Thy speech is fair," answers Rebecca, "and thy purpose fairer, but it may not be—there is a gulf betwixt us." The "gulf"—an image of the unbridgeable, between equal and alien, between the nation's "self-evident truths" and threatening reality—is suitably identified as a racial metaphor. It still remains a stereotyped image of sublimity, of romantic attraction and repulsion for octoroons throughout the nineteenth century.[62]

"Wild and unholy were their thoughts and passions, and the *dark gulf* had been passed": thus the narrator of *The Romantic Story of Miss Ann Carter; (Daughter of One of the First Settlers),* describes her union with "the celebrated Indian Chief," Thundersquall.[63] Milton's "impassable gulf" haunts old-time "Jewesses," while American husbands and prospective fathers, like Middleton and Paul in *The Prairie,* descend not "into this wild abyss the womb of nature" but to the "placid plain" and its "luxuriant bottom" to reach the dying hermaphrodite Natty Bumppo, thus performing a "reversal of the mythic Fall."[64] Magua, the bad childless Indian, is last shown as the presiding character of the gulf, its ancestral totem: "A form stood at the brow of the mountain, on the very edge of the giddy height, with uplifted arms, in an awful attitude of menace . . . " (388). Natty, with an unusually "agitated weapon," fires at his precipitating, laughing, and relentlessly sneering countenance.[65]

Ethnicity as Festive Culture: Nineteenth-Century German America on Parade

KATHLEEN NEILS CONZEN

By 1859, gold rush San Francisco had seen just about everything. But even the most jaded denizen of that raw frontier city must have been bemused on November 10 by the incongruous sight of a flower-bedecked classical bust, accompanied by a bevy of garlanded maidens, being pulled through the city's streets. It was the hundredth anniversary of the birth of Friedrich Schiller, and San Francisco's German citizens were turning out en masse to honor their homeland's national poet. The celebration had begun the night before with a dramatic performance, orchestral concert, and a celebratory prologue specially written for the occasion. The next day, the members of the city's numerous German associations lined up in festive order with colorful sashes and banners, music and marching militia, tradesmen's floats and mounted marshalls, to parade the bunting-draped wagon carrying the poet's bust and its feminine court of honor from the headquarters of the city's leading German society to one of San Francisco's private pleasure grounds. There the bust was enthroned on a speaker's tribune to receive the tribute of a festive oration, concert, and gala ball.[1]

I

Time lends charm to the naive earnestness and solemn festivity of San Francisco's Schiller procession, but its broader significance for the history of ethnicity in America lies in the purposes it was meant to serve and in the festive means chosen to realize them. For the Schiller commemoration was only one local manifestation of what was already by that time a highly visible, elaborate, and ritualized culture of public celebration within the German immigrant communities of America. As early as 1839, before the real onset of mass immigration, Germans held at Dayton an American reprise of the 1832 German national festival at Hambach. The following year Philadelphia's Germans staged an elaborate public parade and outdoor festival in honor of Johannes Gutenberg and the four hundredth anniversary of the invention of printing, and soon German festivities were punctuating the humdrum of American urban life with some regularity.[2]

In early 1843, for example, when Milwaukee's infant German community numbered well under a thousand, it was by marching as a unit in the civic parade celebrating the passage of a harbor improvements bill that the city's Germans decided to announce their claims to political parity. Within a year, they not only virtually monopolized the city's Fourth of July parade, but were also changing the character of the holiday: while the native-born Americans concluded the day as usual with an oration in the Methodist church, the German contingent marched on to a brewery beer garden for music, sharpshooting, games, and ample food and drink. Cincinnati Germans by 1846 were celebrating May Day in the old country manner with a militia parade and country excursions, and two years later the city's leading German association celebrated its first anniversary with an outdoors *Volksfest* of singing, speeches, and food that lasted late into the night and served as a rehearsal for the closing rites of the first great national German singing festival held in Cincinnati the following June. Infant San Francisco witnessed its first German May Fest as early as 1853.[3]

What distinguished such German-American celebrations from those of the American-born or other mid-century immigrants was their frequency, their public yet respectable and orderly character, and above all their pageantry—the parades, the mass assemblies, the ritual performances that were so central a part of the German-American definition of celebration.[4] Everything from Sunday afternoons to national anniversaries was enveloped in a web of group celebration and marked with consciously crafted rites whose symbolism stamped them unmistakably as German-American.

The conspicuous investment of German-American time, energies, and resources in group festivity did not escape contemporary notice. By 1860, one caustic German-American commented that the Germans of New York seemed to be the most pleasure-seeking people in the world. "At least," he lamented, "they put on more popular festivals in a year than take place in a decade in all the larger cities of Europe together. . . . The good people of New York are presented with several festivals a day, and they seem to attend them all in considerable numbers." The festivals, he noted, could last a day or two or even a whole week, and were not cheap. "Where on earth do the thousands upon thousands of workers, who are the main celebrants in these festivities, get the means and time to pursue so many amusements?"[5] Nor were German celebrations ignored by their American fellow citizens. The pages of the new illustrated weeklies soon found in this festive repertoire ample scope for their illustrators' talents, and for the next thirty years German-American public festivities would be regularly documented and publicized to a broad national audience.[6]

Most historians, however, have been content to regard these parades, festivals, and other forms of public celebration as little more than superficial indicators of underlying ethnic community sentiment, tolerantly noting their excesses and seldom inquiring into the deeper significance of this festive commitment.[7] Some scholars, under the influence of anthropological models, recently have begun to look more directly at the rituals and rhetoric of immigrant "festive culture" itself, interpreting them variously as manifestations of an evolving folk culture creating meaning and helping immigrants cope with an alien world, as instruments for the promotion of group solidarity, and as public assertions of group power and demands.[8] The small but growing body of work on more general forms of public celebration in nineteenth-century America views such events from a similar communications perspective as either manifestations of a vernacular oppositional culture or hegemonic efforts by the dominant social class to bring that culture under its control.[9] Such elements were present in German-American festive culture, to be sure, but to interpret an event like San Francisco's Schiller festival only as unself-concious folk culture or propaganda is to miss much of the role that festive ritual played in the evolution of German ethnic identity in America.

Ritualized celebration, theorists tell us, can serve multiple ends. Ritual has been defined broadly by Robert Bocock as "the symbolic use of bodily movement and gesture in a social situation to express and articulate meaning."[10] Like other forms of symbolic communication, its power lies in its ability to quickly and efficiently condense complexity, finesse contradiction, and evoke intuitive comprehension.[11] Ritual can thus function simply as drama or propaganda, aiming at effective communication of a diffuse message to an external audience of passive spectators observing the performance. But its real power lies in its ability not just to communicate to but to actively influence its internal audience, the ritual participants themselves.

Victor Turner's work provides a powerful explication of how this is achieved. "Biology and structure"—that is, the realm of feelings and that of actual social relationships—"are put in right relation by the activation of an ordered succession of symbols, which have the twin functions of communication and efficacy." A tripartite ritual process separates the participant from normality with its roles and statuses, and before reincorporation immerses him or her in a "betwixt and between" threshold state of liminality that not only leaves the participant receptive to the symbolic meanings embedded in the particular ritual but elicits what Turner calls "communitas."[12] "In celebration . . . much of what has been bound by social structure is liberated, notably the sense of comradeship and communion, in brief, of communitas; on the other hand, much of what has been dispersed over many domains of culture and social structure is now bound or cathected in the complex semantic systems of pivotal, multivocal symbols and myths which achieve great conjunctivenes."[13] Communitas for Turner is thus a model of structureless human relationships involving "the whole man in his relation to other whole men" in contrast to the "relationships between statuses, roles, and offices" that constitute the units of normal social structure: "communitas emerges where social structure is not." No society can function adequately, Turner argues, without the dialectic of successive experiences of communitas and social structure that ritual encourages. Untransformed communitas "cannot readily be applied to the organizational details of social existence. It is no substitute for lucid thought and sustained will. On the other hand, structured action swiftly becomes arid and mechanical if those involved in it are not periodically immersed in the regenerative abyss of communitas." Purging and reanimating structure, ritually evoked communitas thereby reinforces it.[14]

Ritual thus offers a way of resolving the problems of meaning that can arise in the course of what Anthony F. C. Wallace has termed "transformations of state," whether recurring or catastrophic, on the part of both individuals and communities. In situations where reasoned resolution is often impossible and where the major goal may be the adjustment of perception to reality or the marshalling of resources— individual, communal, or supernatural—to change reality, the ritual process helps people "feel their way" to a satisfactory integration of bodily feelings and emotions with rational social purposes.[15] Consequently, although modern society is conventionally regarded as secularized and deritualized, in fact its very complexity and mutability encourage the prolific invention of integrating ritual, as social scientists and, somewhat belatedly, historians have come to realize.[16]

Among such invented rituals are often the rituals of ethnicity. There is a certain tendency in current historical interpretation to regard ethnicity in almost primordial terms, to assume that immigrants from a given area share a common culture and a common commitment to preserve it in America, and that both their sense of group identity and the social patterns and institutions that they generate, derive from that culture. But critics have pointed out that the communal activity and consciousness of kind that are the essence of ethnicity in America should be viewed as emergent phenomena that can have many different bases and change over time.[17] Certainly German-Americans lacked a common religion, common regional or class origins, a common political ideology, a common immigrant predicament, in short, most of the generally accepted bases for the crystallization of ethnic sentiment. Yet their history provides clear evidence for the emergence of a German-American ethnic identity, perceptible to insiders and outsiders alike, for a dense array of group institutions, and for periodic instances of sustained common action engaged in by significant portions of what might be termed "the population at risk" of German-American ethnicity.[18]

It is impossible to prove the origins of this very real if distinctive kind of ethnicity without encountering the central role of invented rituals of celebration in its emergence and maintenance. No matter that the German-American community remained cleft even in celebration. Workers and merchants, Catholics and Protestants, literati and toughs, though they might celebrate apart except at moments of unusual intensity, still reflected, both in the values they attached to celebration and in their manner of celebrating, a common festive culture that drew them to one another and set them apart from other Americans. Indeed, as we explore the origins, rituals, and consequences of German-American celebration, we shall begin to discern the lineaments of an ethnicity that in a very real sense *was* festive culture. Their shared need for celebration and the communitas it generated brought German-Americans together, the forms of celebration that they adopted helped them to conceptualize their commonality in ethnic terms, and in defense of their festive culture they entered as a group into American public life, with significant consequences both for American popular culture and for their own collective future.

II

The intertwining of German-American festive culture and ethnic identity was a complex process rooted in the habits of festivity, both traditional and invented, that immigrants carried with them from the homeland. The increasing visibility of German-American public celebration in the 1840s was linked to the intensifying pace of German immigration and to the consequent growth of the German-language press and elaboration of the German *Vereinswesen*—associational life—in America. The immigration provided the numbers, the press the information necessary for public celebration, but the *Vereine* provided many of the occasions and the requisite organization. *Vereine*—in the definition of historian Thomas Nipperdey, free unions of individuals, independent of their legal status in society, for the purpose of attaining certain specific ends—had spread in Germany in the wake of the Enlightenment as an alternative to older household, parish, and corporate-based nonvoluntary forms of social organization. The *Vereine* that emerged in the last third of the eighteenth century and proliferated after 1815 offered a way for individuals set free from the world of tradition and committed to a humanistic belief in progress and a cultivated life—*Bildung*—to join with likeminded others in creating a new set of voluntary social relations on the basis of common interest—in sociability, in mutual benefit and self-improvement, in social reform, in art and learning. In the process, they helped create the basis for a new middle-class identity and culture which, with the spread of the *Vereinswesen* by the later 1840s, not only into virtually every area of bourgeois life but also into the churches, the villages, and parts of the working class, particulary the artisans, was penetrating much of German society.[19]

The sociability and brotherhood central to their functioning readily fostered the institutionalization of forms of celebration within the *Vereine* and their emergence as the guardians of old and the creators of new forms of public festivity. Germans of the period implicitly accepted the basic assumption of their philosophers that man possessed both sense and sensibility, both mind and feeling, that he lived both in a practical world and in a world of art, learning, and friendship. True *Bildung*—the humanistic cultivation that was the goal and the mark of the new educated middle class—gave due weight to both spheres and recognized the important role of *Geselligkeit*—voluntary sociability— in the full development of both sides of the human character. Because women were perceived as having a special aptitude for the sphere of the feelings, once that sphere was admitted to the center of human society, so was the active participation of women in the new world of the *Vereine* encouraged.[20]

A world defining itself in terms of *Bildung* and voluntary sociability was also a world that found it possible to think in terms of the *Volk* as an organism made up of all those influenced in their quest for perfectibility by the same historical and natural circumstances regardless of differences of legal status. It found new value in traditional folk customs as expressions of the nation's soul, and explored the peculiar ability of festivals to generate a sense of national commonality and belonging. Building upon the doctrine of popular festivals enunciated by Rousseau and others and exemplified in the French Revolution, drawing upon pietistic emotionalism and Romantic fascination with folklore and symbol, German nationalists like Friedrich Ludwig Jahn and Ernst Moritz Arndt early in the nineteenth century worked out arguments for the necessity of folk festivals as "a public inalienable human right" and their desirability as an instrument in nation-building. The *Volksfest* would satisfy the need for entertainment and sociability and engender the impression of a classless society of interdependent, responsible individuals through the performance of "meaningful national rites" that could channel "a chaotic crowd into a mass disciplined in part through the performance of 'sacred' acts."[21]

The rituals of these public celebrations thus were "invented traditions" of a classic kind, cobbled together from the remnants of village, guild, ecclesiastical, and courtly customs. Engendering solidarity and communitas in the midst of social change, in the process they also helped the middle-class *Vereinswesen* present itself as the incarnation of the nation and became weapons in what George Mosse has termed a campaign to "nationalize the masses." Rituals, monuments, group performances of songs and drama could literally become secular sacraments, acts creating the national unity they symbolized. In the years between the national uprising that freed the German states from Napoleon and the revolutions of 1848, gymnastic organizations, singing societies, and sharpshooters' groups worked out their own public liturgies, while the rites of the national folk festival as a vehicle for liberal nationalist ideals were pioneered in the Wartburg Festival of 1817 and the Hambacher Fest of 1832. Even a monarch like William of Wurttemberg turned to pseudo-medieval ritual to convert an agricultural fair into a folk festival celebrating the organic unity of Swabian society—the famous Cannstatter Folk Festival copied by the Swabian associations in America—and public monuments evolved from dynastic glorifications to objectifications of the ideals for which the nation was supposed to stand. Nineteenth-century German immigrants thus came to America from a culture that cherished organized sociability and possessed a repertoire of festive forms that consciously and unconsciously spoke in the accents of nationalism.[22]

Vereine spread in America contemporaneously with their elaboration in Germany, carrying with them their culture of sociability and festivity.[23] Their proliferation frequently met practical concerns—needs for insurance, for aid to newcomers, for justice in the workplace—but it also embodied common German perceptions of significant social and cultural inadequacies in American life. German-American observers throughout the nineteenth century were in general agreement that the average German immigrant in many ways Americanized rapidly, in fact almost too rapidly, and that his children were virtually indistinguishable from those of native stock.[24] But they were also aware of the boundaries of this Americanization:

> It is a peculiar thing with us Germans here: we seek and find outward independence, a free, solid life, unlimited industrial trade—political freedom, in short; to that extent we are Americans. But we are Americans, Germans. We build for ourselves American houses, but within glows a German hearth. We wear American hats, but under them are German eyes looking out from a German face. We love our wives with German fidelity . . . ; the good Lord keeps a private German ear for our church services; the American Catawba translates itself into German dreams in our brains, and flows from our babbling tongues in comfortable German tones. We live according to American habits but we hold fast to German morals. We speak English, but we think and feel in German. Our minds speak with the words of the Anglo-Americans, but our hearts understand only the mother tongue. While our gaze hovers over an American horizon, the old German heavens still arch over our souls. Our entire inner life is, in a word, German, and whatever is to satisfy the needs of the inner man must appear before him in German garments.[25]

Accustomed as they were to the cosy sociability and dramatic festivity that enriched middle-class German life, America struck many Germans as too soberly practical, too obsessed with business, religion, and reform, to satisfy the needs of the truly cultivated individual.

They were particularly critical of the lack of the festive in American life, the lack of poesie, grandeur, and richness of public ritual. "The life of the American swings between the market and the church," commented one disgusted immigrant in 1846. "Doing business and praying are the highest moments of the modern republican," and "public meetings are his only real festivals." There was little gaiety in American social gatherings, few places of public recreation. Listen to a German observer describing the opening of the New York Exposition in 1853: "Always the same old story. The militia with its variegated uniforms, in between them the black dress coats of the officials riding in carriages, that was the core of the parade. The only way that you could tell it apart from Henry Clay's funeral procession was that this time the hearse was replaced by the person of the President!" Even the Fourth of July, with its parades, ovations, and fireworks, could not measure up to the "idealistic and artistic" stamp of public celebration to which the immigrants had been accustomed in the homeland. "Everything here becomes profane and common," sighed an 1856 commentator. "The American people lacks naturalness, naïveté, humor, and in a country with a free public life, where every activity, every effort, every viewpoint can express itself without hindrance, we nevertheless find no real *Volksleben*"—no real popular culture expressive of the nation's soul. And again, "the American cannot get enthusiastic about anything; he can't even enjoy himself—for which fact the Fourth of July is a regularly recurring testimony. . . . this is a people that doesn't deserve its festival!"[26]

Americans, of course, had their own modes of socializing, their own festive culture, though its history still remains largely unwritten. By the middle decades of the nineteenth century, the pages of any small town newspaper testified to the varied annual round of picnics and church sociables, lectures, chorales, suppers, balls, sleighing and skating and fishing parties, debates and civic banquets with which the American middle classes filled their leisure time.[27] Historians are also uncovering the rich if less respectable and far more public world of working-class entertainment and celebration, the world of the saloon and the blackface show, of street fairs, militia parades, firemen's revels, and Christmas masking.[28] But the two worlds seldom mixed. Genteel, domestic values insured that when middle-class celebration occurred in public settings, the celebrants grouped themselves in private parties—Sunday school picnics, for example. Holidays were celebrated in the home, like Thanksgiving or New Year's with its "calling" customs, or like the Fourth of July they were increasingly abandoned to the lower classes. Civic and militia parades might bring all classes into festive contact, but at least in Philadelphia by the 1830s, such events had become terrain contested in class conflict. Civic authorities might upon occasion sponsor public celebrations to honor noted visitors or mark historic events, but there was an element of social control to such occasions and the preeminent middle-class American mode of celebration remained the all-male private banquet.[29]

German middle class and artisanal festive culture by midcentury was no less familial in its values than its American counterpart, but it was considerably more public and more sensuous. Much celebration remained confined to the family circle, of course, but German-Americans' veneration of homelife only serves to underscore the significance of the elaborate range of public familial celebration that they also supported. The fact that one New York celebration of the Schiller centennial concluded with a gentlemen's dinner in the American fashion was regarded as scandalous by the mass of German-Americans. American commentators constantly remarked upon the presence of seemingly respectable German families in public places where no genteel Anglo-American woman would venture. Women attended festive dinners even when they were held in taverns; women and children were an important part of beer garden life and of the picnic rituals; they participated in tableaux, rode on floats, indeed little girls even marched as "daughters of the regiment" in New York parades in the 1850s, much to the scandal of Americans—and even of many conservative Germans, it should be noted.[30] Wine and beer were viewed as natural adjuncts to sociability, and Sunday, the one day not dedicated to practical affairs, as most appropriately spent cultivating the other, more sociable and artistic side of the human personality.[31] German-Americans placed explicit positive value on the aesthetic component of celebration: richness of color and costume, lushness of music, intellectual complexity of ceremonial allusion. And unlike Americans, they possessed an explicit tradition of *Volksfeste,* public celebrations whose very purpose was to bring together all elements of the population, using rituals of celebration to erase a sense of class boundaries and generate a feeling of common peoplehood.[32]

Nationality, Germans believed, shaped one's character and modes of thought, creating basic human needs that could not be denied. For Germans, these included sociability and festivity: in effect, periodic infusions of communitas. German-American festive culture, therefore, was not just a byproduct of *Vereine* formed in response to American exclusion or to serve practical ends, but was itself a central goal of *Verein* formation. Immigrants could be American in their workaday world, but if they were to retain a less prosaic sphere to their lives, if they were to maintain the integrity of their personalities, they saw no option but to remain German in their leisure time.

But it was not communitas alone—the experience of direct, unmediated personal relationships—that they sought in festivity; it was also a sense of communion with their brethren in the homeland, a temporary release from homesickness. The highest words of praise that any celebration could earn was that it was "just like in the old homeland." "It was a festival in the genuine German manner," observed one participant of Philadelphia's 1853 singing festival, "and throughout one tasted not a drop of the salt water that separates us from the old fatherland." Carnival celebrants in 1858 Milwaukee were able to imagine themselves transposed back "to one of those glittering masked balls in the old homeland" whose replication "in America, and especially in the 'far west', until now had been regarded as an impossibility." Festivity could help the homesick immigrant forget his exile for a time, and even draw the strength to turn his place of exile into a new home. "The German feels himself newly strengthened and elevated," mused a participant in New York's 1855 singing festival; "he has been able to luxuriate for several days in the loveliest memories of happy bygone days . . . he has forgotten grief and care and abandoned himself completely to the conciliatory influences of noble song."[33]

But that same participant also noted yet another function of German-American festivity: German celebrations unfolded to Americans "one of the loveliest sides of German national life . . . the deep poesie, the inner harmony which form the basic elements of the German character."[34] If German-American festive culture was to survive, its rituals of celebration had to serve not only as ends in themselves but also as a means of bonding the group together and defending its culture from outside attack by creating a more positive image for it. For Americans no less than Germans recognized the incompatibility of the festive cultures of the two groups. To reform-minded, militantly evangelical Americans, Germans might be better workers than the Irish, but off the job they saw them as little more than crude peasants overly addicted to drink and Sabbath-breaking. Middle-class Germans might privately agree with much of the negative judgment of their fellows, but their own disgust with so much of American culture made criticism from Americans difficult to accept. Their pride was at stake. Nor could they ignore the consequences of the mounting temperance, Sabbatarian, and Know-Nothing crusades for the way of life that they were constructing in America.[35]

German-American leaders consequently embarked upon an uncoordinated but conscious campaign to defend their way of life. That involved defining the content of a positive image, ensuring that Germans lived up to it, and communicating it to Americans; it also meant convincing Americans that what Germans termed "nationality" was itself a legitimate category of difference within American society. Their tactics were as much offensive as defensive. Americans at mid-century held out to immigrants the possibility of complete assimilation, provided immigrants conformed to the prevailing ideology and culture of the society. Germans instead drew upon theories of cultural nationalism then prevalent in Europe to assert their right to equal status within American society without conforming culturally. They argued that they had a world-historical mission to elevate and improve American culture through a liberal admixture of German ideals and practices, and that in order to achieve this goal all Germans had a duty to preserve intact the best of their culture for as long as possible. The essence of that culture as they defined it lay in the cultivation of the intellectual and emotional as opposed to the practical world—that side of life that they found so lacking in America; its expressions encompassed not only the sublimities of Goethe and Schiller, Kant and Beethoven, but also the domesticity, conviviality, and *Gemütlichkeit* around which so much of German folk life revolved.

The campaign had to look two ways. On the one hand, it had to mold German immigrants into a group capable of preserving the valued parts of the homeland culture and defending it through the vote if necessary. On the other hand, it had to convince non-German Americans of the two central points of the German position: that the American republic could survive, even thrive, without cultural conformity, and that German cultural differences were valued contributions to America. The intellectual foundations of the campaign were worked out by university-trained polemicists writing in German-American journals of opinion. Their arguments were retailed to the masses in the columns of the daily press and in discussion with the *Vereine,* and to their English-speaking fellow citizens through political debate and the ballot box.

Festive culture was an important weapon in both facets of the campaign. When German-American commentators called for the ritualization of American life, much of what they had in mind was the carefully cultivated liturgy of liberal nationalism that the bourgeoisie had supported in Europe. And when the German masses re-created in America accustomed and comforting forms of public celebrations, they were importing a vocabulary of celebration that spoke almost unthinkingly in nationalistic, and therefore ethnic, accents. Thus the familiar festive culture could look inward, serving as a means to bind German immigrants to the organizations and ideals of the group as formally enunciated by the ethnic apologists; it could also look outward, presenting to the non-German world the positive picture that Germans wished to project, and offering a glittering taste of the glories that German culture could contribute to America if allowed to go its distinctive way.

These varied purposes were made explicit by a prominent German-American journalist in 1855, as he urged attendance at San Francisco's third May Festival. Agitation for political improvement in the homeland, as well as what he termed "the isolated position of the stranger in this country," had created "a perceived need for unity" among the Germans in America, and "it is precisely the May Festival whose celebration offers some satisfaction of that need." It will give the Germans of California "a much-desired chance to enjoy themselves with their fellow countrymen in the old country manner, and thereby to give recognition to the fact that national customs, insofar as a moral significance lies at their base, can be retained even at great distances from the place of origin." But not incidentally, he also pointed out that such festivals were winning for Germans not only the attention of Americans but also their admiration. Another commentator expanded on that theme in promoting the *Turnerfest*—gymnastics festival—in Philadelphia in 1854, which, he said "will give the German element an opportunity to show Americans its most attractive side. German strength, German *Bildung* and joy will step out into the noisy marketplace of American business and public life like reconciling spirits and through their ennobling influence gradually lend it a higher consecration." German *Volksfeste* were teaching Americans how to enjoy life, argued another commentator, and in this lesson lay "their proper significance, their true essence, their real content and most important influence." As a New York editor noted in 1860, "in the German arts cultivated by the singers and Turners we can discern the future of the German element in America," and at the same time "the arts whose triumph is celebrated in the *Volksfeste* are the best means of preventing our children from denying their Germanness."[36]

There is no better example of the ways in which these ends could be intertwined in celebration than the Schiller centennial with which we began. The procession in distant California was only one of hundreds of such festivities that took place on November 10, 1859, in Germany, elsewhere in Europe, and in the German communities of America. The three-day festival closed schools and businesses in many areas of Germany. Citizens engaged in an orgy of parades, statue unveilings, concerts, tableaux vivants, dramatic performances, dinners, speeches, toasts, and crownings of busts, all organized by local volunteer committees. For a people denied either freedom or national unity in the aftermath of the failed revolutions of 1848, Schiller could serve as a symbol of both, and what was on the surface a literary festival and celebration of German cultural strength became in the various German states a festival of the "bourgeois opposition," one in a line of national festivals that helped lend reality to the liberal middle class vision of a single German people.[37]

Across the Atlantic, volunteer planning committees, generally drawn from the ranks of *Verein* members, employed much the same rhetoric and repertoire of public ritual as their countrymen back home. The high points of New York's three-day festival included a bust crowning accompanied by tableaux vivants from Schiller's plays at the Academy of Music, and laudatory tributes at the Cooper Institute presented from a speaker's platform graced with statues of Schiller and the muses Melpomene and Polyhmnia and busts of Goethe, Shakespeare, Lessing, Klopstock, Luther, Herder, Rousseau, Dante, and Homer. Chicago contented itself with theatrical performances, concerts, balls, and banqueting, but Buffalo, Philadelphia, Pittsburgh, Richmond, New Orleans, Cincinnati, and St. Louis, along with many lesser German communities, joined San Francisco in publicly parading their homage to the poet.[38]

These Schiller festivals in exile were clearly a demonstration of solidarity with the vision of freedom and unity for the homeland that informed their German counterparts, a sign that Germans in America still considered themselves part of the greater German nation.[39] But their rituals and rhetoric spoke equally strongly to the special concerns of life in America. To invoke Schiller was to invoke melancholy memories of all that was dear that had been left behind, and to indulge in a feeling of brotherhood for others who shared the same memories. Schiller was also, however, a reminder that the dearest part of the homeland was not its soil but its spiritual treasures, which could accompany the German wherever he went as long as he remained true to his heritage. Indeed, the freedom that Schiller celebrated was the freedom that Germans had found in America. Schiller, proclaimed a speaker at New York's celebration, was the best expression of that side of the German character which most qualified the German despite his distinctiveness to become a true American citizen: the cosmopolitan dedication to the union of all good men in the service of freedom and truth that had become an essential trait of the German character through German classical literature, and especially through Schiller. German-Americans could "rest well in the shadow of his fame."[40]

To celebrate Schiller was thus to celebrate the destiny of America, the German role in that destiny, and a special German commitment to the preservation of the free institutions of America. The fact of celebration and its ritual stages—its processions, speeches, banquets, balls—brought German-Americans together and gave them a consciousness of collective identity; its symbolism—the high culture that it celebrated—provided the justification for that identity. In effect, the rhetoric and rituals of celebration used to evoke a nation in Europe were being invoked in the American Schiller festivals to invent and justify what later generations would term an ethnic identity. The *Vereine* with their festive culture of nationalism had been the cradles of a new class and a new sense of nationhood in Germany. In America, they now became nurseries of ethnicity: an ethnicity that had at its center the commitment to the festive culture that had engendered it, an ethnicity most experienced in the midst of festivity, an ethnicity, in short, not for everyday but for holidays.

III

To understand the implications of an ethnicity nurtured in celebration, we must look more closely at the contours of German-American festive culture—the occasions of celebration, the liturgy and symbols employed, the types of celebrants—and how they changed over time. German-Americans came to apply standard rituals of celebration to a broad continuum of events that they wished to set off from everyday life with appropriate ceremony. At the casual end of the range was the ritualized German Sunday, seen at its best on summer afternoons when festively dressed families, or even whole neighborhoods, made their collective way on foot, by horse car or boat to rural pleasure grounds to enjoy a pleasant stroll, listen to music, drink beer, dance, and sing. The German commitment to "Blue Monday" with its leisurely work pace and male-only public drinking followed naturally from the family orientation of the Sunday. Towards the middle of the festive range were the ceremonies of honor—the evening serenades that greeted distinguished visitors and expressed approbation for local dignitaries, the group rituals that marked funerals and weddings—and the annual round of festivities within the local *Vereine*. The festive highpoints of the year for the *Vereine* were their Christmas or pre-Lenten winter balls and their summer picnic excursions, one or the other of which might also constitute an annual anniversary commemoration, other- wise celebrated with a formal banquet. Singing society concerts, gym- nastic society exhibitions, or even, as in 1848 Cincinnati, the anniver- sary celebration of a prominent society, could become popular *Volksfeste* when opened to the general public, and by the 1850s most communities had one or another such annual event that marked the emotional peak of the local festive calendar. Holidays, too, whether American (like the Fourth of July), German (like May Day or *Pfing- sten*—Whitsuntide), or religious (such as *Fronleichnam*—Corpus Christi), called forth the peculiarly German rituals of celebration. Fi- nally, occasioning the greatest elaboration of parading, pageantry, and public display were the national conventions of the singing, sharp- shooting, and gymnastics associations, held in different cities each year and serving as movable national *Volksfeste*, as well as non-recur- ring anniversary commemorations like the Schiller centenary or polit- ical events like the 1848 revolutions and the foundation of the German Empire.[41]

This range of festive occasions, despite their varying purposes, shared a complex array of ritual elements designed to achieve three main goals of all German-American celebration: evoking a sense of communitas among the group celebrants, stamping it with a specific set of ethnic qualities, and communicating its strength to outsiders. Early efforts at German-American pageantry like the Milwaukee Harbor Celebration seem to have emphasized elements common to both Ger- man and American public ritual, such as the militia parade and the procession of tradesmen, with only the brass bands adding a special German flavor. But the stimulus to public demonstration provided by the 1848 revolutions, the subsequent arrival of exiled revolutionaries, and the elaboration of *Vereinswesen,* soon standardized the formal vo- cabulary and symbolism of celebration on the German liberal nation- alist model.

Fundamental to the first goal of engendering the sense of unmediated membership in a *Volk* that German-Americans sought from celebration was the ritual process itself. This process can be observed in its typical form in the San Francisco May Day celebration noted earlier. Festivi- ties began on Saturday evening with a torchlight parade of the Turners, accompanied by the Union Band, through the city streets to the wharf, where they formally welcomed visiting guests from Sacramento and escorted them to their lodgings. At nine a.m. Sunday there was another parade—with music muted when marching past churches—to Russ' Garden, where the day's observances began with breakfast, an hour and a half of singing and speeches, then popular games and contests, informal family picnics, and an 8 p.m. parade back to the city. The entire program was repeated on Monday as well.[42]

The May Festival included the four basic components of German festive liturgy, corresponding roughly to the traditional elements of familiar religious liturgy. The parade, or *introit,* from some prominent central site to the special place set aside for celebration, whether a summer picnic grove or a winter banquet hall, formally separated celebrants from the workaday world. With the celebrants now in a state of what might be termed liminal receptivity, public speeches and performances, analogous to the sermon and readings of a church service, then communicated both explicit and symbolic messages to the celebrants, whose group song often constituted a formal confession of faith. The communion achieved in these rites was affirmed in the meal and dancing that capped the festivities, after which a more or less formal recessional incorporated newly invigorated group members back into ordinary life. Major festivals could extend over three days or more, sometimes supplemented by pre- and post-celebrations, ensuring the clear demarcation of holiday time from everyday time.

If the ritual process served to evoke a sense of ethnicity, its defining characteristics were communicated by the symbolic vocabulary employed in ritual celebration. The pervasive use of music, banners, costume, and other artifacts bespoke German efforts to intensify the emotional experience of reality in celebration, and the commitment to the world of feelings that distinguished Germans (in their minds, at least) from other Americans. Those same elements simultaneously carried the specific symbolic message of a given occasion, perhaps a springtime celebration of nature, or a carnival release from convention, or a celebration of physical prowess. By identifying the *Vereine,* neighborhoods, or occupations from which celebrants were drawn, they might also serve to delineate the boundaries of the group. The apotheosis of a poet's bust communicated German dedication to higher culture, while representations of Gambrinus and Bacchus asserted both German commitment to these servants of conviviality and the value of conviviality itself. Plentiful food and drink both symbolized and served German appreciation for the physical side of life. Fire's atavistic symbolism was pervasive. Germans claimed to have introduced the torchlight parade in communities where it was previously unknown, combined it with music to honor dignitaries with torchlight serenades, and frequently concluded the evening parades that were the most popular part of any event—because workers could attend—with a spectacular bonfire of torches.[43] Equally popular were symbols of nature. Germans contrasted their love of nature and their appreciation for the physical with the pale and wan indoor life of the American and the constant battle of the American to subdue nature; to celebrate nature was also to affirm a peoplehood based in a natural if not a political order. Thus their choice of outdoor settings under a canopy of trees for their celebrations was an ideological statement, as was their preference for leaves, garlands, and flowers as decoration.

These symbols spoke to the celebrants themselves at every stage of the ritual process; they spoke most loudly to outsiders through the public parade. German-Americans worried that, despite their best efforts, they would never be able fully to recapture the spirit of a German holiday in America: "What is missing is the participation of the entire population. . . . If one is to feel truly festive, everyone, as in Germany, must wear their festive garments, everyone must join in the jubilation. The eye must not be disturbed by everyday business activity, the heart must not be distracted by the thought that one is really escaping from the labor to which the day is legally dedicated."[44] By effectively forcing a holiday mood on the streets through which it passed, the festive parade heightened participants' sense of separation from the ordinary world. But it could also become a powerful vehicle for communicating the German vision of celebration and German self-imagery to American onlookers. Even on the most informal of ethnic occasions, when the picnic itself was the main event, the march to the picnic grounds still acquired a parade-like character from the inevitable bands that accompanied it, and from the common punctuality often forced upon participants by steamboat or train schedules and by some kind of opening ceremony.[45]

It was the national conventions of the singers and the Turners, in particular, that most dramatically exposed American urbanites to the full force of German festive culture by the 1850s and 1860s. These two groups had become the major standard bearers of nationalist ideology in Germany, and were readily turned to ethnic purposes in America. When the eastern Turners held their seventh annual convention in New York in 1857, American commentators quickly ran out of adjectives to convey the spirit of the occasion. They were impressed with the gymnastics displays, the informality of the dances and games, and the lack of rowdiness of the crowd at the festival grounds. "Individuals walk and talk, laugh, dance or sing, as their inclinations suggest: all is given up to unrestrained innocent jollity." But they were particularly struck by the pageantry of the parades. The evening cavalcade, when guest delegations were welcomed, was "with the music, the flags, the insignia, the novel equipments and the brilliant illuminations . . . attractive in the extreme." Americans as well as Germans thronged the streets the next morning to watch the parade from the Bowery to the Green Point Ferry pier, where the Turners embarked for Yorkville Park. "The gorgeous flags, the fantastic costumes, the heterogeneous character of the whole gave it the appearance of a grand carnival. . . . The exhilarating music, the prancing horses, the dazzling uniforms, the unique drinking-horns, and the dense crowd of varied humanity made the scene one such as was never witnessed in the Western World."[46] The 1865 convention of the singers in New York opened with a torchlit mayoral reception and concluded with a "masquerade of the most grotesque description." More than 60,000 persons attended the three-day sharpshooters' festival in Baltimore that summer. Two years later when the singers met in Philadelphia, Independence Hall itself was illuminated in welcome.[47]

Not content with simply teaching by example, Germans attempted to extend their rituals of celebration to American holidays as well. Thus, as in Milwaukee, the Fourth of July parade became one of the earliest battle grounds between conflicting German and American views of celebration. Americans were generally content to celebrate with individual noisemaking, militia parades, and private banquets. Germans thought this great democratic feast worthy of the full panoply of their festive liturgy. They wanted better music, richer artistry, and fuller social representation in the parade, and they wanted a full day of family celebration. Even in the smallest of towns by the later 1850s, Germans were attempting to capture the Fourth; in those years when it fell on a Sunday, they were left to celebrate the "true" holiday alone in a demonstration of their strength that often attracted physical challenge.[48]

IV

These contours of ethnic celebration were "invented" in America largely by the same liberal middle class and artisanal groups that had become the keepers of national ritual in the fatherland. They formed the bulk of *Verein* membership and they dominated the committees that planned the community-wide festivities.[49] Consequently, the ritual symbolism they employed was sufficiently secular and class-specific as to exclude other segments of the German immigration. Church-oriented and purely working-class Germans, however, were as addicted to ritualized celebration as were their secularized middle-class counterparts. They joined in the community-wide *Volksfeste,* and in their own festivities they drew on the same storehouse of celebratory habits. Variations on the same liturgy and symbolic vocabulary (with additions appropriate to the specific group of occasion) governed the festive proceedings of everything from radical workers' organizations to church sodalities, civic celebrations to national conventions.[50]

But equally significant in the decades following the Civil War were gradual changes of stress in the rituals and symbolic vocabulary of group celebration, evidenced by a certain bifurcation within the festive spectrum. Large-scale public festivities became broader and more inclusive in their ethnic symbolism to encourage the widest possible participation. They placed increasing emphasis on pageantry designed to bolster group self-definition and impress an external audience. The definition and defense of ethnicity seemed to become almost an end in itself in these festivities, leaving the rites of communitas and personal integration more and more to the private celebrations of sub-groups within the immigrant community.

The reasons for such trends are not far to seek. Even a temporary illusion of all-inclusive communitas grew more difficult in the face of the ever-increasing diversity within the community encouraged by economic mobility, generational change, and new immigration in these decades.[51] Yet the various sub-groups within the community, sharing elements of a common festive culture as they did, continued to share common defensive concerns in the face of renewed temperance and nativist agitation. At the same time, the Civil War had increased American receptivity to the message of German spectacle. German-Americans were convinced that their part in Republican politics and in the war effort had won them the nation's respect.[52] Moreover, the war had given to Americans a new appreciation for public ceremonial, and to Germans fresh opportunities to show their ceremonial virtuosity.[53] The temptation to play to an external audience was increasingly irresistible.

One sign of this was the growing effort of Germans to manipulate the physical environment of ethnic celebration. Because the increasingly elaborate German-American festivity was by definition public, it required a stage, and found it initially in the city streets and the hillsides and groves surrounding the city. But Germans soon exerted efforts to shape the stage to their liking. German demand supported private parks which supplemented the meager provision of public recreational space, and German associations built their own halls adapted to the special needs of their festivities which, like Cincinnati's Music Hall in the 1870s, could then become important public spaces for all the city's citizens as well.[54] Each city evolved its special geography of German-American pageantry along the routes connecting these enclosed urban halls with the rural private parks where the festive liturgy so often concluded; Germans adapted the rhythms and components of their pageantry to the physical possibilities of potential parade routes, and merchants and residents along the way soon learned to do their part in providing suitable stage decorations. When the Turners met in Chicago in 1869, "wagon load after wagon load" of evergreens and foliage transformed the city's streets, and the parade marched under a specially constructed triumphal arch 30 feet high and 42 feet wide, modeled after the Athenian Propylaen and crowned with a "colossal" allegorical figure of the German fatherland flanked by Liberty and Germania.[55]

There was even an 1860 proposal to create a special suitably designed permanent site for a quadrennial German-American national festival—a German-American Olympus.[56] This failed, but German-Americans soon began to manipulate the permanent built environment to better communicate their message. Initially they were content to build in the standard eclectic styles that dominated the period both in America and in Europe, but by the 1880s, particularly in cities where Germans had achieved a significant measure of status and pride, they self-consciously adopted for public and private buildings the German baroque styles that were being revived in Germany at the time for similar purposes.[57] Even more explicit was the campaign to erect public monuments. Germans were initially shocked by the lack of public statuary in American cities; it was for them just one more sign of American lack of culture. But their surge in numbers in the 1850s coincided with a growing interest in patriotic monuments among native-born Americans, an interest naturally intensified by the Civil War. The result was a series of postwar German-American campaigns, in city after city, to raise money for public monuments glorifying German culture. Initially favored subjects were cultural heroes like Schiller, Goethe, and Beethoven, but they were soon joined by the German-American pantheon by German heroes of the American revolution like Von Steuben, DeKalb, and Herkimer, and then by Civil War heroes like Sigel. An apogee of sorts was reached when the Turners of New Ulm, Minnesota, in 1883 erected on a bluff above their city a copy of the national monument to Arminius, defeater of the Romans, that had been constructed in Germany by public subscription a few years earlier.[58]

Even in this more assertive phase, certain kinds of festivals continued to look mainly inwards, seeking to rekindle familiar memories and familiar feelings of *Gemütlichkeit*. Folk festival associations, appearing by the early 1860s, were one such type. Chicago's Schwabenverein, for example, was formed in 1878 for the express primary purpose of "annually holding the well-known Cannstatter Volksfest and similar festivals according to the fashion of the fatherland, as well as sociable entertainment and the cultivation of German *Gemütlichkeit*." Only secondarily did it also list among its purposes "the support of members and their families as well as general charitable endeavors." It would soon become one of the largest and most important of Chicago's German associations, and never lost its primary focus on the provision of public festivity. By the end of the century, the New York summer calendar included large-scale Badenese, Palatine, Hessian, Swabian, Bavarian, and *Plattdeutsch* folk festivals, most of them several days in length.[59]

Pre-lenten carnival associations were another example. They appeared in most German settlements during the 1850s, and with their mixture of political satire and licensed revelry soon provided an important midwinter punctuation. In New York, the carnival celebrations apparently remained confined to the halls of individual societies, or, by the end of the century, to larger sites like Madison Square Garden, but in other cities they spilled over into the streets in colorful, exotic parades.[60] Prince Carnival visited Milwaukee with the full force of a Rhenish carnival celebration for the first time in 1857, for example. Weeks of masked balls and satirical performances, "fools' parades" and "fools' conclaves" (*Kappenfahrten* and *Kappensitzungen*, traditional parts of the buffonery and mockery of carnival) preceded and accompanied the grand Shrove Tuesday parade. On Rose Monday evening, Prince Carnival received the key to the city, the homage of his subjects, and a theatrical performance in his honor, with the mayor and city council lending their presence to the occasion. The following morning the Prince held a public levee at his "Burg Narhalla" before parading on a grand float through the city streets, dressed in a scarlet cloak with ribbons and orders and a three-pointed fool's cap on his head. His gaudy court included everything from bewigged councillors, an executioner, and a court physician, to Harlequin, Gambrinus on a high throne raising an enormous goblet, Bacchus with his bacchantes looking down on the world from a foliage-crowned wine barrel, a corps of students in appropriate garb, Napoleon with his mounted general staff and life guards, heralds and marshalls on all sides, and satirical groups whose favorite victims included what Germans were accustomed to call "temperance fanatics." The German press dryly reported that the Americans found the whole thing foreign, but showed "great interest and fascination."[61]

But such festivals, although primarily meeting the personal needs of celebrants, could also serve ethnic ends. All efforts to really Americanize the German Carnival failed, noted an early twentieth-century German-American commentator; even American popular songs generally proved uncongenial. "It can be argued without qualification that the so-called Carnival sessions are the only purely and completely German festivities that are put on by the *Vereine* here," he argued, and for that reason they were the most important means of maintaining German sensibilities among immigrants, awakening them in the second generation, and tightening the bonds linking the German-born to one another and to the homeland.[62]

The growing emphasis on communicating with an external audience through festivity, however, and the more inclusive symbolism that it encouraged, reached fullest expression in the three great German-American national festivals of the postwar decades: the Humboldt Centennial in 1869, the Peace Celebrations of 1871, and the German-American Bicentennial Celebration of 1883. The centennial of Humboldt's birth was still cast in the mold of *volksfeste* of the 1848 era. Like the Schiller centennial, it offered German-Americans the opportunity to celebrate themselves and their cultural contributions to America while honoring a renowned cosmopolitan scholar who also happened to be German. "The century that has elapsed since the birth of Humboldt," noted the chairman of New York City's Humboldt Monument Association, "almost coincides with the first century of American independence, and is marked by greater material, moral and intellectual progress than any preceding one in the world's history. That this is due in a great measure to the influence of the free institutions of this country, of which Humboldt was a most earnest and consistent friend and admirer, cannot be denied. There was a two-fold propriety, therefore, that the citizens of America should commemorate the occasion. . . ." New York's commemoration included a daytime parade to Central Park, where a bust of Humboldt—the first monument in the new park—was unveiled, a banquet, and a torchlight parade for those unable to march during the day because of work. Celebrations elsewhere included the usual mix of processions and torchlight parades, dramatic performances, bust crownings, concerts, picnics, and dances; Pittsburgh's celebration was graced by the attendance of President Grant.[63]

The Peace Celebration of 1871 presented a less elitist conception of German-American ethnicity, and one whose right to autonomous existence was based as much on strength as on the abstract value of the putative cultural gifts it could offer America. The Franco-Prussian War, while occasioning a considerable degree of dissension within German-American circles, had also elicited great waves of emotion, pride, and financial support for the Prussian cause, and the Prussian victory and foundation of a united German state were interpreted as grand affirmation of the strength of German culture and nation. When Chicago Germans heard the news of the victory, they sent mounted trumpeters to the German areas of the city to herald a meeting to plan a fitting celebration.[64] Festivities throughout the country would define the German-American community, communicate its sense of strength, and affirm its claim to a place in American life on its own terms.

As Monday, April 10, 1871, dawned, homes, businesses, and clubhouses throughout the lower part of Manhattan were lavishly decked out in flags, drapery, garlands, and transparencies. Through the colorful streets passed a parade of twelve divisions. In the van were military units and the parade's commander, General Franz Sigel of Civil War fame, reminding onlookers of the central role played by German-Americans in the nation's recent crisis. The various divisions of the parade defined the formal elements of the ethnic community: singers, Turners, sharpshooters, and related *Vereine*; militia and veterans' units; secret societies and some 10,600 members of fraternal organizations; brewers, butchers, and other trades; citizens' organizations, social reformers, benefit societies, and ward organizations; and school children. Floats included an elaborate tableau of the Watch on the Rhine sponsored by the singing societies, and brewers' floats with King Gambrinus and his attendants and "a complete brewery in full operation." The cigarmakers distributed cigars, the artificial flower makers distributed artificial flowers, and 500 miners marched alongside a model of a working mine. Other highlights included a colossal bust of Beethoven which "created universal applause," a gigantic top hat contributed by the hatters that represented the crown of Charlemagne under which all of Germany was now united, and a group representing the Kaiser, the Crown Prince, and their retinue. Perhaps as many as 100,000 marchers took part in the four-hour parade, which was reviewed by the governor and the mayor in City Hall Park, and watched by an outpouring of spectators that was "almost unprecedented." The parade broke up in Tompkins Square, where a massive platform capable of holding several thousand people was erected, surmounted by fifty tall poles wreathed in garlands of evergreens and bearing flags, Chinese lanterns, and society emblems. At 5 p.m. a massed choir of 2,000, standing on the platform, opened the formal ceremonies with Luther's hymn, "A Mighty Fortress is Our God." Speeches followed, punctuated by a chorus of "The Watch on the Rhine" and an orchestral performance. Theatrical presentations and other festivities in German society rooms throughout the city capped the day's celebrations.[65]

Twelve years later, the bicentennial of the landing in Pennsylvania of the first organized German immigration provoked equally grandiose and possibly even more wholehearted German-American celebration in numerous cities. If Chicago Germans were too divided to mount a celebration of any kind, reports of celebrations elsewhere often specifically included a category of celebrants who had been conspicuously absent from accounts of earlier national festivals: church and Sunday school groups. Philadelphia, of course, celebrated with a "monster" concert, parade, and picnic, and cities ranging from Newark, Trenton, Pittsburgh, Washington, and Milwaukee to Providence, Des Moines, and even Danville, Illinois, celebrated with their own parades and *Volksfeste*. The parades contained the conventional mixture of associations, trades, military units, and civic groups, but what made them special, and often lent an aura of sumptuous spectacle to the line of march, were the historical units—marching groups and floats costumed and decorated to represent scenes from the German, the American, and the German-American past. No longer were they proclaiming cultural potential; they were celebrating achieved contribution. Where the rhetoric and the representation of the Schiller, Humboldt, and Peace celebrations of necessity focused first on German culture and only indirectly on German-America, in the Bicentennial festivities German-Americans finally had an occasion on which they could indulge unashamedly in self-congratulation.[66]

V

There would be other German-American celebrations. The deaths of Civil War heroes offered cause for remembrance and rededication, and the wave of monument-building that Germans, along with other Americans, indulged in towards century's end offered numerous occasions for festivity. *Verein* conventions, carnivals, and *Volksfeste* continued, and the German Day celebrations that owed their origin to the Bicentennial commemoration became significant occasions in many German-American communities.[67] But the context of German-American festive culture was changing. The generation that had laid its foundations was retiring from the scene, new immigration was shrinking, and older *Vereine* were facing difficulties in attracting members from the second generation. German spectacle competed for attention with the rites of numerous other ethnic groups and with ever more insistent popular amusements. German-American causes—opposition to prohibition or school language legislation, and later support for Germany in World War I—could still provoke large-scale public demonstration. But they seemed less and less the products of a vital and evolving culture, more and more purely defensive.[68] The rites and symbols of ethnicity threatened to become as frozen and static as the rhetoric of cultural superiority that accompanied them. German-American public celebration continued to communicate its message of ethnic strength only too effectively to an external audience, as the anti-German panic of the World War I period documents. But the desperate rhetoric and declining membership of ethnic organizations even in the prewar years suggest the extent to which the rites of ethnic celebration were losing their resonance, and with it their ability to create the consciousness that they symbolized.[69]

In a sense, German-American festive culture became a victim of its own success. The message it had sought to communicate was a complex one. Obviously, simple mass, the weight of numbers, was a central element. The size and frequency of ethnic celebration communicated to Germans themselves the strength of unity, and to Americans the necessity of taking the Germans into account. But specific content was as significant as sheer size. The pageantry routinely defined the formal elements that structured the ethnic community—the societies, the neighborhoods, the trades and businesses, later also the church and school groups. Also explicitly defined was the nature of the bond that united these elements, the cultural heritage that all Germans shared and that distinguished them from other Americans. Music was central—music not only bound Germans together in common emotion, but was the key to winning American respect, asserted German spokesmen time and again. Equally celebrated were other facets of German high culture and their contributions to the liberation of the individual, as well as German appreciation for nature, and the folk customs and costume that signified the organic unity of the German people out of which its higher culture arose. From this flowed also the family emphasis that pervaded German-American rituals of celebration. And finally, German-American celebration glorified *Gemütlichkeit,* and with it wine and particularly beer, those familiar handmaidens of sociability. Gambrinus frequently graced the most elaborate float in any parade.

But equally important was what was missing from the formal symbolism of German-American festivity. American politics played little role—it was too divisive, since Germans divided their political allegiance. Nor, for similar reasons, was religious symbolism stressed, once the anticlericalism of the antebellum years faded. Also absent was much emphasis on loyalty to the politically defined fatherland. Even the celebrations of 1871 glorified peace, not victory, and as newspaper reports emphasized, avoided any stress on the martial accomplishments of the German armies or the specific character of the German state. German nationalism continued to be defined in almost exclusively cultural terms.

Both Americans and Germans proved receptive to much of this message, but in ways that had ambiguous consequences for the survival of the group's festive culture and for the ethnic group itself. Central to festivity for the participants was always the experience of celebration itself. Festivals meant a chance to recuperate from the cares of daily life, to meet with friends and cultivate an emotional sense of brotherhood; the music, the gymnastics, the bust crownings, were usually secondary. For one participant at Milwaukee's 1856 *Saengerfest,* it was "the heartfelt sociability, the harmony and unanimity, everything that we characterize with the much ridiculed name of German *Gemütlichkeit,* that gave this fest its special charm." Such festivals were like oases "in the desert of American public life" where the immigrant could once again, if only for the moment, be "a human among humans," setting aside the work of the day and refreshing his spirit in the cleansing bath of song. "The hours fly at a *Saengerfest,* and the days run by with seven league boots."[70] In the times and places set aside for celebration, through the sacrament of celebration that created what it signified, German-Americans constructed a temporary world where they could again be culturally whole, an ethnic world where they could again feel true kinship with their fellows, a liminal world wherein they could gather the strength to return to the challenges of their American lives.

The sense of ethnic identity nurtured in this world reinforced rather than subverted other bases of identity like religion or class. The very fact that it was linked to no single situational context, no "practical" set of survival issues, meant that diverse sub-groups could draw upon its affective power with slogans like "language saves the faith" to reinforce their own claims to immigrant allegiance in their struggle against the American mainstream. There was always a tension in this relationship, however, to the extent that the secular bourgeois roots of the ethnic culture could never be disguised completely. Leaders hoped to borrow from the emotional force of ethnic communitas without risking any of their own vital interests, yet they rightly feared that too deep an immersion even in "harmless" leisure-time ethnic activities could seduce members from their primary class or religious allegiance, and battles among German sub-groups for control of the festive symbolism of ethnicity played a significant role in the "disharmony" of which German immigrants so often complained.[71]

Thus the ethnicity generated by festivity was a limited one. Efforts to convert the ethnic harmony of celebration into unity beyond the festival grounds generally came to nought. Too many incompatible perspectives were brought together in the consensual rites of ethnic festivity. Most German-Americans remained indifferent to the subtleties of the cultural argument, too readily conflating Bach and Bock and failing to suppport German-language schools, learned societies, journals, or theaters to anything like the extent demanded by the formal ethnic ideology. By and large they proved unable to pass on their language to the next generation, and never succeeded in achieving real organizational or political unity. Lutherans and Catholics remained at odds with one another and with the main thrust of German-American secular culture, and both radical German workers and the German elite also went their separate organizational ways after the Civil War. What united them all was only their shared commitment to the rites of sociability and festivity, though when those rites, or the German language that supported them, were threatened, they proved a force to be reckoned with at the ballot box.[72]

Festivity played an equally ambiguous role in reshaping the American stereotype of German ethnicity. Germans consciously manipulated the symbols of festivity to communicate a particular group image; one measure of their success is the prominent play given to themes of family, nature, high culture, and harmless jollity in the illustrations of their celebrations in the popular press. The images of German drunkenness and immorality that graced the pages of the illustrated weeklies in the 1850s gave way by the 1870s and 1880s to paeans to what later generations might term a "model minority." American observers complimented their German neighbors for the imagination of their spectacles, for the joyfulness that was clearly a part of them, for their family character, and above all for their orderliness and lack of rowdy drunkenness. Irish public celebrations received notice most commonly when they ended in riots; German festivities gave even the beerhall a more favorable image.[73]

But the transformation of the ethnic stereotype was never complete. Temperance and Sabbatarianism would long remain live issues in American public life. And by helping establish the defense of drinking as a central part of ethnic group self-definition—by setting Gambrinus alongside Schiller in the iconology of German culture—German-American festive culture helped set up the ethnic group for the fatal setback it would receive under the twin blows of World War I and Prohibition. German-Americans, commented one caustic self-critic as early as 1869, were in danger of drowning, like Shakespeare's Duke of Clarence, in a butt of Malmsey.[74] But equally significant was the fact that by placing festivity and its attendant drinking habits so near to the center of a culturally defined ethnicity, German-Americans courted the trivialization of their ethnic identity. "The German immigration has been an unmixed good to the United States," commented the *New York Times* in 1883. "Whatever tends to make life better worth living they have not left behind them, and it would be difficult to compute the good that German immigration has done us in importing German music and German beer, and in the labors of the German immigrants as social missionaries, practically showing, what was practically unknown in this country before they came, that it is possible on occasion to be idle and innocent."[75]

That Americans were beginning to entertain the possibility of regarding ethnic cultural distinctiveness as a valuable embellishment rather than as a dangerous deviation was another measure of German success. But neither idleness and innocence, nor the satisfaction of contributing entertainment to American life, are necessarily strong motives for the further cultivation of ethnic distinctiveness, particularly when numerous Americans began to pay German-American festive culture the ultimate compliments of participation and imitation. Franz Sigel, speaking at the 1857 New York Turnerfest, expressed the hope that "the time will come when such festivals shall no longer be spoken of as German, but when all citizens of America, native as well as foreign born, shall participate in them. They are too exclusive now, but I hope the time will come when Americans will either unite with us, or themselves project similar social entertainments. . . ." Mayor Fernando Wood replied that he "fully agreed with the suggestion that Americans should indulge more than they do in social festivals, and thought that the Germans were the best people they could imitate." It was a suggestion echoed time and again in American coverage of German festivities, and by the last decades of the century it was becoming a reality.[76]

In 1869 the *New York Times* could still complain, for example, that "civic processions in this country, except in commemoration of some great event of national significance, are of rare occurrence." By 1883, it could make casual reference to "all the public anniversaries with which these latter years have been crowded for the people of this country."[77] The Civil War had given Americans a stronger taste for public ceremony; the centennial celebrations of 1876, and the periodic civic expositions that punctuated the postwar decades, provided continuing occasions for its elaboration. Civic groups soon began to exploit the possibilities of the parade and public festival for booster purposes. New Orleans had pioneered its organized Mardi Gras in 1857; Memphis followed suit in 1872, Philadelphia with its first more formal Mummers' Parade in 1876, St. Louis with its Veiled Prophet festival in 1878, St. Paul with its Winter Carnival and Pasadena with its Tournament of Roses in 1886, and even smaller summer resorts quickly learned the promotional value of organized festivity. By the 1890s the didactic possibilities of public pageantry had become evident even to reformers, and festivals had acquired a legitimate place in the American civic calendar.[78]

Such trends may have been the natural consequence of the growth of consumer culture and recognition on the part of the authorities that public celebration might at least be controlled and channeled if it could not be suppressed.[79] But it seems probable that immigrant festive culture also played a significant role, both in enhancing the vocabulary of celebration and in demonstrating its potential respectability and commercial profit. The post-Civil War years witnessed an elaboration of the politically oriented St. Patrick's Day parading of the Irish, as well as the entry of other groups like the Scots into the ethnic festival sweepstakes, but Germans remained by far the most visible and successful of festival entrepreneurs.[80] Their carnival tradition early accustomed many American cities to a new richness of parading costume and conceit, including historical allusion; their annual *Verein* conventions and national celebrations heightened standards of parade spectacle and brought scores of thousands of visitors into the city to enjoy themselves; their festive liturgies expanded and deepened the range of American celebratory forms.[81]

Less organized leisure-time activities were also changing. Important elements of the middle and upper classes were beginning to abandon genteel Victorian norms for a more cosmopolitan, public, and leisure-oriented social round, at the same time that commercialized amusements were creating a new mass popular culture stripped of previous plebian or ethnic referents.[82] As early as the 1850s Germans were arguing that their example had done much to lighten American life, and they soon began to exult that the American reception of German festive culture was creating the impression that "America is on the way to becoming a German country." Buoyed by their Civil War contributions and the might of the new German Empire, German-Americans noted that they were exercising "a strong influence on popular life." The "dark, mutually prying and persecuting society" of the past was "yielding gradually to a freer, unembarrassed tone of friendship" in social relations, and society was becoming "Germanized":

> At first the Germans were envied for their harmless merrymaking; their public celebrations were frequently disturbed in the roughest manner; it often ended up in bloody scenes. But gradually the Americans accustomed themselves to them and began to join in, first individually and secretly, but gradually publicly and in droves. Today they themselves organize splendid popular festivals, which include public parades and entertainments of all kinds on the German pattern.[83]

How direct a role Germans really played in the emergence of this new public culture remains unclear. Their musical organizations were clearly an important point of contact with the American middle and upper classes. German entrepreneurs as well as German example had a significant influence on the development of public eating, drinking, and socializing habits, and Germans certainly looked upon the efforts of Americans to establish their new civic festivals with a patronizing eye. By the early 1900s it began to seem to them "as if a large celebration cannot be made a complete success without the enthusiastic cooperation of the Germans. All nativistic objections are cast aside, a large German representation appears on the committee of arrangements, and the singing of the German Männerchöre usually provides one of the most enjoyable events on the programme."[84]

But equally significant was the same author's comment that Germans were participating in these civic celebrations, "not as an element, but as citizens."[85] German street life, German restaurants, dance halls, and beer gardens, German symphonies, parades, and festivities contributed in important ways to the public character of America's emerging popular culture. But as American life took on a more German cast, there was less and less reason for Germans to remain inside ethnic boundaries in order to satisfy their sociable instincts. More and more German-Americans were ready to tackle life without the prop of a formal ethnic affiliation whose cultural basis now seemed to them superfluous, and group organizations found themselves increasingly sounding and acting like conventional defenders of ethnic differences for the sake of difference itself.[86]

VI

German-Americans can take their place in the ranks of nineteenth-century inventors of tradition. Like others in that embattled century, they attempted to use ritual to solve the problem of community and they achieved a real measure of success. The masses of German-Americans may have desired little more than a chance to enjoy a sociable mug of beer or an occasional picnic in congenial company. But their desires intersected with the theories of the cultivated middle classes to create the basis for the only sense of commonality this large and heterogenous group of immigrants possessed. By shaping a purely cultural definition of ethnicity, German-American leaders were able to find a common denominator that enabled the group to generate the sporadic unity needed to defend their way of life when it came under attack, and to support group institutions that provided a cultural bridge for the first generation. But by the same token, when cultural distinctiveness declined and the festive glue dissolved, the logic of German-American ethnicity faded as well, leaving little residue around which some new ethnic definition might crystallize for the group.

In the context of current debates on the nature of ethnicity in America, German-American ethnicity cannot be viewed primarily as primordial, as situational, or even as symbolic, though all of these elements were present.[87] It cannot be explained satisfactorily as some kind of inevitable sociobiological force; it was intentionally evoked by leaders who believed in the reality of a *Volk* but were not above using both argument and ritual to give it form and consciousness. Nor was it simply a set of rhetorical boundaries enclosing a culturally-neutral social stratum or interest group. At the outset at least, culture was not a means to an end of ethnicization but the end in itself. There was real cultural content to the ethnicity, real grounding for the rhetoric. Thus it was also more than symbolic nostalgia, and its exercise demanded actual commitment and group organization. This cultural ethnicity was no less real because of its leisure-time base. There is ample testimony to its influence on the attitudes and behavior of both group and non-group members. German-Americans tended to attribute the weaknesses of their ethnic group—its lack of political power and inability to prevent Americanization—to weaknesses in the culture they imported, to quarrelsomeness and adaptiveness endemic in the German character. It might better be argued that they resulted from the success of the festive culture itself. The rituals of ethnicity never sought more than the simulacrum of community; in assisting personal integration and missionizing American society, they engendered their own obsolescence.

Other immigrant groups followed different paths, and for them festive culture may have played a different role. Nationalism, John Plamenatz reminds us, took separate forms in the West, where cultures possessed the appropriate languages and tools for full participation in modern civilization and had only to worry about their mobilization, as compared with eastern Europe and elsewhere, where radical cultural change was necessary.[88] Ethnic invention in America may reflect similar differences. Festivity would serve different ends for groups more concerned with economic than with cultural defense, or less convinced that their culture had important gifts to offer the nation as a whole.[89] But for the Germans, at least, festive culture was more than a superficial embellishment of ethnic life. It was the medium within which ethnic identity resided, and it was the vehicle with which Germans sought to change the contours of American life.

Defining the Race 1890–1930

JUDITH STEIN

Popular identities, whether racial or nonracial, are constructed as people define their social and political objectives. For instance, in 1848, the abolitionist Frederick Douglass took for granted that blacks were Americans when he asked his audience, "[I]f this is not mean and impudent in the extreme, for one class of Americans to ask for the removal of another class?"[1] This assumption was essential to Douglass's campaign against the American Colonization Society's attempt to remove blacks to Africa. A few months later, he asserted that blacks were a people: "We are one people—one in general complexion, one in a common degradation, one in popular estimation."[2] Addressing northern blacks, who evidently did not identify with the slaves, he attempted to mobilize them behind the cause of southern bondsmen by asserting their oneness. Nevertheless, the two identities were compatible. Douglass believed that blacks, like the Germans and Irish, could be a people and Americans.

The same words can have different meanings. In 1880, sugar workers in Louisiana announced that "the colored people are a nation and must stand together."[3] They were not declaring independence but using a metaphor to unite a group of blacks trying to win a bitter strike. One assumes that six years afterward when the Knights of Labor came into Louisiana's sugar fields and organized both blacks and whites, the manifestoes were different.

The sugar workers' definition of a nation was very different from Cyril Briggs's. Writing in 1919, Briggs thought of blacks as a people and a race. They had specific racial qualities which distinguished them from nonblacks. He thought,

> The surest and quickest way to achieve the salvation of the Negro is to combine the two most likely and feasible propositions, viz.: salvation for all Negroes through the establishment of a strong, stable, independent Negro State (along the lines of our own race genius) in Africa and elsewhere; and salvation for all Negroes (as well as other oppressed people) through the establishment of a Universal Socialist Co-Operative Commonwealth.[4]

Unlike Douglass, he believed that a people required a nation-state of its own. Although unique, blacks were similar enough to other people to require socialism as well as a state.

In 1919, a group of striking longshoremen in Key West, Florida were less theoretical. They called themselves "honest workmen." Their self-conception was probably related to their newspaper appeal to the citizens of the city, "especially the working classes like the members of this union who have to earn their living by the sweat of their brow."[5] Another definition was implicit in the letter of the president of their local union to the National Association for the Advancement of Colored People (NAACP). Asking for support, he said that "the principle involved means so much not only to these Negroes who are on strike but to our race in general."[6] The first appeal stressed membership in a class; the second, a race.

The different names and meanings undermine the common belief that racial identity or consciousness is fixed. The ways people define themselves are determined by their history, politics, and class. They change. The same words have conveyed vastly different meanings and encouraged diverse actions. They mean less and more than they seem. People employ strategic fictions that can be understood only in a context. They always must be understood as one element with other ideological beliefs that have nothing to do with race. And they interact with definitions made by other people, especially by those who exercise power.

John Higham observes that nineteenth-century Americans, living in island communities with minimal connections, did not demand clear definitions of Americans or of peoples. Universal ideology and local dispersal of power permitted varied patterns of ethnic assimilation.[7] This was most obvious for blacks. From the vantage point of the end of the twentieth century, the condition of free blacks was not very different from that of slaves in the antebellum period. But Frederick Douglass's appeal to the former demonstrates that many of them did not think their condition was bound with the latter. The difference between a discriminated-against free person and a slave was enormous. The ending of slavery placed a boundary, imposed by the national state, on the variety of treatment consistent with American ideology. Slave status was now outside the boundary. Because the only people who were slaves were blacks, the national definition of citizenship simultaneously redefined blacks.

White southerners yielded to the force of armies, and then to the power of black votes but refused to accept the substance of the new definition. Throughout Reconstruction black farmers and white planters contended over the meaning of the new citizenship. The struggles reached a climax during the international depression of the 1890s. Responding to a political challenge by black Republicans and white and black Populists, southern Democrats were able to redefine black citizenship and secure order through disfranchisement.[8]

The North was complicitous. After 1896, when its Republican leaders discovered that they did not need black southerners to maintain their national power, the party yielded to southern localism. Northerners found that disfranchisement and Jim Crow did not violate the Reconstruction amendments. Beneath the legal casuistries, they concluded that blacks, and many whites, lacked the "property, virtue, and intelligence" required for political participation.[9] The historian Francis Parkman thought many northerners, too, needed order and rule by groups possessing "hereditary traditions of self-government."[10] The capitulation did not result simply from political pragmatism or reevaluation of their southern, black allies. The massive demonstrations and birth of a "European-style" labor movement in the wake of the punishing depression of 1873 had earlier proved how laboring classes could threaten civilization.

E. L. Godkin, editor of the *Nation,* claimed northern workers and southern blacks composed a dangerous "proletariat" who seemed to belong "to a foreign nation." Because many of their workers were foreigners, northerners voiced fears in class, racial, and nativist language often difficult to separate. Like Godkin, many used southern nomenclature to depict the situation. Native-born residents in Bayonne, New Jersey divided the city's population into two races: "'white men' and foreigners."[11] A few even looked to southern disfranchisement as a solution. However, the challenge of the foreigner, unlike that of the

black southerner, was not political. Elites restructured city governments, eliminated alien voting, and erected new barriers for voters to
trim popular power.[12] But northern institutions were sturdier; industri-
alists had more room to maneuver; and they repulsed the challenge of
a predominantly foreign working class without major alterations in the
northern polity.

However they resolved their problems, northern and southern elites
attempted to forge a new American identity using racial and class fitness as criteria. If their efforts rose feverishly during periods of depression, which were frequent in the late nineteenth century, the new
definitions were rooted in more durable experiences. Industrial capitalism, national markets, and international migration now connected
people who had once lived apart with minimum contact. the more interdependent they became, the greater the differences seemed to be.

Attempting to secure their power and culture, white Protestants demanded clearer definitions of Americans and the other peoples. During
the late nineteenth and early twentieth centuries, Western academics
and publicists studied and ranked the various peoples of the world.
(Europeans were always at the top of the list.) The word "race" came
to mean a biological community with shared characteristics. The scientific underpinning was not so much a sign of precise knowledge as a
rationale for the determination to exclude, isolate, or subordinate,
whichever was appropriate. As much as they could, legally or infor-
mally, elites attempted to protect the body politic—their government,
their schools, their neighborhoods—from others who might pollute it.

There is an extensive and sophisticated literature on the changing
white views of blacks in this period.[13] The new national consensus on
black inferiority did not eliminate the diversities of the nineteenth century any more than the earlier universalist ideology had eliminated discrimination. The new southern order was not replicated in the North.
And even within the South, there were variations. Race and racism
were metonyms for culture and class. Because racial ideology always
intersected with other ideologies and more mundane interests, its impact was not uniform. But joined with the other characteristics of the
new industrial system, the new racism threatened the status and future
of northern blacks, too.

During the late nineteenth and early twentieth centuries, blacks, too,
attempted to define more precisely who they were. Although untar-
nished by the purposes of racism, the way they did it was equally ideological. It also contrasted sharply with earlier black thinking.

Emancipation Elite

Most black leaders who grew up during the period of the Civil War and Reconstruction had not pondered the nature of race. They considered themselves Americans in the nineteenth-century sense. Like white northerners, they thought that civilization was universal: equal laws would reward individual merit. Northern society had ended slavery, allowed them to play significant roles in society, and promised to reward other blacks. Peter Clark, a high school principal in Cincinnati, said in 1874, "The colored people of the United States are not exotic. Centuries of residence, centuries of toil, centuries of suffering have made us Americans. In language, in civilization, in fears, and in hopes we are Americans."[14]

The new industrial society threatened what the elite, composing about one-quarter of the black population, had found so attractive in northern life. Their fragile economic base, in real estate, small business, politics, and the professions was eroded by shifts in public taste, the rise of big business, and the new racism. Earlier they had confidently predicted that hard work and equal laws would also elevate the poor blacks in the North and in the South, where most blacks lived. Now they were not so certain.

They did not respond well to the challenge, because their kind of Americanism emerged from lived experience, not simple rational calculation or opportunism. Frederick Douglass was born a slave, but he became a major American and international publicist. While not all the leaders of his generation had come so far, most had moved from poverty or modest beginnings to positions of respect, culture, and some wealth. Their bourgeois ideas and life-styles and their close work and friendship with elite whites insulated them personally from most of the changes.

Their ties were often to the most reactionary Republican politicians and American businessmen. John P. Green of Ohio was a friend of John D. Rockefeller's; George Myer, an intimate of Mark Hanna's. They looked at the new popular attacks on business as their white friends did. Although they had urged a larger role for the government to ensure equal justice in the South, they opposed government intervention in the North because they saw no threat to democracy or opportunity from the new big businesses. These beliefs stood in the way of a relationship with progressives in the North. Their orthodox economics ruled out their support of government interventions that could

have helped urban blacks; their individualism resisted institutionalized
self-help that could have at least addressed the problems of many
northern blacks.[15]

The generation retained its positions and remained an important part
of the black population, although some "passed." But the group could
not negotiate a transition. Its members became insignificant factors in
racial politics. Their sons and daughters chose a different course out
of their lived experiences. One of them, W. E. B. Du Bois, expressed
the fear that the problem of the twentieth century would be a color
line, meaning "a white effort to limit black progress and development."[16]

The New Intellectuals: Edward Blyden and W. E. B. Du Bois

The words "progress" and "development" were synonyms for Western
civilization, propelled by the engines of capitalism. The Emancipation
generation had believed that Western civilization was open to all, but
the current one concluded that progress was not universal but wielded
by racial groups and nation-states. Educated, urban, and sophisticated,
they revealed in their own lives the limits being placed before them,
even though they were not farmers or workers. They concluded that
they would have to lead and strengthen the race.

Their determination was reinforced and broadened by a historical
coincidence. The American conditions—of Jim Crow and disfranchisement—matured at the same time that Europeans were colonizing Africa. Du Bois acknowledged that Afro-Americans were Americans by
citizenship, language, religion, and politics, but they were also members of a "vast historic race," which was international. The destiny of
blacks was not assimilation of "servile imitation of Anglo-Saxon culture, but a stalwart originality which shall unswervingly follow Negro
ideals." The churchman Alexander Walters declared that "in matters
of race there were no geographic or national limitations." In 1900, both
men attended the first Pan-African Conference, which included blacks
of the United States, the Caribbean, and Africa.[17]

Educated Africans had reached the same conclusion. For most of
the nineteenth century, they, with British liberals, had little doubt that
education, commerce, and Christianity would transform Africa, as
these forces had transformed Europe. Europeans became less optimistic when economic development replaced trade and imperialism succeeded foreign relations. Europeans now found Africans barbarous by

nature, not by culture. While future progress was not foreclosed, Africans required order and domination.

If the Europeans redefined Negroes or Africans (the same people) to serve their new purposes, so did Africans. Edward Blyden, professor, Liberian dipomat, adviser to British colonial officials in Sierra Leone, was the principal theorist of the new view of race. Like the Europeans, he made race the principal motor of history, and "nationality . . . an ordinance of nature." "No people can rise to an influential position among nations without a distinct and efficient nationality," he said. The task of politics and leadership was to develop what nature had decreed.[18]

Blyden retained the idea that bourgeois society was progressive and would improve Africa as it had improved Europe. Therefore, he accepted imperial rule. Foreign power was necessary to remove local divisions and inefficient practices. But alien races could not create an African nation. Colonial rule would permit African leaders to create the nation, the nationality, which would eventually lead to the nation-state.[19]

Blyden, like other nationalists of the nineteenth century, believed that states must be modern and viable, not merely independent. He valued progress more than self-determination. He proclaimed the oneness of people who never had considered themselves part of the same nation and had existed for centuries in states ruled by other peoples. The idea of a nation-state, a state of one nation, was as alien to African history as were the Western institutions Blyden admired. This situation was not unique to Africa. Even after the unification of Italy in 1860, an Italian nationalist exclaimed, " We have made Italy; now we must make Italians."[20]

But while Italian nationalists proceeded from the nation-state to create a nation, the weakness of the African elite required them to build a nation before it could achieve a nation-state. Building a nation meant altering popular culture and removing divisive sovereignties. The only way that could be done was through Western economic, military, and political power. The only way the elite could lead was to lead a colonized people. Asserting the existence of a distinctive culture, black leaders proposed to modify it radically, to make it more like European society.

Blyden never enjoyed a large personal following. His passionate belief in the future led him to minimize the conflicts and variations of the present. His conception of African greatness led to harsh evaluations of the more modest efforts of the Liberian government and African leaders in the colonies of West Africa. Yet his writing and ideas were influential because they provided a compelling, new conception of Africa and its history, which influenced Africans and Americans.[21]

For the moment, the formulation deferred opposition to imperialism. (And the Pan-African Conference of 1900 protested not imperialism per se but its practices.) The concept of race facilitated the unification of the African elite and the identification of its aspirations with those of all blacks. Blyden was born in the West Indies, was educated in the United States, lived and worked in Liberia and Sierra Leone, and acted as an adviser in other areas of Africa. Most of the elite's experiences transcended colony, region, and even continent. They were mobile, united by their ambitions, closer to one another than to Africans in the countryside. The racial identification erased troublesome differences. African history before imperialism was as conflictual as European. The new idea of race removed these divisions by imagining Africa as one.

Pan-African theory accommodated to regional differences. In the United States, most of the new racialists did not look forward to a nation-state for American blacks. This realistic conclusion altered the Afro-American definition of race. While Blyden attributed to Africans all of the qualities which contemporary theorists required of peoples seeking independent nation-states and firmly rooted these in biology, the Americans were more tentative. W. E. B. Du Bois assigned to race a moral and metaphysical significance which reflected the situation of American blacks demanding justice, not independence. For Du Bois, the Negro race had a message. He spoke more often of Negro genius, literature, art, and spirituality than of efficient institutions and distinctive cultures. But if race differences were only "subtle, delicate and elusive", working "silently," how could they be "the central thought of all history?" And, if they were as deep as he assumed, how was it that American blacks "minimize[d] race distinctions?" Du Bois's explanation that Afro-Americans ignored race because its use has been to denigrate them is not convincing if race is as distinctive and central as he alleged. In practice, despite his passion, his work transformed the hierarchy and deep divisions of racial theory into the subtler and more egalitarian ones of cultural pluralism. (He studied with the same men at Harvard as Horace Kallen, the other important cultural pluralist of the period.)[22]

The new racial conception bridged narrower terrain in the Republic. It did not have to overcome differences in sovereignty, religion, language, and culture. American blacks were equal citizens by law in one nation; they all spoke English; most of them were Protestants. Slavery had destroyed most of the distinctions the African elite confronted. The principal barriers confronting the new theorists were those of class and region.

These differences could be considerable. Unlike most southern blacks, Du Bois, as well as Booker T. Washington, accepted southern franchise restrictions during the 1890s. Du Bois assented to "legitimate efforts to purge the ballot of ignorance, pauperism and crime," and, like Blyden, he granted that it was "sometimes best that a partially developed people should be ruled by the best of their stronger and better neighbors for their own good."[23]

During the first decade of the twentieth century, Du Bois opposed disfranchisement when he saw that it struck at the educated as well as the ignorant. Defense of the vote was important for public discourse and use in the North, but it did not modify his program for the race. Du Bois's Anglo-Saxonism mandated racial reconstruction led by a black elite, his Talented Tenth. Black leaders, using the bonds of race, replaced American institutions as the critical civilizing ingredient. The enlarging and uniting of the Talented Tenth became the first item on his political agenda. Du Bois's views of the majority of blacks, the race, was shaped by his elite view of progress, which the concept race obscured.

Arnold Rampersad argues that the real subject of *The Souls of Black Folk* (1903) was Du Bois's "sufferings, his virtues, his gifts,"[24] and, one might add, his values. Despite his sympathy, Du Bois found contemporary black life limiting, narrow, and often immoral. He validated mass potential by celebrating an aspect of slave culture, the spirituals, recognized by whites but no longer the actual culture of southern blacks; by aestheticizing black culture, he made it less threatening.[25] The passion of the book—his own experience of the death of his young son and the story of the two Johns—demonstrated the current worthiness of the Talented Tenth by revealing their achievements, ambitions, and sensibilities. Du Bois ignored actual mass culture, the lived and the artful, and substituted his own imagination and elite white culture's view of the uneducated and poor.[26]

In his novel *The Quest of the Silver Fleece* (1911), a swamp characterizes the culture of the black masses; ignorance, superstition, dreams, and moral delinquincy inhabit this murky region. Salvation comes through labor, the planting of cotton, whose value is taught by two young blacks trained in liberal culture. Du Bois's portrayal paralleled Blyden's depiction of African culture. Black elites needed to "strengthen the Negro's character, increase his knowledge and teach him to earn a living."[27] The remedy of education, even by the well-intentioned, attributed poverty to cultural imperfection and postponed equality until people were fit.

Like his Harvard teacher William James, Du Bois wanted to bring culture to the masses although James's idea of reciprocal exchange rarely appeared in his student's thought. Their notion of culture—the arts, refinement, formal education—was a definition of a leisured class. Gilded Age intellectuals advocated institutions of cultural uplift to restore social harmony, rent by the class conflict of the late nineteenth century. Whatever its efficacy in northern cities, it was unsuited to the reordering of social relations in the South.

Du Bois's formulation persisted in his novel *Dark Princess* (1925). During the Great Depression, influenced by the anticapitalist thinking affecting many intellectuals, Du Bois advocated a black, cooperative, rural economy in the South, led by the Talented Tenth. When George Streator, a young Fisk graduate, currently working as a labor organizer, questioned the goal's feasability and agency, Du Bois reiterated his faith: "I do count on a Negro middle-class to usher in co-operation. I count on the fact that not all of the young Negro leaders are selfish and stupid exploiters. At any rate, either we get leadership from the best part of this class, or we get nothing."[28] Du Bois's journalism continued to remind whites of their injustices and to advance the professional and business aspirations of the Talented Tenth, no matter how imperfect.

Du Bois held too many elite values and ideas to war against the West. Its ideas of leadership, culture, progress, and race were his, too. His passion against its injustices were those of a believer. Categories like morality and corruption, service and selfishness, implied choice. The South did not have to discriminate, the planter did not have to oppress; the capitalist did not have to exploit.

Du Bois addressed the conscience of the middle class, not its institutions. Douglass had united morality and economy when he opposed slavery. His abolitionism was harnessed to the free-labor system of the North, however imperfect, which allowed him to appeal to northern interest as well as morality. Du Bois never found a twentieth-century equivalent. As a result, his egalitarian yardstick functioned as a protest ideal but lacked the power of substantive belief. On the other hand, his racial ideals and elite conception of the route to progress precluded an alliance with labor. (During the 1930s, when many blacks became enthusiastic about the egalitarian Congress of Industrial Organizations, Du Bois acknowledged its virtues but thought it had little significance for racial progress.) In the end, his aspirations transcended equality and justice. He pursued racial greatness, a goal very difficult to define, not to say achieve.

The Racial Ideas of Southern Farmers

Black farmers defined their problems differently. One of them, Nate Shaw, analyzed his situation with some questions: "Now it's right for me to pay you for using whats yours—your land, stock, plow, tools, fertilize. But how much should I pay? The answer ought to be closely seeked. How much is a man due to pay out? Half his crop? A third part of his crop? And how much is he due to keep for hisself? You got a right to your part—rent; and I got a right to mine. But whose the man ought to decide how much? The one that owns the property or the one that works it" [sic].[29]

In 1876, David Graham, from Edgefield County, South Carolina, offered a similar analysis to a congressman who wondered why the planters wanted him "oppressed and downtrodden." Graham told him, "In case I was rich, and all colored men was rich . . . how would he get his labor? He couldn't get it as cheap as he gets it now. . . . His interest is in keeping me poor, so that I will have to hire to some one else."[30]

Shaw and Graham had a sense that they belonged to a people and knew they suffered discrimination. But their sense of discrimination was part of other experiences, alien to Du Bois. Black farmers rooted the racial question in the conflicting aspirations of landowners and workers. Shaw defined himself as "a working man." "Whatever I had," he said, "it come to me through my labor."[31] He took pride in his abilities and identified with other people who worked—black or white—even though he never felt comfortable with whites. He understood that illiteracy made it harder for him, and others like him but he did not believe that culture would bring deliverance. He never doubted the virtues of labor but wondered about the value of labor. The new racial formulation did not accommodate the experiences of farmers because it assumed that plantation labor and sharecropping did not have to be oppressive. Shaw and Graham, like many small landowners and workers, believed that accumulated property required oppressed labor.

Shaw and Graham's conclusions had been shaped by the experiences of slavery, emancipation, and especially Reconstruction. The new Republican party, through its Union League clubs, united polity, society, and economy to protect and enhance black labor and lives. The decline of Republican politics was a crucial blow, as white Democrats well understood, to collective practices. The sharecropping system, too, encouraged more-individualistic values and methods. Added to the falling price of cotton, these changes placed overwhelming burdens on traditions of cooperation, obligation, and the power to enforce them. They were not ended but weakened.

Nate Shaw remarked, "[P]eople wont jump back on their close relationships for money, usually; they'll go to somebody else. . . . Dont want to press them relationships as hard as a money loan will press em." When Shaw, after joining a sharecroppers union in 1931, decided to protest the dispossession of a friend, he described his decision in individualistic terms: "I reared like a mule in a stable, but what crazy person wouldn't rear when he seed the man fixing to take everything he had and he knowed he didn't owe him nothin?"[32] Shaw acted alone on the basis of his conception of justice but without a faith in collective action.

Traditions of collective action are formed, destroyed, reformed on new bases. The southern black communities created by Reconstruction were subsequently fragmented by disfranchisement and the cotton economy. However, if few possessed a living tradition of collective action, the values of the Reconstruction tradition—the dignity of labor, economic independence, participation in the polity—and their daily experiences as farmers and workers stamped their conception of racial progress, and by implication racial identity. The imposed silence of the disfranchised farmer permitted others, black and white, to speak for him.

Marcus Garvey and the New Racial Ideas

The ideas of black intellectuals would have possessed a small constituency had they not been translated into a popular politics. Marcus Garvey brought the new organic conception of the race to the masses: not to the Shaws, but to urban workers. Garvey's success demonstrated that the elite view received more of a hearing in the cities than in the countryside. But he discovered that a diverse urban community had various ideas about how racial bonds should be used, which implied different conceptions of the race. Attempting to put the new ideas into practice brought out many of the problems which the intellectuals could ignore.

Garvey's idea of race was not constructed in Jamaica, where he was born in 1887. The son of a proud artisan, Garvey learned about the international situations of blacks from a group of Pan-Africans in London, where Garvey lived and worked from 1912 through 1914.[33] His politics of uplift emerged partly from them and partly from the contrast between the wealth of England and the poverty of Jamaica. A politics of improvement does not emerge without the making of a comparison. Injustice may be experienced anywhere; underdevelopment, to use the contemporary word, exists only in relation to another society, judged to be developed.

Garvey's description of the mass of Jamaicans revealed his outlook. "As a society we realize that the negro people of Jamaica need a great deal of improvement," he wrote. "The bulk of our people are in darkness and are really unfit for good society. To the cultured mind, the bulk of our people are contemptible."[34] His own chances would be limited by the civilized world's evaluation of the masses. Like Blyden and Du Bois, Garvey believed that popular culture needed to be altered, improved, and ultimately replaced by Western elite culture. If Garvey's indictments of mass culture and subsequent promises of greatness were more fervid than those of Du Bois, it was simply because Garvey was simultaneously fighting to secure his own career as well as analyzing the black situation. But his new Universal Negro Improvement Association (UNIA), which he created when he returned to Jamaica in 1914, and his first project, the building of a school, never got off the ground. Garvey took a common road, migration.[35]

Arriving in Harlem in 1916, Garvey was impressed with Afro-American leaders, who seemed much more progressive than Jamaicans.[36] A new generation of Afro-Americans had begun to act on the advice of Du Bois. Industrial growth, absent from Jamaica, produced a growing movement of southern blacks into cities. The migrants provided the social and economic basis for ideals of racial solidarity, which replaced the individualism of the older generation. Less disinterested than Du Bois would have preferred, the new generation attempted to unite the race with business and institutions of uplift to help the poor.

Although the possibilities of a racial economy within the larger American economy outstripped realism, which the new leaders privately acknowledged, their pragmatism and opportunism allowed them to work in other areas, too. Some serviced immigrant communities, which often lacked professionals.[37] Economically orthodox, like their fathers, most opposed the new reformers and aligned themselves with

the Republican old guard. On the local level, like other ethnic politicians, they made alliances with party bosses for the favors and jobs
that machines offered the faithful. Some dipped into the broader tradition of middle-class reform by attempting to set up institutions to
shelter young women entering the city or advise migrants. They had
not bridged the class gap, but their instruments of racial self-help had
more credibility than the older elite's individualistic prescriptions.
Most of the new leaders lived and worked close to the migrants.[38]

Garvey's purposes fit in very well with the new black trends. He
announced that the UNIA was "doing uplift work . . . to bring them
[the Negroes] in line with the best in our civilization."[39] But during
World War I, Garvey and a growing number of young men in Harlem
became more impatient and critical. The rebirth of popular politics
demonstrated new ways to improve black society.

The New Democracy and Nationalism

The militancy of broad sectors of the American working class affected
blacks, as well. The government's announcement that workers had the
right to join unions and the fall in the unemployment rate to 1.4 percent
led to an upsurge of organization among blacks. The longshoremen
cited at the beginning of this essay were part of the new movement.
By forming a union, they were seeking "the rights that are the just
rights of each and every American citizen regardless of his race or
creed." The new social democratic paths to progress were mapped out
by John Riley, a black organizer for the American Federation of Labor
(AFL) and a member of the International Union of Steam and Operating Engineers, who had worked in the campaign to organize packing-
house workers in Chicago. Union wages and an eight-hour day would,
he thought, "give the ambitious poor boy a chance to make a mark in
life for himself because after he works eight hours a day, he comes
home refreshed and has an opportunity to devote a certain portion of
each day to mind cultivation."[40]

If working-class ideology was one ingredient of black militancy, so
was a new national and racial consciousness, encouraged to some degree by the Allies. Woodrow Wilson's Fourteen Points affirmed the
principle of self-determination. In Africa, as in many other parts of the
world, the mandate system embodied the Great Powers' version of
self-determination in the former German colonies. Afro-American

leaders, influenced by the popular awakenings, hoped that Africans would play a greater role in the governing of the colonies. Garvey, Madame C. J. Walker, a businesswoman, Adam Clayton Powell, Sr., of the Abyssinian Baptist Church, A. Philip Randolph, the young Socialist, and a few others formed the short-lived International League of Darker Peoples in 1919 in New York to represent Africa.[41]

They rooted their claims in racial and democratic theory. Because there were no independence movements in Africa, the league argued that Western blacks and progressive supporters should rule an independent African state. Like Wilson, they agreed that "self-determination in Africa, of course, cannot be absolute." Unlike the president, they rejected supervision by any of the Western powers under the mandate system. The former German colonies should be governed by a commission composed of "the educated classes of Negroes from America, the West Indies, Liberia, Hayti, Abyssinia, and the people of Japan and China and other enlightened sections of the African and European worlds."[42]

Typically, Garvey argued that the white man had "no monopoly of knowledge." Afro-Americans, he held, are "a civilized, cultured people who understand the way of civilization—the way of the world. . . . Africans . . . are innocent of the ways of the civilization that rules the world." It was therefore the obligation of Afro-Americans to save Africans from the fate of native Americans.[43]

Garvey often used this analogy. His invented Africa was "a great forest country, a great wilderness." He said, "We were misinformed about Africa for three hundred years." The ignorance was not about African culture but African wealth. But now blacks know that "Africa is the richest continent in the world."[44] Although the basis of Afro-American rights in Africa was racial, Garvey did not advance a substantive notion of racial distinctiveness. He simply asserted the right to lead and rule on the basis of the western culture of the elite blacks and the organic bonds of race, the appropriate criteria according to the Wilsonian formula. His assumption that African and Afro-American elites should rule African people undercut democratic choice. Garvey's vision slid over the problems that Blyden had addressed and confronted. (Garvey would eventually experience them in Liberia.)

In the end, the African agitation subsided because of its remoteness from the lives of Afro-Americans, not because of its intellectual contradictions. But the identification of self-determination and racial rule was strengthened and applied to domestic situations. The campaign for the first black assemblyman from Harlem defined democracy as racial representation.[45] Some black militants who believed they were equivalents were disappointed.

Garvey was aware of the weakness of his own organization, the UNIA, which he had extended to the United States. He concluded that the ability of Afro-Americans "to move world affairs" was limited.[46] Therefore, the question was not, at the moment, how to liberate Africa but how to produce power. During the war, Garvey had peppered his speeches with references to other resisting groups—the Irish, Indians, Jews. He now turned from the example of oppositional forces, whose victories were less than he and others had hoped or feared, to those who had achieved it. The Anglo-Saxon world had endured and triumphed over its diverse opponents. Western strength was built on business, a surer route to power than agitation or education, abundant commodities in the United States. Personally ambitious and socially rebellious, Garvey attempted to create the infrastructure of the racial community, animated by key western institutions. He hoped to harness the new militancy behind his elite goals.

Black Star Line and Popular Organization

Because the Black Star Line was the instrument that secured the rise and fall of Garveyism, it is useful to examine the culture of its creation. The building of ships, preeminent symbols of national power, had been the highest priority of the United States mobilization. After the war, America's new fleet was to be the core of shipping lines capable of retaining and expanding the foreign markets American businessmen had captured during the war. American officials hoped to penetrate the British monopoly in West Africa. African and West Indian merchants welcomed proposed plans to challenge British shipping, which they thought discriminated against them. The idea of a Pan-African shipping line emerged from a culture that celebrated the importance of shipping, its profitability, and isolated a particular market among black people.[47]

Although initially Garvey thought the local UNIA in New York would be able to own the line, the raising of the necessary capital required appeals to the black public. The original promotion of the Black Star Line was an extension of the recent popular agitation for democracy. Garvey announced that the shipping line was "to be owned by the people, and not owned and controlled by any private corporation or individual, . . . for the fuller economic and industrial development of the race." Garvey identified democratic ownership with racial or national ownership: "like the property of a nation or of a state, the properties of the Universal Negro Improvement Association are the people's, hence no private dividends." Very soon afterwards, however, the Black Star Line was forced to promise "large dividends and profits."[48]

The appeal for money paraphrased the wartime sales campaigns for Liberty Bonds, which identified their purchase with democracy and citizenship. Blacks in New York had been told, "When one becomes the owner of a bond in the United States, he becomes a stockholder in the country. As a stockholder, he will feel a greater degree of interest in the welfare of the country and is entitled to greater consideration in its affairs. Invest in the stocks of Uncle Sam." It was not very difficult to substitute the patriotism of race for that of nation. The idea of accumulating wealth through stocks and bonds had been another by-product of the war and continued into the time of peace.[49]

Garvey targeted the stratum of the underemployed and educated, who held entrepreneurial ambitions. The UNIA's call to "10,000 intelligent young Negro men and women of ambition" fell short of its goal but attracted enough people to launch the enterprise. For them, racial enterprise provided the chance for careers, wealth, significance, and service.[50]

The Black Star Line also appealed to black intellectuals like William Ferris, Joel A. Rogers, and Arthur Schomburg. In 1913, Ferris, a Yale graduate, argued it would be "only when we . . . carry forward our enterprises . . . that the other nations and races of the world will recognize us."[51] After the Black Star Line's ships were acquired, his enthusiasm was unbounded. "We are a new people," he said, "born out of a new day and a new circumstance."[52]

Although Du Bois maintained his distance, he approved of Garvey's work: "American Negroes can be accumulating and ministering their own capital, organize industry, join the black centers of the South Atlantic by commercial enterprise and in this way ultimately redeem Africa as a fit and free home for black men. . . . It [Garvey's plan] is feasible."[53] But Du Bois believed that businesses had to be well run and planned. Garvey's methods, style, and ultimately his failure ruled out anything more than approval of the goal. Nonetheless, Du Bois's words reveal that the Black Star Line embodied many of the racial ideals of the 1920s.

The Black Star Line was a project of a small group. The hope of profit lured many shareholders. But the UNIA, requiring more support and money, attached the agendas of others to it—the ending of lynching, the promoting of equality and industrial opportunity. The line was to be the heart of a new community. Its capital requirements had driven the UNIA to create local organizations, which would both support the shipping line and further develop the community.

But the history of the Black Star Line demonstrated that racial corporations functioned like other corporations. The ships' workers were the first to learn this truth. Some had to sue to obtain their wages when the managers were short of funds. But shareholders and UNIA members had grievances, too. At the root of the conflicts were different priorities and conceptions of racial organization.[54]

Nationalist movements, like nations, often deny that the social divisions of a people are important. The central tropes of nationalist movements are families and communities. Disagreements are often misnamed squabbles and dissension; active opposition, disloyalty and treason. But nationalist movements, unlike nations, lack the power to silence critics. The UNIA's interclass and international composition was the source of intractable problems.

In the United States, one source of conflict was competition among elites in various regions. Racial ideology could not provide answers to the question of which businesses would benefit the black world. The Los Angeles division, preferring to create enterprises close to home, not in Africa or New York, seceded.[55] Other members had ideas of racial organization that flowed from working-class experiences. Some of those who joined the UNIA expected the traditional benefits of organizations they knew, like mutual-benefit associations, to provide protection from sickness and death. Early on, they compelled UNIA leaders to set aside a portion of local dues for death benefits. Their conception of racial organization was rooted in their lives as workers. Often, ownership meant home ownership, the typical form of working-class accumulation.[56] Many believed that racial ties and organization should serve members directly.

The Idea of Race and Afro-Americans in the 1920s

The UNIA's problems were one variant of the failure of the new race concept to encompass the particulars of black life. Denying the social differences among Africans and Afro-Americans by assuming racial unity destroyed the intellectual tools necessary to achieve it. The

NAACP and the National Urban League also assumed that the interests of the race were one. Their actual practices acknowledged diversity because neither organization attempted to organize masses. Both organizations were led by professionals. Culturally assimilated, often second-generation college graduates, they experienced racial discrimination in different ways from most blacks.

A young Fisk graduate's letter to George Haynes, the director of a wartime bureau overseeing the conditions of black labor, revealed the difference. William Kelley had taken a summer job in an automobile factory and now was looking for more permanent work:

> I found that Dodge Bros. was a little hard on Negroes so I left, and went to the American Car & Foundry company here. I have done very well, and am quite satisfied with the change. The plant has been building cars for the Italian government. The contract closes Sept. 8 and of course several hundred men must go in the street. I have studied social conditions there and elsewhere, and could tell you so much. I can really appreciate the fight between capital and labor. I am now wondering if you have anything worth while. I don't want to teach if I can get around it. Hard labor is all right if you are not capable of doing anything else. I hope you are able to place me somewhere.

Haynes recommended going into business. But by the mid-1920s, Kelley was the head of an Urban League chapter.[57]

Like other workers, Kelley discovered that discrimination varied from company to company and made adjustments. But as an educated black he had choices. Kelley learned to appreciate the fight between capital and labor and, understandably, chose to avoid it. Most workers did not have that option. Kelley, more than most Urban League officials, had direct experience with factory labor, but he was not a worker. Kelley was motivated as much by the search for white-collar work as by racial ideology. Like much middle class reform effort, the league was peripheral to the lives of most workers.

NAACP leaders shared similar cultural backgrounds and strategy, but their target was different. Delegating economic problems to the Urban League, they tried to remove racial barriers and regain the rights lost by southern disfranchisement. Unlike the league, the NAACP was a membership organization, but its affairs were dominated by its national leaders. Its local branches were small and inactive and by the end of the decade represented the interests of the new racial elites of the city.

National leaders in both organizations acted on their own agendas, unmodified by popular ratification. Their idea of equality of opportu-

nity for meritorious individuals, the Talented Tenth, was rooted in a
view that the polity was open to moral and legal arguments. They
fought against those proscriptions which affected their own lives.
These goals did not require popular organization or the tactics of extra-
constitutional opposition. Their actions, in David Lewis's words, consisted of "court cases, contracts, contacts, and culture."[58] Ralph
Bunche concluded, "[T]he truth of the matter is that in the thinking of
the Negro elite there is a tremendous gap between it and the black
mass."[59]

Sometimes members of the elite were aware of the gap. Alerted by
the American Federation of Labor, Roy Wilkins of the NAACP
dressed in workman's clothes to investigate conditions of black labor-
ers building dams and levees on the Mississippi. Barely able to convince a knowing landlady that he was a worker, he was horrified at
what he saw. He recalled,

> [W]e tended to be isolated in New York and out of touch with the very
> people we needed most to serve. I knew very well that the N.A.A.C.P.'s
> strategy of carefully selecting lawsuits and political issues and working
> from on high in Congress and the Supreme Court had produced many
> tangible benefits, but from the vantage of those muddy camps on the
> Mississippi, such tactics looked less meaningful than they did from the
> snug offices at 69 Fifth Avenue."[60]

The tactics of the NAACP, or of the Urban League, were not a source
of serious debate or conflict within the organizations until the 1930s.

Although Garvey's methods were different from those of the
NAACP and Urban League, his were equally nonconflictual and future
oriented. If the older organizations assumed that the polity was open
to moral and legal arguments, Garvey assumed that the society was
open enough for blacks together to create economic power, which
would then improve the status of the race. Unlike NAACP leaders,
who had firmer places in American society, Garvey and many UNIA
leaders were more dominated by the immediate needs to use racial organization to establish themselves. Nonetheless, both agendas flowed
from elite experiences and goals: to create more opportunity for the
educated.

But Garvey's economic enterprises, more than lobbying and court
cases, required popular support. Garvey's UNIA was an interclass association, and exhortation was not powerful enough to impose the discipline and financial support that were necessary to maintain an orga-

nization of blacks with different social experiences and objectives. His attempt to keep the organization together through his own person failed.

Leaders often become symbols of nationalist movements when the bonds of community are weak and programmatic objectives capable of uniting the group are absent. In the beginning, Garvey promised concrete benefits. After 1922, he asked for loyalty. He claimed that if he was embattled, so were they. If he succeeded, so would they. He attempted, but also failed, to create a community through himself.[61]

The idea that the person who looks like me represents my interests is compelling in a society where descent has been a means of social division. Yet, Huey Long's Share the Wealth movement revealed a similar dynamic. The uniting of people of various classes with a general grievance and imprecise targets can often only be done by a charismatic leader.[62]

Charisma has limits. The effectiveness of Garvey's was waning even before his imprisonment in 1925 for mail fraud. After the failure of the Black Star Line, in 1922, many, especially the prominent, left. Without big national projects, UNIA divisions turned to local businesses or local politics. Their purposes often reflected the personal interests of leaders; political goals were momentary and often opportunistic. Even though the UNIA became socially more homogeneous, the divisions steadily declined in numbers, despite the devotion of small groups. They simply took their place as one of many black organizations of the working class. The UNIA's difficulties, therefore, did not stem simply from its interclass composition.

The motivations of Garveyites offer a clue to the weakness of the organization. The most active Garveyites were those with the steadiest work, which was usually modest. They were ambitious but pursued their goals singly. The UNIA opened up a more sophisticated world for many. The locals were forums for black and white authors and activists who spoke on a wide range of racial issues, but also world culture and politics. For other Garveyites, the UNIA expressed and confirmed the experience of injustice.[63]

The diverse and loose motivations explain the high turnover. The UNIA was a voluntary organization, not a cult. The ceremonies and parades of UNIA gatherings affirmed achievement, ambition, and solidarity, like other fraternal parading in the 1920s. However satisfying to participants, they were not collective mobilizations for particular goals or actions. These activities were not inconsistent with the individualism that many people found in the 1920s. The UNIA was part of the era characterized by the phrase "New Negro," a singular. Its values were not sharply delineated from other racial institutions in the new cities of the 1920s. Indeed, they were shaped by the same trends.

Black Communities in the 1920s

Black urban elites were well organized and set the agenda for black life even though they had their own social clubs, literary societies, fraternals, and churches. They led political organizations and civic associations and edited newspapers. Despite racial discrimination, they saw signs of improvement for themselves and for other blacks. The prosperity of the 1920s was oversold but not manufactured. In 1929, one leader concluded, "[T]he Negro worker's future, all in all, is roseate and enticing." At the same time, NAACP's executive secretary James Weldon Johnson observed, "[T]he Negro's situation in Harlem is without precedent . . . ; never has he been so securely anchored, never before has he owned the land, never before has he had so well established a community life."[64]

The community life Johnson referred to was created by its elite, not its working class. (Johnson, like Du Bois, would not have expected it any other way.) He acknowledged that Harlem was "still in the process of making." The masses lacked "cohesion" and "social organization."[65] Following the sociology of the Chicago school, Johnson thought that community solidarities would evolve over time. He viewed organization as a natural development, not a social necessity.

Johnson's insight about mass organization was correct. While black elites had achieved national and local organization, the black working class was still in the making. Diversity of occupation and recent arrival worked against organization. By the end of the war, the majority of black men worked in factories. Nonetheless, the black working class was heterogeneous. There had been a "new" black working class, with different economic and racial experiences, at every step in the development of the northern economy since the colonial period.[66] Organizational, cultural, and residential residues of earlier black patterns of work and housing made black life rich but heterogeneous and separated.

After the Civil War, many blacks, often one-third of some black communities, were skilled workers and small businessmen. They had been hard hit by the industrial transformations. Thus, a Pittsburgh firm eliminated its black iron puddlers when the company discontinued puddling. The shift to steel destroyed a craft. Some moved to other localities where puddling shops still operated. Others left the trade. Whatever their personal fate, puddling was not an option for many of them, and certainly not for their sons or new workers. The great demand was for unskilled labor, which became a permanent status, dividing the race as well as races. Blacks remained puddlers at the Penn Iron and Steel company. Their helpers, blacks too, were never promoted. Both the puddlers and the owners called them irresponsible floaters, not surprising, given the prospects of the helpers.[67]

Other work for blacks in the North, like personal service, was an extension of older nineteenth-century and southern work. With industrialization, these jobs were transformed to portering on Pullman cars, for men, or work in commercial laundries, for women. But longshoremen, teamsters, various railroad workers, and construction workers were also common. There was great occupational variety within cities and among cities. The growing demand, however, was for factory labor.

The large numbers who entered the factories during and after the world war to replace departing foreigners added to the diversity.[68] Blacks were latecomers to northern industrialization because most of them were in the South at the time of its beginnings and maturation. Because there was no national labor market, most were isolated from information about industrial work outside their area.[69] Many, like Nate Shaw, used local industry to help them stay on the land, which they did not want to leave. Others worked in southern industry, which, outside the cotton mills, was overwhelmingly black for the same reasons that northern businessmen preferred foreigners. Alabama's mine operators "employed so many Blacks because they were a known and plentiful supply in a labor-scarce, labor-intensive industry."[70]

Those who entered northern industry before World War I came from the Upper South, where small farmers had earlier become dependent upon supplementary wage labor, which often became permanent. Located in towns and cities, they had good information about work. Nonetheless, because many found opportunity, the impetus to migrate north was blunted. Northern firms that set up plants in the South using black labor had no incentive to encourage migration. And, southern planters used many coercive devices to retain their labor force.

Given an early preference for and experience with the foreign-born, northern factory owners were reluctant to experiment with the unknown. They thought that the immigrants were best suited for un-skilled factory labor, which happened to be the labor they needed in this period. Social necessities and experiences were attributed to race.

Many employers altered their racial notions when they needed additional labor during World War I. They then turned to southern blacks. The numbers of northern blacks were insufficient. Then, many northern blacks had no desire to work in the factories. Only in retrospect, after the unionization of mass-production workers, do those jobs seems desirable. The dangerous and unhealthful surroundings and autocratic supervision of the typical factory were surely not very attractive to a black teamster who enjoyed a certain amount of autonomy and fresh air.

Most of the southern migrants had some urban experience, and they were Americans. Lawrence Levine associates the emergence of the blues with "the rise of a more personalized, individual-oriented ethos among Negroes at the turn of the century." Certainly, compared to the foreign-born, the blacks were more ambitious, individualistic, and American in aspiration and thinking. One study found that blacks were more upwardly and downwardly mobile than the security-minded Poles. Black children often kept their wages, whereas foreign-born children gave them to their parents. Black parents kept their children in school longer.[71]

Peter Gottlieb's interviews with migrants confirm the individualistic patterns. Most obtained jobs through personal initiative. They had high expectations about jobs and left them when they found them too limited. Yet these qualities should not be mistaken for the individualism of the middle class. Gottlieb discovered that the migrants used strategies similar to other newcomers to the city to protect themselves from the insecurities of urban working-class life. Migrants were a lot more tentative about the new northern jobs than had been previously thought.[72] Whatever their intentions, they discovered through the depression of 1920–21 that northern work could be impermanent. Many probably returned to the South, at least temporarily. Their actions were thus similar to those of the foreign-born, who, in the earlier period, returned home during depressions. The easy access to the South probably made this solution even more common. If so, the reliance on resources of kin and neighbors in the South explains the paucity of northern organization among migrants.

Black workers whose roots in the North were deeper shared the burdens of class through the cultural traditions of mutualism, reciprocity, and spiritual consolation. These protections often existed outside formal organization. Individual ambitions became secondary when hard-ship—illness, death, unemployment—struck families. Friends and even local merchants would lend a hand when hard times or individual misfortune, which all knew, struck. At their best, and one should not romanticize them, these traditions sheltered the individual from the in-securities of working-class life.[73]

Because historians often study one ethnic or racial group they tend to make kin-related and neighborhood support systems a function of ethnicity. But Alexander Keyssar has found the same culture among the American and ethnic working class of Massachusetts.[74] It also ex-isted among different ethnic and racial groups who happened to be neighbors. Nevertheless, the system was imperfect. For many work-ers, the instability of labor markets made movement a better strategy than mutualism.

For others, unions provided protection, but the decline of the labor movement precluded that solution for most. The power of capital dur-ing the 1920s led to defensive strategies. The AFL made little effort to organize the unskilled and those who labored in factories. The weak-ness of existing unions affected all workers. A former black grievance officer of the Amalgamated Association of Iron and Steel Workers in Warren, Ohio, spoke for many when he said, "Why should I pay dues to the union if my wages get cut anyway?"[75]

The ingredients of black life could have been packaged differently. But the 1920s were dominated by the hegemony of the "new capital-ism" and the weakness of popular politics and organizations. Racial organizations—the UNIA, NAACP, the National Urban League and others—reflected the larger balance of power, not simply black tradi-tions and particularities. Their belief in economic progress, despite the existence of racial discrimination, and sense of racial community, translated into individualistic methods, were very much embedded in the larger culture of the 1920s.

The Demise of the Organic Model

The various forms of community building dominated black politics from the 1890s until the Great Depression, which destroyed the hopes of the Talented Tenth as well as black workers and farmers. As the New Deal state assumed more of a responsibility for providing work and training, racial leaders no longer attempted to create the racial community by relying upon racial bonds to uplift the black population or create businesses to produce jobs and power. They demanded that blacks participate in all government programs or that black workers have the right to join unions.

The demand for jobs, relief, and higher wages recognized the social needs of the black population without mediation and focused black effort on precise targets: the government, the corporation. Becoming more substantial and incorporating working-class issues, politics became the basis for community organization, like the earlier politics of Reconstruction in the South or the later politics of the civil rights movement. The paternalistic relationship between black elites and workers was modified as the weight of the newly politicized voters altered black politics. Leaders spoke less about the special culture of the Negro and more about the social programs for farmers, workers, or the unemployed.

The new language facilitated other bonds and identifications that cut across race. To join an interracial union does not erase racial consciousness but does modify it. With the new power of labor, black leaders not only found new allies but also began to acknowledge the fact that workers, as well as elites, could produce power. When asked why he joined and became an active leader in the Steel Workers Organizing Committee, one black explained, "I guess I was impressed by the success of the C.I.O. in other fields. The idea was sweeping the country and I was swept along with it."[76]

These new trends were often first articulated by new leaders from the black working class and younger intellectuals—Abram Harris, John Davis, Ralph Bunche, E. Franklin Frazier, Sterling Brown. A black journalist claimed, "[T]he new position Negro labor has won . . . has been gained in spite of the older leadership."[77] Like the Emancipation generation at the turn of the century, many established leaders made the transition with difficulty. Garvey and Du Bois never made it.

However incomplete, especially in the South where most blacks still lived, the union movement and new national state created the institutional framework for working-class security and the social and political recognition that ethnic and racial groups had tried to create alone. Neither the racial bonds of elites nor those of workers were able to provide the protections of politics and union organization. The ethnic organizations of the foreign-born were no more successful. The current fashion of viewing American history as an arena of ethnic and racial groups each propelling itself upward often ignores the key actors—broader political movements and economic change—because they are not unique to the group.[78]

As politics changed, the organic model that had dominated black thought since the 1890s lost its power to persuade. Blyden, Du Bois, and Garvey had invented a view of the race to support a politics that addressed the elite discrimination they faced. Like all ideologies, their view of race attempted to interpret the world and direct behavior. Models and goals were taken from Western elite culture. Black elites imagined the majority of Afro-Americans passive and in need of their leadership. The NAACP and Urban League claimed to represent the race by default. Garvey assumed racial bonds that did not exist. Wedded to modern progress, all, in effect, urged shuttling resources—material or moral—within the group. The extreme portrait of social autarchy was impossible to execute, even for its most fervent adherents. Blacks in the United States were too entwined in American life.

The organic model had emerged at a time when popular organization, especially that of Afro-Americans, was particularly weak. The model and the institutions stemming from it reflected that balance of power within the race and the larger society as it deferred the grievances of black farmers, migrants, and workers and filtered out the common experiences blacks increasingly shared with other farmers, migrants, and workers. These social experiences came to the fore in the 1930s in American and Afro-American culture.

It is not surprising, therefore, that there was less race theorizing during the Great Depression. Claude McKay concluded that such efforts seemed "just a waste of intellectual energy" to him.[79] And many blacks easily accepted the working-class identity of the new unionism or the populist ideology of the New Deal and defined themselves in it.[80] A black taxicab driver voted for the Democrats because, he said, they "favor the little man, and I've been a little man all of my life."[81] People did not cease using racial language; it simply meant different things from what it had in the earlier period because people had new ideas of progress, new experiences, new allies, and new politics.

The defining of people of African descent has always been, and remains, associated with the contemporary political purposes. Even when the definition invokes history, it reflects current ideas from the larger culture more than the black past and its traditions, formed by diverse status, region, class, and a four-century residence in the most dynamic region of the world. The literature of definition has been vast because Afro-American history has been at the center of some of the most important events in American history.[82] And the word race has been the principal ideological construct which Americans, black and white, have used to confront the numerous questions stemming from the existence and unraveling of slavery. But the persistence of the term is not equivalent to biological or historical continuity. The search for single, autonomous, and authentic traditions in Afro-American history reflects current politics and essentialist intellectual trends.[83] To give racial identities and language transhistorical meaning is to enter the realm of metaphysics or imagination.

Anzia Yezierska and the Making of an Ethnic American Self

MARY V. DEARBORN

Nathaniel Hawthorne, the master of American romance, is not a writer we commonly think of as ethnic. On closer examination, in fact, Hawthorne appears to have been positively obsessed with ancestry and genealogy, as works like *The House of the Seven Gables* (1851) attest. Moreover, his obsession led him to imagine an invented British ancestry—in short, Nathaniel Hawthorne was an early "invented" ethnic. Thus Hawthorne was fascinated with the legend of a bloody footprint left by a British clergyman on the stone floor of a hall in Lancashire. Over centuries, the footprint was said to remain visible in the stone, "in spite of the scrubbings of all after generations," writes Hawthorne. Hawthorne tried repeatedly to come to terms with this legend—in his unfinished *The Ancestral Footprint* and elsewhere—but could not unravel the mystery of his own invented past. In his dwelling on this ineradicable bloody footprint, Hawthorne participated in a familiar American interrogation of the invention of ethnicity.[1]

Some sixty-five years later, a Jewish-American writer was to make use of another kind of footprint—this one muddy—to inscribe her own ethnic and female identity. Like Hawthorne's, Anzia Yezierska's footprint functions as a kind of narrative conundrum that can open the way for a study of ethnic invention—not as a footprint but as a fingerprint that can identify American identity.

What I will call the incident of the muddy footprint occurs in the

Copyright © 1988 by Mary V. Dearborn. This essay has appeared in slightly different form in the book *Love in Promised Land: The Story of Anzia Yezierska and John Dewey,* published by the Free Press.

opening chapters of Yezierska's *Bread Givers* (1925). Probably her most successful novel, *Bread Givers* is the story of the young immigrant Sara Smolinsky, a daughter who must rebel against her tyrannical Old World father to gain independence and happiness as a new American woman. (It seems at first to be a narrative of the evasion rather than the invention of ethnicity.) *Bread Givers* is a rich text of female and ethnic anger; Sara's identity is achieved through, and the action of the novel is propelled by, acts of narrative violence. These acts for the most part appear in Book 1, "Hester Street," before Sara is consciously aware of her oppression by her father and the patriarchal culture he represents.

Early in the novel, Reb Smolinsky—a Talmudic scholar who considers himself too holy to work and relies on the wages of his wife and daughters—is interrupted at prayer by the landlord's collector lady, demanding rent. Angered by his refusal to look up from his Bible, the collector lady, writes Yezierska, "shut his book with such anger that it fell at her feet."[2] Reb Smolinsky hits her: "Father slapped the landlady [*sic*] on one cheek, then on the other, till the blood rushed from her nose" (*BG*, 18). (Notice that she is now not the collector lady but the landlady herself.) These are, so to speak, the facts of the case—as they are presented in Chapter 1. In the next chapter, Reb Smolinsky is brought to court for assault. His American lawyer asserts that his client is incapable of assault ("He couldn't hurt a fly") but, if he did hit the woman, it was because she "knocked the Bible out of his hands and stepped on it with her feet" (*BG*, 25). When the collector lady protests, the lawyer takes an imprint of her foot on a clean piece of paper and dramatically compares it to a page of Reb Smolinsky's Bible—on which there is a muddy footprint that matches the collector lady's. The evidence is complete; the collector lady, humiliated; the prisoner, discharged, later to be lionized; and the reader, puzzled. Who put the muddy footprint on Reb Smolinsky's Bible?

To solve the narrative mystery, we need to return to the scene of the crime and review the evidence. Immediately before the collector lady's appearance, Sara and the novel's female characters gather to watch Reb Smolinsky chanting from the Bible through a crack in the doorway. The scene is like a stage set: Reb Smolinsky is swaying back and forth in a long black frock coat, a skullcap slipping off his long red hair. The Bible from which he chants is in Sara's experience a patriarchal text, and the passages he chants reflect the impossible promises to which he is prone and that so frustrate Sara: "I will make darkness light before the blind, and crooked things straight" (*BG*, 16). The stage suddenly goes dark, and the "collector lady from the landlord" appears—not, that is, the landlord. This character is, significantly, ethnic (she calls Reb Smolinsky a "schnorrer"), female, and working class—in other words, removed by ethnicity, gender, and class from the dominant culture. She participates, however, in her own oppression; she identifies with that culture to such an extent that she repeatedly demands *her* rent—money that is not hers but her employer's. The narrator, or Sara, believes her and a few lines later begins to identify her as the "landlady." At this point, the narrator's loyalties seem to go irretrievably awry—as do, possibly, her powers of observation. At any rate, a transformative process begins, and a palimpsest of a muddy footprint begins to emerge.

As Chapter 2 opens, Reb Smolinsky is well on his way to becoming a hero; the neighborhood hires him an American lawyer, whose discourse is as false as Reb Smolinsky's own. The collector lady is, in this chapter, described only as the landlady—with one significant exception. When the collector lady protests the lawyer's (and the narrator's) reconstruction of the incident, the narrator writes, "'It's a lie!' shouted the collector lady" (*BG*, 25). Here the narrator is telling the truth, and hinting at the mystery's solution. Generally, however, Reb Smolinsky's version "wins" narratively, and the incident is mythologized, undergoing further transformation. The falsely reconstructed incident, now a parable of immigrant protest, is repeatedly acted out by the neighbors. Reb Smolinsky's blow against the "landlady" (who now becomes the "landlord") is compared to David's against Goliath. This parable-like theater, of course, violently distorts the facts: Reb Smolinsky is, as the action of the novel bears out, solidly on the side of the landlord or the dominant male culture. This distortion is not without good effect; it is important, after all, that the immigrant neighborhood join together to fight oppressive landlords. But, as the narrator reminds us, such a distortion compromises the truth of Sara's—or the ethnic woman's—experience and reinscribes her oppression. "The arguments *always ended*," she writes, "with 'Long years on Reb Smolinsky to fight the landlords for the people!'" (*BG*, 25, my emphasis).

The text itself, however, militates against this odd outcome, so that, in effect, the argument never ends, and the integrity and protest of the narrative voice are preserved. This is, in fact, where Yezierska makes her distinctive narrative statement about gender, ethnicity, and American identity. For it is Yezierska herself, the narrator—or, by extension, the autobiographical heroine Sara—who leaves the muddy footprint on Reb Smolinsky's Bible. It did not exist, and the narrator literally inscribes it. This inscription also operates figuratively. In psychic terms, she dirties Sara's father's things, and the act is a kind of ritual pollution that gives Sara psychic freedom. On an ethnic and feminist level, she walks over the patriarchal text of the Old World—and, in doing so, she leaves her mark: the muddy footprint of American female ethnicity.

If the muddy footprint is a narrative expression of ethnicity in this passage, however, it is clear that it works in a very complex way. In dirtying a Bible, what is the ethnic woman writer saying about her relationship to Judaism? It becomes necessary to question the very nature of her ethnicity: Is it based on her religion, or her foreign birth? She is also making a statement about renouncing her parentage—Is this a comment on her decision to become "born again" as a "true" American? Or is it a recognition that ethnic and American identity involve constant interrogations of genealogy?

Contemporary scholars have rediscovered Yezierska with delight in the past decade. Feminist critics are pleased to find relatively unambivalent portraits of independent women in her fiction; ethnic studies scholars are glad that an important Jewish-American writer has resurfaced.[3] Her fiction is welcomed, in short, because it provides valuable documentary evidence that ethnic women existed. Yezierska's fiction is indeed significant in just this way.[4] But *Bread Givers* and other works like it—Abraham Cahan's *The Rise of David Levinsky,* Mary Antin's *The Promised Land,* Henry Roth's *Call It Sleep*—are too often read only as evidence. They are grouped together as Jewish-American literature because of their content and their authors' ethnicity. I offer the reading above as an example of a response that tries to explore the complex relationship of narrative and ethnicity.

For Yezierska's understanding of her ethnic American identity was indeed complex. Her reputation as an author was based on her ethnicity. When Samuel Goldwyn bought the screen rights to her *Hungry Hearts* (1920) and brought her to Hollywood to write for the movies, the public was charmed by stories about the "sweatshop Cinderella," the immigrant who won her way to Hollywood through her vivid depictions of ghetto life on New York's Lower East Side. "From Hester Street to Hollywood!" proclaimed the headlines announcing her arrival in Hollywood in 1921. Her story was told so often that she became known as the "Sunday supplement heroine."

Anzia Yezierska in 1920 was a product of public relations, itself a recently invented industry at the time. This "Cinderella" was in fact about forty years old; she had struggled for years to find self-expression and independence, realizing along the way that she had better be able to sell herself to the American public. Always conscious of her audience, Yezierska tried to give her public what it wanted. The most superficial consideration of America's response to the immigrant over the early decades of this century suggests the difficulty of the task Yezierska set for herself. In fact, her writing career consisted of constant negotiation with her reading public. In her personal life, she carried on a similar struggle, as she tried to "sell herself" to native-born Americans almost obsessively. In the end, she lost on both counts. She fell from critical and popular favor into obscurity and isolation.

In short, Yezierska's life provides a case study of the invention of ethnicity in American culture. Never was an ethnic woman so consciously "invented." And never was an ethnic woman to realize so fully both the advantages of her invention and its tragic consequences. I will review her life here and then return to what I consider its ethnic junctures—when the complex interplay of ethnicity, American identity, gender, and authorship emerges most clearly.[5]

The "sweatshop Cinderella" who arrived in Hollywood in 1921 had, as I have said, struggled long and hard for her success—a success that hardly constituted a fairy-tale ending. She was born in Plöch, a town in the Polish part of Russia, around 1880; her mother had ten children and could not keep track of their birth dates. The family emigrated in 1893, following the eldest child, Mayer Yezierska, who took the name Max Mayer upon his arrival in 1886. They settled on New York's Lower East Side, the setting of most of Yezierska's fiction, and took the name Mayer. Yezierska became Hattie Mayer.

Yezierska's father was a Talmudic scholar and patriarch, a tyrannical dreamer portrayed in her fiction as relying on the labor of his wife and children for the family's living and from whom Yezierska had to escape to begin her life as an independent woman and a writer.[6] The Yezierska heroine comes to question the practical value of her father's religious system, while he maintains that "the real food is God's holy Torah" (*BG*, 11). Furthermore, the patriarchal nature of Jewish culture her father maintains dictates that the immigrant daughter look elsewhere for her values. Sara Smolinsky's father in *Bread Givers* instructs her, "Only through a man can a woman enter heaven" (*BG*, 137). Like all orthodox Jewish men, he prays every morning, "Blessed art thou, O God, King of the Universe, who has not made me a woman." Nor did Yezierska's mother provide a compelling role model. As the historian Sonya Michel has pointed out, the first-generation Jewish mother was severely oppressed; it was the second generation that came to be eu-

logized as "yiddische mommas" (and then largely by Jewish men).[7]
Mary Antin, roughly Yezierska's contemporary, described in her *The
Promised Land* (1912) a typical Jewish daughter's relationship to her
mother during this period:

> A girl's real schoolroom was her mother's kitchen. There she learned to
> bake and cook and manage, to knit, sew, and embroider. And while her
> hands were busy, her mother instructed her in the laws regulating a pious
> Jewish household and in the conduct proper for a Jewish wife, for, of
> course, every girl hoped to be a wife. A girl was born for no other pur-
> pose.[8]

As Yezierska watched her older sisters be married off to immigrant
men against their wishes, she resolved to learn English and make
something of herself. In a move that was almost unheard of at the
time,[9] Yezierska left her family in 1900 and began to live independently.
This separation from her family, while it freed her from the domestic
fate she had been raised for, was the first of the costs she incurred in
her search for independence.

During the next few years, while going to night school at the Educational Alliance to learn English, Yezierska worked as a domestic and
in the sweatshops as a seamstress, a laundress, and an assembler. In
Children of Loneliness (1923) she remembers that her first job was
working for a family of recently arrived Jews "so successful they were
ashamed to remember their mother tongue."[10] In 1900 she went to live
at the Clara de Hirsch Home for Working Girls, a home that trained
immigrants usually for jobs as domestic servants, where she attracted
the attention of the "uptown" German-Jewish benefactress Sarah Ollesheimer (to whom she was to dedicate *Bread Givers*). Though she
chafed at receiving "charity," she was drawn to the home by her desire
to escape the poverty of the ghetto; she explained, "All I wanted was
a place to live and those white curtains were as far away from me as
the millionaires were."[11] Yezierska came to resent the patronizing nature of the settlement house: Mrs. Ollesheimer, for example, discour-
aged her from becoming a writer and urged her instead to train as a
cook. Still, through the home and the Educational Alliance she was
offered a fellowship to study domestic science at Columbia University's Teachers College. Eager for education of any sort, she went.

Yezierska resented having to accept the mundane fate of teaching
practical arts and rather listlessly taught cooking in the New York City
school system from 1905 to 1913. She later explained her teaching

methods: she would ask if anyone in the class knew how to bake a ham and then direct whoever answered to teach the class.[12]

In the meantime, she enjoyed the life of a young intellectual in the bohemian circles of New York. She attended lectures and lived at the Rand School, which the Yiddish *Daily Forward* called "the socialist yeshiva." There she met the feminist activist Henrietta Rodman, who was to become an important influence in her life.[13] Another influence was the work of the feminist Olive Schreiner, particularly her *Story of an African Farm,* whose heroine proposes a "companionate," or sexless, marriage to her bewildered suitor. This influence, however, proved a more mixed blessing than Rodman's.

In 1911, when she was in her late twenties, Yezierska married a young lawyer, Jacob Gordon. But the newlyweds seem to have misunderstood each other: soon after the wedding Yezierska filed for an annulment, stating that she understood theirs was to be a companionate marriage. The marriage was dissolved, but Yezierska almost immediately married Gordon's best friend, Arnold Levitas, and bore him a daughter, Louise. After a number of alternative living arrangements, finding the roles of mother and writer incompatible, she left Levitas and gave him custody of their daughter. In "Rebellion of a Supported Wife," an unpublished manuscript in her daughter's possession, Yezierska is adamant about the degradation of married life. About motherhood she was more ambivalent. Though she wrote that motherhood is "the ball and chains of the prisoner that keep him chained in his cell," she found leaving her daughter difficult.[14] The two became very close, in spite of their physical separation.

The great turning point in Yezierska's life came in 1917, when she met the philosopher and educator John Dewey. Their brief but intense friendship profoundly influenced both. Dewey, sensing her extraordinary potential, enrolled her in his Columbia University seminar on social and practical philosophy. Many participants in this seminar became leading philosophers and educators, including Albert Coombs Barnes, Paul and Brand Blanshard, Irwin Edman, and Margaret Frances Bradshaw. Barnes's biographer writes that Yezierska was "agonizingly self-conscious in [their] presence" and speculated that she perceived them "as beings of a higher order, of which their formal education was only one sign."[15] With this group and under Dewey's direction, she participated in a study of the assimilation of Poles in Philadelphia; her assignment was to translate and to study the role of women in the Polish home.

Yezierska wrote about her Philadelphia experience in her *All I Could Never Be* (1932) with some bitterness. For she had fallen in love with Dewey, and he, briefly, with her, and the affair ended badly. And when she fell out of love with him, she fell out of love with his ideas as well. Their relationship became an obsessive subject in almost all of her fiction, in which she portrayed cold, rational, successful American-born men who are initially attracted to the ethnic heroines for their warmth and intensity. The ethnic heroine sees in this possible union the chance to "open up" her culture to America, and the possibility of Americanization for herself. "Are we not the mingling of the races? The oriental mystery and the Anglo-Saxon clarity that will pioneer a new race of men?" one of Yezierska's fictional lovers wistfully hopes.[16] Recently, with the Dewey scholar Jo Ann Boydston's discovery of Dewey's poetry—much of it to or about Yezierska—it has become clear that he thought of the contrast between the two in much the same way. In a representative passage (of which Yezierska quotes versions in two of her novels) he writes,

> I am overcome as by thunder
> Of my blood that surges
> From my cold heart to my clear head—
> So at least she said—[17]

But Dewey seems to have tired of Yezierska for the very qualities he once sought in her—her intensity and vitality. "You are an emotional, hysterical girl, and you have exaggerated my friendly interests,"[18] says one of Yezierska's Deweyesque heroes. Yezierska's disappointment was profound, and she seems to have become very wary in her relationships with men after her experience with Dewey.

Among other things, Dewey apparently encouraged Yezierska to write. He gave her a typewriter and brought one of her stories to the editor of the *New Republic*. Yezierska later recalled, "He made me realize that art is the climax of human experience. You don't know what happened until you create with it."[19] As she began to write, she came to feel that her mission was to mediate between her culture and the dominant culture of America. She read about the Pilgrims, a group she called in her autobiography "dissenters and immigrants like me" (*RR*, 207), and felt the need to communicate as a religious revelation: "Fired up by this revealing light, I began to build a bridge of understanding between the American-born and myself. Since their life was shut out from such as me, I began to open up my life and the lives of my people to them."[20]

This strategy of mediation, the attempt to build a bridge between her world and that of the native-born American by opening her culture to America, served her well, at least for a time. The 1920s were, as the Yezierska critic Alice Kessler-Harris points out, a decade of nativism, antiradicalism, and racism, a decade that opened with the Justice Department's deportation of "unsympathetic" aliens.[21] Immigrants made white America anxious, and Yezierska was ideally situated to alleviate this anxiety with her well-meaning efforts to "open up her culture" to America. *Hungry Hearts,* for example, presented to the reader a reassuringly benign picture of the life of the immigrant in the early part of the 1920s. This was the public that acclaimed the rags-to-riches story of the romantic immigrant girl who sold her stories to Hollywood.

Hollywood presented Yezierska with another disillusionment, almost as wrenching as her trouble with Dewey. Initially overwhelmed at the thought of working with such writers as Alice Duer Miller, Elinor Glyn, Gertrude Atherton, Rupert Hughes, and Will Rogers, she soon was put off by the crassness of Hollywood society: "The fight that went on at the pushcarts of Hester Street went on in [the] Hollywood drawing room" (*RR,* 62). She had hoped that the film version of *Hungry Hearts* would mark a new phase in moviemaking; as she later commented, "Hollywood was still busy with Westerns and Pollyanna romances. The studios seldom bought stories from life" (*RR,* 26). But in those days Jewish culture was represented in Hollywood productions by Montague Glass's sentimentalized and broadly comic *Potash and Perlmutter,* and Yezierska was dismayed to see *Hungry Hearts* given a happy ending and burlesque overtones. She fundamentally misunderstood Hollywood's Jewish culture and her place in it.

Worse still, Hollywood made her feel "cut off" from her culture, as if she were "part of a stage-set" (*RR,* 69), and she could no longer write. She confided to Goldwyn her desire to write an "expiation of guilt," a novel to be called *Children of Loneliness,* about children who lose their heritage in their struggle to become Americans. She explains, "I had to break away from my mother's cursing and my father's preaching to live my life; but without them I had no life. When you deny your parents, you deny the sky over your head. You become an outlaw, a pariah." (*RR,* 72). From this time forward, Yezierska commented obsessively about her alienation from her own past, the alienation that resulted from the Americanization she so eagerly sought. One of her college-educated characters laments, "I can't live with the old world and I'm yet too green for the new. I don't belong to those who gave me birth or to those with whom I was educated."[22] Her attempt to mediate between two cultures left her suspended between them.

Yezierska stayed in Hollywood only briefly; her *Salome of the Tenements* was made into a movie as well, though this time she had nothing to do with the process. William Fox tried to lure the "natural-born sob-sister" (*RR,* 45) to his studio with a $100,000 contract, but she turned it down, convinced that Hollywood was ruining her writing. In 1922 she fled to Europe, where she met George Bernard Shaw, Israel Zangwill, Joseph Conrad, and Gertrude Stein—whom she later described as "a very nice big cow."[23] (However inadequate she may have felt, she was clearly a literary lioness at this time.)

Yezierska then returned to New York City, where she lived in Greenwich Village and had such friends as Edward Dahlberg, Waldo Frank, William Lyons Phelps, and Zona Gale. During those years, her daughter writes, "she was an auburn-haired, broad-featured, radiantly handsome woman, with white velvet skin, wide, challenging blue eyes, short, broad-hipped, vigorously healthy."[24] But as the 1920s wore on, she found it more and more difficult to write—she went so far as to take a job as a waitress in order to get material—and her reputation began to fall off. Much as John Dewey had rejected her for the intensity and passion he once celebrated, her reviewers now criticized her fiction for the qualities they had once praised. One reviewer bridled at her "high-handed impatience at the existing order of things." Another said of her *Children of Loneliness* (1923), "[I]f she would learn to command and subdue her emotions, success would be assured." The reading public that had sent her to Hollywood to write the "*Uncle Tom's Cabin* of the immigrant" (*RR,* 61) now dismissed her novel *Salome of the Tenements* as a cheap movie.[25]

Nevertheless, she continued to try to write. She spent 1928–30 at the University of Washington on a Zona Gale Fellowship and the early 1930s in Arlington, Vermont, trying to live cheaply and write. In choosing a small New England village for a refuge, she set herself up for another disappointment: she could not understand her neighbors, and they were bewildered by her. A friend, the novelist Dorothy Canfield Fisher, remembers that "her efforts to get in touch with the Vermonters of Arlington, their efforts to help her—all proved futile."[26] Yezierska's real and invented ethnicity once more interposed, and she left Arlington weeping and distraught, again disillusioned.

Yezierska's Hollywood success ironically backfired in the 1930s when she returned to New York City and found that the legend of her success dissuaded prospective employers from giving her the menial jobs she was then forced to seek. When the WPA Federal Writers Project began, she eagerly applied for relief and was taken on the project. Her semiautobiographical *Red Ribbon on a White Horse* describes her WPA experience in detail, including her friendship with the aspiring novelist Richard Wright. At first she was allowed to produce creative work for pay, but with a change in leadership she was put on the guide detail and sent to catalog trees in Central Park. The WPA experience clouded her feelings about charity still further.

For fifteen years after leaving the WPA in 1935, she lived in relative obscurity. Though she still wrote tirelessly, she was unable to find a publisher. She lived alternately in New York and with her daughter in California, exploring Christian Science, dabbling in mysticism, and attending the lectures of Krishnamurti. Then, in 1950, Scribner's agreed to publish her *Red Ribbon on a White Horse*. W. H. Auden wrote an introduction in which he singled out her search for a vocation as the overriding principle in her work. And, in *Red Ribbon,* the autobiographical heroine is able to report that she has found some peace. She has learned that she need not seek elsewhere for fulfillment: "All that I could ever be, the glimpses of truth I reached for elsewhere, was in myself" (*RR,* 220).

Initially the publication of her autobiography did little to improve Yezierska's material existence—in 1953 she wrote to Charles Olson at the Black Mountain School asking if "there wasn't some humble spot such as teaching English or helping in the kitchen where [she] might earn a roof over [her] head."[27] But she now entered a new phase in her writing career. In the 1950s she reviewed over fifty books for the *New York Times.* And in the years before her death in 1970, she became something of an old-age activist, writing numerous articles and stories about the plight of the elderly.

It has been necessary to review the facts of Yezierska's invented life in detail because in the business of making her Cinderella self a number of facts about her previous self became obscured. This was easy business for the publicity mills of Hollywood, perhaps, but the skill with which Yezierska learned to change the facts of her own life is astonishing. Her daughter remembers her mother as "incapable of telling the plain truth. . . . [S]he had a talent for dramatizing and enlarging her life for an appreciative listener."[28] Yezierska's mythmaking mostly involved, but was not confined to, her vital statistics. As I have noted, she was herself unaware of her own age and, in fact, accounts of her age vary by as much as ten years. When a studio publicist asked her age in Hollywood in 1921—when Yezierska was at least thirty-five—he speculated, "I'd say you were about thirty-five." She responded coolly, "I'll say I am about thirty" (*RR*, 80). A nod less to vanity than to necessity, Yezierska's untruths about her age were formulated in order to keep the Cinderella success story aesthetically intact. This necessitated that she present herself as fresh out of the ghetto in 1920— thereby neatly erasing about twenty years of her own life. Her years as a teacher, her marriage (either of her marriages), her child—none of these important features of her life appeared in her official and unofficial versions of herself. She always depicted herself as coming straight from the sweatshops to Hollywood splendor, omitting the intervening years of a young working woman whose life was, if relatively cheerless, by no means squalid. So, in a 1920 interview with *Good Housekeeping,* for instance, Yezierska presents herself as if the year were 1901 and she were just emerging from the ghetto.[29] In a 1920 review of John Dewey's *Democracy and Education,* she describes herself reading the book over a sandwich on her lunch hour at the factory—a charming picture indeed, but an unlikely one.[30]

If Yezierska distorted the facts of her life, the picture is further confused by the autobiographical nature of her fiction. For Yezierska used her own or anyone else's experience to shape her plots. One of her sisters bore ten children and had to struggle to make ends meet; this sister's life was convenient for such stories as *Bread Givers* and "The Free Vacation House," in *Hungry Hearts. Salome of the Tenements,* about a young immigrant girl who wins a millionaire WASP husband, only to find the differences between them unbridgeable, might remind readers of Yezierska's relationship with Dewey—certainly it is where she sets forth most clearly her sense of that relationship—but it was based on the much-publicized contemporary event of the immigrant reporter Rose Pastor's Cinderella marriage to the millionaire Graham Stokes. "Wild Winter Love" is again about an immigrant woman writer who has a relationship with a Deweyesque hero, which in this case drives her to suicide. Yet Yezierska's daughter explains in a reprint of *Hungry Hearts* that the story was based on Yezierska's response to the attempted suicide of Rose Cohen, an immigrant writer whose *Out of the Shadows* did not win the acclaim Yezierska's work did.[31] In the uncollected story "The Love Cheat" (1923), Yezierska rehearses her favorite WASP/ethnic love affair plot, but this time she makes the heroine a repressed and stuffy native-born American who cannot respond to the passionate ethnic hero.[32]

The relationship with Dewey that caused her so much pain became an obsession not only for psychological reasons but because she clearly saw its aesthetic appeal. The sense one gets is that she pointed out the stereotypical contrast implicit in the relationship just in case anyone missed it. In her letters to Dorothy Canfield Fisher, her friend in the 1930s, Yezierska repeatedly waxes rhapsodic over the differences between them. On sending Fisher *Bread Givers,* Yezierska wrote, "It will show you how wide apart are the worlds from which we come. But for all the myriad differences—between your people and mine—deep within, the same heart beats in all."[33] On occasion, she became a little snippy on the subject: when Fisher recommended some changes in the morals of the heroine of Yezierska's manuscript of her *All I Could Never Be* (1932), Yezierska responded that, though she had made some of the changes, "a Russian Jewess could never achieve the heroic power of restraint of an Emily Dickinson."[34] Complaining about a negative review of one of her books, she (not incorrectly) attributed the reviewer's shortsightedness to the same mythic contrast: "Mr. Brown found a few passages that jarred the Anglo-Saxon in him and he sentenced to the ash-heap my whole new world of dreams."[35] Hoping for a better review for her *Red Ribbon* in 1950, she wrote to Malcolm Cowley, "[My book] is as different from the book you reviewed last Sunday as the Hester Street ghetto is different from puritan New England."[36]

Given that Yezierska saw the dramatic potential of her story so clearly, it is not surprising to learn that she briefly attempted an acting career. With her friend Marcet Addams Haldeman, who was to marry Emanual Julius, the publisher of the Little Blue Books, Yezierska studied at the New York Academy of Dramatic Arts in 1909. Her niece Rose Goldberg remembered of her aunt's acting "screaming, feigning faints, body control and floor contortions in line with her dramatic disciplines." Another niece, Viola Simpson, saw Yezierska's acting as a "desperate effort to evolve an identity in keeping with her own emotional intensity."[37] About the only records that remain of Yezierska's acting are the letters that document her friendship with Marcet Haldeman-Julius—which tells us, among other things, that Yezierska told her friend that she was naming her baby girl Marcet, a tribute Haldeman-Julius remembered fondly in a letter to her own daughter fifteen years later.[38] Yezierska, in fact, named her daughter Louise.

These untruths do not impugn Yezierska's reliability; rather, they show how well she took to the mythmaking process and the extent to which she could turn events to her advantage. Though Yezierska was in fact "made" by others, by the nascent public relations industry, it is important to keep in mind her conscious participation in the process.

In was *her* idea—not a Hollywood publicist's or a press agent's—that she change her name back from the Americanized Hattie Mayer, the name she was given upon her arrival in America, to the impossible and foreign-sounding Anzia Yezierska. Records show that she was calling herself Anzia in 1910, a full ten years before she was "discovered." We cannot be sure whether she had already rediscovered her own Jewishness or was looking forward to reinventing it. What is clear is that Yezierska had a fully formed sense of what being Jewish and ethnic meant in the early decades of this century. The author of "We Can Change Our Noses But Not Our Moses" and "You Can't Be an Immigrant Twice" knew well the advantages and pitfalls of invented ethnicity.[39]

I have suggested that Anzia Yezierska, the sweatshop Cinderella, was a creation of public relations. But the phrase "public relations" was not yet in use in 1920, and in fact a whole range of influences created the "historian of Hester Street." It is well documented that the 1920s saw the birth of modern advertising, but the rise of public relations is at least as characteristic of the age and perhaps more significant.[40] The 1920s saw the rapid growth of the movie industry and an explosion in communications—phenomena at once conducive to and productive of public relations efforts. It is easy, too, to see the need for public relations as a response to the sheer mass of society that the growth of communications and media revealed to American citizens. The "hordes of immigrants" were part of this mass, and a particularly frightening part. One writer of a public relations handbook attributes the rise of the industry to just this need: "Public relations started as publicity . . . because, as it became harder for people with different backgrounds to understand and know about each other, the first necessity was for one group to tell another about itself."[41] Edward L. Bernays, considered the "father" of modern public relations, attributes the growth of the industry to the work of the muckrakers and explicitly connects its real beginnings with the need for good Americanization publicity for immigrants in the war years.[42] By 1925 H. L. Mencken could poke fun at the profession, declaring, "Every politician, movie actor, actress, and prize fight has a publicist," and likening the euphemism of "publicist" to that of "mortician."[43]

In the nativist 1920s, immigrants needed all the good publicity they could get. Set against the mysterious and anarchic Sacco and Vanzetti, this frank red-haired lady storyteller was a public relations triumph. The gospel of Anzia Yezierska was first spread by a former minister turned Hearst columnist, Frank Crane. Yezierska's "The Fat of the Land" had been published by Glenn Frank, the editor of *Century* magazine, selected by Edward O'Brien as the best short story of the year, and *Hungry Hearts* had been published by Houghton Mifflin in 1920. But, though critically praised, the book did not sell well. Long used to entering editors' offices dramatically and throwing herself on their mercy, Yezierska seems to have presented herself to Crane as an Old World specimen. He wrote up their encounter in his syndicated column:

> I got a new slant on America from Anzia Yezierska. She walked into my office one day and brought the Old World with her. She had not said three words before I saw farther into the heart of Russia and Poland than I had ever been able to do by reading many heavy books. She was Poland. She was the whole turgid stream of European imagination. The waters of the stream laved by consciousness.[44]

Frank Crane's column came to the attention of an employee of Samuel Goldwyn, who in turn told Yezierska's story to his boss. Goldwyn had recently initiated his "Eminent Author's" series, itself a triumph of public relations. Annoyed by the growth of the "star system," which allowed the actors and actresses in his films to demand larger and larger salaries, Goldwyn hit upon the idea of billing the writer over the star. When the series began, in 1919, the following statement appeared in the trade publications:

> Eminent Authors Pictures, Inc., organized by Rex Beach and Samuel Goldwyn, unites in one producing organization the greatest American novelists of today. It insures the exclusive presentation of their stories on the screen and each author's cooperation in production. The authors are—Rex Beach, Rupert Hughes, Leroy Scott, Gertrude Atherton, Governeur Morris, Mary Roberts Rinehart, Basil King.

Goldwyn declared, "The picture must pass the severest critic that it will ever meet—the author of the story."[45] Not the greatest reader of all time—the only book he ever read through was *The Wizard of Oz*—Goldwyn reportedly also wanted to get Washington Irving to do *The Legend of Sleepy Hollow* as a vehicle for Will Rogers, until Rex Beach informed him he was sixty years too late.[46] Undaunted, Goldwyn tried to sign George Bernard Shaw, who declined (though Goldwyn did sign the equally eminent Maurice Maeterlinck, who seems to have taken the studio for something of a ride).

The "Eminent Authors" scheme was a publicity stunt, an attempt to "cash in" on the literary business. It was an attempt that failed, though the long tradition of writers "going Hollywood" can be seen as a kind of stepchild of it—mostly because in the days of silent films nobody really had much of an idea what a script consisted of. The Eminent Authors, it seems, were paid to come up with ideas, which "scenario writers" then wrote into scripts. In reality, the authors were used as publicity dummies.

The rise of Hollywood, as I have said, was in symbiotic relation with the rise of public relations. Even Edward L. Bernays found the business of "star-making" too heavy-handed. In his autobiography, he describes working for Fox to promote Theda Bara in the 1917 *Cleopatra*. Devising slogans like "The high cost of kissing the modern Cleopatra is cheap compared with the price Ceasar paid," Bernays not only tried to lure the general public but also devised strategies to appeal to high school principals by stressing the film's educational qualities and to milliners and dressmakers by providing fashion inspiration. Bernays remarked wryly on the packaging of Theda Bara, who was "sold" as an illegitimate daughter of a French artist and an Arab woman. Though *Bara* is *Arab* spelled backward, the star was another invented ethnic heroine, Theodosia Goodman from Cincinnati. Bernays wrote that Goldwyn, whom he met three years later, reminded him of a "salesman in a perpetual rush." Resolving never to work for the movies again, Bernays commented, "It was a crude, crass, manufacturing business, run by crude, crass men."[47]

As Lary May and other film historians have pointed out, the early movie moguls were almost all immigrants, East European Jews, who had come out of the sales business. Carl Laemmle, the founder of Universal Pictures, was a clothing salesman who compared selling movies to selling clothes; Adolph Zukor sold furs; and Sam Goldwyn, né Goldfisch,[48] sold gloves. Goldwyn was so attuned to public opinion that he used to sit in movie theaters with his back to the screen, watching audience reaction. He once stated,

> If the audience don't like a picture, they have a good reason. The public is never wrong. I don't go for all this thing that when I have a failure, it is because the audience doesn't have the taste or education, or isn't sensitive enough. The public pays the money. It wants to be entertained. That's all I know.[49]

Mary Roberts Rinehart and Gertrude Atherton, two of Goldwyn's original Eminent Authors, remembered their Hollywood experiences with some disillusionment. Rinehart remembered that she felt she had no place at the studio: "I was precisely as useful as a fifth leg to a calf." But both remembered their publicity functions. Goldwyn tried to send a blimp to greet Rinehart on her arrival in Hollywood; when she declined, he sent an open car filled with flowers instead. Rinehart wrote very little in Hollywood but was photographed constantly, in any variety of settings.[50]

One can imagine the public relations opportunity Anzia Yezierska presented to Goldwyn and his staff. It is emblematic that she was glorified not for any stories she had written but for the story of her life. Indeed, the "sweatshop Cinderella" stories were the product of Goldwyn's publicity machine. In *Red Ribbon on a White Horse,* she recounts a Goldwyn assistant's enthusiasm about selling her story to the tabloids: "'A natural for the tabloids! Millions couldn't buy this build-up for the picture.'" Yezierska reflects,

> As long as I remained with Goldwyn I was in a glasshouse with crooked mirrors. Every move I made was distorted, and every distortion exploited to further the sale of *Hungry Hearts.* The dinner parties, the invitations . . . , all that had seemed to be the spontaneous recognition of my book was but the merchandising enterprise of press agents selling a movie. Money and ballyhoo—the fruit of the struggle to write. (*RR,* 80–81).

Though Yezierska was among Jews in Hollywood, she felt a great gulf between herself and them. When she met William Fox, she felt "East Side had met East Side" (*RR,* 84), but she found him unsympathetic to her struggles with writing and ultimately turned down a lucrative writing contract he offered her. About Paul Bern, the director of *Hungry Hearts,* she wrote, "He had a dark, Hester Street face, but slick as a picture on the cover of a movie magazine" (*RR,* 44). She was enchanted with the stage sets of East European shtetls and Hester Street kitchens built for her film, and she felt the scenario writer had improved on her own material. But she was horrified to learn that Montague Glass had been hired to do the "post-mortem"—to "doctor"—the final version of the film. Yezierska described Glass, the author of the *Potash and Perlmutter* stories, as "the man who made a living burlesquing Jews for *The Saturday Evening Post.* . . . Americans reading his Potash and Perlmutter stories thought those clowning cloak and suiters were the Jewish people" (*RR,* 81). Glass was to provide "laughs and a happy ending" for the film (*RR,* 82), which disgusted her. The entire Hollywood experience left her disillusioned. "I had dreamed of Olympian gods and woke up among hucksters," she wrote (*RR,* 62). Afraid that the turmoil she suffered would affect her writing, she fled Hollywood and eventually returned to New York.

Yezierska fled Hollywood, but she could not flee her public image. Whenever one of her books was published, the press revived the "sweatshop Cinderella" story. Yezierska milked it herself for a few years, writing magazine articles like "This Is What $10,000 Did for Me."[51] But she was finally undone by it. Critics called her fiction overemotional and uncontrolled, criticizing her for the "ethnic" traits they had once enjoyed. W. Adolphe Roberts, in a typical review of *Salome of the Tenements,* called her work an orgy of the emotions," "sentimental, illogical, hysterical, naive," adding somewhat cryptically, "I have assumed this incoherence to be racial. Yet I would hesitate to call it Jewish."[52] (It is interesting to note that *Salome* tells the story of an immigrant girl who "cashes in" on her uniqueness, winning the love of a WASP millionaire attracted to her "passionate intensity"—perhaps reviewers were made nervous by immigrants who did not remain in the picturesque ghetto.) Yezierska battled this kind of response tirelessly, pointing out to her critics exactly what they were doing: condemning the person they themselves had helped create. In a portrait of her by Burton Rascoe in "A Bookman's Day Book," Yezierska explains how she tried to persuade reviewers not to dismiss her work as hysterical: "These people in the ghetto are high-strung, inarticulate. They are so hungry for little bits of sympathy, love and beauty; they are like children; what seems to be hysterical or overemotional to Anglo-Saxons in them is a natural state, because they feel so deeply and are not educated enough to articulate their emotions."[53] Yezierska's desire to "open up her culture" to native-born Americans was thus reduced to a plea for sympathy.

It would be a mistake to interpret the invention of Anzia Yezierska's ethnicity as a mere publicity event, however, with Yezierska dumbly manipulated by forces beyond her control. She was an active agent in the process—and remarkably successful, at least for a time. It would be equally wrong to underestimate the pain Yezierska felt when the invention backfired. Her rise from the ghetto and her inability to leave it behind left her feeling terribly divided. In one of her letters to Dorothy Canfield Fisher, she again revives the conceit of her mysterious "difference," but she expresses it with real poignancy. She writes that she wants to discuss a book idea with Fisher, "'the question of the establishment of people from different cultures in a society new to them.'" "It is a subject," she goes on, that has been close to my heart for many years. Not only that house painter who had found work in Arlington or Prof. Solveni—there's Lafcadio Hern [*sic*] who was able to feel at home in Japan or D. H. Lawrence in Mexico or Italy or T. S. Lawrence [*sic*] in Africa [*sic*]—These men had found the center of their work in themselves and could go on with their work in any part of the world. But there is also a Stefan Zweig—a versatile novelist—who was driven to suicide because of his uprootedness.[54]

At the end of *Red Ribbon*, Yezierska reflects on the immigrant woman's victimization by a consumer culture, recognizing the falseness of that culture's discourse:

> I saw that Hollywood was not my success, nor my present poverty and anonymity, failure. I saw that "success," "failure," "poverty," "riches," were price tags, money values of the market place which had mesmerized me and sidetracked me for years. (*RR*, 219)

For Yezierska, the "price tags" were high. Seduced and betrayed by her public, by "the money values of the market place," she was doomed to disillusionment. She had dramatically high hopes for realizing herself and for finding what she called "truth," hopes that were almost always dashed. But she never stopped fighting. Will Rogers once said to her, "You're like a punch-drunk fighter, striking an opponent no longer there. You've won your fight and you don't know it" (*RR*, 68). Her daughter said that "to know Anzia was to be close to an emotional volcano, always ready to erupt." Given her high expectations, writes her daughter, "she was the loneliest person I knew."[55] It is too easy to see Yezierska as crippled by the false values of Hollywood or victimized by a nativist and sexist American public. Rather, it was an extraordinary complex of circumstances that contributed to the making of this controversial and difficult ethnic American heroine.

Deviant Girls and Dissatisfied Women: A Sociologist's Tale

CARLA CAPPETTI

[M]y past . . . seems very remote to me. The changes in ways of life have recently been so great as to separate all of us from our early years profoundly, and in my case this separation seems to be more profound because I was born in an isolated region of Old Virginia, 20 miles from the railroad in a social environment resembling that of the 18th century, and I consequently feel that I have lived in three centuries, migrating gradually toward the higher cultural areas. The fact that I reached civilization at all is evidently due to some obscure decision on the part of my father to attend an institution of learning. . . . In this decision he provoked a certain amount of resentment from his own father, a Pennsylvania Dutchman, rich in land but with peasant attitudes.[1]

—WILLIAM ISAAC THOMAS, *"My Life,"* 1928

Had he been a European immigrant with such literary talent, Thomas might have contributed to the immigrant narratives that have become a genre in American literature. The American-born William Isaac Thomas, however, became a sociologist. And when, at the turn of the century, he joined this still infant discipline at the University of Chicago, Thomas brought two crucial assets: his identity as a migrant who had come from rural Virginia to urban Chicago and a special sensibility for words, for storytelling, for personal narratives.[2] By 1918 Thomas had become—with his coauthorship of *The Polish Peasant in Europe and America* (1918–20)—the founding father of American urban sociology.[3] Making extensive use of immigrant letters and life histories, Thomas had combined science and storytelling and produced what, in

124

1937, was voted the single most important contribution to American sociology.[4] Most important, he had successfully staked out sociology's claim to immigrant narratives, a privilege that had remained largely the territory of autobiographical writing.

Although *The Polish Peasant* has been acknowledged as a turning point in American sociology, Thomas's work still awaits recognition as having been crucial to the developing discourse on the city and its inhabitants that took shape in those years. Centered in Chicago, this discourse produced an impressive series of sociological studies and novels on the city, on immigration, and on deviance. It eventually shaped the representation of urban America between the two world wars, becoming known as the Chicago school of urban sociology and the Chicago school of urban literature.[5]

A fragment of this intellectual scenario can be explored by focusing on W. I. Thomas's *The Unadjusted Girl: With Cases and Standpoint for Behavior Analysis* (1923).[6] The sociologist's earlier effort to explain the maladjustment that occurred when Polish immigrants moved from the "old" to the "new" world, from the rural villages of Poland to the industrial cities of America, became, in this later study, an attempt to understand the maladjustment that all people experience—not just immigrants from rural Europe—when they migrate to "modernity," that abstraction which is so often synonymous with "city." In *The Unadjusted Girl*, the deviant girl and women in general replace the Polish immigrant as an emblem of all the hopes and threats implicit in the transition.

At the core of *The Unadjusted Girl* are a number of social phenomena—female deviance, corruption, prostitution—that had become increasingly visible during the first two decades of the century. The rapid urban growth of the period, nourished not only by foreign immigrants but by internal migrants from the rural regions of America as well, was the most obvious cause of such social problems. When he decided to study juvenile female deviants, Thomas implicitly decided to retell his favorite story—the story of the immigrant voyage across centuries and toward "civilization"—with new characters and a new setting. The result was a new story of migration and change from a premodern, rural, traditional, ethnic community to a modern, urban, freer, often deviant society. It is this shift that makes *The Unadjusted Girl* a portrait of "unadjusted modernity" and, as such, most valuable for a study of the representation of urbanization in American culture.[7]

This view of the text as a sociological monograph that, somewhat like a literary text, attempts to represent modernity raises certain questions. If *The Unadjusted Girl* is simply a study of female deviance, of young prostitutes and female criminals, then why is there a substantial section on middle-class mature women who are often unconventional but rarely criminal? Why is the delinquent girl rather than the delinquent boy the center of attention, and what symbolic role does she play in Thomas's social program? How does a sociological type—the deviant girl—relate to literary types—Maggie, Sister Carrie—that belong to the same tradition? What kind of aesthetic is embedded in the methodology of personal documents and in the form of montage that underlie the text, and what relationship exists between the form of this sociological monograph and its subject matter?

In what follows I pursue a threefold argument. A storyteller of sociology, Thomas constructed this study of female deviance as a bildungsroman of modern society, a story of growth and development in which migration and deviance—both literally and metaphorically intended—play a crucial role. Within such narrative, and in spite of what the title of the study might suggest, not one but two main characters occupy center stage: the mature and respectable woman on the one hand and the young lumpenproletarian girl on the other. Although both engage in morally subversive forms of behavior, they play substantially different roles. Last, borrowing from the aesthetic of montage, Thomas uses personal documents in a way that makes *The Unadjusted Girl* not only part of the modernist project to capture the fragmentation and dislocation of the modern world, but also a revealing picture of the close ties that link science and art.[8]

The Country and the City

The female deviant in the modern world exists, in Thomas's study, in the space defined by two main axes: on one side is a theory of human behavior that combines psychological, anthropological, and physiological concepts; on the other is a theory of social change that describes and narrates the decline of the old world and the rise of modern society.

Thomas's theory of human behavior and personality provides two basic concepts for his portrait of deviant modernity: the "wishes" and the "definition of the situation."[9] Thomas identifies four basic wishes as universal and innate behavioral components: the wish for new experience, the wish for security, the wish for response, and the wish for recognition. Without delving into the details of this taxonomy, one notices that these wishes form two sets of complementary opposites. The wish for "new experience" originates in what Thomas considers the best traits of our primitive ancestors—courage, anger, disregard for death, impulses of attack and pursuit.[10] The wish for "security," on the other hand, points to the negative attributes of our forebears—fear, avoidance of death, timidity, flight, caution.[11] Transferred to the modern universe, the two wishes divide people into two main groups: those who want change, disregard standards, and have no fear of instability and those afraid of change, especially of economic insecurity. The second set of wishes locates the individual among other human subjects. The wish for "response" inspires, in fact, all desires for love and appreciation, finding expression in activities relating to love.[12] The wish for "recognition," on the other hand, animates the pursuit of political, artistic, or scientific careers, and the desire for fashionable and elegant dresses. In this mirror of behavioral dualities, not only do the four wishes form two sets of complementary opposites—Pasteur versus the philistine, Florence Nightingale or Jane Addams versus Napoleon—but each wish contains complementary and morally opposite types as well—the inventor and the vagabond, the philistine and the miser, the self-sacrificing woman and the promiscuous one, the leader and the exhibitionist:

> The moral good or evil of a wish depends on the social meaning or value of the activity which results from it. Thus the vagabond, the adventurer, the spendthrift, the bohemian are dominated by the desire for new experience, but so are the inventor and the scientist; adventures with women and the tendency to domesticity are both expressions of the desire for response; vain ostentation and creative artistic work both are designed to provoke recognition; avarice and business enterprise are actuated by the desire for security. (38)

By showing that moral judgments are socially and culturally defined and by revealing their tautological nature, Thomas sets the stage for a procession of cases illustrating precisely the complementarity of morally and socially dichotomous behaviors.

After he dismisses the question of whether certain forms of behavior are "good" or "evil," Thomas raises two new questions: First, what causes one or the other wish to become predominant? Second, what causes two individuals who are equally directed by the same wish—for example, the wish for new experience—to become an artist, a scientist, a hobo, or a criminal? In order to account for the highly individual nature of behavior, Thomas at this point introduces two new ingredients: temperament, a physiological one, and social experience, a cultural one. While the first is "a chemical matter dependent on the secretions of the glandular systems" (39), the second is a record of all the external influences acting upon the individual.

Little interested in the "chemical" component of his scheme, Thomas turns his attention to the interaction between wishes and social experience. Such interaction distinguishes "man" from the "lower animals" and allows the former the privilege of choosing whether to obey stimulations, a choice exercised on the basis of memory and of "past experiences" (41):

> Preliminary to any self-determined act of behavior there is always a stage of examination and deliberation which we may call *the definition of the situation*. And actually not only concrete acts are dependent on the definition of the situation, but gradually a whole life-policy and the personality of the individual himself follow from a series of such definitions. (42)

Parting company here with social, economic, and biological determinism, Thomas courageously theorizes that personality—and even the whole life of an individual—is the product of choice. Only one obstacle stands in the way of such a behavioral utopia:

> But the child is always born into a group of people among whom all the general types of situation which may arise have already been defined and corresponding rules of conduct developed, and where he has not the slightest chance of making his definitions and following his wishes without interference. . . .
>
> There is therefore always a rivalry between the spontaneous definitions of the situation made by the member of an organized society and the definitions which his society has provided for him. The individual tends to a hedonistic selection of activity, pleasure first; and society to a utilitarian selection, safety first. (42)

The theory discloses here its double nature. On the one hand, by postulating a culturally and socially defined subject, Thomas provides the tools to free the individual from Darwinian as well as Lamarckian forms of determinism. On the other, by positing a collective and more powerful subjectivity, Thomas is forced to deny the newly discovered freedom and to defer liberation to a near sociological future.

If the "wishes" and "the definition of the situation" provide the conceptual framework for Thomas's discussion, it is the narrative of how the old world declined and the modern world rose that, by introducing time and history, illuminates the sociologist's program toward past and future:

> Originally the community was practically the whole world of its members. It was composed of families related by blood and marriage and was not so large that all members could not come together; it was a face-to-face group. I asked a Polish peasant what was the extent of an *"okolica"* or neighborhood—how far it reached. "It reaches," he said, "as far as the report of a man reaches—as far as the man is talked about." And it was in communities of this kind that the moral code which we now recognize as valid originated. (44)

This is the once-upon-a-time of Thomas's tale, the magic formula evoking a time and a place where the physical space occupied by the kin completely contained the universe of an individual. Through this narrative formula Thomas historicizes the dominant moral code of his time, implicitly denying its innate and everlasting validity, especially in times of social change.

Resistance to change, repression of individual wishes, and, ultimately, power to uphold immobility are, according to Thomas, the primary traits of these older communities:

> In small and isolated communities there is little tendency to change or progress because the new experience of the individual is sacrificed for the sake of the security of the group. . . .
>
> In the small and spatially isolated communities of the past, where the influences were strong and steady, the members became more or less habituated to and reconciled with a life of repressed wishes. The repression was demanded of all, the arrangement was equitable, and while certain new experiences were prohibited, and pleasure not countenanced as an end in itself, there remained satisfactions, not the least of which was the suppression of the wishes of others. (70–72)

When the community successfully exercises control, upholds uniformity, and maintains order,

> as it does among savages, among Mohammedans, and as it did until recently among European peasants, no appreciable change in the moral code or in the state of culture is observable from generation to generation. (70)

"Savages," "Mohammedans," "old Europe," and, in other passages, even "rural America" all fall within the compass of Thomas's compact, premodern world, which stretches in time and space to include "primitive" and "rural" communities of different ages and continents. Primitive and rural worlds emerge as identical, held together by monolithic worldviews, one-dimensional norms, and intolerant rules and standards. The dichotomy that splits human nature into a wish favorable to change and a wish opposed to it finds its sociological complement here in the polarity between individuals who desire change and a community that opposes it; it also finds narrative complement in the polarities between immobile, traditional communities and historical, modern societies.

Several documents concerning the lives of immigrants both in the old world and in the new bring Thomas's model of social control in traditional societies to life. Two travelers are called in as witnesses of how communal decisions are taken in the old world:

> 25. We who are unacquainted with peasant speech, manners and method of expressing thought—mimicry—if we should be present at a division of land or some settlement among the peasants, would never understand anything. Hearing fragmentary, disconnected exclamations, endless quarreling, with repetition of some single word; hearing this racket of a seemingly senseless, noisy crowd that counts up or measures off something, we should conclude that they would not get together, or arrive at any result in an age. . . . Yet wait until the end and you will see that the division has been made with mathematical accuracy. . . . In the end, you look into it and find that an admirable decision has been formed and, what is most important, a unanimous decision. (45)

> 28. It sometimes happens that all except one may agree but the motion is never carried if that one refuses to agree to it. In such cases all endeavor to talk over and persuade the stiff-necked one. Often they even call to their aid his wife, his children, his relatives, his father-in-law, and his mother, that they may prevail upon him to say yes. . . . It seldom occurs in such cases that unanimity is not attained. (48–49)[13]

These travel notes are not unlike, in tone and form, the ethnographic writings that had resulted from the observation of more "exotic" people. Both participate in a discursive practice that pushes peasant societies into a "prehistorical" past—incidentally, a contradiction in terms—with other "primitive" cultures, a discourse to which Thomas himself was clearly contributing.

The unanimity that prevails in the old world, Thomas points out, does not immediately break down upon immigration, even though such dislocation undermines and threatens to dissolve it. The classical example, not surprisingly, is the Romeo and Juliet fable of love across ethnic boundaries, of love as a breakdown of old identities.[14] The letter of a Jewish woman of Hungarian descent who has secretly married a "gentile boy of German parents" recounts how she was cast out by parents and friends first and by her own husband later:

> 29. . . . I cannot stand the loneliness and do not want to be hated, denounced and spurned by all. My loneliness will drive me to a premature grave. Perhaps you can tell me how to get rid of my misfortune. Believe me, I am not to blame for what I have done—it was my ignorance. I never believed that it was such a terrible crime to marry a non-Jew and that my parents would under no circumstances forgive me. I am willing to do anything, to make the greatest sacrifice, if only the terrible ban be taken off me. (51–52)

Immediately below this document, Thomas juxtaposes the letter of a Jewish father whose daughter has married an Italian and who cannot solve the riddle between belief in freedom and rejection of a gentile son-in-law:

> 30. . . . My tragedy is much greater because I am a free thinker. Theoretically I consider a "goi" [gentile] just as much a man as a Jew. . . . Indeed I ask myself these questions: "What would happen if my daughter married a Jewish fellow who was a good-for-nothing? . . . And what do I care if he is an Italian? But I can not seem to answer these delicate questions. The fact is that I would prefer a refined man; but I would sooner have a common Jew than an educated *goi*. Why this is so, I do not know, but that is how it is, of that there is no doubt. And this shows what a terrible chasm exists between theory and practice! (52)

By means of the travel reports and the immigrant letters, Thomas composes an image of the old community—both in Europe and in the immigrant colonies of America—as a society where the individual is controlled by the family, where situations and emotions are predetermined, where gossip is a powerful form of social control.

And even after the individual migrates to the modern world and to the American cities, the community continues to exercise its control across the ocean. Stepping momentarily outside his sociological role to enter as a witness, Thomas asserts,

> In examining the letters between immigrants in America and their home communities I have noticed that the great solicitude of the family and community is that the absent member shall not change. . . . And the typical immigrant letter is an assurance and reminder that the writer, though absent, is still a member of the community. (57)

In describing the old community, Thomas projects onto it all that is opposed to change: permanence and stability, of course, but also conservatism and opposition to progress.

What could be more antithetical to this monstrous stasis than the fragmented and contradictory nature of the modern world?[15]

> But by a process, an evolution, connected with mechanical inventions, facilitated communication, the diffusion of print, the growth of cities, business organization, the capitalistic system, specialized occupations, scientific research, doctrines of freedom, the evolutionary view of life, etc., the family and community influences have been weakened and the world in general has been profoundly changed in content, ideals, and organization. (70–71)

At the opposite end of the spectrum appears a world of change, novelty, and metamorphosis—the world of cities, industry, consumer capitalism, and, most important, science. Through a neomaterialist theory of evolution, Thomas disrupts the immobility of the old world, introducing time and history. Material and technological developments mark the transition to this generic "modern" world, which clearly shows, however, the industrial and urban developments of early-twentieth-century America.

When he condemns the past as irrelevant and hails material evolution as the agent of change, Thomas's prose breaks out of its scientific and objective disguise:

> The typical community is vanishing and it would be neither possible nor desirable to restore it in its old form. It does not correspond with the present direction of social evolution and it would now be a distressing condition in which to live. . . . [I]t represents an element which we have lost and which we shall probably have to restore in some form of coöperation in order to secure a balanced and normal society,—some arrangement corresponding with human nature. (44)

Far from being a nostalgic reformer—the old community shall *not* be restored—Thomas explicitly responds to those who looked backward in time, who yearned for the village as a prelapsarian world and damned the city and industrialism for the sins and evils of human nature.

Endowed with all that was missing in the village, the modern world signifies for Thomas free individual choice, social participation for women, sexual freedom for all. The process resembles the opening of a frontier where the barriers represented by communal and kinship groups are finally torn down. In the process, physical migration overlaps with social evolution while both converge toward a "higher" modern world, one that promises the possibility of new individual identities:

Young people leave home for larger opportunities, to seek new experience, and from necessity. Detachment from family and community, wandering, travel, "vagabondage" have assumed the character of normality. Relationships are casualized and specialized. Men meet professionally, as promoters of enterprises, not as members of families, communities, churches. Girls leave home to work in factories, stores, offices, and studios. Even when families are not separated they leave home for their work. (71)

Once they step outside the communal boundaries, however, young people find themselves in a world that is "large, alluring and confusing" (78), a world that contains both freedom and conflict, liberation and corruption. The modern world is also synonymous with "vagueness," "rival definitions," "indeterminateness" (82). Here, clashing codes coexist, to the confusion of the young girl, simultaneously influenced "by the traditional code . . . [and by] the passing show of the greater world which suggests to her pleasure and recognition" (82). Captured by this spectacle of glittering beauty, the sociologist himself seems to become hypnotized—much like the people he is discussing— by the unceasing mutability of that world.[16]

Thus in a city the shop windows, the costumes worn on the streets, the newspaper advertisements of ladies' wear, the news items concerning objects of luxury define a proper girl as one neatly, fashionably, beautifully, and expensively gowned, and the behavior of the girl is an adaptation to this standard. (82)

Emblem of innocence and sophistication, nature and culture, purity and corruption, the girl at once contains and defies these opposites. Precisely at this juncture the ambivalent nature of the modern world and of the modern girl becomes apparent. Along the elegant avenues of the city, in the theatrical character of its show, is where Thomas locates the central conflict of the modern world:

[T]he modern world presents itself as a spectacle in which the observer is never sufficiently participating. The modern revolt and unrest are due to the contrast between the paucity of fulfillment of the wishes of the individual and the fullness, or apparent fullness, of life around him. All age levels have been affected by the feeling that much, too much, is being missed in life. This unrest is felt most by those who have heretofore been most excluded from general participation in life—*the mature woman and the young girl.* (72, my emphasis)

These are the archetypes of change that occupy Thomas's sociological universe and clamor for a freer future: the young girl and the mature woman. Somewhat like the other historical class, they have nothing to lose but an old system that excludes them from life.

The Restless Woman

The overall narrative of *The Unadjusted Girl* follows the paths of vanishing communities and disappearing families. Yet the literary substance of the text materializes where the existences of real people are introduced through letters, autobiographical sketches, and case histories. Women and girls, prostitutes and peasants, hobos and thieves, give life to Thomas's mosaic of human behavior in times of change. "The Regulation of the Wishes," "The Individualization of Behavior," and "The Demoralization of Girls"—the three chapters where most of the documents appear—reproduce even in the titles the narrative progression from traditional community to modernity. Beneath these titles are dozens of moving personal accounts, testimonies uttered by a multitude of modern marginals. Among them stand out the mature woman and the young girl. They symbolize the old world that Thomas wishes away. Their life histories reveal the control that the old community continues to exercise even after they have moved away and migrated to America, to the city, or to modern society; at the same time they reveal the dangers awaiting them in the midst of modernity.

The nature of the modern world and the changing norms that regulate the Gorgon of female sexuality in that world provide two recurrent themes in the stories of women and girls. The modern world, however, seems to inspire and cause different desires and behaviors in the woman and in the girl. For the mature woman, modernity translates into a desire to participate in social life, to be free from Victorian conventions and domesticity; for the young girl, modernity signifies a desire for clothes, movies, and all those objects that consumerism potentially makes available to everyone. In the stories of women and girls who are all in rebellion against dominant conformity, Thomas detects the signs—dissatisfaction, rebellion, deviance—of a relentless erosion of communal power.

Age is the most visible but least important mark distinguishing the mature woman from the young girl. Whether bourgeois or petit bourgeois, middle-class or working-class, most of the mature women appear to live in fairly stable social and economic conditions. The documents recount stories of women who are dissatisfied with marriage; women who, unable to find fulfillment in marriage, have betrayed their husbands; women who have rejected marriage conventions and are now living as concubines. The complexities of love and the frustrations of marriage receive here the sanctions of science. Unconventional and even "immoral" behavior is theoretically and sociologically legitimized on the basis of the four wishes that Thomas has posited as essential components of human nature.

Thomas introduces one such case as the "cry of despair . . . from a woman who limited her life to marriage . . . and is now apparently too old to have other interests" (87). The letter, like many documents concerning mature women, was written to the *Forward,* a New York Yiddish newspaper. It expresses in confessional form the tensions splitting a woman's consciousness between sanctioned role and unquenched desires:

> 37. There is a saying about the peacock. "When she looks at her feathers she laughs, and when she looks at her feet she cries." I am in the same situation.
>
> My husband's career, upon which I spent the best years of my life, is established favorably; our children are a joy to me as a mother; nor can I complain about our material circumstances. But I am dissatisfied with myself. My love for my children, be it ever so great, cannot destroy myself. A human being is not created like a bee which dies after accomplishing its only task.
>
> Desires, long latent, have been aroused in me and become more aggressive the more obstacles they encounter. . . . I now have the desire to go about and see and hear everything. I wish to take part in everything—to dance, skate, play the piano, sing, go to the theatre, opera, lectures and generally mingle in society. As you see, I am no idler whose purpose is to chase all sorts of foolish things, as a result of loose ways. This is not the case.
>
> My present unrest is a natural result following a long period of hunger and thirst for non-satisfied desires in every field of human experience. It is the dread of losing that which never can be recovered—youth and time which do not stand still—an impulse to catch up with the things I have missed. . . . If it were not for my maternal feeling I would go away into the wide world. (72–73)

Two antipodal worlds loom over the letter: on the one hand is the world of settled domestic contentment; on the other, the world of contingent human experience and social participation. The woman speaks to an audience that might misread her motives and compels her to emphasize, "I am no idler whose purpose is to chase all sorts of foolish things, as a result of loose ways" (73). This audience might too readily conclude that she is dangerously leaning on the precipice of deviance and sin. To some extent, this is the same audience Thomas is addressing in his book, the audience whose moral standards he is attempting to modify. To such an audience Thomas hopes to prove that the wish for new experience—a natural wish present in everyone—and not latent corruption is the source of domestic despair.

The restlessness and rebellion still contained within words in the previous case translate into actions in subsequent ones. A woman who has betrayed her husband recounts a touching story of adultery and guilt. The letter narrates the story of a woman whose husband brings a cousin into the house as a boarder and who, as a result, begins to lose control over her emotions. The central paragraphs of this long letter retrace the dramatic struggle leading to sin:

10. . . . I almost never spoke to him, and never came near him. God only knows how much these efforts cost me, but with all my energy I fought against the diabolic feeling in my heart. Unfortunately, my husband misinterpreted my behavior as a lack of hospitality. His resentment compelled me to assume a more friendly attitude toward his relative, as I wished to avoid quarrelling. What followed may easily be inferred. From amiability I passed to love until he occupied my whole mind and everybody else was non-existent for me. Of course no one was aware of my predicament.

One day I decided to put an end to my sufferings by confessing all to my boarder and requesting him to go away or at least leave our house and avert a scandal. Unfortunately, my hope of a peaceful life was not fulfilled, following my confession to the cousin. He remained in our home and became more friendly than ever towards me. I began to love him so intensely that I hardly noticed his growing intimacy with me and as a result I gave birth to a baby whose father is my husband's cousin. . . .

I am unable to describe to you one hundredth part of the misery this has caused me. I always considered an unfaithful woman the worst creature on earth and now . . . I am myself a *degraded woman*. . . . The mere thought of it drives me insane. My husband, of course, knows nothing about the incident. . . . Every day in the week is a day of utter anguish for me and every day I feel the tortures of hell. . . . I can not stand my husband's tenderness toward the child that is mine but not his. When he gives the baby a kiss it burns like a hot coal dropped in my bosom. Every time he calls it his baby I hear some one shouting into my ear the familiar epithet thrown at low creatures like me . . . and every time he takes the child in his arms I am tempted to tell him the terrible truth. . . . And so I continue to suffer. (15–16, my emphasis)

The protagonist of this domestic drama constructs her sin as an evil fate, as a series of events that accidentally lead to her fall.[17] Stressing from the beginning that as a child she conducted herself "decently" and that as a young girl she "strove to marry some good young man and live contentedly," in the attempt to establish her moral and behavioral credentials, the author of this letter, like the preceding one, evokes the moral context surrounding her. She asks her potential judges that they not discount her tale of betrayal on the basis of innate corruption or youthful depravation. The guilt she imposes on herself and her description of herself as a "degraded woman" measure the moral order she and her audience share. Most important, they measure the repressed desire released in the forbidden act. A forbidden sin committed and then represented as "real" rather than fictional: this is what gives the confession its quasi-cathartic quality. At once representing and forbidding, the letter articulates the fear-desire of becoming a "degraded" woman. In this case, as in many others, Thomas follows the advice of his patroness, Ms. Dummer, who opens her foreword to *The Unadjusted Girl* by quoting Spinoza's "Neither condemn nor ridicule but try to understand" (v). In keeping with the exhortation of the Dutch philosopher, Thomas abstains from judgment and points out instead that the wish for a response explains the woman's behavior.

A special case adds new elements to Thomas's gallery of middle-class deviance and illustrates how far the limits of unconventionality could stretch for the middle-class woman. This is the story of Margaret, related not in letter form but through a case history.[18] Her story illustrates what social landscape was available outside the confines of moral conventions:

> 38. I had been looking for Margaret, for I knew she was a striking instance of the "unadjusted" who had within a year come with a kind of aesthetic logic to Greenwich Village. She needed something very badly. What I heard about her which excited me was that she was twenty years old, unmarried, had never lived with a man or had any of that experience, had worked for a year on a socialist magazine, was a heavy drinker and a frequenter of Hell Hole, that she came from a middle class family but preferred the society of the outcasts to any other. Greenwich Village is not composed of outcasts, but it does not reject them, and it enables a man or woman who desires to know the outcast to satisfy the desire without feeling cut off from humanity. Hell Hole is a saloon in the back room of which pickpockets, grafters, philosophers, poets, revolutionists, stool-pigeons, and the riff-raff of humanity meet. Margaret loves this place and the people in it—so they told me—and there she did and said extreme things in which there was a bitter fling at decent society. (73)

The narrator proceeds to quote the story in Margaret's own words and to fill in the details of a middle-class existence that, after turning against its own class, has drifted toward the margins of society. From these moral outskirts are uttered Margaret's concluding words:

> "I want to know the down and outs," said Margaret with quiet, almost fanatical intenseness. "I find kindness in the lowest places, and more than kindness sometimes—something, I don't know what it is, that I want." (76)

For Thomas, Margaret's is simply a case of "revolt." Thomas has already provided, in the theory of human nature and in the narrative of social change, both the behavioral ingredients (the wish for new experience and for response) that combine in this type of life history and the sociological ingredients (modern revolt and unrest, desire to participate, rejection of the old system) that accompany it. What Thomas fails to notice is that Margaret's story is a romantic quest for the humble but ideally good transposed into the modern city. It is a Wordsworthian-Byronesque search for the lost self among the lowly or the exotics, a search that parallels Margaret's voyage from the rejection of a "respectable, middle-class family" to the discovery of "sex" and "hard street life," to embracement of "socialism" "poetry," and "anything that expressed a reaction against the conditions of my life at home" (73), and, finally, to the waterfront, the saloon back rooms, and their prostitute and criminal guests:

> And I liked them. They seemed human, more so than other people. And in this place were working men. One man, with a wife and children, noticed I was going there and didn't seem to belong to them, and he asked me to go home with him and live with his family; and he meant it, and meant it decently. (75)

By the end of her quest Margaret has come full circle. She has opened and closed her story with family images, and her symbolic adoption into the family of the "down-and-outs" immortalizes the success of her quest for a new self.

The Immoral Professor

Not included in the documentary selection of *The Unadjusted Girl*, yet central to its portrayal of middle-class deviance, is an important episode of Thomas's own life history, an episode that warrants a short digression.

On April 12, 1918, just below the full-page title "FLANDERS LINE STIFFENS" and surrounded by more war news, the *Chicago Daily Tribune* carried on its front page the following headline:

EXTRA—DR. THOMAS AND WOMAN TAKEN IN LOOP HOTEL

The article, several columns long, recounted how the manager of the hotel, suspecting a couple of not being married, had complied with a new law, alerted the FBI, and brought about the arrest on charges of violating the Mann Act and of registering under false pretenses. The article went on to inform its readers, "Prof. Thomas is the author of the widely discussed book 'The Mind of the Woman.' His wife has been known as an ardent exponent of pacifism and was one of the supporters in the Ford peace ship enterprise."[19] During the following days it became known to readers of the press that Thomas was fifty-five years old and Mrs. Granger, the adulteress, only twenty-four; that Thomas was a professor of sociology at the University of Chicago and Mrs. Granger the wife of a lieutenant serving in France (this fact was reiterated every day for a week); that Mrs. Thomas had welcomed Mrs. Granger into her own house during the pretrial hearings. The heavy-handed symbolism of this scenario was unmistakable: fantasies of incest taboos, unspeakable sexual sins, betrayal of the country, and sexual triangles could be made out behind the daily news accounts.

Thomas's career suffered a sudden and irreparable rupture when this scandal broke out. Regardless of his twenty years of service, he was dismissed from the university—never again to hold a permanent professorship—amid a fanfare of well-publicized remarks over his "eccentric" ideas, his "shocking" behavior, and, worst of all, his teaching "The History of Prostitution" to classes attended by both men and women.[20] The University of Chicago Press immediately interrupted the publication of *The Polish Peasant*, "as if to complete the expunging of W. I. Thomas from the Chicago scene."[21] His next study, *Old World Traits Transplanted*, had to appear under the name of his colleagues Robert Park and Herbert Miller, because the Carnegie Corporation—sponsor of the study—would not have its name associated with that of Thomas. A proposed appointment to the Americanization project was vetoed, and in 1928, when he was finally elected president of the American Sociological Society, voices were still casting doubts on his moral fitness.[22] From this point on, Thomas became an academic "marginal," sharing directly, if on a different level, some of the experiences of the immigrants, women, and criminals he studied. In due time he issued a defense statement:

> I am therefore not guilty of this charge as it is understood, but I am guilty of the whole general charge in the sense that I hold views and am capable of practices not approved by our social traditions. Society should not interfere with the free association of mature persons capable of leading their own lives and seeking their own values.[23]

Labeling as "practices" actions that his contemporaries considered immoral and the law treated as criminal, and dismissing as "social traditions" the moral truths of his age, culture, and class, Thomas was subjecting that reality to the estranged gaze that characterizes cultural, political, and historical outsiders—immigrants and ethnographers most typically; he was proclaiming himself outside the moral jurisdiction of the tribe, the same tribe he labored to consign to the past in his studies.

Some of the basic facts of this scandal remain obscure. Morris Janowitz has suggested that it was perhaps in order to discredit Mrs. Thomas, whose political activities were "under official surveillance," that the scandal was so vicious.[24] As Deegan and Burger have pointed out, Thomas himself was closely associated with Jane Addams, Hull House, and Chicago reform activities:

> Thomas' ties to Addams and her close associates were not only professional but also private. He frequently dined with Jane Addams; his first wife, Harriet T. Thomas, was intimately involved in the Suffragist Movement in Chicago and an active member of the JPA and the Women's International League of Peace and Freedom, a controversial group of which Addams was one of the founders.[25]

Commenting on the almost complete absence of personal papers concerning the most prominent figure of American sociology in the archives of the University of Chicago, Janowitz has noted that it "appears to the intellectual historian as if there may have been an effort to obliterate the record of W. I. Thomas as a man."[26]

The Unadjusted Girl loudly resonates with the scandal that brought Thomas down from his academic seat. Viewed in this context, *The Unadjusted Girl* yields one more element of its agenda: the attempt to confront from a scientific point of view—as objective, empirical observations—the system of power that oppresses many of the mature women discussed by Thomas and that eventually causes his own fall. More important than Thomas's theory or the minimal interpretations that he provides, the case histories of restless and rebellious women represent efforts to assert the reality and the existence of such behaviors, to bring them back from the netherworld of "deviance." *The Unadjusted Girl* is an attempt to erase the line that separates deviance

from normality—a line in which Thomas himself had become caught—
and to modify the law of irreversible regression that governed the discourse of female deviance.

Exemplary in both respects is the long autobiographical document
that closes the chapter on mature women, "The Individualization of
Behavior." The opening lines, surprisingly, announce that this is a
story with a happy end:

> 54. I am a college graduate, 27, married five years and the mother of
> a three-year-old boy. I have been married happily, and have been faithful
> to my husband. (93)

The reasons for placing the end of the story at the beginning soon become clear. Brought up well within conventional boundaries, the
woman recalls her childhood love for a boy whom, from age six, she
has decided to marry but who dies in the Iroquois fire, leaving her
adolescence "dreary for a long time" (974). After a number of years
she leaves home to go to college, where her best friend initiates her
into the secrets of sex:

> [My best friend] saw an upper classman [girl] falling in love with me, and
> she came to me with the news. Then she saw how innocent I was and
> how ignorant, and my sex education was begun. She told me of marriage,
> of mistresses, of homosexuality. I was sick with so much body thrown
> at me at once, and to add to the unpleasantness some one introduced me
> to Whitman's poetry. I got the idea that sex meant pain for women, and
> I determined never to marry. (94)

Soon thereafter, however, her feelings begin to change as she falls in
love with a girl and as a new world of experiences open up to her:

> She told me her ambitions, and I told her mine; it was the first time I had
> ever been a person to any one, and I was her loyal and loving friend. I
> kissed her intimately once and thought that I had discovered something
> new and original. We read Maupassant together and she told me the way
> a boy had made love to her. Everything was changed, love was fun, I
> was wild to taste it. I cultivated beaux, I let them kiss me and embrace
> me, and when they asked me to live with them, I was not offended but
> pleased. I learned my capacity, how far I could go without losing my
> head, how much I could drink, smoke, and I talked as freely as a person
> could. I discussed these adventures with the other girls, and we com-
> pared notes on kisses and phrases, and technique. We were healthy an-
> imals and we were demanding our rights to spring's awakening. I never
> felt cheapened, nor repentant, and I played square with the men. I al-

ways told them I was not out to pin them down to marriage, but that this intimacy was pleasant and I wanted it as much as they did. We indulged in sex talk, birth control, leutic infections, mistresses. . . . (94–95)

Perhaps to the surprise of the contemporary reader, this proto-sixties hymn to sexual liberation turns out to hide sexual amusements that may appear relatively innocent by contemporary standards:

I could have had complete relations with two of these boys if there had been no social stigma attached, and enjoyed it for a time. But instead I consoled myself with thinking that I still had time to give up my virginity, and that when I did I wanted as much as I could get for it in the way of passionate love. (95)

The encounter with a man "fine, clean, mature and not seemingly bothered with sex at all" (95) prompts a second important shift in the life history. With this new companion the conversation shifts from sex to "music and world-views and philosophy." She is more experienced sexually, while he is more experienced intellectually. When they eventually marry, they have a happy marriage based on friendship, respect, honesty, frankness—a marriage about which she writes, "I don't feel that I possess my husband, nor that he does me" (96).

Through this case history Thomas was attempting to proclaim a new scientific model for women's behavior, a model in which deviance would not be irreversible. The document ultimately sums up Thomas's reform program with regard to mature women and clarifies the reason for their inclusion in a study of juvenile female delinquents. It proves that women who have been "promiscuous" or who have experimented with nonheterosexual relationships are not necessarily harmed for life, condemned forever to drift among the "variants." It is possibly in reference to such unorthodox beliefs that, when the scandal broke out, the *New York Times* provided its readers with the following description of "Thomas' teachings":

Women are better off for having had their fling as men do.

Dissipated women often make excellent wives.

Calvary is the persistence of the old race habit of contempt for women.

Any girl, mentally mature, has the right to have children and the right to limit their number.

The morality of women is an expediency rather than an innate virtue.

Marriage as it exists today is rapidly approaching a form of immorality.

Matrimony is often an arrangement by which the woman trades her irreproachable conduct for irreproachable gowns.

Children are not the result of marriage, but marriage is the result of children.[27]

This is a summary that hardly contains the outraged sneer of the audience.

The Delinquent Girl

Thomas's portrait of the "unadjusted" girl begins not far from, and indeed overlaps with, that of the "restless" woman—and, one should add, of the "immoral" professor. Neither science nor morality drew fine distinctions between these types. They belonged to the same group—congenitally corrupt or perverted early in life.[28]

Most of the cases of juvenile delinquency appear in the chapter "The Demoralization of Girls." The general social phenomenon here is much the same as before: girls who break away from norms and rules. This time, however, the focus is primarily on girls from the poorest classes—recent European immigrants or girls who have run away from poor midwestern farms and villages. While the mature woman is attempting to stretch or break open the domestic circle defined by the moral boundaries of love, sex, and marriage, the young girl is more precisely trapped in a circle of theft, prostitution, vagabondage, and drugs.

Neither confessions, nor cries for help or advice, nor outbursts of frustration, the personal documents concerning young girls contain mostly factual narratives and detached scientific observations, the kind of narratives one finds in institutional case records. Most of these documents come, in fact, from the records of social agencies and institutions. The caseworker is the main author, the one who summarizes and orders the events, and establishes causal connections between them. Sometimes the record includes long direct quotations or paraphrases of the girl's words, testimony, or reflections. In these documents, more so than in the letters written by the mature women, one can overhear the complex dialogue that defines the relationship between the observer and the observed.

Two elements compose Thomas's portrait and diagnosis of the delinquent girl. On the one hand, poverty, demoralization within families, and urban allures—amusement, adventure, pretty clothes, and so on—

emerge as primary causes of delinquency; on the other, social workers, social agencies, and juvenile courts emerge as agents of reform and ideal surrogate families.

Poverty and the degradation of families, or their absence altogether, form the opening theme in several case histories:

> 59. Helen comes from a large family, there being eight children. Her father is a miner and unable to support the older girls. She was told at the age of fourteen that she was old enough to support herself and to get out. She came to Chillicothe because of the draftees from Western Pennsylvania. . . . In a few weeks she had developed from the little red hood and mittens with the stout shoes of the foreigner into a painted-cheeked brow-blacked prostitute. She had her name and address written on slips of paper that she passed out to soldiers on the streets. (102–3)

> 60. Evelyn claims to know absolutely nothing of her family or relations. Was found in a room in a hotel, where she had registered as the wife of a soldier. Seemed entirely friendless and alone. . . . Did not seem to feel that she had done anything very wrong. It seems to be a case of society's neglect to an orphan. She was taken to the Isolation Hospital for treatment for syphilis infection and escaped within 24 hours. (103–4)

> 63. Carrie is a colored girl, 23 years of age at the time of her commitment. She was sentenced . . . for possessing heroin. She was born on Long Island—the illegitimate child of a notorious thief and prostitute known only as "Jenny." She was adopted when fifteen months old. . . . Her foster mother states that she was always a difficult child and very stubborn. When she was as young as nine years old the neighbors complained of her immoral conduct with young boys on roofs and cellars. She seemed to have no feelings of shame. (107–8)

This type of analysis, a version of Lamarckian sociology, understands families and communities as part of the social environment. In the way the physical environment can cause deformation to the body, the social environment can exercise a negative influence on the mind and eventually cause severe forms of "maladjustment."

The social environment includes not only the kinship group but also the modern urban world. A perceptive observer of that world, Thomas identifies in some of its manifestations more factors that ignite the process of deviance.

> 62. . . . Catherine got acquainted with her brother's sister-in-law, Jennie Sopeka, a girl ten years older, with an exceedingly bad reputation. . . . Catherine said she knew nothing of this girl when she came to see her and proposed they go to Chicago "to have a nice time and nice clothes." (106)

68. "When I saw sweller girls than me picked up in automobiles every night, can you blame me for falling too?"

Pretty Helen McGinnis, the convicted auto vamp of Chicago, asked the question seriously. She has just got an order for a new trial on the charge of luring Martin Metzler to Forest Reserve Park, where he was beaten and robbed. The girl went on:

"I always wanted good clothes, but I never could get them, for our family is large and money is scarce. I wanted good times like the other girls in the office. Every girl seemed to be a boulevard vamp. I'd seen other girls do it, and it was easy." (114–5)

71. American girl, twenty-one years old, semi-prostitute, typical of a certain class one grows to know. Works as a salesgirl in one of the high class shops—a pretty girl, languid manner but businesslike. . . .

Sex had been a closed book to her and, as she was naturally cold and unawakened, she was not tempted as some girls are. She did not care about being loved, but the wish to be admired was strong within her and love of adornment superseded all else, particularly when she realized she was more beautiful than most girls.

The department store is sometimes a school for scandal. Many rich women are known by sight and are talked over, servants' gossip sometimes reaching thus far, the intrigues between heads of departments and managers are hinted at and the possibility of being as well dressed as someone else becomes a prime consideration. (122–23)

Arguing in part against a vulgar Freudian view that sought in the abnormal or maladjusted sexuality of the individual the causes and effects of all major problems, Thomas turns his gaze, instead, toward the main symbols of consumer capitalism:

The beginning of delinquency in girls is usually an impulse to get amusement, adventure, pretty clothes, favorable notice, distinction, freedom in the larger world which presents so many allurements and comparisons. . . . [S]exual passion does not play an important rôle, for the girls have become "wild" before the development of sexual desire. . . . Their sex is used as a condition of the realization of other wishes. It is their capital. . . . Mary (case No. 64) begins by stealing to satisfy her desire for pretty clothes and "good times." . . . Katie (No. 65) begins as a vagabond. . . . In the case of Stella (No. 66) the sexual element is a part of a joy ride. . . . Marien (No. 67) treats sexual life as a condition of her "high life," including restaurants, moving pictures, hotels, and showy clothes. Helen (No. 68) said, "I always wanted good clothes." (109)

Fashion, money, and amusement thus play a double role in Thomas's narrative. On the one hand, they signal the birth of the modern world,

the end of the era of repression, and the beginning of the era of titilla-
tion.[29] On the other, they corrupt young girls and encourage them to
follow the road of deviance. Not congenital sexual drives out of control, but that beautiful world of clothes, shows, and restaurants, which
liberates the individual and allows the expression of long-repressed
wishes, is what triggers theft and prostitution, generating female delinquency.

Central to this chapter is the record of Esther Lorenz, a young
woman native of Prague, Bohemia, born to a family described by the
caseworker as "poor and very foreign and unprogressive" (172).

> 86. Statement from the Laboratory of Bedford Hills Reformatory for
> Women:
> Esther Lorenz was committed to the institution March 23, 1914, from
> Special Sessions, N.Y.
> Offense: Petit Larceny. (172)

The record reveals the interaction between family poverty, theft, and
desire for a "good life." More important however, it exposes in a
striking dialogue of voices, the relationships of power disguised under
the label "deviance." The dialogue includes the voice of Esther, in the
form of letters to a friend and to the parole officer; the voice of the
caseworker, sketching Esther's background and the events leading to
her conviction; the voice of the parole officer, who, writing to the superintendent of the reformatory, recommends that she not be given
another parole and, possibly, that she be deported; finally, Thomas's
voice, reinterpreting Esther's letters so as to show the "ideal human
material" in a girl who was ruined by the penitentiary.

The letters are part of an epistolary exchange between Esther Lorenz and Lillian Marx over a period of several months. The two friends
were first caught stealing clothes at Macy's, were then convicted and
sentenced to serve probationary sentences, and are now working as
domestics in two different families in upstate New York from where
they are corresponding. Written in Bohemian, the letters have been
translated into English—the parole officer informs his reader—by a Bohemian woman who attempted to reproduce the style "of the few letters written in English by Esther" (174).

Esther's letters contain two recurrent themes: the harshness of work
and life in the family where she is a servant, and the desire for nice
men, wealthy men, and for the good times of dances and movie theaters. Her description of work could be part of a number of maids'
journals, real or fictionalized:

October 1, 1914. . . . Dear friend, I apologize not to answer you right away. I have lots of work. I have two people and little baby girl. I have so much work; I haven't got even time to wash my face.

November, 1914. . . . Dear Friend, if you could come with me to moving pictures, there we would meet nice mens [sic]. Wouldn't that be nice? I have my hand so hard like a man from hard work, so you can imagine how hard I am working.

Dear Friend: . . . I have such a cranky lady. If I stay here another two months with her I think I go crazy. I was very sick the other Sunday. We had 8 people and so you can imagine what work I had. Only if you would see me you would get frightened how I look; I am only bone and skin and pale in face. You would say that I go by and by in grave. Everybody ask me what's the matter with me but you know I can't tell everybody I come from Bedford.

February, 1915. . . . I am crying so much—I have such a hard work. Everything hurts me; I am all broke down. If I can only come free I wouldn't mind to have not even a shirt. I would give everything if we can be free. (174–87).

Esther, however, unlike those servant girls who let themselves waste away from overwork and consumption, has strong and clear ideas about who, what, and where the fun is.

October 1, 1914. . . . Dear sweetheart, you ask me to come to see you but how can I do that; I haven't got no shoes and no money, I am very poor. If you can you come over on Saturday evening and sleep with me. I got big bed. On Sunday . . . we go in a place where we can have a good time and lots of kissing. We going to look for some nice man but something better, not only working man; we shouldn't have to go to work.

My dearest friend: . . . If you want to marry one of the officers, you know what they are, they are ever the other [army] men. They can't marry only a poor girl. If they want to marry they got to have a girl with lots of money 20,000 Kronen, and they got to put the money down for guarantee. If happens something to your sweetheart officer, then you get the money back. Do you understand me, Sunday School? But dear we hav n't got the mens yet, we have to wait for them. If we going to get mens [sic] like that, cause we not rich.

November, 1914. . . . Dear friend, I am going to moving pictures every Wednesday and every time when I going out I see the nice young mens [sic]. How they love them, the girls, and we can't help that. I met one nice man and he some kind of detective. . . . Dear friend, if you could come with me to moving pictures, there we would meet nice mens. Wouldn't that be nice?

> Dear Friend: . . . I received letters from my sister and they were so happy. . . . My sweetheart is not killed yet, so I am going to take him when I get home. He always asks about me if I'm angry at him. I rather take him than American; they only want to have girl got to have money. The poor girl they don't want her and those which are not rich they are nothing worth. Don't you think so friend, I am right?

> [March, 1915] . . . Friend, I got to go school every Wednesday but next Wednesday I wouldn't go, I go to the dance. I have white dress under black skirt and long coat and she going to think that I go to school. I leave my skirt and my books in my friends house and I go to the dance, ha, ha, ha. Come with me ha, ha, I have there lots of nice young boys and the man who brings me the eggs and lots of other young man, so I going to have nice time. . . . I be very glad if you can come with me, but don't tell on me that I'm going to the dance. My lady she don't know anything about it. She think I am innocent girl, No 1. I am, don't you think friend? When I think I have three years, I start to cry, I don't know what to do. But when I think of nice mens, I start to jump in the kitchen and singing. (174–88)

More complex than most representations of servant girls, Esther is a suffering victim, a cunning schemer, an aspiring vamp, a pragmatist, and an expert on the laws that govern the marriage market.

Eventually Esther's letters are discovered by her friend's lady and sent to the parole officer. Their content brings Esther back to jail for breaking the parole. It is at this point that the parole officer writes to the superintendent of the institution where Esther is incarcerated to express an opinion:

> I think much of the subject's suspiciousness and deceitfulness is racial and there is small chance of her adjusting to American customs. I remember that you considered deporting her in the first place and while I still think it would be very bad for subject to have the stigma of deportation added to that of her arrest, I do feel that her own country is the best place for her and that she will be far more apt to live a straight, normal life there with the restraints of her family and their standards to help her than she will here. Do you think it may be possible to send her back on her own money when conditions of war permit? (192)

The officer invokes and juxtaposes two different sets of categories. On the one hand there are "suspicion" and "deceit"—presumably two forms of "racial" behavior stereotypically associated with the peasant. On the other hand are "American customs"—the opposite of distrust and, at any rate, something one is not born with but adapts to. Implicit in the officer's comments is the verdict that Esther has failed to pass the admission test into modernity; for this reason she must regress to the hypothetically stable and cohesive family of the old world.

Thomas's comments on Esther could not be farther from the parole officer's, or more revealing of the distance that separates the old technicians of deviance from the new school to which Thomas belongs. For Thomas Esther's desire for clothes, dance, and men signals a "strong and social" character. Her machinations to regain freedom and her fight against "organized society" reveal an intelligent and even imaginative mind at work. Esther needed stimulation through "creative work," participation in some "form of society," "recognition," "gratification," but the court failed to recognize these needs.

At this point Thomas begins to unfold his agenda for the reform of delinquent girls, an agenda with which he hopes ultimately to transform this type of story into one with a happy ending:

> But some years ago the juvenile courts were established. It had become apparent that numbers of disorderly children, mainly from broken homes, were being brought into the criminal courts for escapades and sexual offenses, placed in jails with hardened criminals and thereby having the possibility of the formation of a normal scheme of life destroyed once and forever. Certain women were the first to protest and to act, and the result was the formation of a court for children which dispensed with lawyers and legal technicalities, and *treated the child* as far as possible *as an unruly member of a family*, not as a criminal. . . . Their service has been very great in checking the beginnings of demoralization. The court is wiser than the parents of the children and incidentally does much to influence home life. (194–95, my emphasis)

Here the narrative, which has been suspended for pages while the sociologist digresses through dozens of case histories, regains momentum as Thomas forecasts a future world in which juvenile courts and social agencies will displace families in regulating and shaping human personality. If the elimination of "lawyers and legal technicalities" euphemistically describes the elimination of the basic constitutional rights for a large class of people, the substitution of families with judiciary courts and social workers stages the power struggle between kinship group and state, and the victory of the latter.

The successful reform of several girls whose case histories Thomas reports provides a contrast to Esther's failed redemption. Two cases, in particular, exemplify the progression from deviance to reform that Thomas propounds. The first is that of Helen Langley, nineteen years old in 1918, immoral daughter of an immoral mother and a drunkard father, depraved from the age of twelve when, according to the record, "she began to 'go crazy over the boys', to attend dance halls and to go out on motor trips with unknown men" (167); at the age of fourteen she was sexually attacked by a neighbor "and since that time her life has been a series of immoral relations with sailors and civilians" (167). Her tortuous pilgrimage finally halts when she is confined to a hospital in order to be cured of tuberculosis. The caseworker goes on to describe her condition there, after she is adopted by a sympathetic physician and a motherly nurse:

> 85. . . . Helen has gained several pounds and looks like a new person, is content and happy, *sleeps most of the day* and said she feels rested for the first time for years. She takes all the care of her own cottage, has become very tidy in her habits, *enjoys washing her dishes* etc., and *keeping things in order.* Helen said that her plan when she is discharged is to find a good place where she can do housework. She intends to have nothing further to do with men, particularly sailors. She *loves to do sewing and handwork* and showed the most astonishing amount of embroidery which she has done for one of the nurses. (170, my emphasis)

Paradoxically, the oppressive domesticity that Thomas indicates as the cause of rightful rebellion in the case histories of well-to-do women emerges now, in the cases of deviant girls, as the sign of readjustment and normality. If Helen ever did find the desired job as a domestic, she killed two birds with one stone: she cured herself of deviance and also freed a wealthier sister of her domestic fetters.

The story of Mary, even more clearly than Helen's, shows in which direction Thomas was moving to find an appropriate ending for his narrative of deviant modernity. Daughter of a promiscuous mother and an uncertain father, Mary grows up surrounded by a "complete lack of ordinary sex morality and social standards" (204). Her early experiences "break down completely any sex inhibition she might have had, aroused sex needs and accustomed her to the habit of sex expression" (206). Eventually discovered by a social worker, she finds her life taking a turn for the better. First the psychological examiner "indicates the sex situation," next the psychometric tests "showed her to be well up to average in intelligence," and finally the social worker takes charge of Mary:

> 89. . . . There seemed to be every basis for a satisfactory adjustment to life if the environmental opportunities could be provided so that her work and social interests would have a chance to develop and help to organize a more socialized sex expression. . . .
> Meantime the case worker built up the social background, finally

raised scholarship money and Mary went into the second year of the commercial course in a good High School.

There was never any attempt to deal with the sex side by repressive methods, never any interference with her social life, nor any form of restraint. When she wanted to go to visit her mother, the whole situation was talked out with her and she was given the worker's attitude frankly and honestly but decision was left to her. She did not go. She has continued to associate with boys on an unusually free basis. She will go to see a boy friend at his home exactly as she would visit a girl. She could not be made to see why she should not accept a boy's invitation to go to New York City for a sightseeing excursion. . . . Her standards are changing rapidly with her developing tastes and interests. She has made good in her school work consistently. She has been rash and unconventional in the extreme but has never, apparently, overstepped the boundaries of morality on the sex side. For a year and a half she has made steady progress and there is no indication that she will ever again become a delinquent. (209)

If Helen's and Mary's case histories can shift from *Maggie, a Girl of the Streets* to *Little Women,* it is because, unlike fiction, case records need not follow a particular style or literary mode with absolute devotion and consistency. Loaded with the authority of empirical reality, this sociological literature can afford to disregard the narrative law of plausibility and to create, instead, new plots, causations, resolutions. Here, where sexual morality, unconventionality, and delinquency meet, where the mature and middle-class woman is made to stand next to the young and lumpenproletarian girl, the previously questioned line separating deviance and norm is reestablished.

Thomas's tale finds the desired happy ending by disclosing, first, a shift from authority to influence as the means to elicit conversion and readjustment; second, a view of deviance as a temporary phase rather than a permanent trait; and, finally, the role of the social worker as hero. Commenting on juvenile delinquency and on the larger social issues surrounding this "social problem," Thomas is now ready to conclude that "the child should be taken in charge by society as soon as it shows any tendency to disorganization" (211). Quoting from "one of the most systematic proposals," he adds,

. . . Each city, probably each county would require an extension or reorganization of its personnel to include a department of adjustment to which teachers, policemen and others could refer all children who seemed to present problems of health, of mental development, of behavior or of social adjustment. For good work this would require the services

of doctors, nurses, psychiatrists, field investigators, recreational spe-
cialists. . . .

The ideal would be to have the school act as a reserve parent, an unusually intelligent, responsible and resourceful parent, using whatever
the community had to offer, making up whatever the community
lacked. . . .

All neglected, dependent and delinquent children, whether of school
age or not, would fall within the province of [the department of adjust-
ment]. (211–12)

After shifting to the subjunctive mood, Thomas's narrative closes with
a ghastly sociological vision. What begins as a story of how the family
and the community are declining, and must disappear as modern society is born, suddenly undergoes a striking metamorphosis, to emerge
as an apotheosis of those very entities transposed into the state and its
institutional branches. In this Kafkaesque universe, social workers,
judges, and teachers will be the parents of a brood of citizens sub-
sumed by way of adoption into a new megafamily—modern society.

Through the young girl and the mature woman, Thomas carries out
a scientifically encoded attempt to explain and posit a new era of "individualism," where individuals exist apart from the immediate surroundings. It is, in the last analysis, the behaviorist version of an old
American myth—the (male) individual as his own class, community,
and family—a myth born as the emblem of the western frontier and
now reinterpreted to serve the purposes of an urban frontier. At the
same time, the wish for "security" and the wish for "new experience"—earlier presented as antithetical elements of the individual personality—become, by the end of the discussion, a dichotomy between
individual and group:

Society desires stability and the individual desires new experience and
introduces change. But eventually all new values, all the new cultural
elements of a society are the result of the changes introduced by the
individual. (234)

This was Thomas's solution to the origin of variation, an unresolved
riddle in Darwin's theory of evolution, in the sphere of social evolution.
With this reformulation Thomas came very close to celebrating deviance—a behavioral variation—as *the* agent of social change. Thomas's
apotheosis of individual deviance and rebellion, however, ultimately
contains two distinct programs. One program speaks *for* the middle
classes and preaches a message of liberation; the other speaks *of* the
underclasses and preaches a message of social control. If social evo-

lution is to progress, individuals must "derange the existing norms"; yet, ultimately, a sharp line separates prostitutes and criminals as "merely destructive of values and organization" from the unconventional woman, the scientist, or the inventor as "temporarily disorganizing but eventually organizing."

Sociological Modernism

The methodology underlying *The Unadjusted Girl* was first developed by Thomas and is now well known in the social sciences as the "personal documents" methodology. It is essential to understand this methodology in relation to the type of reality Thomas was trying to grasp; it is equally essential to view it in the context of the modernist aesthetic of the period and of the epistemological crisis intrinsic to modernism.

Thomas never discussed at length the methodology of *The Unadjusted Girl*. His instinctive empiricism and suspicion of abstract theorization made such a self-conscious analysis difficult. However, in the last chapter of the monograph—"Social Influence"—amid the concluding remarks, Thomas did include the fragments of a methodological and poetic position. The unconventional form of the monograph rests on his belief that "the 'human document,' prepared by the subject, on the basis of the memory . . . is capable of presenting life as a connected whole and of showing the interplay of influences" (249–50). In the personal documents, not in the physical body of the deviant, the former philologist and professor of literature proposed to discover the laws of human behavior. Much like the biologist who collects selected organisms, Thomas suggested, the sociologist collects personal documents for the purpose of studying selected personalities: "Ordinary and extraordinary personalities should be included, the dull and the criminal, the philistine and the bohemian. Scientifically the history of dull lives is quite as significant as that of brilliant ones (253–54)." Such documents at once measure social influences and reveal the interplay between subjective and objective, internal and external factors, the interconnections of influences, values, and attitudes. The first-person document, in the diverse literary forms it takes, emerges as the ideal sociological source.

The documents that Thomas selects, edits, and arranges in *The Unadjusted Girl* proclaim the existence of people living on the outer margins of the physical and moral city: the restless woman and the deviant girl. These same documents, however, reveal strategies that are far from identical. The personal documents concerning mature women include a large proportion of letters written in the first person and only a small proportion of case histories written in the third. The ratio is inverted with regard to young girls. The written record of their lives is inseparable, in fact, from their arrest and institutional confinement. The mature woman writes herself into a confession, an outburst, a cry for help. The young girl, on the contrary, "is written" into either of two case histories: the unhappy-ending one of spiraling and everlasting deviance; or the happy-ending ones of illness and cure, corruption and recovery, sin and redemption. Obviously critical of sociological "omniscience," Thomas asked social scientists to forgo the practice of ventriloquizing their subjects' thoughts and words and, instead, to exercise their proper function by selecting, editing, and ordering the documents already in existence. Thomas was compounding into a sociological methodology and a literary practice the skills of journalists, fiction writers, and social workers with those of psychologists, ethnographers, and biologists. Imagined as a collector of literary fragments, the sociologist would have to make these utterances intelligible through juxtaposition and sequence. This applies to the author in the age of montage and sociological observation: "I trace the origin of my interest in the document to a long letter picked up on a rainy day in the alley behind my house, a letter from a girl who was taking a training course in a hospital to her father concerning family relationships and discords."[30] More than simply inviting sociologists to leave the aseptic and safe walls of academia, Thomas told them to go out and find sociological treasures among the urban debris.[31] As it emerges from the *The Unadjusted Girl,* the modern sociological author is an archaeologist of the modern self who excavates the records of juvenile courts, girls' bureaus, probationary associations, charity organizations; who digs for fragments among discarded epistolary exchanges and hunts in Miss Lonelyhearts columns. He hopes to discover the secret laws of human personality and behavior.

When Thomas lectured on primitive and modern people, a student recalled years later, a phantasmagoria of colored slips would flip in front of students' eyes:

He brought into the classroom materials from his research recorded on small slips of paper. Bibliographical items were on blue slips, extracts from books and articles on yellow slips, and his own comments on white slips. His custom was to read quotations from the literature upon a given topic, supplementing these by his own inimitable comments. Students in his courses were alternately shocked and thrilled by an extract on behavior widely different from our own or by a penetrating interpretation

which showed among the great diversity of human behavior a manifestation of human nature akin [to] if not identical with our own.[32]

Montage—the basis of his lectures and of his writing—was inextricable
from the nature of modern society; it was the aesthetic form that could
both contain and convey the fragmented and dislocated nature of that
reality. The colored slips of paper that he brought to his lectures were
the treasures that the sociologist had accumulated during his expedi-
tions to the borders of urban civilization. Ultimately, through these
multicolored fragments, Thomas familiarized the "strange"—deviant
behavior—and estranged the "familiar"—middle-class morals—thus
bridging the gap that separates the modern, urban, middle-class, male
self from the primitive, the immigrant, the female, and the deviant.

Conclusion

> The book is intended for social workers and students of criminol-
> ogy, but the layman will find it a major thrilling human document
> than the great majority of fiction. It is the raw material of which
> fiction is made.[33]
>
> —*Bookman*, 1923

> This is an anthology of existences. Lives of a few lines or of a few
> pages, countless misfortunes and adventures, gathered together in
> a handful of words . . . for such is the contraction of things said in
> these texts that one does not know whether the intensity which
> traverses them is due more to the vividness of the words or to the
> violence of the facts which jostle about in them. Singular lives,
> those which have become, through I know not what accidents,
> strange poems:—that is what I wanted to gather together in a sort
> of herbarium.[34]
>
> —MICHEL FOUCAULT, 1977

At the center of Thomas's study of female deviance in the modern
world stands the most emblematic figure of early urban literature: the
girl who leaves the village for the city and there finds the excitement
of freedom but also the danger of corruption. An archetype of city
tales, the young woman in the city bespeaks at once the promise of
regeneration and the threat of degeneration; she captures the hope for
freedom, culture and refinement, and the fear of deviance and decay.
The concern with urban deviance, women's liberation, and immigrant
transition locates *The Unadjusted Girl* at the thematic core of some

important fictional works of the period. Stories of girls corrupted by the slum or by the wealth and sophistication of the city are at the center of a literary tradition that includes Stephen Crane's *Maggie, a Girl of the Streets* (1893) and Theodore Dreiser's *Sister Carrie* (1901). Like these authors, Thomas found the girl who goes to the city both a well-established type and an appropriate means to explore, imagine, and represent the modern world. Like Edith Wharton, he participated in the struggle to bring about a post-Victorian era for women, of freedom from nineteenth-century ideas of morals, conventions, and domesticity. Like James Weldon Johnson's *The Autobiography of an Ex-Colored Man* (1912), Abraham Cahan's *The Rise of David Levinsky* (1917), and Sherwood Anderson's *Winesburg, Ohio* (1919), Thomas's work strove to capture and promote the experience of leaving the village, the family, the community, and one's old identity behind. Finally, with *The Unadjusted Girl,* Thomas foreshadowed the best urban novels of the 1930s and early 1940s and their stories of delinquent boys in the urban jungle. James T. Farrell, Richard Wright, and Nelson Algren would soon bring forth a literature that made room for the subjectivity of the criminal, of the delinquent, of the lumpenproletarian male; their novels would soon transform the delinquent gang boy from helpless victim of heredity and environment or passive recipient of social workers' good intentions to active historical and existential subject.

While using the girl to retrace the transition to the modern world as dangerous but also inevitable and necessary, Thomas redefined the female "types" that could be recognized as legitimate and therefore "real":

> [F]ifty years ago we recognized, roughly speaking, two types of women, the one completely good and the other completely bad,—what we now call the old-fashioned girl and the girl who had sinned and been outlawed. At present we have several intermediate types,—the occasional prostitute, the charity girl, the demi-virgin, the equivocal flapper, and in addition girls with new but social behavior norms who have adapted themselves to all kinds of work. (230–31)

He brought new female types into sociological existence by allowing their voices to be heard, their stories to be told, their actions to be understood. Thomas's labeling the cases as responding to this or that wish, it becomes ever more clear, is often but a flimsy pretext to let suppressed behavioral discordances be heard. Scattered and, at times, hidden under a layer of "objective" scientific prose—"the sexual passions have never been completely contained within the framework of marriage" (68)—are Thomas's corrosive strokes—"A clean and pro-tected moron is not far from corresponding to the ideal woman of the Victorian age" (166).

While primarily concerned with the sociological phenomenon of female deviance, Thomas's study produced an allegorical representation in which deviance stands for the "other" possibilities shut off to "normal" women by conventional Victorian morality. In this allegory the image of the deviant provides the weapon with which to criticize the moral order, to make visible the constructed nature of its rules, and, finally, to redefine a new behavioral order altogether. A relationship of transference joins the unrest of middle-class women and the deviance of lumpenproletarian girls, so that the delinquent girl exists empirically as a sociological phenomenon to be studied, as a social problem to be solved, and as a social illness to be cured; at the same time she exists metaphorically as that part of the female self that bourgeois morality has ruled out. Around these two figures—as they foreshadow the impending doom of conventional domesticity and Victorian morality—Thomas wove a double-edged gospel: on the one hand, *deviance as freedom* for the middle-class rebellious woman; on the other, *deviance as degeneration* to be cured by social workers and psychologists for the young lumpenproletarian girl. While the first will be saved *through* deviance from the prison house of Victorian domesticity, the second must be saved *from* deviance through a conversion to middle-class female morality. It is perhaps this remarkable ambivalence that has caused Thomas to be reclaimed as a protofeminist by some feminist historians and castigated as sexist by others, two contradictory positions that leave the task of assessing Thomas's work still largely un-accomplished.[35]

Ethnic Trilogies: A Genealogical and Generational Poetics

WILLIAM BOELHOWER

While narrative trilogies in American literature have not been neglected by literary historians, they generally have been seen as isolated instances or as unique moments in the overall career of a particular author. One immediately thinks of John Dos Passos, Theodore Dreiser, James T. Farrell, or even Josephine Herbst. But in the first four decades of the twentieth century, and especially during the late 1920s and 1930s, the trilogy served as a major experimental vehicle for appropriating and interpreting the crisis of modern American culture. Given the relatively concentrated span of time in which trilogies began to appear and the number of those who practiced this form, the task of reevaluating its hierarchical importance within the literary system of genres then prevailing automatically proposes itself. This revisionary act, however, takes on added importance when one considers that most of the trilogy practitioners were immigrant or ethnic writers: John Cournos, Ole Rølvaag, Sophus K. Winther, James T. Farrell, Daniel Fuchs, August Derleth, William Carlos Williams, Pietro Di Donato, Vilhelm Moberg.[1]

Consonant with the trilogy project in its broadest dimensions, they too sought to go beyond the semantic crisis investing the cultural foundations of turn-of-the-century America. But the paradigms they used for effecting this cultural passage are based on the perspectival system inherent in the immigrant experience, which is patterned on the spatial shift from Old World to New World and is naturally concerned with the attempt to establish a trajectory of continuity out of what might be called a catastrophic act of topological dislocation. In other words, the

This essay is an enlarged version of "The Ethnic Trilogy: A Poetics of Cultural Passage," in *MELUS* 12. 4 (Winter 1985 [published in 1988]), 7–23.

ordering principle behind the poetic program of the ethnic trilogy is intrinsically genealogical in that it is fundamentally generational. Contrary to the "nativist" trilogy, then, the ethnic trilogy interprets the crisis of foundations within a different and broader order of historical facts. On this basis, it is able to achieve poetic closure and a semantic refoundation of American culture where the nonethnic trilogy cannot. Indeed, this positive resolution at the narrative level is directly related to its affirmative evaluation of ethnicity. To the extent that this form succeeds in incorporating the intercultural perspective of the world of the immigrant fathers as its germinal principle, to that extent can its narrative parabolas successfully embody both the imaginative possibilities and the limits of the two faces of nineteenth- and twentieth-century American experience. In this way the ethnic trilogy returns to American fiction a significant part of its premodernist tradition, only now, as we shall see, in radically different hermeneutical terms.

To understand the literary significance of the ethnic trilogy (and of the trilogy project as a whole) in relation to other narrative poetics of the period, one must consider, even if briefly, its specific historical juncture, so that its genesis and the consolidation of its narrative program can be explained in context. By moving from the nineteenth to the twentieth century, from the farm or the small town to the factory and the city, the American self moved into the modern world as a highly mobile numerical unit of a mass society in which it was increasingly hard to find a legitimating cultural framework. The genealogical principle ordering so much of nineteenth-century culture was itself no longer valid, as these words of T. S. Eliot's suggest:

> What are the roots that clutch, what branches grow
> Out of this stony rubbish? Son of man,
> You cannot say, or guess, for you know only
> A heap of broken images. . . .[2]

It is also in Eliot's "unreal city" of "The Waste Land," with its perspectival fragmentation, radical contingency, uprootedness, and unceasing machine-ordered motion, that the condition of cultural paralysis and impotence came to be considered normative. Indeed, it was the peculiar spatial dynamics of the metropolis that evoked the response of spatial form in modernist texts, which emphasized synchronic relations at the expense of diachronic development, collage juxtapositions at the expense of temporal cause-and-effect sequencing, the mythic method with its static simultaneity at the expense of purposeful historical processes, endless description and the stream-of-consciousness technique at the expense of the story and objective narration.[3] In short, the semantic catastrophe that set the twentieth century adrift from nineteenth-century culture was also expressed at the level of literary genre by the shift from realism and its classical procedures of representation to modernism and its obsessive experimentation with new formal techniques. Insofar as these new modes became the dominant literary means for organizing narration, they clearly registered the radical shift in the construction of a new cultural episteme; but as it became increasingly clear from the vantage point of the thirties, these same texts revealed an ideological impasse in the very nature of their aesthetic choices. They were, in other words, often unable to cope with the new type of challenge the Great Depression would eventually present.

Within the same period, although as a whole slightly later, a significant number of writers took to the trilogy form to interpret the very shift of which modernism seemed in part to be a mimetic victim, or at least they sought to elaborate a broad poetics of recovery that would sublate the technical acquisitions of modernist texts. In this suturing poetics lies the ambitiousness of its narrative program as well as its claim to dominance within the hierarchical ordering of the literary system of genres as a whole. Of course, the only way the trilogist could go beyond the modernist cul-de-sac was by reevaluating the agency of the subject and his perspectival possibilities, by reintroducing a dialogical relationship between the subject and his environment, by redefining reality as a specific historical construct rather than as an unmediated universal condition.

On the other hand, at the metanarrative level of its dialogue with other fictional modes, the trilogy sought to recover elements from the realist tradition in order to *re*-present the crisis of cultural foundation through the distancing filter of history. Simply put, this meant the recovery of story as well as the *re*-use of the genealogical principle for creating a "hierarchy of relevance" in the repertory of representational procedures, now further enriched by modernism.[4] With such a regulating principle in hand, the trilogy tries, with varying degrees of success, to mediate between those same isotopic categories that are capable of creating either narrative catastrophe or fusion:[5] continuity versus discontinuity; coherence versus incoherence; conservation versus change; stability versus instability; construction versus deconstruction. Needless to say, they generate and sustain the very narrative tension that characterizes the trilogy's unique quest for a principle of coherence. Furthermore, the way the genealogical principle is perceived and the extent to which it is allowed to function as a germinal principle for the entire trilogy format are what distinguish "nativist" from ethnic solutions to the cultural shift exemplified in modernist texts. The choice of the semantic contents for the above, purely formal isotopes, then, is ultimately a question of *which version of history* the trilogist chooses to represent as a mediating filter, as a structural homology, for narrative production.

It is, in other words, very much a question of deciding on a particular *terminus a quo* and *terminus ad quem*. For Dos Passos's *U.S.A.* trilogy, for example, there simply are no dominant or winning immigrant moments and no dramatized phenomena of mass immigration: an interesting historical problem, the solution of which can be read in Dos Passos's very limited employment of the genealogical principle, which is ultimately used to deconstruct itself. His characters, so many unhoused exiles, end up drifting without remembering where they originally came from or desiring some definite goal. And lacking the two framing contexts of the categories of house and goal, no journey can ultimately make sense and no character convert mere space into a series of significant places. As a structure of knowledge, history too is flattened to the present tense, to the randomness and imperviousness of the newsreel sections, and to a spatial configuration that both negates the notion of qualitative change and implies the defeat of the human subject as an active historical agent and source of memory. Needless to say, the old words of the immigrants—mentioned in the penultimate, "Camera Eye" section of the *U.S.A.* trilogy—go pathetically unheard. As a result, even the faintest appeal to genealogical or generational construction is eliminated. What one inevitably has here as *terminus ad quem* is the reconfirmation of the modernist impasse. The ethnic trilogy, on the contrary, introduces that metacultural distancing factor which Dos Passos lacks or refuses to activate: the "world of our fathers."[6] Thanks to it, a genealogical circle is indeed possible, but this time as a real and not a pseudo-dialogical principle, for implicit in the proper noun of the immigrant name is a prefabricated story that has its beginning in a radically different culture.[7]

This much Henry Adams, in his *Education,* sensed when he complained, "Not a Polish Jew fresh from Warsaw or Cracow—not a furtive Yacoob or Ysaac still reeking of the Ghetto, snarling a weird Yiddish to the officers of the customs—but had a keener instinct, an intenser energy, and a freer hand [than he the born American]. . . . "[8] Suggested here is the new, transhistorical and intercultural *terminus a quo* that the ethnic trilogy relies on for closure. Because of it, the trilogy's narrative *verbum* is programmatically caught between two different models of cognition; and, in the further light of an ethnic *terminus ad quem,* we can now see that the poetics of recovery, which I mentioned earlier, is also a poetics of reinterpretation. In short, the new genealogical alignment, the new cultural foundation that the ethnic trilogy produces, is established through ethnic interpretation, which in turn draws its hermeneutical authority from the very stereoscopic perspectivism the immigrant subject introduces.

How crucial this type of mnemotechnical practice of return is to ethnic-trilogy poetics becomes apparent when one turns to the narrative paradigms that order it. In fact, precisely to the extent that the ethnic trilogy dramatizes positively the first of its three paradigms (the immigrant or foundational paradigm) will it be able to resolve the problems of closure in the third (or most properly ethnic) paradigm. Inversely, if the trilogy fails to give due attention to the first paradigm, the attempt to establish an ethnic hermeneutics as an ordering principle becomes highly problematical. Thus, Joe Stecker's decision to build a house of stone "to last two hundred years," at the end of William Carlos Williams's *The Build-Up,* the final novel of the trilogy, is an answer to his Norwegian-American wife's founding dream "of an estate to be named Alverheim after the ancestral home of her forebears," even though her only son and youngest child has recently died in a hunting accident and her husband now seems to be a mere shadow of himself, defeated by the loss of his "heir."[9] Indeed, were it not for a deeper sense of origins, this trilogy would have no way to transcend the personal tragedy engulfing the Steckers. As it is, the house stands as an open-ended metaphor for a new burst of energy, a new beginning, and one more verse added to the book of generations as suggested by chapter 5 of Genesis. They decide to build the house, knowing that their daughter Flossie is expecting her second child. As Cotton Mather put it in 1719, "Sirs, I have told you the *Story* of *Life.* This is the *Story.* In the V Chapter of *Genesis,* you have the *Story* told, Nine times over, so; *The Man Was Born, he had an House, and he Died. That's all!*"[10] Here the genealogical circle and the sense of the generational model as an orienting, story-making device are made quite explicit. In the narrator's words in *The Build-Up,* "As Gurlie [Stecker's wife] thought back to her ancient lineage, now broken, she felt herself predestined to re-establish it."[11]

The point I wish to make here, since it addresses directly the topic of cultural passage, is that the trilogy paradigms themselves form the best structural context for evaluating the specific uses of ethnic-trilogy poetics, for they alone can offer a complete narrative grammar of the trilogy's genealogical imperative. At this metanarrative level, then, one can see how the ethnic trilogy speculates on the very possibilities of the genealogical principle by offering ethnicity as its cultural filter for reading cultural crisis. In short, the trilogy paradigms spell out the various ways in which the quest for narrative coherence can be structured in specific discursive manifestations.

The trilogy paradigms are formal elaborations of the narrative program by which trilogies regulate themselves. They are canonic and procedural and offer a processing system for interpreting the effectiveness and complexities of specific narrative montages.[12] At this point we can take up the necessary task of identifying a trilogy poetics, which literary critics and cultural historians have so far left unarticulated, thus consigning a major narrative form to a marginal status. That the ethnic trilogy, as a concerted effort, has constructed a new model of aesthetic communication, however, is most evident at the paradigmatic level.[13] Here, then, I will only try to prepare the way for a new appreciation of ethnic trilogies by describing their particular perspectival *jeu,* their shifting modalities, the structural capacities of their various characters: in short, the typology of paradigms that generate their text-world.

As has already been suggested above, the ethnic trilogy, while having the same genealogical aspirations as its nativist counterpart, structures them according to a different hierarchy of significance based on a unique stereoscopic perspective. Put in another way, what changes a potentially weak series of narrative paradigms into a tightly connected sequence of typological permutations is the originating immigrant paradigm, whose dialogical unfolding sets up the juxtaposition of two cultural systems and is generational. Thus, we have old world–new world and an actantial typology of a) fathers and mothers (founders); b) fathers and mothers versus sons and daughters; c) sons and daughters. Here, arranged in chronological order, is the first indication of our three paradigms, each having its own narrative program, tensional logic, actantial roles, and chronotopic space.[14] It bears repeating that the three paradigmatic moments of this genealogical parabola transcend the limits, while embodying the possibilities, of any particular textual manifestation. Furthermore, they are intended merely as descriptive models for identifying, and not necessarily defining, the trilogy poetics. In no way are they meant as rigid devices of exclusion. To continue, the master topics that account for the semantic coherence of the three paradigms are, respectively: (*a*) CONSTRUCTION; (*b*) DECONSTRUCTION; (*c*) RECONSTRUCTION. Each paradigm also has its dominant modality and in corresponding order they are: (*a*) *vouloir-faire;* (*b*) *pouvoir-faire;* (*c*) *savoir-faire.*[15]

First Paradigm: Construction

In the first paradigm, the ancestors, the fathers and mothers, dominate. Their story is governed by a foundational project (implicit in the act of emigration/immigration) or by the projection of a possible world. The idea is to begin life over again. In Part 2, "Home-founding," of *Giants in the Earth,* Rølvaag expresses the theme of construction this way:

> The talk had now drifted to questions of a more serious nature, mostly concerned with how they should manage things out here [in the Dakotas]; of their immediate prospects; of what the future might hold in store for them; of land and crops, and of the new kingdom which they were about to found. . . . No one put the thoughts into words, but they all felt it strongly; now they had gone back to the very beginning of things. . . .[16]

As this exemplary passage suggests, the narrative logic of this paradigm is based on the category of the possible; the catalyzing hypothesis is that expectations can come true; wishing can make it so. *Vouloir-faire,* therefore, both as competence and performance, is the dominant mode and accounts for an idealization of the topology of the real. All this is evident in these words from the opening chapter of Pietro Di Donato's *Christ in Concrete:*

> That night was a crowning point in the life of Geremio. He bought a house! Twenty years he had helped to mold the New World. And now he was to have a house of his own! What mattered it that it was no more than a wooden shack? It was his own![17]

Things are done with an eye to the future. If the present intrudes, as it constantly does, it is read in the key of "not yet."

The thematic roles are almost exclusively those of founding, but they are particularly conjugated in terms of a single, extended, and often great act. As Vilhelm Moberg says in the preface to the third volume of his tetralogy, *The Settlers,* "He [the immigrant] had come to make a living for himself and his family, he must build a house and establish a home; he must build up a new society from its very foundation."[18] There is in this passage, and in the first paradigm as a whole, a self-conscious sense that the immigrant undertaking is a mythological or epic exploit, that it is a history-making act. Indeed, the topographical movement from one country to another, that is, the motif of the journey, suggests that the dominant conception of space is that of a homogeneous (because as yet undiscovered) ideal habitat. The utopian and fantastic impulse of the emigrants and their clarity of vision also create this type of spatial model, as is evident in John Cournos's *The Mask:*

> It was settled that they should go to the new land of milk and honey. But where? What city? Again Vanya came with the suggestion. He read aloud from his geography book: "Philadelphia, 'the city of brotherly love,' is celebrated for its public institutions, its hospitals, its schools, its free colleges of learning." . . . [L]ike children they all believed implicitly the words in the geography book. The vision of Vanya's career rose like a mirage in Gombarova's thoughts, journeying thousands of miles.[19]

The protagonists (above all, the fathers) cannot help taking on a certain heroic stature in such a context, and their Homeric potentiality is often confirmed not so much by their actions as by the fact that the latter are frequently communal (see Rølvaag's Norwegians, Moberg's Swedes, Di Donato's Italians, Derleth's Germans and French).

At any rate, doing tends to dominate over the modality of thinking, for, in Peter Grimsen's words in *Take All to Nebraska,* "There was scope for action here."[20] Furthermore, with construction as the master topic, goals are still relatively uncomplicated; motives are few, simple, public in character, and usually agreed upon by all. The *vouloir-faire* of the project inspires consensus. It also goes without saying that the first paradigm unfolds a very transparent view of reality, this too being part of the epic dispensation. The characters refuse to admit a fallen world, since definite truths and noble principles can and do prevail.

Indeed, it is this poetic moment of the trilogy parabola that comes closest to recapitulating the foundational, prehistoric myth of America spawned by Renaissance explorers and that comes closest to recalling the romance tradition of nineteenth-century American literature. It follows that the type of literary conventions governing the representational modes of this paradigm tend to be drawn from epic-style fiction, the adventure story, the romance, the saga, the fairy tale, the utopia, folklore, and the Bible. This is especially true for those trilogies that have a pastoral or prairie or farm setting, as opposed to those set in the urban habitat (those of Di Donato, Cournos, Fuchs). Both versions of this first paradigm, however, are closely identified with what I have defined elsewhere as the immigrant novel, where a system of ideal expectations provides one of the major structuring moments.[21]

It is primarily through the activation of narrative elements from this genre that a rather detailed map of an immigrant/ethnic worldview is charted: a stock of themes, characters, actions, situations, objects, customs, beliefs, institutions, and so forth—all of which make up a bound cultural encyclopedia. A good part of the epistemological space of this first paradigm is taken up with the perspectival world of the parents, which is often rather explicitly rooted in Old World reality. For example, Cournos's trilogy begins in Russia, while Moberg's begins in Ljuder Parish, in the province of Småland, Sweden. What makes the originating cultural encyclopedia strong is not the fact that the story of the first paradigm begins in the old country, although this is certainly important, but that it is bound (intrinsically held together) by the fathers and mothers. In short, it constitutes a world at this point, and not yet a fragment, even if this world is a rather tightly restricted ghetto, as is often the case. The individual is still part of the family, and the family a part of a homogeneous community. Relations tend to be preeminently *intra*cultural. Indeed, in Rølvaag's *Giants in the Earth* the sudden presence of so-called foreigners like the Irish or a band of Indians causes a great deal of fear and consternation, while in Di Donato's *Christ in Concrete* the protagonists speak almost exclusively in Italian. Apart from the specific map of discourse, then, it is this originating world that germinates the other two paradigms, that acts as a kind of narrative locomotive. If developed, if made normative at the discursive level, it inevitably inoculates the trilogy against fragmentation. How it does so remains to be seen, but this is a matter for the third paradigm. Suffice it to say that this first paradigm can even be rather sketchy or marginal and still be the genealogical center of the trilogy. It can, in fact, even function as an absent presence and have its desired effect. Everything depends, as I shall show, on the sons and daughters.

Second Paradigm: Deconstruction

The second paradigm defines space in a much more local and restricted sense than the first does and strips the latter of its sublimity and panoramic reach. This is one of the reasons why its master topic may be appropriately labeled "deconstruction," for it is governed by repeated acts of definition, verification, and analysis of the *real* possibilities of carrying out a constructive project. The very difficulty of owning a house or keeping it (as in Di Donato, Winther, Derleth, Williams, Cournos, Fuchs) is often a major issue. The dominant modality, therefore, is *pouvoir-faire;* imagination no longer seems able to control circumstances. The characters must settle for what can be done within clearly defined limits. Fuchs's characters (Max Balkan, Philip Hayman, and even Herbert Lurie) learn to accept their ghetto environment; learn, in Balkan's words, that it is impossible "to live like the men in the old days and in the great tragedies."[22] Or, as Philip Hayman says of his immigrant father, "This was not his time nor world. . . . "[23] The dominant culture begins to invade the immigrant or ethnic world, often through the major source of tension: fathers and mothers versus sons and daughters. Indeed, the family itself now tends to be a major chronotopic space, although in this paradigm the very notion of a ruling homogeneous space is sacrificed to a series of disconnected local spaces. The family is here broken up, with the children going away (either psychologically or physically) or the parents dying off or losing their authority. One immediately thinks of Rølvaag's Beret Holm, particularly in *Peder Victorious,* when she no longer has the support of her husband, and of Winther's Meta Grimsen in *Mortgage Your Heart.* In the latter, Peter Grimsen could note, when thinking of his inability to understand his sons, "Two sets of thoughts lived side by side in this house in the corn field."[24]

The narrative logic of this paradigm, in other words, is ruled by conflict, while *pouvoir-faire* becomes a series of specialized and discontinuous performances. With the act of discovery concluded and physical boundaries established, various kinds of institutions—social, political, economic, religious—define more and more what can and cannot be done, and in terms of highly restricted topologies. Perhaps there is no better expression of this sense of limits than this scene describing the Gombarov family's living quarters in Philadelphia, from Cournos's second novel, significantly entitled *The Wall:* "That cul-de-sac! That wall at the end of it, barring all progress, shutting them in. Was not that a symbol of their lives?"[25] A little later in the novel, the main protagonist defines his own possibilities in terms of a series of constricting topologies:

> His struggle with himself was one thing; his struggle with the world and material considerations was another; his struggle with his family was a third. These were three formidable walls. Life was a city which had fortified itself against him with three strong walls.[26]

Such frames, then, provide a set of microcultural scenarios that channels experience into often unrelated, highly atomized segments. For instance, the American school, with its introduction of new kinds of knowledge, now rivals the family, as is the case in Winther's trilogy. In Rølvaag's novels, political parties and different creeds divide a once homogeneous community and leave the individual bewildered and secretive about his motives. In short, the sense of totality peculiar to the first paradigm is lost. Gestures are smaller, more unsure; experience, a series of discrete "nows"; goals, so many missed targets. Deeds are local, modest, partial, and often inconclusive. It is a commonplace world, and the characters come up against its fallenness, its everydayness, by testing and analyzing it, by discovering its limits. Instead of simplifying an original project, they tend to complicate it, lose their way in it. The best cognitive stance is perhaps the one that Philip Hayman learns to adopt in *Summer in Williamsburg:*

> Philip walked down the street clinging close to the tenement houses for the shade. If you would really discover the reason, you must pick Williamsburg to pieces until you have them all spread out on your table, a dictionary of Williamsburg. And then select. Pick and discard. Take, with intelligence you have not and with a patience that would consume a number of lifetimes, the different aspects that are pertinent. Collect and then analyze. Collect and then analyze.[27]

There is here a very strong sense of contact with a disenchanted reality, a reality that gives itself to being surveyed, classified, and defined but that refuses to be shaped according to a constructive project, no matter how hard one tries. Indeed, the second paradigm is based on a dissipative dynamic and a topology of micro-catastrophes, if you will. The originating paradigm suffers cultural contamination, while cultural passage enters its most critical stage.

There are, in fact, trilogies in which this paradigm dominates. In Farrell's *Studs Lonigan* series, for example, the genealogical principle is deconstructed precisely because the ethnic world has lost its authority, cut loose as it is from the germinal "world of our fathers," which is left undeveloped. The return of Patrick Lonigan (Studs's father) to his old immigrant neighborhood, at the very end of the third volume, only confirms the fact that the cultural traces of his originating world are now mere archaeological ruins and evoke the type of pathetic relationship he had with his son throughout the trilogy. This choice of discontinuity as the dominant poetic principle restricts Farrell's use of representational conventions to the cultural impasse of naturalism. In

Fuchs's trilogy, on the contrary, the paradigm of deconstruction, although the most fully developed at the level of discourse, is reinterpreted through the perspective of the paradigm of construction, which has a marginal but normative significance for his total poetic program. One might say that here the conventions of ghetto fiction, so similar to the static structures of naturalistic determinism, are seen as mere conventions and certainly not as the last word in narrative invention. As Fuchs shows by ultimately relying on the genealogical principle of the first paradigm to structure his narrative sequences, it is through the poetics of the ethnic trilogy that the conventions of modernism and naturalism (normative in Farrell and Dos Passos, for example) are proven to be restrictive.

In keeping with its closed narrative perspectives, its situations and themes, the limited possibilities of its inventory of character types and the fragmentation of their worldview, the second paradigm tends to employ a set of corresponding representational modes taken from the domestic novel, the realist novel of psychological or social complication, the naturalist novel, the political or proletarian novel, bottom-dog fiction, and the modernist novel (with its techniques of interior monologue, multiple point of view, and stream of consciousness). While this paradigm places the maximum degree of emphasis on discontinuity, change, incoherence, and instability, thus calling into question the possibility of a praxis of genealogical continuism, the third paradigm recovers the principle of coherence and continuity. This it does not by nullifying the deconstructive moment but by sublating it through yet another interpretative shift.

Third Paradigm: Reconstruction

The final narrative program is governed by interpretation; the once impermeable and now deconstructed fact is here inserted into a new inferencing field whose ordering forces are these: Project—Memory. In this context facts are given a new reading through a process of ethnic semiotics, even if their problematic status remains. Thus, Winther's Grimsen family remains disinherited and does not win back the farm, and Meta can do nothing to vanquish the past, which she must now face alone; but Hans, the favorite son, can face the future positively by opening up, by producing, a new hermeneutical space. It is worth quoting from the third volume of the trilogy, significantly entitled *This*

Passion Never Dies, in which the "passion" is clearly defined as an act of ethnic *return:*

> "Resignation is a dog's philosophy," he said aloud. "Has mother been resigned? Did she sit with folded hands when trouble came to her?" . . . Her hands moved in scene after scene as they flashed into his memory. Suddenly the scenes came in perfect chronological order until finally he saw her hands smooth back Peter's white hair, as Peter gasped, "Tell Hans never . . . " "By God that's what he was trying to say," Hans almost shouted. It was like a command from his father in the days when Peter's word was law that no son of his dared disobey. Peter's words were carried out, and promptly. . . . A new life beat in Hans, the life of a man who has known how to meet the hard work on the farm.[28]

The genealogical principle is here reaffirmed through the semiotic space of ethnic reconstruction. The dominant modality, *savoir-faire,* suggests the type of circular closure that can be obtained by activating a new competence and a new type of performance. Doing (*pouvoir-faire*) cannot reconstruct an original lost world or bring back the past (which would inevitably run the risk of a pathetic anthropology, a nostalgic wringing of hands over the absence of origins), but knowing can recover it through interpretation, by interrogating the *traditio* inscribed in the first paradigm. An apparently comic version of this interpretative dynamic can be found in Cournos's novel *The Wall,* where the Jewish protagonist, after donning an oriental costume for the art schools' autumn ball, suddenly realizes,

> Above all, the astonishing fact flashed across his mind: he was and had never ceased being an oriental; an ancient Jew of the East. . . . Strange unaccustomed thoughts entered his head: memories, as it were, of some other wholly forgotten existence, lived elsewhere and at some other time, more harmonious with his real temperament, which was now over-crusted and obscured by drab thoughts and a drab life, as unfitting to him as the drab garments of his remembered life.[29]

It is, after all, this ethnic perspective that links together the ineradicable discontinuities of the second paradigm, not simply by defining them as continuities, for the basic fact of their nontransparency remains as so many fragments; but by reading the *traditio* itself as an act of constructive interrogation rather than as a set of constructed answers. This much Hans, in the above passage from *This Passion Never Dies,* makes clear, as do the other ethnic-trilogy protagonists in their own, specific ways.

In the paradigm of reconstruction the *traditio* itself is read in terms of both memory and ongoing project. While the project refers to the first paradigm as *originating* source, memory refers to it as *originated* fact. Just as the originating dimension makes the production of ethnicity in the third paradigm possible (by presenting its constructive *vouloir* for interpretation), so does the originated dimension provide a set of historical and archaeological facts recoverable through memory. Thus, the originating and originated are actually the two faces of a single source and are equally instrumental in generating an ethnic semiotics, as we can see from this passage of Cournos's *The Mask:*

> "A man's life," observed Gombarov . . . , "is on the surface a series of isolated pictures, yet in some mysterious way connected or grouped into a harmonious if not always a perfect pattern. And this invisible, continuous design, which runs through a man's life like a *motif* through a musical composition, is called character by some men, destiny by others. . . . " Altogether this personality represented in its make-up a clash of races . . . a clash of reflective and energetic forces, and having been torn up by the roots from its original mould, and replanted in another place, then reshuffled elsewhere—having, moreover, come under the influence of the unstable, shifting arts and moralities of the age, and yet kept something of the nature of its ancient soul—this personality was almost a physical symbol of the tenacious persistence of old spirits under the pressure of an age of iron, twentieth-century cosmopolitanism.[30]

The "series of isolated pictures," referring as they do to past events and an achieved patrimony, make up an originated culture, but as snapshots they are also irreducibly discontinuous moments lacking an explicit narrative thread. The "clash of reflective and energetic forces," on the other hand, is semiotically produced by the ethnic "personality," whose "tenacious persistence" is ultimately due to the "invisible, continuous design" of the originating project. But the project itself is made "visible" only through the retrieving act of interpretation, even if thinking differently (that is, according to an ethnic perspective) means thinking the difference, or self-consciously interrogating the genealogical gaze, of the first paradigm.

The very ability of the sons and daughters to move positively back and forth between the cultural perspectives of our three narrative paradigms also suggests how time and space are redefined in this program of reconstruction. The basic ethnic strategy of cultural contrast and comparison implies a *jeu* of shifting temporal dimensions in which the bare present is redeemed through genealogical enrichment. Time is now released from its static and reductive *nunc* through the tenses of Project and Memory. In this way, the crisis of the present (so characteristic of the second paradigm) is historicized through what might now be called ethnic time. As for the space of the real, its naturalistic limits are exploded from within by the insertion of the wick of ethnic semiotics. Monocultural space, and the crisis that has invested it, now reveals a polymorphic physiognomy of ethnic traces, associations, symbols, and images. It is through his/her genealogical relationship with these spatial and temporal fragments of the founding *traditio* that the ethnic protagonist is in a position to go beyond the entropic conditions of the cultural crisis of the second paradigm, for the perspective of the immigrant fragment as hermeneutical object is itself paradigmatically outside the culture of crisis. (Earlier, I referred to this perspectivism as metacultural and transhistorical.) With this ethnic *savoir-faire* we now have an interpretative going beyond or, as Cournos expressed it in the above passage, the insertion of a dialogical "clash" that redimensionalizes the chronotopic restrictions of the deconstructive paradigm. Closure, in other words, is achieved through a normative hermeneutical gesture.

Of course, at this point the trilogy might be dismissed as being ineffectual, as producing a floating *pensiero debole* or weak epistemology incapable of creating its own paradigm.[31] Indeed, Fuchs and Cournos might even be cited here as providing evidence insofar as they casually define this marginal cognition of an absent presence as a praxis of *zakhar* (remembering),[32] or, in the words of Fuchs, as a mere game of old men who "play tick-tack-toe with the great Talmud":

> old men who find synagogues in a tenement basement store with the terrible toilets facing the back yards. These old men nodding over the yellow, holy-odored volumes, arguing in a straight line of tradition that extends over the world in width, in depth to the earliest times, in length to God himself.[33]

But it is this very "weakness" that generates a new subversive here/elsewhere, a unique semiotic space that breaks down all cultural limits through its very interpretative nomadism. Cournos, for example, admits that his protagonist, Gombarov, is a misfit, a wandering Jew,[34] but he also admits that the long life of his people runs through him like "a mystic force, a living fluid running down the spine."[35] Fuchs's protagonists, on the other hand, decide finally to remain schlemiels, stubbornly refuse to accept the degradation of ghetto conditions. Even if they do remain in Williamsburg, they do not "dumbly submit."[36]

The main thematic role of the protagonists in the third paradigm is to reinterpret the status of the referent in the second paradigm. This involves putting the real between the parentheses of project and memory, so that present time and space become a false floor, which gives way to the semiotic space of Rølvaag's *Their Fathers' God*. The parameters of this world are indeed elusive and fluctuating, for at any moment and in any place, traces of it may uncontrollably and involuntarily reappear in a face, an accent, an object, a gesture. With the disestablishment of the originated world of the first paradigm, the *traditio* may be deterritorialized, no longer clearly signified (except as a product of quotation, stereotype, anthropology, archaeology). But the *traditio* itself now becomes the hermeneutical object, the signifying source that makes the difference.

Ethnic Semiotics as the Criterion of Ethnic Fiction

If it was in the second paradigm that the problem of cultural passage became most critical, it is in the third that it is resolved and narrative closure made possible, depending on the extent to which the protagonists respond to the program of an ethnic *savoir-faire*. The narrative conventions specific to the paradigm of reconstruction, therefore, are those based on ethnic fiction proper, just as the conventions of the immigrant novel and those of modernism best corresponded to the first and second paradigms, respectively. Ethnic fiction, in other words, can be classified as such to the extent that it *produces* ethnic interpretation, to the extent that the interpreting protagonist produces a positive strategy of perspectival contrast and comparison through a genealogical interrogation of his/her *traditio*. This dominant modal act can be a starting point or a point of arrival, as it is in Rølvaag's *Their Father's God*. The gesture of narrative closure, of a radical appropriation of the modality of ethnic semiosis, is here made in the very last lines of the novel, after Peder's (the protagonist's) mixed ethnic marriage has gone on the rocks:

> And going to the corner back of the door he began hunting among the clothes that hung there, aimlessly and with slow movements.
> "Looking for something?" asked Jacob Fredrik.
> "That old cap of mine," he answered, absently, and continued turning the clothes. . . . "What time did she leave?"
> "This morning, shortly after I came down," gulped Jacob Fredrik.
> Peder found the cap, which all the time had hung in plain sight, put it on, and went out.[37]

The novel and the trilogy end here. The act of putting on his old cap (ironically "in plain sight"), while not offering a new transparency or an end to his problems, does suggest a perspectival commitment, a hermeneutical return. Granted, Peder simply "went out"; we do not know where. But we do know with what competence, it seems to me. Rølvaag's open ending indicates that the semiotic space of ethnic fiction is now everywhere and nowhere at the same time: everywhere because Peter's going out is topographically unlimited; nowhere because his ethnic perspective is based on the absent presence of the hieroglyphic gaze of his dead father iconically framed at the end of *Giants in the Earth*. Thus, through Peder's role as ethnic semiotician this nowhere becomes a cultural everywhere. As the Norwegian minister warns in *Their Fathers' God*, "A people that has lost its traditions is doomed,"[38] but Peder adds, "It would be folly to try to build up the different European nations over here. The foundation is new, the whole structure must be new, and so it shall be!"[39] Of course, Peder is right in affirming that ethnic reconstruction is not so much a repetition as it is a dialogical production. At the metanarrative level, the trilogy program is *about* genealogy precisely because this third paradigm produces a poetics of continuity through the act of interrogating the "world of our fathers." It is ultimately the signifying system of the first paradigm that genealogically originates the ethnic interpreter and his praxis of ethnic interpretation.

The ethnic narrative program, with its perspectival *jeu,* is, therefore, very much one of reinterpreting the *traditio,* which was elaborated in the first paradigm as a homogeneous cultural encyclopedia with its own internal cohesion. This encyclopedia (with its various institutions and systems—religion, folklore, cuisine, and so on—and their set of scripts involving actors, actions, settings, goals) is the best means we have for verifying the degree to which a given ethnic culture is functioning in a specific text and its specific semiotic potential. The protagonist's narrative status as ethnic interpreter is based on his recovery and *re*-use of this encyclopedic material. A text invests in ethnicity to the extent that it is stocked with various ethnic *savoirs* taken from this encyclopedia; or, more specifically, ethnic fiction is based on the type of its encyclopedic selections and the degree of their frequency, expansion, distribution, and intensity. The very possibilities of an ethnic semiotics depend on this investment.

It should not be forgotten, however, that in comparison to its status in the first paradigm, the encyclopedia may now lack the intrinsic ordering principle (the ancestors) that had previously made it possible to organize its various systems into a totality. Indeed, it may now be without a binding or a center, largely virtual and present only as a series of mobile sequences and free-floating motifs. In this sense, much ethnic fiction is epistemologically weak, but this weakness can also become its peculiar semiotic strength. Ethnicity may now be only optional and symbolic, a hermeneutical device of double awareness, which has no intention of creating a new system, a retotalization of a buried encyclopedia, but which also has no intention of abandoning the practice of ethnic semiosis. The ethnic self, therefore, may now choose to elaborate a local cultural map or float about in the dominant culture as exegete or interpreter of the ethnic traces inscribed everywhere (but nowhere) in the American topology. According to this strategy, ethnic semiotics is nothing but the ongoing interpretation of the genealogical history that the ethnic perspective produces. In conclusion, this type of narrativity, often the result of a radical discontinuity between the ethnic self and his *traditio,* is the very story of a cultural difference: not only the story of an ethnic perspective but the story of its genealogical reconstruction.

Blood in the Marketplace:
The Business of Family
in the *Godfather* Narratives

THOMAS J. FERRARO

Giorgio introduces me to his friend Piero Paco, hero of the Italo-American breach into American literature. He looks like a massive gangster but turns out to be a plain, nice guy with a lot of folksy stories and no complexes. He doesn't feel guilty about blacks, doesn't care about elevating Italo-American prestige. He's no missionary for wops. No gripes about the Establishment. He just decided in the best American way to write a book that would make half a million bucks because he was tired of being ignored.

"You don't think struggling Italo-Americans should stick together and give each other a push up from the bottom of the pile where they've always been?" I ask him. But he's no struggling half-breed anymore. He's made his pile; he's all-American now.

"I'm not going to push that crap," he says engagingly.

—HELEN BAROLINI, *Umbertina* (1979)

I

What, after all, could be more American than the success stories of penniless immigrant boys clawing their way to wealth and respectability by private enterprise? What legitimate American business tycoon ever objected to being called "ruthless," to being credited (like the good boxer) with the "killer instinct" . . . ?

What is more, *The Godfather* could be seen to represent not only some of the continuing principles of the American way of life, but the ancestral ideals it had somehow inexplicably lost on the way. In Don Corleone's world bosses were respected and loved by their subordinates as surrogate fathers. Men were men and women were glad of it. Morality ruled unchallenged, and crime, for the most part, was kept off the streets. Families stuck together under patriarchal control. Children obeyed—fathers, and virtuous wives were not afraid of losing their status to mistresses. . . . No wonder *New York* magazine exclaimed (according to the paperback edition's blurb): "You'll find it hard to stop dreaming about it."

—E. J. Hobsbawm, *"Robin Hoodo"*

In his 1969 blockbuster, *The Godfather,* Mario Puzo presented an image of the Mafia that has become commonplace in American popular culture. Since Puzo, it has been taken for granted that the Mafia operates as a consortium of illegitimate businesses, structured along family lines, with a familial patriarch or "godfather" as the chief executive officer of each syndicate.[1] Puzo's version of the Mafia fuses into one icon the realms of family and economy, of southern Italian ethnicity and big-time American capitalism, of *blood* and the *marketplace.* "Blood" refers to the violence of organized crime. "Blood" also refers to the familial clan, and its extension through the fictive system of the *compare,* or "co-godparenthood." In *The Godfather,* the representation of the Mafia fuses ethnic tribalism with the all-American pursuit of wealth and power. Since its publication, we have regarded this business of family in *The Godfather* as a figment of Puzo's opportunistic imagination, which it remains in part. But the business of family in Puzo's Mafia is also a provocative revision of accepted notions of what ethnicity is and how it works—the new ethnic sociology in popular literary form.

During the late seventies and early eighties, there was a short outburst of scholarly interest in *The Godfather* and its myriad offspring. A consensus about the meaning of the saga's popularity emerges from the books and essays of Fredric Jameson, Eric Hobsbawm, John Cawelti, and John Sutherland. The portrayal of the Corleone family collective allows Americans, in the post-Vietnam era, to fantasize about the glory days of "closely knit traditional authority." The portrayal of the power and destructive greed of the Mafia chieftains permits Americans to vent their rage at "the managerial elite who hold the reins of corporate power and use it for their own benefit."[2] The family and business thematics are, in each instance, disengaged from one another. As Jameson puts it: on the one hand, the ethnic family imagery satisfies "a Utopian longing" for collectivity; on the other hand, "the substitution of crime for big business" is the narrative's "ideological function."[3] In standard treatments like these, Puzo's narrative is regarded as a brilliant (or brilliantly lucky) instance of satisfying two disparate appetites with a single symbol. This perspective, formulated in the late seventies, seems to have settled the issue of the novel's popularity.

I want to reopen that issue. We need to return to *The Godfather* because we have too easily dismissed its representation of the Mafia as a two-part fantasy. Of course, *The Godfather* is not reliable as a roman à clef or as a historical novel: Puzo's details are fuzzy, mixed-up, and much exaggerated.[4] "There was things he stretched," as Huck would put it, and everyone knows it. But critics have been too ready to accept his major sociological premise—family and business working in tandem—as pure mythology. The importance of *The Godfather* lies not in a double mythology, I would argue, but in its taking of the fusion of kinship and capitalist enterprise *seriously*. Its cultural significance lies not in the simultaneous appeals of "family" and "business" imagery but rather in the appeal of an actual structural simultaneity: *the business of family*. By failing to pause long enough to consider its surface narrative, critics have underestimated not only the strategies of the novel but the insights and intuitions of its huge audience as well.

Readers have underestimated the business of family because little in traditional theories of the family, ethnicity, and advanced capitalism has prepared them to recognize it. In both scholarly and popular treatments, ethnic culture and extended kinship are interpreted as barriers to the successful negotiation of the mobility ladder, particularly its upper ranks. Southern Italian immigrants and their descendants have long been thought to exemplify the principle that the more clannish an ethnic group, the slower its assimilation and economic advancement.[5] Herbert Gans's *Urban Villagers*, Virginia Yans-McLaughlin's *Family and Community*, Thomas Kessner's *The Golden Door*, and Thomas Sowell's *Ethnic America* essentially update the social-work perspectives of writers such as Phyllis H. Williams and Leonard Covello.[6] In 1944, Covello wrote,

> Any social consciousness of Italo-Americans within "Little Italies" appertains primarily to sharing and adhering to the family tradition as the main motif of their philosophy of life. . . . The retention of this cultural "basis" is essentially the source of their retarded adjustment.[7]

This long-standing tradition of identifying the Italian family structure as a dysfunctional survival runs aground on the Mafia.

Historians and sociologists attest to the difficulty of interpreting the Mafia in terms of a linear model of assimilation and upward mobility. All commentators recognize that the Mafia was not simply transported here; that it grew up from the multiethnic immigrant streets, rather than being passed on from father to son; and that Prohibition was the major factor in shaping its growth. In *A Family Business,* the sociologist Francis A. J. Ianni concedes these points, only to stress the family structure of the syndicates and the origin of this familialism in southern Italy:

> [The Lupullo crime organization] *feels* like a kinship-structured group; familialism founded it and is still its stock in trade. One senses immediately not only the strength of the bond, but the inability of members to see any morality or social order larger than their own.

Ianni's research tempts him into abandoning the tradition of placing ethnic phenomena on a linear continuum running from Old World marginality to New World centrality.[8] His research supports and his analysis anticipates (if it does not quite articulate) the cutting edge of ethnic theory. It is time for the criticism of ethnic literature generally, and of *The Godfather* in particular, to take advantage of such theory.

Scholars in a number of fields are working to change the way we think about ethnicity, ethnic groups, and ethnic culture. In identifying the social bases of ethnicity, theorists are shifting emphasis from intergenerational transmission to arenas of conflict in complex societies. They argue that we need to examine ethnic cultures not as Old World survivals (whatever their roots) but as strategies to deal with the unequal distribution of wealth, power, and status. In this light, ethnic groups are seen to include not only socially marginal peoples but any groups who use symbols of common descent and tradition to create or maintain power. From a historian's perspective, European family structures and traditions do not necessarily dissolve in the face of capitalism but rather, as they have always done, evolve to meet its changing needs.[9] Herbert Gans has spoken of "cost-free" ethnicity among the middle classes, but ethnicity is often *profitable* as well.[10]

In his work, the anthropologist Abner Cohen conceives of ethnic groups as "interest groups," in which ethnic symbols function in lieu of more formal structures such as the law. By the symbolic apparatus of ethnicity, he means the emphasis on common history and tradition, endogamy and social boundary maintenance, religion and ritual, and everyday encoded behavior, including "accent, manner of speech, etiquette, style of joking, play," and so forth: the rhetoric and codes of "blood."[11] As Cohen explains, the symbolic apparatus of "ethnicity" incites genuine loyalty and emotion, whose power and idiosyncrasy should not be underestimated. But the apparatus also serves utilitarian purposes within society at large, including the economic marketplace. In many of our most familiar examples, the function of ethnic ritual is primarily defensive, organizing a group on the margins of society: but the uses of ethnicity can be quite aggressive as well. The Italian-American Mafia is a case in point. As Ianni and others have demonstrated, it is the ethos of ethnic solidarity that puts the *organization* into Italian-American organized crime.

In her discussion of *The Godfather,* Rose Basile Green comes the closest of any critic, I think, to unpacking in Cohen's fashion what she herself calls the "socioeconomic ethnic image" of the Corleone crime syndicate. Unlike almost everyone else, Green takes seriously Puzo's portrayal of the syndicates not as a historical novel about actual gangsters but as a treatise (however romanticized) "dealing with the contemporary strategy of gaining and securing power." Yet her analysis splits into typical parallel paths: crime as a means for social mobility versus the family as a locus of traditional southern Italian responsibility. Although Green identifies "a subtle line between personal interest and structural power," she too fails to make the strongest connection between the private family life ascribed to Don Corleone and the illegitimate enterprise he heads. When Green says that *The Godfather* explores "the contemporary strategy of gaining and securing power," she means by "strategy" the tactics of bribery, intimidation, the brokerage of votes, intergang warfare, and so forth, with which Don Corleone conducts business outside the confines of his own organization. But the most noteworthy device for gaining and securing power in Puzo's depiction is internal to the Corleone syndicate. The device is not a gun or payola but, quite simply and obviously, that mystified entity the "southern Italian family."[12]

II

"Tell the old man I learned it all from him and that I'm glad I had this chance to pay him back for all he did for me. He was a good father."

—MICHAEL CORLEONE

As narrator in *The Godfather,* Puzo adopts the familiar role of cultural interpreter, mediating between outside readers and an ethnic secret society. Puzo's agenda, implicit yet universally understood, is to explain why Sicilian-Americans have made such good criminals. The answer, generally speaking, is their cult of family honor. The Corleones believe, with a kind of feudal fervor, in patriarchy, patronage, and protection. *The Godfather* is saturated with the imagery of paternity, family, and intimate friendship; with the rhetoric of respect, loyalty, and the code of silence; with references to Sicilian blood and the machismo attributed to it; with the social events—weddings, christenings, funerals, meals, and so forth—that embody the culture of family honor. Always the business of crime is interlaced with the responsibilities of family. In the film, for instance, Clemenza frets over a request from his wife even as he presides over the execution of Paulie Gatto: "Don't forget the cannolis!" Don Vito himself is a true believer. He believes in the mutual obligation of kinfolk. He seeks to expand his wealth and power to protect his dependents and to make his protection available to more and more people. He recruits from within his family to keep the business "all in the family" for the family's sake. "It was at this time that the Don got the idea that he ran his world far better than his enemies ran the greater world which continually obstructed his path."[13] At the same time, "not his best friends would have called Don Corleone a saint from heaven"; there is always "some self-interest" in his generosity (*G,* 215). For everyone recognizes the wisdom of family honor—Corleone's honor—given the special exigencies of operating in a big way in an outlawed underground economy.

In his analysis of the ethnic group as an interest group, Abner Cohen stresses the growth potential wherever there is a sector of an economy that has not been organized formally:

> Even in the advanced liberal industrial societies there are some structural conditions under which an interest group cannot organize itself on formal lines. Its formal organization may be opposed by the state or by other groups within the state, or may be incompatible with some important principles in the society; or the interests it represents may be newly developed and not yet articulated in terms of a formal organization and accommodated with the formal structure of the society. Under these conditions the group will articulate its organization on informal lines, making use of the kinship, friendship, ritual, ceremonial, and other symbolic activities that are implicit in what is known as style of life.[14]

The ethnic ethos means sticking together, respecting the authority of the group rather than that of outsiders, defending the group's turf, and abiding by tradition. The reasoning comes full circle, for tradition is equated with group solidarity. The family is the core element of the group and its most powerful symbol. Under the appropriate conditions the ethos of "ethnicity" is by no means anachronistic in the advanced stages of capitalism, no matter how rooted such values might be to the past of particular groups. Wherever ethnicity can facilitate enterprise, capitalism as a system can be said to be one of ethnicity's primary motors, not its antithesis. Focusing on the old moneyed elite of London, Cohen has argued that ethnicity functions among the privileged as well as the impoverished and among "core" castes as well as racial and national minorities. In another case study, the historian Peter Dobkin Hall implicates family and tradition in the mercantilism of Massachusetts elites, 1700–1900.[15] As both Cohen and Hall contend, a precondition for capitalized ethnicity is a legal vacuum. Here I wish to add a corollary based on the history of the Mafia: the desire to engage in enterprise, not simply in a vacuum (where there is no law or formal arrangements) but in an economic zone outside the law and *against* formal arrangements, makes some form of family and ethnic organization a necessity.

The seemingly "feudal" ethos of family honor, deeply internalized, cements individuals together in American crime, structuring syndicates and giving them their aggrandizing momentum. Loyalty and devotion to group honor are the values around which individuals are motivated, recruited, judged, and policed in the Mafia. These values are especially good in binding criminals together and in making criminals out of those otherwise not drawn to the outlaw life. They came into the forefront in America when Prohibition created an enormous unorganized sector of the national economy, legally proscribed, but promoted by immense appetites and the willingness of the actual legal structure to play along, especially "for a price." They are also especially needed to hold together the large-scale enterprises, not structured or protected by law, that prohibition creates but that survive after it: rackets devoted to gambling, loan-sharking, prostitution, various forms of extortion, and eventually drugs. In legitimate business, a prized executive who sells himself and perhaps a secret or two to another company is regarded as an unexpected operating loss. A *caporegime* who becomes a stool pigeon can bring the whole system down. The ideology of tradition and of group solidarity, principally of the family, is ideal for rationalizing crime syndicates, in both senses of the term "rationalize": ideal for organizing them because it is ideal for justifying their existence and their hold over their members. Scholars report that actual mafiosi crime syndicates are family based. In *A Family Business,* Ianni analyzes the structure of a major American Mafia clan—the "Lupullo" family—abstracting four general rules of organization:

> the merging of social and business functions into one kin-centered enterprise; the assignment of leadership positions on the basis of kinship; the correlation between closeness of kin relationship and the hierarchy of positions; and the requirement of close consanguineal or affinal relationship for inclusion in the core group. . . . [16]

Ianni produces several diagrams to illustrate his thesis: a genealogical table of actual and fictive (godparent-godchild) relations; a flowchart of the subdivisions and their operations within the crime syndicate; and a third table, which combines the preceding two.[17] The third table diagrams what Ianni calls the "power alliances" (relations of respect and deference) between leaders within the Lupullo crime hierarchy. The pattern of authority within the syndicate mimics the pattern within the patriarchal clan.

In *The Godfather,* Mario Puzo provides a narrative equivalent of the Lupullos' power chart. During the wedding scene, Puzo introduces the Corleones in terms of their dual roles as family members and company executives. Vito Corleone is president and chief executive officer, as well as father or godfather to everyone within the organization. Genco Abbandando, *"consigliori"* (right-hand man), has been his best friend during his American childhood, his honorary brother, the son of the man who took him in and gave him his first job. But Genco is dying, and it is suspected that Tom Hagen, Vito Corleone's "adopted" son, will be taking over as counselor. Vito's eldest, Sonny, operates one of the principal three divisions or *regimes* of the family. The other two division leaders (*capo-regimes*), Tessio and Clemenza, are *compari* of Vito, godparents to each other's children. Fredo, the second son, serves his father as bodyguard and executive secretary. Michael, the youngest son, is the black sheep of the family and has nothing to do with its business. By tradition, the women are "civilians." But Connie's groom, Carlo Rizzi (an old boyhood chum of Sonny), expects, through this marriage, to rise quickly in the syndicate.

The network of nuclear family, extended kin by blood or marriage, and honorary kinship is not simply a structural convenience. The ideology of family operates neither as false consciousness in the vulgar sense nor as rhetoric that is entirely and self-consciously hypocritical. The rhetoric of solidarity works to organize the Corleone syndicate *because* of its hold over the imaginations and passions of leaders and those in the common ranks alike. As Cohen explains it, ethnic symbols function in lieu of formal structures precisely because of their trans-utilitarian, emotional appeal. This "dual" nature of symbolization is illustrated especially well in Puzo's depiction of Tom Hagen's admission into the Corleone syndicate.

Sonny Corleone had brought Tom Hagen, an orphaned waif of German-Irish extraction, into the Corleone household, where he was allowed to remain. "In all this the Don acted not as a father but rather as a guardian." Only after Hagen goes to work for Don Corleone is he treated as a fourth son:

> After he passed the bar exam, Hagen married to start his own family. The bride was a young Italian girl from New Jersey, rare at that time for being a college graduate. After the wedding, which was of course held in the home of Don Corleone, the Don offered to support Hagen in any undertaking he desired, to send him law clients, furnish his office, start him in real estate.
>
> Tom Hagen had bowed his head and said to the Don, "I would like to work for you."
>
> The Don was surprised, yet pleased. "You know who I am?" he asked.
>
> Hagen nodded. . . . "I would work for you like your sons," Hagen said, meaning with complete loyalty, with complete acceptance of the Don's parental divinity. The Don, with that understanding which was even then building the legend of his greatness, showed the young man the first mark of fatherly affection since he had come into his household. He took Hagen into his arms for a quick embrace and afterward treated him more like a true son, though he would sometimes say, "Tom, never forget your parents," as if he were reminding himself as well as Hagen. (*G*, 51–52)

In the scene above, Hagen moves into the Don's inner circle. It is a *dual* movement, enacted simultaneously, into the inner realm of Don Vito's familial affections and into the ranks of his crime organization. Tom touches the Don's heart by volunteering, despite his origins, to submit himself to the Don's will and risk his life and freedom in the company. By the same token, the Don rewards Hagen's voluntary show of respect with a symbolic "adoption" that signifies the bond of loyalty upon which their futures as gangsters will depend. The symbol of paternity here works emotionally and pragmatically at the same time. Indeed, the father-son bonding is all the more powerful because of its economic component, while its utility depends, in the absence of biological paternity, quite precisely upon the psychological density of the tie.[18]

So far I have been juxtaposing the sociology of ethnic and familial interest groups with various elements of *The Godfather,* treating the latter as if it were merely an illustration of the former—as if *The Godfather* were a kind of sociological tract or social-work guide to the Mafia. Of course, *The Godfather* is not exposition, but a novel; not sociology, but story. Yet the populist, fictional composition of *The Godfather* does not mean it is any less effective than the scholarship of Cohen or Ianni as a medium for implicating the ethnic family in capitalism. Puzo uses the resources of fiction—imagery and rhetoric, characterization, and, most of all, narrative—to make a case for the interpenetration of family and business. In the instance of Tom Hagen's admission to the Corleone family, Puzo rigs a set of circumstances and unfolds an event in such a fashion that the strands of father-son emotion and corporate personnel management are not phenomenologically separable. Hagen's recruitment/initiation functions as a microcosm for the interpenetration of family and business in the narrative as a whole. Through melodrama, Puzo undermines the still common assumption that family and business operate as separate spheres. Puzo combines family and business within the same narrative site. He also subverts the reader's desire, in keeping with a purified notion of the family and a vilified notion of the economy, to subordinate one phenomenon to the other, as cause and effect, in any given instance. In *The Godfather* the syndicate never, or almost never, uses family imagery *merely* to structure itself in lieu of better alternatives, thereby "corrupting" the forms and values of an otherwise sacrosanct ethnic tribe. On the other hand, the family never engages in business *simply* to support itself, dirtying its hands to keep head and heart clean. Always the two phenomena are causally intermingled. By the deviousness of situation and event, Puzo contextualizes the ethnic family within the capitalist economy while excavating the contribution of ethnic culture and the rhetoric of ethnicity to illegitimate enterprise.

To a greater extent perhaps than we have become used to in analyzing modernist, high-brow literature, the story line is crucial to *The Godfather.* Even the critics most hostile to Puzo admit that his great gift is storytelling, including the creation of memorable characters, but especially the creation and maintenance of suspense—of beginnings that captivate, middles the keep you going, and endings that satisfy. In

The Godfather, Puzo narrates two plots that lock together into a single, resounding conclusion.[19] When the novel opens, a breakdown in filial obedience exposes the Corleone syndicate to "a hostile take-over bid" from the Barzini-Tattaglia group. At the same time, business matters threaten the lives of Corleone family members and precipitate dissent among them. This double crisis is the hook that captures our attention: a business in trouble, a family in trouble. We cheer for a solution to both crises—nothing less will satisfy—and Puzo contrives brilliantly to give it to us. Both crises, potentially disastrous, are solved when Don Vito's youngest son, Michael, ascends to his father's place and successfully squelches the Barzini-Tattaglia threat. It is a stunning illustration of the structural logic of family business in narrative terms. The return of the prodigal son alleviates the problem of managerial succession, while the resurrection of the syndicate's power base restores the primacy of family values and commitments. Puzo's story is "dual" in the sense that the ethnic symbols of the Mafia are dual and that Tom Hagen's adoption as a Corleone is dual. So tightly constructed is Puzo's plot around the theme of duality that the novel's denouement seems inevitable. To save the business, you must regroup the family; to save the family, you must regroup the business.

In *The Godfather,* Puzo uses Connie Corleone's wedding to illustrate the overlapping structures of family and business in the American Mafia of the 1940s. In the *Godfather* film (the lens of which constantly obscures our view of the novel), Coppola plays with a contrast between the beneficent private life of the Corleones (the sunlit wedding feast) and their business escapades (inside the darkened house, inside their hearts of darkness).[20] Yet, Coppola's moral allegory reifies a distinction between the private and the corporate, home and work, explicitly undermined by the novel. In Puzo's design, business associates *are* the proper wedding guests, because one's family and friends are one's proper coworkers and retainers. The specter of communal solidarity, embodied in the wedding, marks a plateau of harmonious unity from which the Corleones are about to fall. As Puzo introduces the members of the Corleone family at Connie's wedding and their environment, he not only unpacks the functional interdependence of family and business. He explicates and foreshadows a disturbance in family-business equilibrium, reciprocally engendered, mutually threatening, that is the medium for the *Godfather* narrative. As Puzo imagines it, the incipient threat to the Corleone empire is analytically inseparable from the breakdown in the familial solidarity of the syndicate—including Genco's death, the Don's creeping senility, Sonny's disobedience, the disloyalty of Carlo and Tessio, Hagen's intransigent foreignness, Michael's rebellion. At the same time, tensions in the family arise directly out of the involvement in the business of crime.

At the opening of the novel, Don Corleone is nearing retirement, which has him justifiably worried about the leadership of the syndicate. In standard corporate management, such a problem can be handled either by promotion of the best available personnel from within company ranks or by recruitment from outside the company (intercorporate "raiding"). But for the Corleones, of course, the problem of the company executive is strictly a family matter, and that makes it a problem indeed. The right-hand man, Genco Abbandando, dies on the day of the wedding, leaving Don Corleone no choice but to promote Tom Hagen, an adopted son whose German-Irish descent precludes consideration for the top post of don. Both Clemenza and Tessio, the two *capo-regimes,* are nearing retirement themselves; moreover, they are not quite family enough. Of the don's own sons, neither Sonny nor Fredo seems finally to have the mettle to be don, while Michael, once favored to head the family, is now an outcast:

> [Sonny] did not have his father's humility but instead a quick, hot temper that led him into errors of judgment. Though he was a great help in his father's business, there were many who doubted that he would become the heir to it. . . . The second son, Fredrico . . . did not have that personal magnetism, that animal force, so necessary for a leader of men, and he too was not expected to inherit the family business. . . . The third son, Michael, did not stand with his father and his two brothers but sat at a table in the most secluded corner of the garden. (*G,* 17)

The leadership vacuum, familially engendered, is the weak link that tempts the Barzini-Tattaglia consortium (fronted by Sollozzo, the drug dealer) to take over the Corleone rackets. Weaknesses in the character of family members and in their relations with one another expose the Corleone family to, quite literally, a hostile takeover bid.

Concomitantly, and inseparably, business tensions have precipitated disputes within the intimate family circle. Michael has fallen out with his family because he objects to the way its members make a living, committing himself instead to the defense of his country and the "straight arrow" mobility of a Dartmouth education. Connie's old-fashioned Sicilian wedding seems to symbolize the unity of the Corleone generations. Yet the garden celebration actually screens dissent between Connie and her father, traceable to Corleone involvement in the rackets. "Connie had consented to a 'guinea' wedding to please her

father because she had so displeasured him in her choice of a husband"
(*G*, 20). The persistence of the Corleone syndicate means that one of
the qualifications for a Corleone son-in-law is potential for criminal
leadership. Don Corleone objects to Carlo Rizzi as his daughter's husband not because he doubts Carlo's qualities as a mate but because he
questions Carlo's ability and trustworthiness as a gangster. For his own
part, Carlo marries Connie not only out of love but also because he
hopes to rise in the Corleone syndicate. When Don Corleone violates
the principle of familial promotion, providing Carlo with a living but
not an executive role, Carlo seeks revenge on his father-in-law and the
family. Carlo sets up the assassination of Sonny, bringing the syndicate
to the brink of disaster. By Puzo's design, as demonstrated in this instance, any analysis of family-business disrepair comes full circle: we
trace family problems to business questions, only to find the intrusion
of business into family life returning to haunt the business.

Carlo's betrayal, like that of Paulie Gatto and ultimately of Tessio
himself, illustrates the point of vulnerability in a family business within
a competitive market. The principles of maximizing profits and employing insiders are not always compatible. Syndicate leaders are
tempted, for the sake of performance, to slight certain inept family
members. Syndicate members are tempted, for personal gain, to betray
their organizations. As long as a doctrine of familial loyalty is obeyed
to the letter, neither temptation wins the day. But when family principles break down, the company is in danger.

The leadership vacuum in the Corleone syndicate is filled by the re-
establishment of order in the Corleone patriarchy, when Michael returns to his family, his descent culture, and his filial "destiny." In *The
Godfather,* the crisis of managerial succession is a crisis, as Cawelti
notes, of "family succession"which can be solved only *familially*.[21]
Puzo resolves the dual crisis by having Michael grow a familial conscience and an ethnic consciousness, mandating his ascent to his father's position as patriarch. At the novel's opening, Michael is a family
pariah—*scomunicato,* excommunicated.[22] Before the war, Michael
was the chosen heir to his father's regime, but later he refuses to have
anything to do with the business and barely anything to do with the
members of his family. He courts an "Adams" for a wife. Puzo's narrative counteracts the seeming decline of the Corleone syndicate by
charting Michael's rebirth as a Corleone family member and a businessman of crime.

Michael's return as a once prodigal son is enacted in a steplike progression that mirrors the rhythms of religious initiation—baptism, con-

firmation, the sacrament of marriage or the priesthood. Killing Sollozzo and the police captain, Michael commits himself to his father's honor and a life of crime, *simultaneously*. In Sicily, he is symbolically rebaptized a Sicilian, learning the history of the Italian Mafia, converting to the old traditions, even taking a local wife (subsequently killed). Back in America, he is apprenticed to his father. When Don Corleone dies, Michael takes over the business and the family, becoming godfather to Connie's firstborn and "Don Michael" to his business associates. During the actual christening of his godson (as Coppola depicts it), Michael's henchmen execute a series of murders that restore the internal solidarity of the Corleone syndicate and enlarge its boundaries and standing. When he acts his father's part, even Michael's face begins to resemble Don Vito's in his prime. Puzo's drama of monarchical, Oedipal succession reverses the familiar convention of second-generation "orphanhood" with which the novel begins.[23]

Any analytic attempt to separate what Michael does out of an emotional recommitment to his father or his ethnic past from what Michael accomplishes out of a pragmatic enlistment in his father's company is doomed to echo in the wilderness. Readers even vaguely familiar with the *Godfather* narrative know that the brutal simultaneous killings at the end of the novel reestablish and indeed improve the Corleones' standing in the American Mafia. But it is less well recognized, and the film underplays, how the ending reintegrates the Corleone household. Critics argue that Puzo deploys family imagery to win sympathy for Michael's otherwise morally egregious plans. Critics misconstrue the strategies of the novel, however, when they subordinate the familial pleadings of the narrative to its capitalist melodrama, as if the reintegration of the family were merely an ideological cover for the reincorporation of the syndicate. The two structures are interrelated; neither can rightly be subordinated to the other.

Standing godfather to his nephew, Michael accepts family leadership and embodies family unity, literalizing his newly won title as patriarch of an extended family, crowned "Don" Michael Corleone. Michael tightens the family circle around him. Hagen returns from Nevada. Traitors to family honor—Gatto, Rizzi, Tessio—are weeded out. Michael's success in restoring the Corleone empire is as much the act of a truly obedient son as his godfatherhood is a basis for taking over the syndicate, for the crime organization becomes a structure on which the Corleones are reunited. Coppola's film version leaves us with a trace of dissent in the air, ending with Kay's recognition of Michael's ruthless criminality. In the novel, Puzo restores the equanimity of husband

and wife and, by symbolic extension, of the Corleone family at large. Tom Hagen explains to Kay why it was necessary, from the standpoint of their ethos, for Michael to order the executions of Carlo Rizzi, Tessio, and the others. Kay acquiesces to Hagen's explanation and Michael's desire that she come home. She undergoes a rite of cultural self-transformation, to make herself into the kind of Italian-American woman the criminal environment expects. Whereas the film ends with Kay's anguish, the novel ends with Kay's conversion to Catholicism. Every morning she goes to mass with her mother-in-law, there to say, in the final words of the novel, "the necessary prayers for the soul of Michael Corleone" (*G*, 446). The peace of the Corleones is thereby restored. Michael does not mend matters with Kay simply to make the company perform better, any more than he restores the power of the syndicate simply to win his wife back and reintegrate his family; as Puzo has rigged the plot, the two go hand in hand.

III

The single aspect of *The Godfather* that seems to have made the deepest impact on the American public is Puzo's use of the central symbol of "the family." This symbol's influence has virtually changed overnight the American public's favorite term for a criminal organization.

—John Cawelti

For its depiction of an ethnic subculture that functions as an interest group, *The Godfather* would warrant attention from scholars—even if, like *The Fortunate Pilgrim*, the novel had disappeared into obscurity upon publication. But the novel has had a major impact on popular culture. The figure of "the godfather" outstrips all but the most ubiquitous cultural symbols, falling somewhere between Huckleberry Finn and Superman, perhaps better known than Uncle Sam himself.[24] The novel has possibly been the best-seller of all time. By 1971, when the first film was released, there were over one million hardcover copies in circulation—multiple copies in every library in every town in America—with at least ten million more paperbacks.[25] Historically, the reading of the novel framed the film—not, as in academic criticism, the other way around. The novel still sells, another five or ten million to date, in a $1.95 paperback series of "classic bestsellers." The most

immediate spin-offs were the two films; versions of those films rearranged for television; and the video format, which frequently offers
both films on a single cassette. By 1975, 260 more books on the Mafia
theme had been released, principally of the hard-boiled variety.[26] In
1984, Puzo himself tried again with *The Sicilian,* his fictional account
of Salvatore Giuliano. Ethnicity in crime has figured in several major
films, including *The Cotton Club* (coscripted by Coppola, Puzo, and
William Kennedy), *The Gang Who Couldn't Shoot Straight, Mean
Streets, Broadway Danny Rose, Heart of the Dragon, Scarface,* and
Once upon a Time in America. The popularity of the family "dynasty"
sagas, especially in their many ethnic varieties, can be traced in part
to Puzo's model. More telling still has been the ceaseless production
of *Godfather* clones, emphasizing the fusion of family and crime. Practically a genre of their own, they include (auto)biographical works like
Gay Talese's *Honor Thy Father,* Joseph Bonanno's *Man of Honor,* and
Antoinette Giancana's *Mafia Princess*; novels like Vincent Patrick's
Family Business and Richard Condon's *Prizzi's Honor*; academic studies like Francis A. J. Ianni's *A Family Business*; and films and tele-
plays, including "Our Family Honor," ABC's ill-fated attempt to combine Italian-American gangsters with Irish-American cops.

What are we to make of the lasting fascination with *The Godfather*?
Since its appearance, scholars have recognized *The Godfather* as an
artifact of what is called, perhaps misleadingly, the "new ethnicity."
The timing of the novel and its immediate offspring, from the book's
publication in 1969 to the television series in the late seventies, corre-
sponds to the rise of a celebratory attitude toward ethnic identity. This
celebration encompassed not only groups by and large still marginal—
blacks, Indians, newcomers from Asia and the Hispanic Americas—
but also the descendants of European immigrants, including the Italians, who were increasingly well established in the middle classes.
Necessarily, the connections drawn between the increased salience of
ethnicity and *The Godfather*'s popularity have been premised on the
prevailing interpretation of *The Godfather* as a two-part fantasy, in
which family sanctuary and successful corporate enterprise are polar
opposites. My reading of *The Godfather,* emphasizing the complicity
of family and business, calls for a reexamination of the novel's role in
the new ethnic self-consciousness. Both the popularity of *The Godfather* and the celebration of ethnicity are complex phenomena, reflecting a myriad of attitudes toward race, class, and gender as well as toward ethnicity—attitudes often in conflict with one another. By
claiming that *The Godfather* articulates the business of family, I do not
wish to mute these other voices. My ambition is to point the way to-

ward evaluating the voice of family business within the larger cacophony of debate.

Scholars like Jameson and Cawelti, working within the frame of traditional *Godfather* interpretation, seek to locate in the novel an anticapitalist energy—not an overt critique so much as an impulse, the energy of a potential critique partially veiled and misdirected. Both critics argue that Puzo portrays the Mafia as the center of a capitalist conspiracy and, simultaneously and irreconcilably, as a refuge from the conspiracy of capitalism. Because Puzo's Mafia functions as "the mirror-image of big-business," its brutality provides a focus for anticapitalist anxiety and an outlet for anticapitalist anger.[27] Similarly, the juxtaposed, equally powerful image of the family reflects, in Jameson's terms, a "Utopian longing" for escape from the prison house of capitalism. "The 'family' is a fantasy of tribal belongingness," echoes Cawelti, "that protects and supports the individual as opposed to the coldness and indifference of the modern business or government bureaucracy."[28]

In the standard view, *The Godfather*'s putative double fantasy reflects the misdirected energies of the new ethnicity; the new ethnicity arises from frustration with capitalism yet mutes its resistance in clamor about the decline of the family and traditional values.[29] My analysis of *The Godfather* suggests we might hesitate, however, before accepting the majority opinion, that the family in the novel embodies a refuge from capitalism. We need especially to question whether a case for the subsersive nature of *The Godfather* can rest on the myth of the Italian-American family as a precapitalist collectivity, when Puzo mounts all his forces to undermine this false dichotomy. The representation of the southern Italian family in *The Godfather* is not the kind of saccharine portrayal of innocent harmony—the haven in a heartless world—that scholars take as the benchmark of ethnic nostalgia. In *The Godfather,* capitalism is shown to accommodate, absorb, and indeed accentuate the structures of family and ethnicity. Americans respond to *The Godfather* because it presents the ethnic family not as a sacrosanct European institution, reproduced on the margins of America, but as a central American structure of power, successful *and* bloodied.

The desire of scholars to identify ethnic pietism as a locus of anticapitalist energy has blinded them to an alliance between the new ethnicity and procapitalist celebration of the family. This alliance is an insufficiently recognized strain in recent popular culture. At least until World War II, and perhaps into the 1970s, the dominant attitude toward the ethnic family in the United States assumed its incompatibility with capitalism, whether ethnicity was favored or not. The rabid Americanizers of the early decades attempted to strip immigrant workers of their familial and cultural loyalties. Among immigrants themselves, many feared that the price of upward mobility might be family solidarity, even as most in their midst deployed the family as a basis for group enterprise and mutual financial support. And intellectuals who were skeptical of capitalism, whether partly or wholly, based one strand of their critique on the damage that capitalism supposedly inflicted upon traditional family cultures. These family doomsayers tend less and less to be nativist Americanizers and guardians of ethnic tradition, but the nostalgia among scholars remains loud and clear. While the myth of the natural ethnic family still holds sway among intellectuals, the general public has come increasingly to accept and indeed welcome the idea of compatibility between ethnicity and capitalism. To accent the Italian example, for instance, public figures ranging from Lee Iacocca to Geraldine Ferraro and Mario Cuomo emphasize the contribution of family values to their own success stories, occasionally stretching our imaginations.[30] Similar rhetoric appears in the reemergence of the critique of the black family, in the widespread lauding of Asian- and Caribbean-American merchants and their schoolchildren, and in the general appeal for a new American work ethic. In this light, *The Godfather* feeds upon a strain of American rhetoric and expectation that has reached full salience only in the last decade.

Perhaps no artifact of American culture, popular or serious, has made the case for the business of family with quite the force of *The Godfather*. At no time in United States history has ethnicity enjoyed the vogue that it first achieved in the years of *The Godfather*'s greatest popularity and, in large measure, now maintains. The congruence is no coincidence. *The Godfather* does indeed participate in the new ethnicity by celebrating the ethnic family. But the Mafia achieves its romantic luster not because Puzo portrays the Italian-American family as a separate sphere, lying outside of capitalism, but because the Italian-American family emerges as a potent structure within it. The ethnic family in *The Godfather* feeds off a market sensibility rather than undermining it.[31] The Corleones can provide protection from the market only because they have mastered it. Indeed, the height of romance is reached in *The Godfather* with Puzo's choice of the Mafia as a model for family enterprise, for illegal family enterprises are capable of growing and expanding to an extent that the structure and regulation of legitimate capitalism will ultimately not support.

If *The Godfather* does indeed harbor anticapitalist energies, as a thorough reading of the novel might suggest, then perhaps scholars have been looking for that energy in the wrong places. Jameson concludes,

> When indeed we reflect on an organized conspiracy against the public, one which reaches into every corner of our daily lives and our political structures to exercise a wanton and genocidal violence at the behest of distant decision-makers and in the name of an abstract conception of profit—surely it is not about the Mafia, but rather about American business itself that we are thinking, American capitalism in its most systematized and computerized, dehumanized, "multi-national" and corporate form.[32]

Jameson and the others may be correct in insisting that fascination with *The Godfather* is motivated, at a deeper level, by anticapitalist anxiety. But the real scare occasioned by *The Godfather,* however much suppressed, is about capitalism not in its "most systematized and computerized, dehumanized" form, but rather in its more "intimate" varieties—ethnic, familial, personal. My reading of *The Godfather* suggests that if we wish to press charges against capitalism, we press charges against family and ethnicity, too. One strand of rhetoric in twentieth-century America, familiar to us from Howells's *Hazard of New Fortunes* and sources pervasive in our culture, suggests that Americans can go home to escape the specter of capitalism. Professionals often complain about taking work home with them, mentally if not literally. How much more frightening, then, is the alternative represented by Puzo: when some Americans go home to papa, they end up confronting the boss. Critics have been quick to interpret the brutality of the Mafia as a symbol for the violence to the invididual inherent in capitalism, and to assume that the family represents an escape from that violence. Yet the melodrama of *The Godfather* implicates the family not only in the success of the Corleone empire but in its cycle of self-destructive violence as well. Michael reintegrates the family business only *after* burying a brother, murdering a brother-in-law, alienating a sister, and betraying the trust of his wife. For Americans who experience family and economy as interwoven pressures (if not actual combined enterprises), the Mafia genre may allow a focusing of resentments, even if, inevitably, a Mafia analogy overstates them. For the cost of employing blood in the marketplace is finding the company at home.

My speculations notwithstanding, there is no direct way to study popular opinion and pinpoint the popular interpretation of *The God-father*. Indeed, it would be a mistake to assume there is any single interpretation (any more than there is a single "mind of the masses"). The great strength of popular literature may be its ability to entertain different, even contrary readings. But we can at least consider how other American artists catering to mass audiences have read the message of Puzo's novel. Two of the novel's best offspring—the film *God-father II* (1974) and *Prizzi's Honor* (1982) by Richard Condon—illuminate the novel's reception. Although Puzo receives credit for the *Godfather II* screenplay, along with Coppola, the film offers a perspective on the Corleones very different from either that of the novel or that of its reasonable facsimile, the first film. Pauline Kael actually throws almost all the credit for *Godfather II* to Coppola: "This second film . . . doesn't appear to derive from the book as much as from what Coppola learned while he was making the first."[33] For our purposes, however, it is not essential to distribute praise or blame, but simply to note that the film differs significantly enough from the original narrative to constitute a "rereading" of it (even if it is, in part, Puzo's own). Whereas the original *Godfather* narrative winds the fates of the Corleone family and the Corleone business together, Coppola's *Godfather II* separates the two strands. In *Prizzi's Honor,* on the other hand, Richard Condon uses all the devices in Puzo's novel, plus some of his own, to bond family and business tighter than ever. *Prizzi's Honor* surgically extracts Puzo's theme from underneath his excesses and Coppola's sermonizing and exposes it to a scintillating parody. The greatest testament to *The Godfather* has been paid not by critics or scholars but by Condon and John Huston, who directed the 1985 film version from Condon's own screenplay. Together, *Godfather II* and *Prizzi's Honor* can be construed as leading voices in a debate about the meaning of Puzo's novel and the future of the genre in which all three works participate.

IV

> This time I really set out to destroy the family. And I wanted to punish Michael.
>
> —FRANCIS COPPOLA[34]

Among scholars and film critics, *Godfather II* is commonly regarded as a greater work of art than the first movie, and infinitely preferable to the novel. In the standard interpretation, the second film sheds the Mafia of its sentimentally familial wrappings and reveals it for what it is and perhaps has always been: capitalistic enterprise in its most vicious form. Pauline Kael interprets this revelation moralistically. *Godfather II* is to be praised for eliminating the illusion that there might be anything desirable about the Corleone crime family.[35] Fredric Jameson stresses the historicity of *Godfather II*. For him, *Godfather II* explodes the illusion of the Mafia's "ethnicity" by attributing its origins to social arrangements in "backward and feudal" Sicily and its growth in America to the advanced stages of capitalism. The second film, according to Jameson, submits the themes of the first "to a patient deconstruction that will in the end leave its ideological content undisguised and its displacements visible to the naked eye."[36] For both Kael and Jameson, the deconstruction of the family and the ethnic group is a precondition for truth. But to my mind, it is they along with Coppola himself, not Puzo, who run the greatest risk of romanticizing the Sicilian-American family.

Godfather II narrates the further adventures of Michael Corleone, interspersed with flashbacks to the early days of his gangster father, Don Vito Corleone. The film is a political morality tale with a vengeance. In the original narrative, as Don Vito's business goes, so goes his family: their fates are intertwined. But in *Godfather II* Michael promotes his criminal enterprise at the expense of his personal family, group solidarity, and the Italian-American heritage. The central plot is a Byzantine series of maneuvers between Michael Corleone and the Jewish gangster Hyman Roth (modeled on Meyer Lansky). In their struggles, both Michael and Roth use a Corleone *capo-regime,* Pentangeli, now living in the old Corleone house on Long Island, as a pawn. To counter Roth, Michael manipultes the imagery of the criminal "family"—Roth as Michael's "father," Pentangeli as his "godson"—with complete cynicism. He succeeds by deliberately evacuating the idioms of family and ethnic solidarity of all meaning *except* as short-term (and short-sighted) instruments in a (transethnic, transfamilial) quest for power.

In the process, Michael's multinational crime outfit is reduced to merely a conglomerate of illegal enterprises. The network of ties with his father's retainers back in New York City unravels; Michael's nuclear family falls completely apart; and the southern Italian ethos that structured his father's world is vanquished entirely. Michael's evil is measured on a scale marked out in emphatically familial and ethnic units. The detail is endless. At the novel's end, Michael arranges the deaths not only of Roth (his "father") and Pantangele (his "son") but of his natural brother Fredo. Fredo has traded information with Roth; but he has also served as the only real father that Michael's children have ever known. Michael wins the trust of his partners and underlings only by blackmail, bribery, and the promise of mutual profit; such trust lasts only as long as convenient for all parties; and such relations frequently end in death as well as dissolution. Family and community have disintegrated among the Corleones. In the opening scene, the band at his son's first-communion party cannot play a tarantella but at Pantangele's frustrated urgings, comes up with "Three Blind Mice." In his portrayal of Michael, Coppola draws upon one of the most familiar of ethnic themes—second-generation infidelity—chastising him accordingly.

The loss of family/ethnicity, coupled with the consummation of Michael's business deals, spell one thing: Michael has *Americanized.* The Corleone empire has become, in Hyman Roth's phrase, "bigger than General Motors and AT&T." But it has cost Michael and his people their inheritance. It is an old story. By the film's end, Coppola has used Michael to update Abraham Cahan's *The Rise of David Levinsky,* outfitting the Russian-Jewish merchant as a 1970s CEO in Sicilian garb. Like Levinsky, Michael trades his roots for rubles. The film exploits that peculiarly American paranoia of cultural and social orphanhood amid fortune and fame. Isaac Rosenfeld called Cahan's novel "an exemplary treatment of one of the dominant myths of American capitalism—that the millionaire finds nothing but emptiness at the top of the heap."[37] Reviewing *Godfather II* in *Commentary,* William Pechter concluded that Michael was "another instance of that unrevivably exhausted cliché: it's lonely at the top."[38]

By comparison, Michael's father had found the top of his heap quite rewarding:

> And even Don Corleone, that most modest of men, could not help feeling a sense of pride. He was taking care of his world, his people. He had not failed those who depended on him and gave him the sweat of their brows, risked their freedom and their lives in his service. (*G,* 215)

At the end of the original narrative, Michael has lost his brother Sonny and the enforcer Luca Brasi to the five-family war; his *capo-regime* Tessio and brother-in-law Carlo Rizzi to treachery; and, possibly, his sister Connie, because of Carlo. But around him coalesces a new family regime: his mother, new wife Kay, Fredo, Tom Hagen, Clemenza and his men, the new capo Rocco Lampone and his men, and Albert

Neri. In Puzo's *Godfather,* family and business work in tandem, although with no guarantee of perfect profits or perfect harmony. *Godfather II* rends them asunder once again.

Ironically, *Godfather II* would seem to have been more hospitable than the original narrative to the twin appetites identified by Cawelti, Jameson, and other critics. Formal analysis suggests that if Americans in the seventies needed to vent rage at capitalism or fantasize about ethnic solidarity, then *Godfather II* would be the better vehicle for doing it. In the original story, the "mirror-image corporate capitalism" thesis is compromised, as Stanley Kauffmann has noted, by the unconventional "blood-bonds of loyalty" in the Mafia.[39] In *Godfather II,* those bonds are broken and Michael Corleone's operations are identified as mainstream big-time capitalism. In the original story, nostalgia about the Italian-American family is compromised by the Corleones' criminal enterprise. In *Godfather II,* the linear narrative of assimilation (Levinsky-style) feeds a yearning for a time when the Sicilian family withstood the ravages of individualism, personal greed, and the capitalist dynamic. For the television special (a mini-series first broadcast in 1977), Coppola rearranged films I and II into chronological order, neatly literalizing this romantic revision.

From directors to actors and critics, the professional film community bestowed raves upon *Godfather II,* hailing it as a sign that Hollywood could still produce art and rewarding it with the "Best Picture" Oscar for 1974. Yet the public reacted with an indifference that was more than a little surprising, given the unparalleled success of the novel and first film as well as the usual appetite for sequels. William Pechter accurately noted at the time, "I know of no one except movie critics who likes *Part II* as much as part one."[40] Public coldness to *Godfather II* has, if anything, deepened over the years. Curiosity brought millions into the theaters to see *Godfather II* the first time around, but most viewers told their friends afterward not to bother, nor did they return for a second showing. America's notorious disdain for unhappy endings may account for the film's unpopularity. Yet, having said so, we need to specify what, after all, makes Michael's triumph over his enemies, both Hyman Roth and the Senate Investigation Commission, so unsatisfying for so many.

As I have argued, *Godfather II* reasserts in unmistakable terms an antithesis between ethnic familial solidarity and success in capitalist enterprise. Perhaps the unpopularity of the film signals in part a resistance to this delusive dichotomy. Many intellectuals favor the film because they cling to the idea of a naturalistic, precapitalistic family.

Most Americans, on the other hand, increasingly believe in the compatibility between family values (which ethnics are now thought to epitomize) and the capitalist system. The original narrative promotes changing expectations; the sequel disappoints them. Certainly, the general audience resents the condescension in *Godfather II*, in which Coppola assumes he must strip the Corleones of all redeeming value in order to communicate the social costs of their megalomania. Moviegoers are unhappy less with the villainy of Michael's empire, which they acknowledge, than with the film's underlying, regressive sociology: that the breakup of family life is a necessary precondition for syndicate expansion. The tendency in our own era is no longer to underestimate the compatibility of the ethnic family and capitalism. The desire is now to overestimate, and hence romanticize, the growth potential and structural flexibility of the ethnic family business. In the final analysis, *Godfather II* strips the original narrative of its populist sociology, returning to the well-worn conventions of "up from the ghetto" novels. In *Prizzi's Honor*, on the other hand, Richard Condon restores the Mafia genre to its original source of strength—the icon of family business—generating a parody of Puzo's novel that is, at the same time, an interrogation of the business of family.

V

> They had to have at least two minds: the group mind that made them need to be a part of a family, and a separate individual mind that let them survive inside the grinding, double-crossing mass of their families, betraying their own people for money again and again, fifty thousand times. She was sure that it was the *macho* disease that made the Sicilians so fucking dumb. The family lived only for power—and money, because it meant more power. . . . Money, beyond a point that they had left behind long before, was only grease for the chariot. All those who followed behind the chariot gained money but, in appropriate measures, they were following the chariot because of the prodigious power on the chariot.
> —IRENE WALKER

Prizzi's Honor, like *The Godfather*, begins with a wedding as an occasion to bring the Prizzis together and explain the structure of their syndicate and their relations with other families:

> Corrado Prizzi's granddaughter was married before the baroque altar
> of Santa Grazia de Traghetto, the lucky church of the Prizzi family. . . .
> Don Corrado Prizzi, eighty-four, sat on the aisle in the front pew, right
> side of the church. . . . Beside Don Corrado sat his eldest son, Vincent,
> father of the bride, a cubically heavy man. . . . Beside Vincent was his
> brother, Eduardo, and his third "natural" wife, Baby. . . . Directly be-
> hind Don Corrado sat Angelo Partanna, his oldest friend and the family's
> counselor. . . . Behind the first two rows on the right side of the church,
> captured like pheromones in the thickening smell of hundreds of burning
> beeswax candles, in serried ranks, row upon row, were lesser Prizzis,
> one more Partanna [Charley], and many, many Sesteros and Garrones.[41]

Men from these four families—Prizzis, Partannas, Sesteros, and Gar-
rones—constitute the upper levels of the Prizzi organization. The central character of the novel, Charley Partanna, bears a surname that is
the name of a town in Sicily (destroyed by earthquake in 1969), like
Vito Corleone. On the internal cover of the hardcover (immediately
following the epigraph page of the Berkley paperback), the web of
command is diagrammed in a chart reminiscent of Francis A. J. Ianni's
breakdown of the Lupollo family (see appendix). This structural dia-
gram combines genealogy with company organization, suggesting that
not only corporate leadership but also the relation between the units
themselves is familial. A web of marriage unites the Prizzis with other
Mafia families. "Heavily larded among them were relatives from most
of the principal families of the *fratellanza* in the United States. Sal
Prizzi had married Virgi Licamarito, sister of Augie 'Angles' Licamarito, Boss of the Detroit Family . . . " (*PH*, 12). Condon explains the
system of "profitable repair" operating between the Prizzis and the
noncriminal sector of society—"the New York City Police Department
. . . the multinational conglomerates, the Papal Nuncio, the national
union leaders, . . . the best and brightest minds of the media, the dis-
trict attorney's office, the attorney general's office, and the White
House staff"—all of whom are represented at the wedding (*PH*, 12–
13). To an even greater degree than Puzo, with more irony yet more
telling detail, Condon explicates the mechanisms of power, responsibility, cash flow, and production: precisely how the semiretired don,
counselor Angelo Partanna, boss Vincent (chief operating officer), and
underboss Charley, who is in disfavor with Vincent but not with the
don, are related; how Eduardo heads the legitimate side of their operations, which does the laundering for the rackets, in what ways the
Prizzis differ from other Mafia crime outfits; and so forth. "They took
a poll and sixty-seven percent of the American people think that what

they all call the Mafia is the most efficiently run business organization
in the whole country," quips one of Condon's characters (*PH*, 122).
At times in *The Godfather*, Puzo's narrative commentary suggests a
tongue-in-cheek guide to the manners and mores of the Mafia. *Prizzi's
Honor* serves the Mafia as Lisa Birnbach's *Preppy Handbook* serves
the old-boy, old-money networks of the Northeast. The Prizzis call
themselves a brotherhood—*fratellanza*—but they mean by that not a
coterie of equals but a male hierarchy: "you must obey your superiors,
to death if necessary, without question," swears the initiate, "for it will
be for the good of the brotherhood" (*PH*, 43). The Prizzis operate as a
unit in both their personal and their business lives, decisions being controlled from the top and always with a mind to "Prizzi's Honor." The
main protagonist, Charley Partanna (Jack Nicholson's role) personifies
the system. In the opening scenes of the film, we see, in quick succession, the birth/baptism of Charley Partanna, the brass knuckles he is
given for a birthday present, and his blood-rite initiation into the Prizzis. Charley's father is Don Corrado's *consigliere*.[42] Charley is the
don's godson. Charley calls Don Corrado "padrino" ("little father"),
a diminutive meaning "godfather." At seventeen, Charley becomes a
made man in the family; in his thirties, he becomes the enforcer and
underboss; now, in his mid-forties, he is the heir apparent to the family,
after the don's son Vincent ("Domenic" in the film) and the don himself. "As we protect you, so you must protect Prizzi Honor" is the
Mafia creed (*PH*, 42). There is no functional distinction, as the Prizzis
understand it, between Charley's "birth" into the Prizzi family and his
"initiation" into it. From birth, he has been destined to be, in turn, a
dependent of this clan, a soldier, its chief executive in charge of security, and, ultimately, boss and don. "Both men, father and son, had
been bred to serve their feudal lords" (*PH*, 53). There is no more distinction between Charley's biological descent and cultural election
than between the familial and professional nature of the Prizzi organization.

Condon focuses throughout the novel on the interdependence of
family and business, the personal and professional, playing his comedy
on the tensions between them. No pretense of separation is maintained. Boss Vincent resents underboss Charley, for a scandal caused
by his own daughter, Maerose; so Vincent deals not through Charley,
as custom dictates, but through his father, Angelo. The personal pen-
etrates the professional, and vice versa. Business is conducted in
homes as well as in offices, and frequently over meals. Don Corrado
lives in a grand old city mansion, "as befitted a business executive,"

but owns neither the home nor any of its contents, out of respect for both "the rules of humility and austerity" and the diligence of the Internal Revenue Service. Don Corrado's house, literally, is his business quarters. The lack of private lives is underscored by the virtual absence of women in the inner sanctum of the Prizzi family, a literalization of both Mafia mythology and Puzo's narrative precedent.[43]

The structural hierarchy, male bonding, and Sicilian cult of honor constitute the context for the action of the novel. Like that of *The Godfather*, the plot in *Prizzi's Honor* involves a botched caper that exposes the Prizzis to hostile maneuvers by the other New York families and leads to a crisis of managerial/familial succession; familial double-crosses, with Charley acting Michael's role as the prodigal son, who temporarily turns against the family; and a murderous resolution that brings the appointed heir to power, restores the primacy of the crime organization, and resolidifies the nuclear and extended family of the new don. The details in Condon's novel and in Huston's film echo those in Puzo's and Coppola's works in an amusing game of one-upmanship. A wedding initiates both works, but Puzo/Coppola produce an adman's fantasy of a Sicilian garden party. Condon and Huston, on the other hand, produce a credible representation of an actual Brooklyn wedding: the women dressed in black, not white; a VFW hall, rather than a garden; Sinatra tunes as well as old folk songs; and so forth. The closer attention one pays, from first phrase to last, the funnier and more pointed the connections. More important than the refinement of *The Godfather*'s cultural milieu is Condon's brilliant plot conceit, which highlights and at the same time satirizes the family-business mentality of the Prizzis.

Prizzi's Honor is, in the words of a *Playboy* reviewer, "the best episode of *As the Underworld Turns* since Puzo's *Fools Die*."[44] The reference to the soap opera is not gratuitous, since the action of *Prizzi's Honor* involves a problem marriage between its central characters, Charley and Irene (née Maida Walcewicz) Walker, who is a free-lance assassin, or "contractor," in the occasional employ of the Prizzis. The marriage between Charley and Irene violates the sanctity of the Prizzis' family business. Irene is a Catholic Pole, whose former husband (murdered by Charley on orders from the don) is a Russian Jew. "How come you aren't a wop and I meet you at Teresa Prizzi's wedding?" asks Charley, who falls in love and marries her against that logic (*PH*, 33). Irene's foreign background is merely a symbol for her real outsiderhood. "You and this woman see everything with the same kind of eyes," Maerose tells Charley, knowing better and setting Charley up for a fall (*PH*, 96). True, both Charley and Irene kill people for the mob; otherwise, though, their operations are like night and day. "Let's see how it goes," warns Angelo. "A mixed marriage" (*PH*, 144). The film plays up the comedy of middle-class manners between Charley, an Italian chauvinist, and his wife, Irene, who wants to keep on working after marriage. In the novel, Irene's sexual autonomy is, quite explicitly, a corollary of her independence in the marketplace of crime. Irene is a loner, a one-woman company, an entrepreneur whose approach to business exemplifies the norms of a free market:

> The fantastic thing about Charley was that he *was* a Boy Scout. Charley paid his dues to his life. Charley believed. . . . Charley knew he was serving a purpose, not a buck. . . . It was different for [Irene]. . . . She wasn't locked into any family, she was a straight, commercial freelance who couldn't expect any protection from anybody if she didn't do the job right. . . . (*PH*, 117–18)

While Charley is a *sottocapo,* Irene is a *contractor.* The idiom is perfect. Irene makes deals independently, strictly on a cash basis, accepting no retainer and maintaining no ties to any particular outfit. As a cover, Irene is a tax consultant. To her the world operates simply as the circulation of dollars; loyalty is just a matter of the origin of the next paycheck. She is therefore the perfect foil to a family-business mentality.

Just prior to the novel's denouement, the Prizzis appear to be in shambles. No money is coming in, the Filargi caper has soured, and the other families are maneuvering to take over the entire business. Vincent has been assassinated, and Charley is turning traitor. The Prizzis suffer as the Corleones suffer after Sonny's death. Condon resolves the crisis by duplicating one strand of *The Godfather* 's narrative logic, turning the family over to the rightful heir—in this case, Charley. Don Corrado offers Charley the position of boss, second-in-command, with the promise of that of don after Don Corrado's death. The Prizzis need Charley, yet Charley needs to earn that promotion. Charley must repair the family's relations with the other syndicates and with the police; and, in the dual logic that organizes these narratives, Charley must prove his fidelity. The price is steep: he must deliver Irene to the cops himself—dead. "Zotz her? Clip Irene?" (*PH*, 294). The borderline in Charley's decision is clearly demarcated. Will he honor his contract with Irene or the Prizzis' ethic of familial loyalty?

"The family were what he had been since Sicily started breeding people. They were his food. They had been with him forever. There were hundreds of thousands of them, most of them ghosts, some of them bodies. They were all staring at him, waiting to know what he would do" (PH, 296). The weight of all the Prizzi tradition, his respect for his *padrino* and father, who are waiting for his decision, and Charley's training and dreams overdetermine the decision:

> He thought of becoming Boss of the Prizzi family. His entire life had pointed him toward that. He had trained for that since he was thirteen years old and now it could happen. He could feel the power as if it were the texture of fine, strong cloth between his fingers. He could taste it as if his mother had come back to cook one more glorious meal for him. He thought of the money . . . eight million dollars a year, every dime tax free, every dime safe in Switzerland. . . . (PH, 269)

Becoming boss means filling his father's shoes, his mother's expectations: family is money is destiny when you are born into the Prizzis. Eight million dollars and Mom's home cooking, too! In *Prizzi's Honor,* as in *The Godfather,* the working out of the Oedipal crisis prompts the return of the prodigal son and the reintegration of the crime family. Charley's quest for power runs along pathways of filial obedience; the strength of the Prizzis depends on Charley's urgency to obey. Being asked to become don is for Charley, as for Michael, an offer he can't refuse.

Charley sets Irene up for the kill, by telling her that the don accepted her terms of settlement, paying all she asked. Irene knows that Charley is lying, because the don would never settle the Las Vegas score by returning the money she stole from the Prizzis.[45] She considers the love-match canceled. In accordance with her own methods, Irene prepares to kill Charley, transmuting the marriage contract into a murder contract in her mind: "She didn't feel the grief anymore. Charley was a contract she had put out herself, and had given to herself; full fee" (PH, 305). In contrast to Irene's cold-bloodedness, Charley feels the righteous conviction of Prizzi duty:

> [Irene] had a different and much paler, thinner meaning when he judged her beside the total meaning he got from his family. He was now Boss of that family. He had to set an example that would be remembered as long as the family stood. He saw dimly that it was right to sacrifice the woman he loved so that the family could go on and on fulfilling its honor, which was its meaning. He suddenly saw clearly that Irene had stepped so far out of line that there was nothing left to do but to whack her. (PH, 300)

Charley kills Irene before Irene is able to kill him. Charley wins not because he is technically more proficient or luckier but because he has the *emotion* of Prizzi honor motivating him and the full force of the Prizzi clan backing him up. However much the business of family causes friction (the "grinding, double-crossing mass of their families"), still there is a corporate front (*PH*, 103). Irene dies because she stands alone, without a family, without protection.[46] The structural equivalent in *The Godfather* is the death of Carlo Rizzi, kin by marriage, but an outsider, a traitor. In the ending of each novel, the integrity of the crime family is reinstated by sacrificing a "family" member whose membership was suspect in the first place and compromised by that member's activities. The murder of Irene is also an ironic footnote, highlighted in the film, on the conventions of romantic love so favored in American popular culture.

"The surprise ending will knock your reading glasses off!" runs a blurb on the paperback, credited to the *New York Times*. Yet the eliminating of Irene, and Charley's having to do it, is a perfect culmination for the novel's strategy of playing feudal capitalism off against free-market independence. Alternatively, Charley and Irene could flee the Prizzis and go together to Hong Kong, where they would be outfitted with new identities. (Irene's past misdeeds to the Prizzis, and the current difficulties with the police, preclude Irene's remaining with the family.) This alternative ending would require a conversion in Charley's character, to the point where he could see himself turning his back on history for autonomy and romantic love. But at least such an ending would remain consonant with the hypothesis of the narrative—namely, that feudal capitalism, which dominates the American underworld, operates by sacrificing individualism to the group. Readers and film viewers are surprised because they expect a dreamy ending, in which Charley gets his family and Irene, too. Such an ending, however, violates the business of family in the world of the Prizzis. The principle of family honor precludes romantic love because romance presumes a free-market logic of one-to-one relationships. In the film, the overlay of sappy music and the casting of Nicholson as Charley, who acts superbly but is mistaken for Nicholson the loner, tips expectations in the direction of a romanticized ending. To conclude with Charley as the don, while still happily married to Irene, would be to entertain a fantasy of irreconcilables (of the sort that scholars characteristically misattribute to *The Godfather*). In the final chapter, Charley calls up Maerose, initiating their reconciliation. Maerose and Charley are now both outcasts who have returned to the family. Maerose's claim on Charley is ethnic. She reminds him in the film, "We grew up together, Charley. We are the same people." By marrying Maerose, Charley reunites the Prizzis and Partannas in the incestuous bond that maintains the power of their family.

What are the implications of *Prizzi's Honor* as a revision of *The God-father*? Like Puzo, Condon makes it clear from start to finish that *the* theme to be pursued in a Mafia narrative is the question of business and family. Condon's comedy is effective because we, as readers, already understand the structural interdependence of business and family in the Mafia and accept it basically as truth. Condon does not mean, of course, to celebrate the business of family. Whereas Puzo provides a thin coat of narrative irony, Condon paints in layers and layers of satire, usually comic, but occasionally courting a grimmer dimension. From start to finish, Puzo eliminates no more than a dozen or so mobsters, who deserve it anyway. Condon burns down the Palermo Gardens nightclub, with 89 people dead, 217 severely burned, and 4 blinded, most of them innocent guests and "civilians." Condon also corners his main character into killing his wife. Both *Godfather II* and *Prizzi's Honor* submit the Mafia to moral scrutiny. *Godfather II* depends on a romanticized ideology of family for its critique, so that Coppola, in the final analysis, is caught within a family-business hermeneutic circle. *Prizzi's Honor* adopts a position truly contrary to that of the family-business mentality; it assumes, in the figure of Irene, the possibility of a free marketplace, in which individuals function independently of one another and the realm of the personal is uncluttered by the operations of business. In so doing, Condon is able (like Puzo in the first novel) to question the naïveté of free-market spokesmen and ethnic romanticizers, who think that the domains of "family" and the "group" are extra-economic. But Condon accomplishes something far more emphatically than does either Puzo in *The Godfather* or Coppola in *Godfather II*: that is, to chart the special costs of doing business familially.

In *Prizzi's Honor*, the family business grows beyond its members' need for wealth, annexing their freedom to its own dynamic, the growth of the syndicate. "Money, beyond a point that they had left long before, was only grease for the chariot" (*PH*, 103). The Prizzi organization empowers its members, but it also imprisons them, psychologically and literally. Other, more legitimate forms of family business may not police their boundaries with quite the brutality of the Prizzis, but they may not prosper as much either. In *The Godfather*, the loss of individual liberty among the Corleones, however implicit, is buried under the glorification of familial loyalty, whereas Richard Condon's carefully developed "surprise" ending etches in the popular consciousness an image of familial tyranny to give nightmares: Charley knifing Irene, in the throat, from the marriage bed.

As an analysis of the mechanics of family capitalism and a critique of its appeal, *Prizzi's Honor* supersedes *The Godfather*. Let us not forget, however, that Puzo made the way for Condon's accomplishment. Puzo is often maligned for exploiting the stereotype of Italian-American criminality, which has long been used to discriminate against the general Italian-American population. But, in the final analysis, *The Godfather* does not so much rehash an old tale, whatever its strands of inheritance, as tell a new one. In *The Godfather,* Puzo refashions the gangster genre into a vehicle for reversing the traditional antithesis between ties of blood and the American marketplace. In so doing, he transforms the stock character of the Italian-American outlaw into the representative super(business)man; and he transforms the lingering image of immigrant huddled masses into the first family of American capitalism.

Appendix: THE PRIZZI FAMILY
(1918–   )

CORRADO PRIZZI

VINCENT PRIZZI
Boss

ANGELO PARTANNA
Consigliere

EDUARDO PRIZZI
Legitimate Enterprises and Political
Activities

Beniamino Sestero   Arrigo Gerrone
Lieutenants

CHARLES PARTANNA
Underboss

CAPIREGIMES
Rocco Sestero
Salvatore Prizzi

Gambling (National Sports Book. Numbers and
Policy, Casinos in Nevada, Atlantic City, Flor-
ida, Bahamas, Aruba, London). Narcotics.
Loan Sharking, Labor Racketeering. Extortion.
Pornography, Alcohol, Others

SOLDIERS
(Grouped under Capiregimes)
980 Active—1120 Inactive

CRIMINAL INCOME REINVESTMENT

Banking, Insurance, Interstate Trucking, Electronics,
Heavy Construction, Real Estate Investment and
Management (81 downtown and midtown buildings in
9 cities), Cable Television, Brokerage and Underwrit-
ing, Personal Loan Companies, Wineries, Food Manufacturing and Importing: Fast Food Chain Franchis-
ing, Theatrical and TV Motion Picture Production,
Phonograph Records, Video Manufacturing, Hardcover and Paperback Publishing, Magazine Publishing, 3 Law Firms (NY, LA, Zurich), 11 Hospitals, 1
Flower Farm, 137 Hotels, 23 Laundries

GROSS ANNUAL BUSINESS
$1,770,000,000

Police, Judiciary, Legislative, Executive Government
at Federal, State, County, Municipal and Ward Levels

GROSS ANNUAL BUSINESS
(Tax Free)
$490,000,000

TO OVERSEAS BANKS
Switzerland, Panama, Bahamas, Nigeria

Comping for Count Basie

ALBERT MURRAY

I

In autobiography as in fiction, nothing has more to do with what the story is really about than the voice of the narrator. So the main thing was to get his voice on the page. Everything else came after that. Incidents mean only as much as the way they are told makes them mean. If you couldn't help him sound like himself in print, you'd probably be better off working on a book about Count Basie than on one by Count Basie about himself.

Obviously it is the voice of the narrator that establishes not only the physical point of view, including the relative sharpness or vagueness of focus and the limits of the field of vision, but also the listening post, which determines the reader's distance from the alarums and excursions, if any, and also whether what is being said is heard verbatim or at second remove—and how much is to be heard in either case.

It is also the storyteller's voice that creates the overall atmosphere as well as the specific mood for each situation and sequence of action. The on-the-page equivalent of vocal cadence, tone, and timbre, together with vocabulary, syntax, and imagery, determines just *how* whatever is being recollected and recounted is to be taken. Whether the narrator is deadpan or scowling or smiling or laughing or has his tongue in his cheek makes all the difference in the world. The tone of voice may not only represent a sense of life that is not otherwise stated; it may also of its very nature counterstate or cancel out any direct assertion or avowal.

Unlike the narrator of stories in the third person, who can either maintain one position and one voice or shift position and voice source at will, the autobiographer speaks in his own voice at all times. Even when the conversation with and between others is quoted as if with total recall, it is still only an approximation. It is, in fact, the narrator's mimicking of others with his own voice barely disguised, and indeed what really counts is the impression he wishes to convey. Sometimes he may go so far as to put words and phrases that are obviously his own into the mouths of others in order to create a desired effect. But after all, this is only a storytelling device that has been employed since the days of "talking animals," during the age of fable, and that also permits the ever-so-earthy peasant language of the aristocrats in most folktales.

Third-person dialogue, on the other hand, can almost always be taken as literal transcription. Moreover, such is also the convention of third-person narrative that the degree of intimacy and omniscience the storyteller chooses enables him to represent and indeed give voice to as many memory banks and individual streams of consciousness and to reveal as many private thoughts, anxieties, fears, wishes, confusions, and even motives as suit his purpose.

Even when fiction is narrated in the first person, there are many more options than the autobiographer has. You may be an outsider with only a spectator's view of things, or you may be personally involved in the action to some small or large degree. Or you may exist at the very center of all the action, with everything happening around you and to you.

As autobiographer, you have only one position, and that is at the center of everything that matters. Even though you may represent yourself as being only a passive witness to the times, you still occupy what Henry James called the "commanding center." Yours is the central informing intelligence, the comprehensive or overall sensibility that determines the operative frame of reference. And so it is that the autobiographer's voice is the vector of the basic sense of life, of attitude toward experience, and hence of the value system that everything in the story represents.

And so it is also that the limitations of the autobiographer's awareness are ultimately also an important part of what his story is about. Inferences may also be drawn from deliberate omissions. After all, since what is at stake is a matter not of guilt but of attitude, there is no literary Fifth Amendment. Language, as Kenneth Burke once said, is symbolic action, the dancing of an attitude. So, under certain conditions, is silence. In the context of a discourse, ellipsis, omission, and silence are also verbal actions and as such also represent the dancing of an attitude.

The point is that it is always the storyteller's story because it is his voice that is the vector, even when he is anonymous, as when he is working in terms of the third person and seems totally concerned with depicting somebody else at the compositional center, if not the protagonist. It is still his voice that provides the emotional as well as the physical context in terms of which everything else is defined.

II

And yet, as literary craftsman, the cowriter of an as-told-to autobiography is also present on every page. Never as a partner in a duet, to be sure, but he is there nonetheless. Actually, his role is very much the same as that of the piano accompanist who comes onstage with the solo vocalist or instrumentalist. Once the performance gets under way, it is as if the very best accompanists are neither seen nor heard.

Even as the accompanist vamps until the soloist is ready, what he plays is like so many bars of preparatory silence. And the same is almost as true of his obbligatos and fills. Everything he plays is specifically designed to enhance the presence and the unique traits of the featured soloist, not to divert attention from him in any degree whatsoever. Nor does such background support compromise the integrity and authenticity of the solo as solo statement. Few soloists perform a cappella. Many singers accompany themselves on the piano, and perhaps even more do so on guitar.

Sometimes the accompanist, for all his unobtrusiveness, actually leads and prompts the soloist. Sometimes he only follows, perhaps most often as if he were whispering yes, yes, yes; and then, and then, and then; go on, go on, go on; amen, so be it. Even when he engages in call-and-response exchanges, it is always as if the soloist is carrying on a dialogue with someone who is either absent or totally imaginary. But always the accompanist is there to keep the melodic line and its frame of reference intact, and the soloist in key, in tune, and in time.

For all that, however, it is only at the end of the performance, when the bows, if any, are being taken, that the accompanist shares a brief moment in the spotlight with the soloist. And yet two of the most prominent and influential contemporary American musicians, both of whom were easily identifiable by their piano styles, were also two of the very best comp artists who ever did it. One was Duke Ellington, and the other was Count Basie himself.

III

Count Basie's conception of the role of the literary craftsman (and re-search assistant) as cowriter of an as-told-to autobiography was just about everything you could want it to be. All-time exemplary band-leader and performing artist as improviser that he always was to his very fingertips, he was completely aware and appreciative of the fact that what he was involved in was an act of composition. He knew very well that getting his voice down on the page was not simply a matter of making a literal transcription of his recollections and then tidying them up for the printer.

As for dictating sequences and anecdotes into a tape recorder, very few people seem able to do that in their most natural or characteristic cadence, syntax, and tone of voice. More often than not, they become so self-conscious and spend so much time choosing words, revising their phrases, and measuring their statements that they not only inter-rupt the normal flow of discourse but even lose the train of thought from time to time and have to begin again, and again, only to end up sounding stilted, at best. To be sure, there are those who do manage to maintain a steady on-mike flow. But usually they sound more like overstylized media types than like the individuals they project other-wise. Indeed, in such instances their words are only likely to become on-the-page equivalents of masks and costumes. In any case, Basie knew that the microphone patter that he used onstage and in interviews with entertainment-page reporters would not do for the kind of book he had in mind.

In point of fact, a small Sony tape recorder with a tiny clip-on mi-crophone was used at every working session over a period of six years, and transcriptions were made from most of them. The trick was to get him to respond to questions by speaking not into the microphone but to you in a casual, person-to-person conversational tone and tempo. And that meant getting him in the frame of mind that made him try to take you back into his past with him, in much the same way as he was soon to do when he took you to Kansas City and later on to Red Bank, New Jersey. Then, instead of addressing himself to abstract issues as such, he would simply become anecdotal and evoke people and details about places and days and nights and ongoing actions and relationships. Once he got an anecdote going, the "I said," "he said," "she said" particulars tended to fall into place with no effort at all.

The whole procedure worked as smoothly as it did because it was not really a new approach to composition for Basie. After all, he had been collaborating with staff arrangers and free-lancers as well for almost fifty years. Also entirely in line with his definitive orientation to improvisation, he had his own, functional conception of dictation. For him it was mostly a matter of feeding suggestions and instructions directly from the keyboard to band members during rehearsals, or perhaps during an actual performance. In either circumstance, it was only sometimes that his statements were repeated literally. At other times they were to be complemented—perhaps through counterstatement.

So, he was already all set to utilize the services of a cowriter as the literary equivalent of both the piano accompanist or comp artist, who would supply him with chordal structures and progressions in the form of documentary notes, press clippings, photographs, recordings, and data from various colleagues over the years. At the same time you were also to be his staff arranger and copyist, who would prepare tentative score sheets, which the two of you would rework and polish together, as if rehearsing the band.

This made you Count Basie's literary Count Basie and also Count Basie's literary extension of such legendary arrangers as Eddie Durham, Buck Clayton, Buster Harding, Jimmy Mundy, Andy Gibson, Ernie Wilkins, Frank Foster, Frank Wess, and Thad Jones all rolled into one. No mean task or honor for you, but everyday stuff for him. And when he realized that you, for your part, already conceived your own writing in terms of vamps, choruses, riffs, call-and-response patterns, breaks, chases, and so on to out-choruses and tags, all he could do was point his finger at you as if at a sideman and say, "You got it." Which, forever after you began addressing him by this nickname in the Gonzelle White troupe, only to have him turn it back on you, became "You got it, Mister Bateman. Where the hell are we, Mister Bateman? How did I get off on this, Mister Bateman? Get me out of here, Mister Bateman. Stop pointing and just get us out of here, Mister Bateman. Hell, you the one with the dates, Mister Bateman; you tell me when I was supposed to do whatever it was, and I'll tell you what I remember about it."

Not only did he appreciate the fact that getting the voice on the page with all of its distinctively personal inflections was the sine qua non of an autobiography; he also understood that, once there, it had to function as a series of paragraphs and chapters in a book. And what he wanted was the kind of book that made you see and hear as you read. Indeed, he really wanted a book that would unfold like a movie script, with long and medium camera shots and close-ups, with montage and flashback sequences, and all the rest, including panning, zooming, cutting to, crosscutting, fading in and fading out.

IV

Very much in line with the many recapitulations and revisions required by an as-told-to autobiography was the fact that, being a performing artist, Basie was as used to regular rehearsals as he was to improvisation, so you could count on taking him back over some details time after time until the replay turned out to be a statement that he was willing to release to the public. As should surprise no one, he was no more inclined to release raw material as a writer than he was given to doing so as a musician.

He did not think that unguarded or loose expression represented one's true, honest, and material self. It represented one as careless, unorganized, and confused. As far as he was concerned, one should always get oneself together before making any kind of presentation to others. This was not unusual for a bandleader. Very rarely do any musicians worthy of the name ever presume to play, or even rehearse, anything without first tuning up their instruments and getting in key, if only to get deliberately out of key. In any case, as fresh and impromptu as the best Basie bands always sounded, they were always well drilled. Even the widely celebrated unwritten, informal, or head arrangements were worked up during rehearsal and reworked during subsequent rehearsals. Although many riff patterns and ensemble figures also came into being during actual performances, those that became a part of the repertoire were reworked and refined in rehearsal after rehearsal. Such arrangements were called "heads" mainly because the band had memorized them long before they were copied out on the score sheets.

Relaxed and basically geared to improvisation as Basie's bands always were, his musicians always looked well-rehearsed and together. Nor was there ever any ring-around-the-collar sloppiness about their appearance. Their uniforms were sharp, and their deportment on the bandstand was beyond reproach. There was always room to hang loose and swing, but careful preparation was as characteristic of the Basie approach to performance as were the unexpected accents, on-the-spot obbligatos, and extended vamps, solos, and out-choruses. One more time, indeed.

V

Even when it is offered as an entirely unprepossessing personal record of one's own life, undertaken with great reluctance, an autobiography is still of its very nature an exercise in exemplification, concerned with the narrator's sense of endeavor, fulfillment, and failure. As such it is really a species of fiction. It is a story with an explicit or implicit moral.

Sometimes it may be structured in terms of a dramatic plot (one thing's *leading* to another) that unfolds on the dynamics of tragedy, comedy, melodrama, or farce. Or, perhaps just as often, its story line may be only a simple matter of one thing's *following* another, as in the genre of the picaresque novel, that literary extension of the logbook, diary, or journal (and perhaps also the rogue's deposition!). In either case, it is a story, and as such it takes people and events from the context of vital statistics and the facts of everyday life into the realm of legend, myth, fairy tale, and fable (which, by the way, also has the effect of transforming the profane into the sacred).

It is the stuff of legend, myth, fairy tale, and fable, not the concrete facts per se, that accounts for the widespread interest in such classics of autobiographical writing as the *Confessions* of Jean Jacques Rousseau, the *Autobiography* of Benjamin Franklin, the *Narrative of the Life of Frederick Douglass, a Slave, Written by Himself,* and *The Education of Henry Adams* (written in the third person!) that persists from generation to generation. It is not that factual precision is unimportant but rather that such books are read less for the information than for the story.

The autobiography is a form of history, even so. Being a personal record of one's own life, it is of its very nature an exercise in chronological documentation, which, however skimpy in the details, is obviously intended to convey historical data. Thus it is a historical document that may be the subject of scholarly investigation, and its usefulness as such depends on its accuracy and its scope, both of which may be limited in some degree (but not necessarily compromised) by the author's inevitable subjectivity.

Whatever its limitations, however, the autobiography is still an indispensable form of historical documentation. So, along with all considerations based on the assumption that style functions as statement in autobiography, much the same as it does in fiction, there is also the matter of content: what is included and to what purpose, and what is omitted either by design or through oversight. After all, whatever the story line of an autobiography is, the book itself is made up of factual details about real people involved in actual events.

VI

What Basie had in mind was a book giving his own account of some of the highlights of some of the things he had been involved in during the course of his career as a musician and bandleader over the years, including a few incidents thrown in for laughs. As far as he was concerned, there were no axes to grind, no special ideological points to make, and no old scores to settle. He did not even express any overall urge to set the record straight. He simply dealt with longstanding misrepresentations and misinterpretations as they came up in the normal sequence of putting the book together.

That was the way he put it for the cowriter at the very outset of the collaboration, and not only was it justification enough for the undertaking of an autobiography at any time; it was also precisely what was most urgently needed: not a gossip- or sensation-oriented show-biz confession, which, as far as he was concerned, was out of the question anyway.

What was needed was the first book-length treatment of the Count Basie story by anybody at all, because although he had never suffered a lack of publicity and promotion but had been one of the most famous men of his time for nearly five decades, with a musical signature that is to this day still perhaps almost as instantly identifiable in international circles as the national anthem, there had at that time been only one book about him. It was entitled *Count Basie and His Orchestra* and had been written by an Englishman named Raymond Horricks, but it was mostly about the personnel of this orchestra over the years, with only a thirty-four page sketch of Basie himself. *The World of Count Basie*, by Stanley Dance, didn't come out until Basie's own project was under way, and it too was mostly about members of the band.

Moreover, the personality sketches that had appeared as features in various journalistic publications were, for the most part, either based on very brief entertainment-reporter interviews, usually given on the go or backstage and almost always off the cuff, or derived from secondary-source materials, including other articles and unverified eye-witness and hearsay accounts.

Anyway, what Basie wanted the cowriter to help him put together was a book giving his own version of what struck him as the key elements and turning points of his life. And he was very aware of the fact that, once released, it would become the prime source (as likely to be double-checked as taken at face value) and point of departure for more detailed, monographic studies and attempts at full-scale biographical undertakings as well.

The most obvious model for what he had in mind was the souvenir booklet that record companies sometimes include in deluxe boxed sets. It would contain more information about his childhood in Red Bank and Asbury Park, his apprenticeship in Harlem and on the entertainment circuits, and also his years as a Kansas City journeyman than had ever been published anywhere before. In addition, it would provide the most comprehensive running account of the band's extensive travels over the years, because he wanted future readers to realize that the band did not spend most of its time in theaters and dance halls in places like Harlem or Chicago's South Side but that it was a national as well as an international institution.

Also, instead of providing a formal discography as an appendix, he decided to treat the performance and reworking of key items in the band's repertoire as the integral part of the main action of the narrative that they indeed were. When he thought of the book as a bound volume, he visualized it as standing on the record shelf at one end of the Basie collection, with a complete discography by experts like Jorgen Jepsen or Chris Sheridan at the other.

VII

Most of the major omissions from *Good Morning Blues* were intentional. Naturally, some were due to faulty memory, but some lapses were also deliberate. As Freddy Green pointed out to the cowriter early on, Basie was a much more reliable source of historical particulars than most of the self-styled experts. But he was also the type of person who would pretend not to know something just in order to find out what somebody else knew. He was never one for showing that he knew more about anything than somebody else. But when he said, "Is that where that happened? Boy, my memory is gone! I thought that was out in Washington," anytime he said something like that, you'd better recheck your sources!

Sometimes he would say, "Let's skip that, because I might not have it right, and I don't want anybody saying, 'See there, he don't know what he's talking about.'" But in writing about Kansas City, for instance, he just simply had no intention of going on record with everything he had seen or heard about the workings of the Pendergast Machine, the business interests and invisible associates of Ellis Burton and Piney Brown, or the political connections of Bennie Moten. About the Reno Club, for instance, he said,

> Goddammit, somebody is always asking me to paint them a detailed picture of everything that went down in there, and name names. But why the hell should I get into that? My business in there was music, and that didn't have a damn thing to do with naming names and meddling around in somebody else's gig. Hell, ask them about it, not me. If they make a movie and show some other stuff, that's okay as long as it's true. But I don't want it in my book. Don't care how true it is. You don't have to go around talking about other folks' business just because what you're saying is true.

On the matter of the tells-all confession memoir, Count Basie was no less insightful than Somerset Maugham, for instance, who in *The Summing Up* said,

> I have no desire to lay bare my heart, and I put limits to the intimacy that I wish the reader to enter upon with me. There are matters on which I am content to maintain my privacy. No one can tell the whole truth about himself. It is not only vanity that has prevented those who have tried to reveal themselves to the world from telling the whole truth; it is direction of interest. . . .

There was also Basie's unimpeachable sense of propriety. Never a blabbermouth, once he became a public figure he was not only extremely concerned with not becoming embroiled in controversy of any kind; he was also always very much alert to the untold damage a mean or even a careless word from him could do to other people's reputations and careers. Nor did he recognize any statute of limitations on promises made in the course of tipping on the Q.T.

If the story he has chosen to tell is thereby made short on scandalous self-exposé, it is also short on outrageous self-inflation. If it is short on explanation, it is also short on false claims and pretentiousness. It is obviously a success story, but he does not presume to have a formula.

And if it is short on advice, it is also short on condescension and pontification. If it also is short on the usual protest and polemics that are so predictable in the personal accounts of many other Afro-Americans, it is also short on gratuitous (and politically naïve) self-degradation and the rhetoric of sackcloth and ashes or phony despair.

Behind all of that supercool, laid-back understatement, Old Base was mostly having himself a ball, and in his daily contacts with white people over the past forty-five years, he was much less concerned with keeping from being done in by hostile ones than with keeping from being bored to utter exhaustion by worshipful ones (saying Bill this and Bill that in no time at all, curiously oblivious to the fact that true intimates were calling him Base). He did not presume to speak for other Afro-Americans; instead, he set them an impeccable example of how to carry yourself in a way that always commands respect as well as admiration and even awe.

VIII

In the case of *Good Morning Blues,* some key answers to very basic and entirely appropriate questions about the influence of the cowriter whether insidious, thinly disguised, or obvious, on both form and content are already a matter of public record. There was *Stomping the Blues*. There was the essay entitled "Duke Ellington, Vamping Till Ready." There was *The Omni-Americans,* and there was also *The Hero and the Blues*.

The invitation to collaborate with Count Basie on his memoirs was a signal honor indeed, but it was also a great responsibility, which was accepted not only because the subject matter was interesting but because it fell neatly into the context of section nine of *Stomping the Blues*—so much that it was like working on an elaborate representative anecdote as an extension of "Kansas City Four/Four and the Velocity of Celebration" to be called "For Instance Count Basie and His Orchestra."

There were also the notions about the special shortcomings of much Afro-American biographical documentation as expressed in "Duke Ellington, Vamping Till Ready," for instance:

Seldom are such books concerned with making anything more than a political statement of some kind or other, mostly polemical. Rarely do they reflect very much personal involvement in the texture of everyday actuality as such. On the contrary, most often they are likely to leave the

impression that every dimension of black experience is directly restricted, if not inevitably crippled, by all-pervading (and always sinister)
political forces.

And also:

More often than not, it is as if all of the downright conspicuous orientation to style in general and stylistic clothes in particular, all of the manifest lore of good cooking and festive music and dancing and communal
good times (both sacred and secular), all of the notorious linguistic ex-
uberance, humor and outrageous nonsense, not to mention all of the
preoccupation with lore and lore making (that blues lyrics are so full
of)—it is as if none of these things, otherwise considered to be so characteristic of the so-called black American's lifestyle, is of any basic significance at all once the so-called black American becomes the subject
of biographical contemplation.

And also:

Actually, most biographies and autobiographies of U.S. Negroes tend to
read like case histories or monographs written to illustrate some very
special (and often very narrow) political theory, or ideology of blackness,
or to promote some special political program. Such writing serves a very
useful purpose, to be sure. But the approach does tend to oversimplify
character, situation and motive in the interest of political issues as such,
and in the process human beings at best become sociological abstrac-
tions. At worst they are reduced to cliches.

None of which should come as any surprise to anybody already familiar with *The Omni-Americans,* for one of the most obvious concerns
of that book is that any image of Afro-American experience that is
geared to the standard, materialist assumptions about human fulfillment underlying most of the so-called findings of American social-
science technicians is very likely to reinforce the folklore of white supremacy and the fakelore of black pathology.

The Hero and the Blues, a book about the nature and function of the
heroic image in fiction, is based on the assumption that endeavor,
whether in quest, in conquest, or in defense, is what storytelling is
really about. Accordingly, it rejects protest and elects to view the eternal necessity of struggling not only as the natural condition of mankind
but also as a form of antagonistic cooperation, without which there is
no achievement and fulfillment, no heroic action, no romance.

There were also specific assumptions about the Basie project. One
was that, in addition to providing useful documentation of Count
Basie's successful career as a bandleader, it would be in effect a natural

history of the very distinctive Basie style. Little interest though he himself ever had in analyzing and explaining how and why he played the way he did, as a casual account of what he was doing from time to time in place after place his book would also be a story of his musical evolution. For example, when he went west on the vaudeville circuit, he used the striding left hand of an eastern ragtime piano player, but when he came back home from the stomp-oriented West, the stride hand had somehow been all but replaced by the walking bass of Walter Page.

Another of the cowriter's very personal assumptions was derived from a discussion about the refinement of aesthetic statement in "The Style of the Mythical Age," by Hermann Broch, published as the introduction to Rachel Bespaloff's *On the Iliad*. In a passage about expressing the essential and nothing but the essential, as in childhood before one enters the cluttered world of subjective problems and in old age after one leaves behind the clutter, Broch goes on to discuss the style of old age, which he describes as being not so much the product of maturity as

> the reaching of a new level of expression, such as old Titian's discovery of the all-penetrating light which dissolves the human flesh and the human soul to a higher quality, or such as the finding by Rembrandt and Goya, both at the height of their manhood, of the metaphysical surface which underlies the visible in man and thing and which nevertheless can be painted; or such as *The Art of the Fugue* which Bach in his old age dictated without having a concrete instrument in mind. . . .

There Broch defines it as "a kind of *abstractism* in which expression relies less and less on the vocabulary, which finally becomes reduced to a few prime symbols, and instead relies more and more on the syntax. . . . "

Count Basie himself had no particular concern with such observations, but to the cowriter they were directly applicable to the evolution of the quintessential style of understatement that Basie, not unlike Ernest Hemingway in literature, achieved and received universal recognition for—and at a relatively early stage of his career. Indeed, as far as the public at large was concerned, it was as if both had expressed themselves that way all along.

Another pet notion of the cowriter was that the distillation and refinement achieved by the all-powerful yet laid-back and understated Basie style were analogous to both the seemingly purely pragmatic but poetic and indeed ritualistic prose of Ernest Hemingway as well as to the visual simplifications of Henri Matisse, especially but not exclusively during the late years when Matisse settled on the cutouts as if to echo Hokusai, the great Japanese master who, at ninety and at the peak of his mastery, said, according to Broch, "Now at last I begin to learn how one draws a line."

There was (or so the cowriter liked to think) also a noteworthy resemblance between the music of Count Basie and the paintings of Matisse during the years of their apprenticeship. There were the tinkling, sparkling, and cascading notes and the fancy runs and finger-busting figures of young Basie during his Harlem-stride or eastern-ragtime phase, culminating in the "Prince of Wails," recorded with Bennie Moten's orchestra in 1932, just as there was, or rather had already been, the mosaic density, sometimes of brushstrokes and sometimes of detail, that characterized many of the early van Gogh and Pointillist-influenced Matisse paintings, such as *Luxe, Calme et Volupté* (1904–05), *The Open Window, The Moorish Screen,* and the various odalisques, in which, as John Russell has said, he aimed "to fill the entire surface of the canvas with a unified decorative pattern and to achieve ever more exciting interactions of color." Also, behind Basie there was the all-pervading influence of Louis Armstrong, much the same as there was that of Cézanne for Matisse.

Naturally, the analogy does not apply in all particulars. Analogies seldom, if ever, do. Nevertheless, here are two more: Both men foreshadowed their mature reliance on syntax in much of their earlier work, but neither seems to have realized at the time that the subsequent development and refinement of their craft would take them back in the direction of their early efforts instead of away from them. Young Matisse seems to have regarded his simplifications not as distillations but as preliminary sketches and studies—and as such they were really throwaways. Basie regarded his purely functional vamps, riffs, and obbligatos as the stock-in-trade of the comp artist, which made them throwaways in the theatrical sense of the throwaway line.

The point here is not that either old master was ever dead-set on eliminating all density from all the later work on the basis of some rigid principle. It is rather that such density as is obviously there is even more obviously a matter less of vocabulary and detail than of syntax. In Matisse's *Tabac Royal* (1942), *The Egyptian Curtain* (1948), *The Parakeet and the Siren* (1952), and *Ivy in Flower* (1953), the density is based on fewer colors, less color nuance, and less detailing than in *The Moorish Screen* (1921), *Decorative Figure on an Ornamental Background* (1927), or *Odalisque in Red Pantaloons* (1922).

As a performing maestro, Basie, who thought in terms of perennials as well as new productions, always included items from every period of his repertoire with no noticeable preference for the less complex ones. However, when earlier recordings of such vintage items as "Jumping at the Woodside" (1937) and "9:20 Special" (1941), for example, are compared with later ones—even when the sidemen are obviously geared to a rococo-like density, strongly influenced, no doubt, by Charlie Parker—the overall statement is still more a matter of basic blues—idiom syntax than of lush additions to the vocabulary. Indeed, against the unison and ensemble backgrounds so typical of the later Basie arrangements, the effect of the high-speed-note solos is not unlike that of Matisse's use of decorative figures against the flat backgrounds in such final cutouts as *The Sorrow of the King* (1952) and *Large Decoration with Masks* (1953).

Anybody who has hung out with him knows very well that Count Basie had no concern whatsoever with such juxtapositions and speculations. He regarded them as being academic at best and a bit too highfalutin in any case. The suggestion that Matisse's reproductions be used as Basie album covers struck him as being very nice and appropriately contemporary. But so far as the rest was concerned: "Okay. I see what you mean, but that's you saying that now, not me."

Matisse, on the other hand, was highly conscious of musical parallels in his painting. He was theorizing in terms of "harmonies and dissonances of color" as long ago as 1908, and in 1946 he spoke of black as "taking a more and more important part in color orchestration, comparable to that of the double-bass as a solo instrument." And, of course, over the years there were *Harmony in Blue,* which became *Harmony in Red, Music, Dance, Joy of Life, Piano Lesson, Music Lover,* and so on. Then, in fruitful old age, there was the book of twenty prints (from cutouts) that represented "crystallizations of memories of the circus, of popular tales, or of travel," which he called *Jazz* because they were composed on unspecified principles of improvisation, but which resemble no other jazz in existence more than that of Count Basie's band in general and Count Basie's piano in particular.

One of the best possible models for keeping all of these and other personal assumptions and opinions under control was Count Basie himself. Universally popular as his individualistic piano style made him, few soloists, vocal or instrumental, ever sounded more as if they had all their own, special attributes and nuances under more effective control than when they had him in there doing what he did in his own, special way in the background, usually unattended by most of the audience.

Even so, there is finally no getting around the fact that regardless of how self-effacing certain accompanists might seem to be, what they do has a crucial and even definitive influence on the manner as well as the substance of the performance of any soloist. Thus, no matter how distinctively individual your personal identity remains, when, say, Duke Ellington supplies the accompaniment, you are apt to sound even more like yourself than ever, to be sure, but at the same time your voice becomes Ellington music. And when you perform with Count Basie, the chances are that you are going to sound very much like yourself on a Basie beat.

The implications of this aspect of the as-told-to autobiography for oral-history projects in general should be obvious enough. After all, such projects are hardly ever initiated by the narrators, who are seldom in a position to exercise any basic control over context, theme, direction, emphasis, or nuance. Indeed, far from having any definitive editorial prerogatives, many do not know what use will be made of the data their interviews produce.

This was certainly not true of Count Basie and *Good Morning Blues*. In the first place, he himself initiated the project in his own, good time. Then he chose an accompanist who met criteria he himself had established. Moreover, in doing so he enjoyed the same position of unassailable authority that gave such headliners as Billy Eckstine, Sarah Vaughan, Ella Fitzgerald, Tony Bennett, and Frank Sinatra the option of being showcased by Ellington, Basie, Nelson Riddle, some pickup combo, or an anonymous studio aggregation.

In any case, it was not for nothing that, for all his widely celebrated gracious deportment toward the press corps throughout his long career, he was one of the most reluctant and reticent of interviewees. He was admittedly extremely sensitive to and wary of the crucial influence that the reporter's frame of reference and editorial slant could have on what was to be printed as an objective rendering of verbatim quotations, and he dreaded the misrepresentation and destructive distortions that were often the result. Then there was his longstanding suspicion that reporters were mostly concerned about getting credit for some sensational revelation, regardless of who was embarrassed or hurt in the process. There was also the matter of sharing idiomatic experiences with an insider rather than having to explain routine details to someone who, however curious and genuinely sympathetic, was nevertheless an outsider. Obviously, this is not a matter of "for your ears only" but rather of "for your ears first," with everybody else getting the benefit of the more relaxed, natural, and revealing discourse. That storytellers do better with some audiences than with others should surprise no one.

When Basie asked prospective as-told-to collaborators what kind of book they thought his story would make, he already knew that he himself wanted a literary equivalent of the "class act" that his no less refined than down-to-earth orchestras always were. He also knew that he did not want to become involved with anybody who was going to try to maneuver him into reducing the chronicle of his career as one of the most successful of American musicians to a polemic about racism. He wasn't one to brag about his achievements, which were considerable; but he didn't stand for any putdowns either. The condescending rhetoric of do-gooders turned him off.

He was all for including anecdotes for laughs and for humor in general, and especially for jokes on himself. But as for publicizing delicate indiscretions of no fundamental significance to his development as a musician, he felt that any man well into his seventies who did that was only putting tarnish on his own trophies and graffiti on his own monument.

"Is Ethnicity Obsolete?"

ISHMAEL REED, SHAWN WONG, BOB CALLAHAN, and
ANDREW HOPE

*Statements based on a discussion at the First Annual Alaska Native
Publishing Conference in Sitka (January, 1986) and partly edited from
a transcript of impromptu remarks.*

ISHMAEL REED: **America's "Black Only" Ethnicity**

So what is ethnicity, and who is ethnic? I teach a course at the University of California at Berkeley, and I have encouraged students to write from the experience of their ethnic background. I have mostly American-European students who, when given this assignment, often write stories about a "black" person. So I guess in the United States, ethnicity is interchangeable with being black. In other words, "blacks" are the only ethnic group in the United States.

I'll give you an example. Early in 1986, three writers appeared on David Brinkley's ABC show. An Irish-American, a Jewish-American, and an Afro-American; William Kennedy, E. L. Doctorow, and Toni Morrison. They were invited to give their views about the state of contemporary American society. Of the three, only the Afro-American writer's ethnicity was cited. Toni Morrison was introduced as a "black" feminist writer, yet Doctorow wasn't introduced as a Jewish-American writer, nor William Kennedy as an Irish-American writer.

Yet, when Toni Morrison told an international P.E.N. audience, in January 1986, that she never felt part of America, as a black person, her remark was greeted by groans, and she was deemed ungrateful by *Newsweek,* a magazine that once carried her photo on the cover, and which constantly prints articles about "black" America, as though this lazy metonymy referred to an actual territory with its own economy, and political, and cultural hegemony.

226

White ethnicity has been swallowed up by what we call "White America." You know, we have these two basketball teams in the United States right now—"White America" and "Black America." "Black America" has its leaders, usually coronated by the media. The leaders of "White America" are "Black America's" leaders as well, so in the eyes of the media, "blacks" are viewed as having a dual loyalty. If someone came from another planet and asked a "black" person "take me to your leader," the alien would be there two or three weeks before his informant finished reciting the names of "Black America's" leaders.

All of this reminds me of an observation made by Chester Himes, one of our greatest novelists, who, of course, had to go to Europe in order to recognized, because he wrote the truth.

Anyway, Chester Himes said that "to live in a racist society is to live in a situation of absurdity, and this designation of "blacks" as America's only ethnic group is an example of that, because what the media refer to as "blacks" are among the least ethnic of America's ethnic groups. "Blacks," in the United States, have a multi-ethnic heritage. If Alex Haley had traced his father's bloodline, he would have traveled twelve generations back to, not Gambia, but *Ireland*.

W. E. B. Du Bois said that the "pure" African disappeared after the first generation of Africans in America. So that's how rampant cohabitation was. As a matter of fact, cohabitation was an election issue in one of Abraham Lincoln's campaigns. All these Mulattoes all over the South—they didn't know what to do with them. I remember reading one of Andrew Johnson's speeches, where he said he went through Tennessee and didn't know what was what. He saw "black" women with "white" children and what appeared to be "white" women with "black" children. That's how we got about five new races in the Americas. Five new races have originated in this country and in South America and in the Caribbean. You go down there and it's the same situation. Blacks have difficulties claiming the multi-ethnicity of their heritage because such a claim renders millions of people less "white." We threaten people. We can't define ourselves fully because it threatens people. And it's amazing how even Afro-American intellectuals define themselves according to how others see them. If "whites" don't take note of their existence, then they consider themselves to be "invisible men."

It is common knowledge that many southern families have both a "white" and a "black" branch. Toni Cade Bambara, one of our great writers in the United States, said that she was walking down the street in Atlanta, Georgia, with a black person who said, pointing to a person on the opposite side of the street, "Oh, there's cousin Al," or somebody; cousin Al was blond and blue-eyed. You go down South and all the people are like relatives. A dark-skinned person may have a blond blue-eyed cousin. This is America's secret—the secret of miscegenation that is glossed over with terms like "whiteness" and "blackness." Very few Americans are willing to cast aside these superstitions, are willing to admit that "white blood" and "black blood" have been intermingled over the centuries. Racial bias, as we all know, has been a disaster that has tainted American scholarship so that even those in the intellectual professions sometimes appear to promote popular mythology instead of enlightenment. Recently a team of University of California anthropologists traced the origin of the Polynesian people to China, whereas anybody who has visited those islands will not have failed to notice people with an obvious African ancestry, including some early Queens of Hawaii. Presumably those people with an African ancestry came from outer space. I told a professor of Celtic studies at Dartmouth of my Irish-American heritage; he laughed. This was an intellectual at one of our great Ivy League colleges.

So we permit millions of people to acquire what passes in the United States as prestige without their having to earn it. All one has to be is "white." For them to be "white," to permit them to be "white," to liberate themselves from what they regard as the shackles of ethnicity, there has to be "blackness." Ethnicity is treated like a kind of disease. We get such a violent response to our work in the United States not only because of racism but because we remind people who are "passing" for Anglo of their immigrant grandfathers. This is a good point that Bob Callahan brought up. We remind people—we're like walking examples, or emblems of ethnicity. That makes people uncomfortable.

Sometimes it appears that the American dream is one that grants whiteness to those who wouldn't be considered white in Europe. In Frankfurt, Germany, last year, I encountered Italians who were darker than I am, and who had kinky hair. I thought I was in a soul café. It was in an Italian café, with all these black people with kinky hair. In the United States, Italians, whose ancestors mated with Africans, are considered "white," even though the Africans were in Italy for more than 300 years. As Nat King Cole sang, you won't learn that in school—it's amazing all the things you can't learn when you go to the so-called "educational system," right? We still use racial definitions that were created by slave masters in order to save money. If you could say that the offspring of an African and a European was "black," you could save money. "Black," then, is a commercial term. Theodore Bernstein said that the media chose "black" over "Afro-American" because "black" was easier to set in headlines.

America's "black-only" ethnicity has become a narcotic which permits "white America" from dealing with its problems. "Blacks" become the surrogate targets, and the stand-ins, the performance artists for all of America's ills. Take the black male/black female conflict that's become such a commercial rage for publishers, theatre producers, film-makers, and the "conference" industry.

All one has to do is read articles by Jewish feminists, in such publications as *Tikkun,* and *Shmate,* to discover that the conflict between Jewish-American men and women is as intense. *The Dream Book,* an anthology edited by Helen Barolini, discusses the friction between Italian-American men and women, and Irish-American women writers describe the relationship between Irish-American men and women as not being all-together rosy. Before the movie *The Color Purple,* there was a movie called *The Quiet Man,* about Irish male chauvinism.

I found it ironic that a mass newsmagazine—which regularly entertains its readers with articles about "the underclass," (originally a racist euphemism for black petty criminals)—hired an Asian-American scholar and reporter to comment about the divisions between black men and women, when Asian-American intellectuals are constantly warning about Asia-America's extinction that will result from the intermarriage of whites and Asians.

Male/female discord, welfare, narcotics addiction, teenage pregnancy, and crime—even though Congress's Asian-Gang Task Force reveals that members of the media's model minority is making more money at it—are all erroneously viewed as exclusively problems of "Black America," and the current media and political line is that it's "Black America's" fault that "Black America" has these problems.

As long as such public attitudes about "Black America" are maintained, ethnicity will never become obsolete. By blaming all of its problems on blacks, the political and cultural leadership are able to present the United States as a veritable utopia for those who aren't afraid of "hard work." A place where any goal is possible, for the "strong hearted" and "the brave," and other cheerleading myths. And, so, instead of being condemned as a "problem," the traditional view of the "black presence," the presence of "blacks" should be viewed as a blessing. Without blacks taking the brunt of the system's failures, where would our great republic be?

SHAWN WONG:

Ishmael brought up the topic of the model minority. Model minority is a term invented by the media. Each time model minority is used it's synonymous with Asians in America. Yet there is the sense that all minorities were in some kind of great acceptance and suffering sweep-stakes. Which minority suffered the most, yet achieved the most. Which minority was able to assimilate the fastest. And, of course, there's a price to be paid for acceptance. Asians in America, according to the media, were willing to pay the price. And in America, if you're willing to pay the price, there are great rewards. The media touts our higher than average income, education, and loyalty. "Loyalty" meant, for Chinese, that we weren't Japanese during World War II and we weren't black during the sixties. Model minorities don't cause trouble. In America silence was love.

Ethnicity will never be obsolete in America as long as there are eth-nic minorities in America. Just as there are so-called model or loyal minorities there are disloyal minorities also. The media exploits that image. When Eldridge Cleaver's *Soul on Ice* became a best seller, American publishers rushed into print the black militant, the black poor, the black ex-con—and no one else.

In the heart of all the "black fire" and "black rage" themes, Ishmael Reed edited an anthology of writing titled *19 Necromancers from Now* (Doubleday, 1970) which featured nineteen black, Chicano, and Asian writers. On the cover of the anthology there was no mention of black writing, militancy, or ethnic rage, just the subtitle: "An Anthology of Original American Writing." Ethnicity was not the selling point of the book. For the time it was a very radical move for Ishmael.

What's ironic about this is the prediction by population growth ex-perts that by the year 2010 there will no longer be a white majority in America. Ethnicity may become obsolete because emphasis on an eth-nic "minority" will no longer serve a purpose, that is, set one minority group off against another. Publishers of the books in twenty-first-cen-tury America may follow Ishmael's lead and simply defuse ethnicity as a selling point.

Colleges which are experiencing very high percentages of Asian en-rollment are abandoning the baggage of a term like "minority enroll-ment" for "under represented populations."

If we use colleges as a microcosm of American society the model minority of today might become the "model under represented population" of the future. Ethnicity will no longer be a "concern," a "problem," an "issue" in America—it will be a way of life.

BOB CALLAHAN: **The European Immigrant Response**

In American society today, the illness of racism still confuses just about everything—so much so that you can't even begin to talk about ethnicity without having to place almost primary emphasis on the underlying question of race.

Now the only thing that Ishmael Reed has said today that I would somewhat disagree with is that by the year 2000 America will become a multi-cultural society.

It certainly appears to be true that by the year 2000, in certain regions of our country, the non-white population will begin to outnumber the white, or Euro-American population.

But the simple fact remains, that, regardless of white to non-white proportions, America already is a multi-cultural society. It has been that way since even before the days of Christopher Columbus.

With reference to that fact, we have operated the Before Columbus Foundation for more than ten years now under the assumption that there are at least five major cultural traditions to be accounted for if you wish to speak accurately about anything as wide, and as diverse, as American Culture as a whole.

America is its Native-American tradition, its Afro-American tradition, its Euro-American tradition, its Asian-American tradition, and its Hispanic-American tradition.

And, as everybody knows, within each of these broad traditions, there are dozens—if not hundreds—of distinct and recognizable individual traditions just bursting at the seams, attempting to establish new or renew old cultural agendas of their own.

And, as everybody also knows, this represents far too much diversity for our popular media to bear. Because of this, our media is likely to seize on only one of these cultural movements at a time. As a result, in the great escalator belt of American popular recognition, some one of these individual traditions is going up, while all others are going down, all the time.

I'd like to speak a little, if I may, about the political consequences of these facts. The topic "Is Ethnicity Obsolete?" has, I think, a particularly urgent edge to it here in the dying days of Ronald Reagan's administration.

I realize that there were other factors involved, but you could almost say that, in part, it was Ronald Reagan's manipulation of the ethnic issue that helped to sweep him into office for a second term.

I take this as a very ironic accomplishment because my own father was a very fine, and wonderful old ward boss in the great Irish Catholic, New England Democratic manner.

I'm fairly sure my father would have turned over in his grave if he learned how Ronald Reagan by 1985 had managed to reverse all the old mirrors.

By 1985, you see, the Democratic party had more or less abrogated its previous leadership role in terms of ethnic politics, and had more or less concluded that ethnicity had become exactly the same thing as race.

Let me give you an example or two of what I am talking about.

At the time I was working in the book department at the *San Francisco Examiner,* and I picked up a story about certain changes that had occurred in terms of new operative guidelines then being furnished by the California Arts Council. At the time, for a series of complicated reasons, the California Arts Council had felt compelled to spell out in some detail just who might be eligible for "minority" arts support. In so doing—and in the name of a good deal of contemporary Democratic thinking on the matter—the California Arts Council concluded that only non-white peoples should properly be considered minorities for the purpose of receiving cash subsidies to support certain neighborhood culture programs and institutions.

In reading about this, I felt we had reached a rather major turning point in terms of the ethnic history of this country. Suddenly, and almost overnight, the Jews were no longer a minority anymore. Suddenly, and almost overnight, the Italians were no longer a minority anymore. Suddenly, and almost overnight, the Armenians were no longer a minority anymore. Suddenly, and almost overnight, the Irish were no longer a minority anymore.

As I wrote that week in my *Examiner* column, I became so excited by this piece of news that I rushed down to my favorite Irish luncheon pub and confronted my friend Paddy Nolan, the proprietor, telling him: "Guess what, Paddy, the California Arts Council has just done what over a thousand years of British Imperial History failed to do."

"Put on your best suit, Paddy," I said. "It looks like you are finally free."

Now all of this would be the funny joke it almost is if it weren't for the fact that, at the same time the California Arts Council was busily abolishing almost two hundred years of European immigrant history, Ronald Reagan was attempting to build his own second-term campaign on the very same building blocks that the Democratic party was then in the process of abandoning.

Do you remember where Reagan began that second campaign?

To refresh your memory, I think it is important to recall that he began it not in Iowa, or New Hampshire, but from a small Irish village called Ballyporeen.

Now Mr. Reagan's actual Irish "roots" are rather suspect. He is the son of a hard-drinking, left-wing Irish American union-organizer, but Reagan's mother and father divorced when Ronald was just a small child, and he didn't actually drift back into Irish circles until the call went out for Irish lead actors in Hollywood in the late thirties, and early forties.

Reagan was called "Dutch," you might also recall, almost up until the time he was elected governor of the State of California.

But the point is that, in 1985, Ronald Reagan began his campaign among his lost Irish cousins in Ballyporeen; and then, when the Democrats countered somewhat with Geraldine Ferraro—whose role on the ticket was obviously the result of sexual, and not ethnic politics—Reagan showed up the next day in New Jersey with the Italian-American Catholic Archbishop on one arm, and Frank Sinatra on the other.

At the end of the day, as they say in Belfast, Reagan carried every major European immigrant group in this country—except for the Jewish community—by commanding majorities.

He recognized these communities, while his opponent took them for granted—or suggested that they did not even exist—and that single act was no small part of the manipulative genius of his re-election campaign.

To the question, then, "Is Ethnicity Obsolete?" I suggest the answer we can draw from the political side of this equation is that I wouldn't go out and campaign from that particular position if I cared a whit about getting elected to office these days from almost anywhere in this country.

On the contrary, just as we are learning in the fields of American literature and culture, the worst thing you can try to do to any people is to try to strip them of their history.

And this certainly includes European immigrant peoples, as well.

In fact, it would seem that the educated American author—much like the successful American politician—is someone who is able to build something from the diverse cultural building blocks that have gone into the construction of American culture as a whole.

Sophistication in these matters—it would also seem—is to try to never drive a wedge into this history by following the illusions this country continues to create largely in the name of the politics of race.

ANDREW HOPE:

The definition of "minority group" has become more and more diluted. You have the elderly, you have the handicapped, you have the gays, you have the white married women, you have the smokers, the non-smokers, etc. Just so that more and more white people can qualify as one minority group or another, and I don't think that ethnicity is even a question. Take Jesse Jackson's Rainbow Coalition. You know he had to go for all the "yuppie" votes to get anywhere, and he didn't get them. In American politics real ethnic issues that should be addressed aren't addressed. All these non-entities jump on the bandwagon and take over the platform. And the real, meaningful things, the ethnic questions, aren't really addressed. They are shoved aside.

I just tried to think of Native Americans and Alaskan Indians as an ethnic group, but then, how do you break it down from there, because there are about five hundred different language groups within the Native American community? And it crosses all the borders just like, I guess, the immigrants crossed all the borders. And there are about a thousand tribes in the United States, and Senator Inouye from Hawaii has been successful in designating Hawaiians as tribes recently. It's one of the kind of amusing things that happen in the Congressional Appropriations process. Or you look at Alaska and try to say Alaskan Indians are an ethnic group. Well, you know, there are about forty different language groups in Alaska, and they cross all borders. There are Siberian Yupic people, Canadian Athabascans, Canadian Tlingits, Canadian Haidas, Canadian Tsimshaws. Then you have the tribal groups, and there more than two hundred of those in Alaska. And so by no means is there any kind of unified, ethnic, Alaskan native group.

Ethnicity differs from tribalism since tribal government is not based on race. The relationship among the tribes and to the United States is not based on race. The tribes determine their own membership, because they are governments. The status of tribal governments is one of the fundamentals of American political liberty. Yet many people make the mistake of thinking that somehow Indian tribes are an affirmative action issue of some kind or another. So the question remains: how does American "ethnicity" relate to Native Americans?

Notes

Introduction

1. Coover, *Pricksongs & Descants* (1969; New York: New American Library, 1970), 40. Kingston, *China Men* (New York: Knopf, 1980), 118. The array of postmodernists from Donald Barthelme to Clarence Major who have played with the idea of "invention" is formidable.

2. The anthology edited and translated by Allan H. Gilbert, *Literary Criticism: Plato to Dryden* (Detroit: Wayne State Univ. Press, 1962), provides a helpful introduction to the uses of "invention" in Renaissance poetics. Jacopo Mazzini, *Discorso in difesa della "Commedia" del divino poeta Dante* (1587; trans. Gilbert), for example, focuses on what happens

> when the poet takes something from history and then goes on to add many things from his own invention. This can come about in two ways. The first is when the history is not known in detail. In this instance the poet has before him a wide field in which he can enlarge and particularize the history by introducing his own inventions without fear of transgressing the credible. This sort of regal story is better and more perfect than all the others. The second kind of this impossible credible taken from history appears when the poet transmutes and falsifies history that is true or at least recorded in some writer; this procedure is also according to my opinion fitting to the poetically credible. (390)

Lodovico Castelvetro, *Poetica d'Aristotele vulgarizzata et sposta* (1571, 1576; trans. Gilbert), emphasizes originality:

> But if any thief of the inventions of others ought to be mocked at and punished, the poet who is a thief should be, for the essence of a poet consists in his invention, since without invention he is not a poet. (324)

In the section on comedy, Castelvetro, too, sketches the relationship of invention to tradition, truth, and history:

Now to compose the plot of a comedy the poet searches out with his own powers a happening in its universal and particular aspects, and because everything is invented by him and no part is given to actual events or to history, he gives names to the persons as it pleases him and is able to do with no inconvenience and in a reasonable way. . . . [I]f he wishes to be thought a poet in the true meaning of the word, that is an inventor, he ought to invent everything, because, since the private material makes it easy for him, he is able to do it. But no one should think that he who composes the plot of the comedy has license to make up for himself new cities that he has imagined, or rivers or mountains or kingdoms or customs or laws, or to change the course of the things of nature, making it snow in summer and putting harvest in the winter, and the like, for it befits him to follow history and truth, if in forming his plot it happens that he needs such things, just as it equally befits him who forms the fable of a tragedy or of an epic. (320)

In all these instances, as well as in uses of "invention" made by Georges de Scudéry (Gilbert 582) and Edward Phillips (Gilbert 672), there is, of course, never any metaphysical doubt about the existence of truth and history (as there is, for example, in the epigraph by Coover).

3. Among the many relevant authors and titles, I am here thinking especially of the following: Roy W. Wagner, *The Invention of Culture* (Chicago and London: Univ. of Chicago Press, 1981); Gerald L. Bruns, *Inventions: Writing, Textuality, and Understanding in Literary History* (New Haven: Yale Univ. Press, 1982); Mauro Ferraresi, *L'invenzione nel racconto. Sulla semiotica della narrazione* (Milano: Guerini e Associate, 1987); Philippe Ariès's chapter on the discovery of childhood in *L'Enfant et la vie familiale sous l'Ancien Régime* (1973); Barbara Sichtermann on the invention of the "loss of childhood" in her contribution to *Karl May der sächsische Phantast. Studien zum Leben und Werke* (Frankfurt: Fischer TB 6873, 1987); Joseph Adelson, *Inventing Adolescence: The Political Psychology of Everyday Schooling* (New Brunswick: Transaction Books, 1985); on motherhood: Elisabeth Badinter's *L'Amour en plus* (German transl. Zürich: Piper, 1981), and Ann Dally, *Inventing Motherhood: The Consequences of an Ideal* (New York: Schocken, 1985); Thomas B. Trautmann, *Lewis Henry Morgan and the Invention of Kinship* (Berkeley, Los Angeles, London: Univ. of California Press, 1987); John O. Lyons, *The Invention of the Self: The Hinge of Consciousness in the Eighteenth Century* (Southern Illinois Univ. Press, 1978); on the invention of America: the books by Edmundo O'Gorman, Peter Conrad, and, most recently, Garry Wills—as well as the famous dialogue from Henry James's *The American* (1877): "Did you ever hear of Christopher Columbus?" "*Bien sûr*! He invented America, a very great man. And is he your patron?"; Bruce Tucker's essay "The Reinvention of New England, 1691–1770," *New England Quarterly* 59 (September 1986): 315–40; Alvin Greenberg on *The Invention of the West* (New York: Avon, 1976); Earl

Conrad, *The Invention of the Negro* (1967); Thomas Hunt King, "Inventing the Indian: White Images, Oral Literature, and Contemporary Native Writers," Diss., Univ. of Utah, 1986; Bernard Sherman, *The Invention of the Jew* (New York: Yoseloff, 1969); Bernard Dubourg, *L'Invention de Jésus* (Paris: Gallimard, 1987): Hyam Maccoby, *Paul and the Invention of Christianity* (New York: Harper & Row, 1986); Nicole Loraux, *The Invention of Athens: The Funeral Oration in the Classical City* (Cambridge, Mass., and London: Harvard Univ. Press, 1986); Morris J. Vogel, *The Invention of the Modern Hospital: Boston, 1870–1930* (Chicago: Univ. of Chicago Press, 1985); Rudolf Pörtner, *Oskar von Miller. Der Münchner, der das Deutsche Museum "erfand"* (Düsseldorf, Wien, New York: Econ, 1987); Alain Jouffroy, *La Vie reinventée: L'exploration des années 20 à Paris* (Paris: Laffont, 1982); Alan Trachtenberg on our ability to "see" photographic pictures in a lecture "Field and Foundry: A Working Contrast," Lexington, October 1, 1986; Stephen Tatum, *Inventing Billy the Kid: Visions of the Outlaw in America, 1881–1981* (Univ. of New Mexico Press, 1982); James J. Farrell, *Inventing the American Way of Death, 1830–1920* (Philadelphia: Temple Univ. Press, 1980); and Jacques Derrida at Harvard University, April 1986. Cf. also Kathleen Neils Conzen's address, "German-Americans and the Invention of Ethnicity," in Randall M. Miller, ed., *Germans in America: Retrospect and Prospect. Tricentennial Lectures Delivered at the German Society of Pennsylvania in 1983* (Philadelphia: German Society of Pennsylvania, 1984).

4. Hayden White, "Foucault Decoded: Notes from the Underground" (1973), in *Tropics of Discourse: Essays in Cultural Criticism* (Baltimore and London: Johns Hopkins Univ. Press, 1982), 252. Ibid., 252–53, is a discussion of metaphor and metonymy, which, derived from Giambattista Vico, also informs White's *Metahistory: The Historical Imagination in Nineteenth-Century Europe* (1973; Baltimore and London: Johns Hopkins Univ. Press, 1985).

5. Hayden White, "The Fictions of Factual Representation" (1976), in *Tropics of Discourse*, 122. For a recent attempt to tackle the task of the postmodern biographer, see David B. Nye, *Invented Self: An Anti-Biography from Documents of Thomas A. Edison* (Odense: Odense Univ. Studies in English 7, 1983).

6. "Introduction: Partial Truths," James Clifford and George E. Marcus, eds., *Writing Culture: The Poetics and Politics of Ethnography* (Berkeley: Univ. of California Press, 1986), 5, 6.

7. Michael J. Fischer, "Ethnicity and the Post-Modern Arts of Memory," in *Writing Culture*, 195. See also his statement "the search or struggle for a sense of ethnic identity as a (re-)invention," 196. It is interesting to see how the anthropologist Fischer, whose essay opens with excerpts by Jean-Pierre Vernant and Emanuel Levinas, arms himself with Jacques Derrida, Jacques Lacan, Michel Foucault, Jean-François Lyotard, and Michel Serres but avoids interpreting the ethnic texts he reads—works by Maxine Hong Kingston, Charles Mingus, Marita Golden, Jose Antonio Villareal, Richard Rodriguez, N. Scott Momaday, Leslie Silko, or Gerald Vizenor—as "inventions" (and this although he would find many clues in their books—see, for example, the passage by Kingston used as an epigraph here) or even in the context of anthro-

pological ethnic theory. This results in an unusual delineation of those American writers' shared sensibilities, but also in a reinstatement of (perhaps exaggerated) ethnic differences "between cultures, between realities" in the United States (230). Though the essay places itself in an avowedly postmodern, post-religious, and post-immigrant, technological and secular universe, it is hardly post-ethnic in its a priori valorization of the cultural "richness" of the various groups that form the "tapestry" of "pluralistic universalism" as opposed to the supposedly "homogenized" "blandness" of "majority discourse." Yet the essay raises the question to what extent the postmodern strategies of "preserving rather than effacing differences" (which Fischer detects in his texts) are, in fact, the essentials of modern American "majority discourse." This process of inadvertently reaffirming ethnicity in a deconstructive enterprise is reminiscent of Tzvetan Todorov's recent observation that in an American collection dedicated to view "race" (in quotation marks) as a trope, the quotation marks could disappear again very easily in the process of the analysis or in the presentation of contributors as white deconstructionists. What I am suggesting, then, is that the efforts which have led ethnography or history to be interpreted as fictions be also directed at ethnicity itself.

8. *Imagined Communities: Reflections of the Origins and Spread of Nationalism* (1983; London: Verso, 1985), 62. Ernest Gellner, *Thought and Change* (London: Weidenfeld and Nicholson, 1964), Anderson 15. Anderson's correlation of print-capitalism and nationalism might fruitfully be compared with Robert B. Stepto's thesis of the Afro-Americans' double quest for freedom and for literacy in *From Behind the Veil: A Study of Afro-American Narrative* (Urbana: Univ. of Illinois Press, 1979).

9. Eric Hobsbawm and Terence Ranger, eds., *The Invention of Tradition* (Cambridge: Cambridge Univ. Press, 1983); the contributions by Hugh Trevor-Roper (on Scotland), Prys Morgan (on Wales), and Terence Ranger (on Africa) seem especially startling and, as far as I know, without parallel in American ethnic studies. E. S. Shaffer has also called attention to the ways in which "'origins' are often invented—and reinvented—in order to make highly polemical reformulations of national character and purpose" in his "Editor's Introduction" to *Comparative Criticism* 8 (1986): xviii, an extremely valuable special issue on "National Myth and Literary Culture."

10. Hobsbawm, "Introduction: Inventing Traditions," 14. Many questions are generated by this approach. For example, when did the 14th of July become the *quatorze juillet,* or the Fourth of July *the* American national holiday? How did flags and anthems become de rigueur for the establishment of nationhood? When did American Southerners begin to feel like Southerners and to develop a need for a "Southern history and culture" approach to legitimate their new identity? When did the idea of a quasi-separate "women's culture" first emerge? How did genealogical literature support modern national and ethnic claims? How could the highly inauthentic English song *Yankee Doodle* become

a national symbol of the emerging United States, just as they were engaged in armed struggle against *Yankee Doodle*'s country of origin?

11. W. Lloyd Warner and Paul S. Lunt, *The Social Life of a Modern Community* (New Haven: Yale Univ. Press, 1941). See Werner Sollors, *Beyond Ethnicity: Consent and Descent in American Culture* (New York: Oxford Univ. Press, 1986), 23 and 183.

12. Fredrik Barth has made the *boundary* (and not the "cultural stuff" that it encloses) the central feature of ethnic divisions and has directed us to focus on the *emergence* of ethnic consciousness rather than on the survival; Fredrik Barth, *Ethnic Groups and Boundaries: The Social Organization of Culture Difference* (Boston: Little, Brown, 1969). Abner Cohen has investigated the emergence of ethnic distinctions against the background of power relations and has insisted on ethnicity as a category that describes dominant as well as dominated groups; Abner Cohen, *Urban Ethnicity* (London: Tavistock Publications, 1974). George Devereux has studied the essentially "dissociative" nature of ethnic consciousness: it always needs something non-ethnic in order to present itself. To be an "*x*" means "not being a *y*". This confrontation of Jew/Gentile, black/white, Chicano/Anglo, French/foreign, or (pan-)ethnic "richness" vs. assimilated "blandness," is thus essential to the (inherently antithetical) establishment of an ethnic identification; yet across such divides modernization takes command by "antagonistic acculturation," the process of becoming more alike even in conflict, antithesis, or protest (for instance, against the melting pot mainstream); George Devereux and Edwin M. Loeb, "Antagonistic Acculturation," *American Sociological Review* 7 (1943): 133–47; George Devereux, "Ethnic Identity: Its Logical Foundations and Its Dysfunctions," in George de Vos and Lola Romanucci-Ross, eds., *Ethnic Identity: Cultural Continuities and Change* (Palo Alto: Mayfield, 1975), 42–70. Herbert Gans has studied the ways in which "symbolic ethnicity" functions as a weak symbol system, as part of a leisure culture, and, perhaps, even as an integrative force in a modern industrial society, since symbolic ethnicity generates gentle diversification in an assimilative context; Herbert J. Gans et al., eds. *On the Making of Americans: Essays in Honor of David Riesman* (Philadelphia: Univ. of Pennsylvania Press, 1979).

13. "Story in Harlem Slang," in *Spunk: The Selected Stories of Zora Neale Hurston,* ed. Bob Callahan (Berkeley: Turtle Island, 1985), 83, 88.

14. Hamilton Holt, ed., *The Life Stories of Undistinguished Americans As Told by Themselves* (New York: James Pott & Co., 1906), 289.

15. Henry W. Grady, "In Plain Black and White: A Reply to Mr. Cable," *Century Magazine* 29 (1885): 911.

16. Charles W. Chesnutt, "Race Prejudice; Its Causes and Its Cures: An Address Delivered before the Boston Historical and Literary Association," *Alexander's Magazine,* 1 (July 1905), 25.

17. Transl. J. Pierron (Paris: Mame, 1987).

A Plea for Fictional Histories and Old-Time "Jewesses"

1. As an early reviewer wrote, "If our feelings are tried, it is that this gentle maiden, with more of nature's nobility than belonged in aggregate to all the other characters of the tale, must be sacrificed in the degradation of her unhappy race, when she has served her purpose, 'to point a moral and adorn a tale,' without a sigh for her self devotion, or future destiny." *Edinburgh Monthly Review* 3 (1820), 198. An adaptation of *Ivanhoe* for the stage performed on January 24, 1820, has Rebecca stay on in England, rejecting many marriage offers and building up her fame as a benefactress. H. A. White, *Sir Walter Scott's Novels on Stage* (New Haven: Yale Univ. Press, 1927), 197. In his parody *Rebecca and Rowena,* W. M. Thackeray finally brings Ivanhoe to marry Rebecca, after many an adventure. In his "Proposal for the Continuation of *Ivanhoe*," he sums up the general discontent: "Of all the Scottish novels, however, that of which the conclusion gives me the greatest dissatisfaction is dear old *Ivanhoe.* . . . From the characters of Rowena, of Rebecca, of Ivanhoe I feel sure that the story can't end where it does." *Fraser's Magazine* 34 (1846), 238.

2. Walter Scott, *Ivanhoe* (London: Dent, 1980), 5. Page references to this edition are given in parentheses in the text.

3. See Georg Lukács's discussion of *Ivanhoe* in *The Historical Novel* (Boston: Beacon, 1962), 49.

4. *Old Mortality* (London: Thomas Nelson, 1905), 497.

5. I am here using Werner Sollors's suggestive dialectical categories relating myths of origins to their culturally founded discourses of self-realization and amalgamation in *Beyond Ethnicity: Consent and Descent in American Literature* (New York: Oxford Univ. Press, 1986).

6. Alexander Welsh, *The Hero of the Waverley Novels* (New Haven: Yale Univ. Press, 1963), vii; John Colin Dunlop. *History of Prose Fiction* (London: Bell: 1888), 3.

7. See W. H. Gardiner's review of James Fenimore Cooper's *The Spy,* in *North American Review* 15 (July 1822), 250–52.

8. See "*Ivanhoe,*" in *Western Review and Miscellaneous Magazine* 2 (May 1820), 204–24; *Port-Folio* 9 (1820), 300–36; 10 (1820), 95–98; and 13 (1822), 493–501. See also, for a general appraisal of the novel's reception in the United States, James T. Hillhouse, *The Waverley Novels and Their Critics* (Minneapolis: Univ. of Minnesota Press, 1936), 78–81.

9. In the historical novel the practice of footnoting often underlines the "authenticity" of the place described with reference to real topology; landscape description provides a lexicon and a perspective through which geographical entities become objects of taste (romantic picturesqueness) but also palimpsests of the past workings of man's history and culture, showing the fictional construction of national genesis through a semiotically reconstructable setting. See, for example, the first description in *Ivanhoe,* 27–28. During Scott's life

and working time, moreover, several place illustrations with a double reference to real topology and fictional description were published, like James Skene's, whose telling title is *Series of Sketches of the Existing Localities Alluded to in the Waverly Novels, Etched from Original Drawings* (Edinburgh: Cadell, 1829).

10. Edgar Rosenberg, *From Shylock to Svengali: Jewish Stereotypes in English Fiction* (Stanford: Stanford Univ. Press, 1960), 85.

11. Review of *Ivanhoe*, in *Edinburgh Review* 33 (1820), 53.

12. See the introduction to *Letters of Rebecca Gratz* by the editor, Rabbi David Philipson, (Philadelphia: Jewish Publication Society of America, 1929).

13. Quoted in W. S. Crockett, *The Scott Originals* (New York: Scribner's, 1913). For further Rebecca Gratz/Scott's Rebecca stories see G. Van Rensselaer, *Century Illustrated Monthly Magazine* 24 (1882), 679–82, and *Border Magazine* 4 (1899), 210–11.

14. *Letters of Rebecca Gratz*, 32.

15. Crockett, *Scott Originals*, 291.

16. Miriam Biskin, *Pattern for a Heroine* (New York: Union of American Hebrew Congregations, 1967), 58.

17. Compare Mark Twain's well-known accusation in *Life on the Mississippi* (1896): "The South has not yet recovered from the debilitating influence of his books. . . . " This is echoed by, among others, H. J. Eckenrode, in "Sir Walter Scott and the South," *North American Review* 206, no. 2 (1917), who goes so far as to blame Scott for the evils of slavery: "[I]f democratic movements had not been checked by disillusion and the revival of mediaevalism, slavery would have continued to aid the progress of the world. . . . The South, through slavery, was able to realize Sir Walter's mediaevalism to no small extent" (601). As for the modern tournament,

> it was popular in the South for decades. The reason for this popularity lies in the fact that the tournament, so called, is nothing more or less than the representation of the passage of arms at Ashby-de-la-Zouche, so admirably described in *Ivanhoe*. The rewarding for a tiresome day of tilting at rings was the ceremony of the crowning of the queen of love and beauty by the victorious knight. The Middle Ages all over again! (602)

Ivanhoe is, on the other hand, recognized as the sacred urtext for Anglo-Saxon racial pride and Caucasian purity by Reginald Horsman in *Race and Manifest Destiny: The Origins of American Racial Anglo-Saxonism* (Cambridge: Harvard Univ. Press, 1981), 39–41, 160–61.

18. Rena Walden (Thoreau's very name for Nature) takes up her brother's self-styled name when passing for white. Warwick, the kingmaker, is the protagonist of Edward George Bulwer-Lytton's *The Last of the Barons* (1843). See William L. Andrews, *The Literary Career of Charles W. Chesnutt* (Baton Rouge: Louisiana Univ. Press, 1980), 159.

19. Charles W. Chesnutt, *The House behind the Cedars* (London: Collier, 1969), 48. Further page references are given in parentheses.

20. Gertrude Stein's mulatto character, Melanctha, also dies abruptly of a (tuberculous) fever (*Three Lives*, 1909). As if echoing Scott's readers' dissatisfaction with the ending of *Ivanhoe*, Robert A. Bone comments on *The House behind the Cedars* that "in the end, Chesnutt avoids his artistic responsibilities by arbitrarily putting his heroine to death." *The Negro Novel in America* (New Haven: Yale Univ. Press, 1965), 37. When Chesnutt sold the movie rights of the novel to the Micheaux film corporation, Micheaux decided on a new ending, in which an educated Frank, the poor ex-slave, marries the heroine. See Frances Richardson Keller, *An American Crusade: The Life of Charles W. Chesnutt* (Provo: Brigham Young Univ. Press, 1978), 270.

21. *Fenimore Cooper: The Critical Heritage*, ed. George Dekker and John P. McWilliams (London: Routledge & Kegan Paul, 1973), 70.

22. Charged with forgery by European readers for Logan's speech in *Notes on the State of Virginia*, Thomas Jefferson answers by praising it "as a specimen of the talents of the aboriginals" of the country, in the belief that "Europe had never produced anything superior to this morsel of eloquence"; but he also adds a final pun: "But wherefore the forgery; whether Logan's or mine, it would still have been American." *Notes on the State of Virginia* (New York: Harper & Row, 1964), 209–10.

23. *The Indian Chief: or, Tokeah and the White Rose* (Hildesheim: Olms, 1972), 4:252.

24. "Recent American Novels," *North American Review* 21 (1825), 82. Walter Scott's consistent use of Scottish dialect made necessary a glossary, with his own translations, as an appendix to his novels.

25. The romantic usage of folklore, legends and songs, also popularizes an anthropological knowledge of the Indian: see, for instance, Philip Freneau's footnote to "The Indian Burying Ground" (1788). For Indian death songs, see Albert Keyser, *The Indian in American Literature* (New York: Oxford Univ. Press, 1933), 20–45.

26. "In New England," writes Heckewelder, the Indians "at first endeavoured to imitate the sound of the national name of the *English*, which they pronounced *Yengees*." *An Historical Account of the Indian Nations* (Philadelphia: Small, 1819), 130.

27. *Indian Chief*, 4:79.

28. James Fenimore Cooper, *The Last of the Mohicans: A Narrative of 1757* (Albany: State Univ. of New York Press, 1983), 186. Further page references to this edition are given in parentheses.

29. James Fenimore Cooper, *The Pioneers* (Albany: State Univ. of New York Press, 1980), 23. Further page references to this edition are given in parentheses.

30. Henry Nash Smith, *Virgin Land* (1950; Cambridge: Harvard Univ. Press, 1973), 58–70.

31. Natty's personal melancholy and melancholic fate are often stressed, even by those who rightly point out his successful hermaphroditism, as a suitable rhetoric for the future of the nation. See D. H. Lawrence (*Studies in Classic American Literature*, 1923), Richard Chase (*The American Novel and Its Tradition*, 1957), and R. H. Pearce (*Historicism Once More*, 1969). Beyond romantic melancholy and the biological death of a character, what Natty stands for is also the national future. In the relation past-present in *The Pioneers*, Natty is presented as a "figurative frontier," "the neutral ground of national becoming." See Edwin Fussell, *Frontier, American Literature and the American West* (Princeton: Princeton Univ. Press, 1965), 27–68. Natty's own project at the end of the novel is to "go low toward the Pennsylvany line," "the foremost in that band of pioneers who are opening the way for the march of the nation across the continent." His past is to be reproduced in the future. See my "La Frontiera del tempo nei Leatherstocking Novels di James F. Cooper," *Storie su storie: Indagine sui romanzi storici (1814–1840)* (Vicenza: Neri Pozza, 1985), 65–94.

32. *Fenimore Cooper: The Critical Heritage*, 196, 252.

33. Cooper is here echoing and adapting to fictional needs the contemporary universalist theories of language derived from the analysis and the comparison of Sanskrit with European languages. See R. H. Robins, *A Short History of Linguistics* (London: Longman, 1979), 132–59.

34. For the polemics on Cooper's historical accuracy, his relying on "unreliable" sources, see the early attacks of W. H. Gardiner and Lewis Cass in the *North American Review* 23 (1826), 166–67; and 26 (1828), 357–76; as well as W. Rawle, "A Vindication of the Rev. Mr. Heckewelder's History of the Indian Nations" (1825), repr. in E. Rondthaler, *Life of J. Heckewelder* (Philadelphia: Ward, 1847). See also James Franklin Beard, "Historical Introduction," to the State University of New York Press edition of *The Last of the Mohicans* and Robert Clark, *History, Myth and Ideology in American Fiction, 1823–52* (London: Macmillan, 1984). I am concerned here not with what is "true" either in Cooper's sources or in his novels but with what was considered or made to appear as such in the discourse of both the novel and its historical sources.

35. For cyclical time in Cooper's novels see Allan M. Axelrad, *History and Utopia: A Study in the World View of J. F. Cooper* (Norwood: Norwood Editions, 1978), and J. P. McWilliams, *Political Justice in a Republic: J. F. Cooper's America* (Berkeley: Univ. of California Press, 1972).

36. *Fenimore Cooper: The Critical Heritage*, 197. The Indian ability of decoding was already pointed out in George Imlay's widely read *Topographical Description of the Western Territory of North America* (London: Debrett, 1797), 102–3. It is detailed both by Heckewelder in his *Account* and by Jonathan Carver in *Three Years Travels through the Interior Parts of North America* (1784). See the explanatory notes to the State University of New York Press edition of *The Last of the Mohicans*, 364.

37. Quoted in Don Russell, *The Lives and Legends of Buffalo Bill* (Norman: Oklahoma Univ. Press, 1960), 377.

38. *The Life of Hon. William F. Cody Known as Buffalo Bill* (1879; Lincoln: Univ. of Nebraska Press, 1978), 30.

39. Frank Norris, "The Frontier Gone at Last," *The Responsibilities of the Novelist,* in *The Complete Works of Frank Norris* (Port Washington: Kennikat Press, 1967), 7: 55. For Natty's "authentic" descendants see also John G. Cawelti, *Adventure, Mystery and Romance* (Chicago: Univ. of Chicago Press, 1976).

40. Validation through violence appears in Philip Fisher's reading of *The Deerslayer.* Proper names "are as open to contest as the names of places which directly reflect rights and forms of ownership" in the bloody Indian/White quarrel over the land and national identity; an identity "not invented" but occurring "in the act of suppressing the identity of another." See *Hard Facts: Setting and Form in the American Novel* (New York: Oxford Univ. Press, 1985), 35–53. For a mythic strategy concealing violence, see also Richard Slotkin, *Regeneration through Violence: The Mythology of the American Frontier, 1600–1860* (Middletown: Wesleyan Univ. Press, 1973).

41. Yury Lotman, "Mito, nome, cultura," *Semiotica e cultura* (Milan: Ricciardi, 1975), 121.

42. James Fenimore Cooper, *The Prairie* (San Francisco: Rinehart Press, 1950), 365. Further page references are given in parentheses.

43. Discussing the importance of class structure for the modern novel, Lionel Trilling discards the possibility that "'minority' groups" would provide a class substitute in American fiction, since there seems to be no "real cultural struggle, no significant conflict of ideas," and no "satirical ambivalence toward both groups." "Art and Fortune," in *The Liberal Imagination* (1950; Garden City: Doubleday, 1953), 253. Yet the half-breed in *The Pioneers,* a historical novel of manners, shows an affinity with the foundling and its class transvestism, which is transformed into a racial and cultural transvestism. The fake half-breed is in itself both a compromise between two different cultures at struggle with each other and a symbolic, if not satirical, structure of ambivalence.

44. *Hope Leslie: or, Early Times in the Massachusetts* (New York: Harper, 1842), 2: 12.

45. As pointed out in Carolyn L. Karcher's introduction to Lydia M. Child's *Hobomok and Other Writings on Indians* (New Brunswick: Rutgers Univ. Press, 1986).

46. In an 1851 stage adaptation of *The Wept of Wish-Ton-Wish,* the distracted Narramattah is made to say, "Ah! I have been dreaming, I suppose; again dreaming that I was an Indian girl, and married to a Chief—yes, I have just dreamed that he was going to be killed and that I leaped quickly to his side and saved him,—I dreamed too that I had a child, 'tis very strange, 'twas but a dream." (New York: Samuel French, n.d.), 22.

47. Vauthier, Simone. "Textualité et stéréotypes: Of African Queens and Afro-American Princes and Princesses: Miscegenation in *Old Hepsy.*" *Regards sur la littérature noire américaine,* ed. Michel Fabre. (Paris: Publications du conseil scientifique de la Sorbonne Nouvelle—Paris III, 1980), 65–107.

48. Jared Sparks, "Recent American Novels," 87.

49. Lydia Maria Child, *Hobomok, a Tale of Early Times,* [by an American], (Boston: Cummings, Hilliard, 1824), 16.

50. For superstitions and the supernatural in Scott's novels, see Enrica Villari, "La resistenza alla storia nei romanzi giacobiti di W. Scott," *Storie su storie,* 5–30.

51. James Fenimore Cooper, *The Wept of Wish-Ton-Wish* (New York: Townsend, 1859), 197. Further page references are given in parentheses.

52. Tragic deaths in literature are textually constructed through multiple symbolic denials, as Francesco Orlando has shown in *Lettura freudiana della Phedre* (Turin: Einaudi, 1971).

53. See Hayden White, "The Forms of Wilderness: Archeology of an Idea," in *The Wild Man Within: An Image in Western Thought from the Renaissance to Romanticism,* ed. Edward Dudley and Maximillian E. Novak (Pittsburgh: Univ. of Pittsburgh Press, 1972), 3–38, especially for his analysis of the archetypal wild men of the Old Testament, and the taboo of their mixed origins.

54. *Fenimore Cooper: The Critical Heritage,* 93, 100.

55. The relation between the Wandering Jew and the mulatto is made by Daniel Aaron in "The Inky Curse: Miscegenation in the White American Literary Imagination," *Social Science Information* 22 (1983), 169–90.

56. In *Ivanhoe,* the Templar, a man without a nation, is the lustful alter ego of the Saxon hero. He resembles Magua, a man without a nation and the Mohican Uncas's evil double. In *The House behind the Cedars,* Rena Walden falls into a maddening fear in the forest where the Anglo-Saxon George Tryon and the black lustful schoolmaster, a man who has feigned property and propriety, are both concealed in order to surprise her.

57. In "Ligeia" (1846) Rowena and Rebecca are intertextual presences; the veiled alchemist Ligeia (Rebecca) has, of course, "raven black" hair, *"blacker than the wings of the midnight."* American dark ladies may indeed be Rebecca's descendants, as Fiedler noted in *Love and Death* (New York: Stein and Day, 1975), 297.

58. James Fenimore Cooper, *Notions of the Americans* (Philadelphia: Carey, Lea & Carey, 1832), 2:287. Cooper considers Indians a vanishing people; therefore intermarriage is not seen as menacing. In the essay a logic of disappearance rationalizes the distaste for mixing expressed in the novels; as for the blacks—for whom the objections to mixing are greater—they too do not constitute a serious problem, because of their very low birth rate. However, Cooper adds, "matrimony is very much an affair of taste" (69–70), a personal choice, beyond progressive amalgamative beliefs. "Taste," he writes in *Home as Found* (1838), "whether in the arts, literature, or anything else, is a natural

impulse, like love." (New York: Capricorn Books, 1961), 79. In Thomas Dixon's *The Leopard Spots* (1902) the following dialogue occurs between George Harris and the liberal Honorable Everett Lowell, who denies him permission to court his daughter: "It is a question of taste," snapped Lowell. "Am I not a graduate of the same university with you? Did I not stand as high, and age for age, am I not your equal in culture?" "Granted. Nevertheless you are a negro, and I do not desire the infusion of your blood in my family." "But I have more of white than Negro blood, sir." "So much the worse. It is the mark of shame." (New York: Doubleday, Page, 1902), 391.

59. Thus, Aphra Behn's *Oroonoko* (1688) had no American followers. Sarah Wentworth Morton's "The African Chief" (1792) seems to be an isolated instance of the portrayal of a black as a noble and doomed African prince. In George Washington Cable's *The Grandissimes* (1880), Bras-Coupé seems to be the stoic counterpart of Oroonoko, who, Indian-like, does not show any concern for the tortures inflicted upon him. In France in the second half of the eighteenth century, an adulterated translation of *Oroonoko* became instead a generative text for the representation of black characters. See L. F. Hoffmann, *Le nègre romantique: Personnage littéraire et obsession collective* (Paris: Payot, 1973), 59–62.

60. Tamenund's speech seems reminiscent of Rebecca's as well as of Freneau's "The Prophecy of King Tammany," which is often given as Cooper's source.

61. In an American poetic rewriting of *Ivanhoe*'s final scene, a Rebecca styling herself as a potential slave will not only find a place in heaven but will there also be reunited with Rowena and Ivanhoe: "I go away/To other lands—men shall not say,/That the poor Jewess lives a slave!/No, my despised, degraded race/In this fair land can have no place./Yet though the darkly-rolling wave/Divide us, while we live on earth;/we meet again . . . we meet in Heaven." "Rebecca to Rowena," *United States Literary Gazette*, July 15, 1824, 125.

62. See Werner Sollors, "Never Was Born: The Mulatto, an American Tragedy?" *Massachusetts Review* 27,2 (Summer 1986), 293–316.

63. *Boston, Two Hundred Years Ago; or, The Romantic Story of Miss Ann Carter, (Daughter of One of the First Settlers,) and the Celebrated Indian Chief, Thundersquall; with Many Humorous Reminiscences and Events of Olden Time* (Boston, 1830), 14.

64. As noted by Ørm Overland, *The Making and Meaning of an American Classic: James Fenimore Cooper's The Prairie* (New York: Humanities Press, 1973), 171.

65. The genealogy of such a gulf figure goes back to Milton's Satan and his novelistic counterpart, Ambrosio, in Matthew Gregory Lewis's *The Monk* (1796), whose final death flight strikingly resembles Magua's. For the Milton romantic tradition, see Mario Praz, *The Romantic Agony,* English trans. Angus Davidson, 2nd. ed. (Oxford and New York: Oxford Univ. Press, 1951).

Ethnicity as Festive Culture

I gratefully acknowledge the support of the Woodrow Wilson International Center for Scholars and the Stiftung Volkswagenwerk for the research on which this essay is based.

1. *Illustrirte Zeitung* (Leipzig), Jan. 14, 1860, 25–26; for background, see Jacob F. Haehnlen, "Die Deutschen am stillen Ocean," in *Schiller-Album zur hundertjährigen Feier der Geburt des Dichters: Eine Festgabe der Freunde Schiller's in der neuen Welt* (Philadelphia: Schäfer und Koradi, 1859), 152–59.

2. Emil Klauprecht, *Deutsche Chronik in der Geschichte des Ohio-Thales* (Cincinnati: G. Hof und M. A. Jacobi, 1864), 174; Gustav Körner, *Das deutsche Element in den Vereinigten Staaten von Nordamerika, 1818–1848* (Cincinnati: A. E. Wilde & Co., 1880), 75–76.

3. Kathleen Neils Conzen, *Immigrant Milwaukee, 1836–1860: Accommodation and Community in a Frontier City* (Cambridge, Mass.: Harvard University Press, 1976), 1; *Wisconsin Banner* (Milwaukee), June 28, July 5, 1845; *Cincinnati Volksfreund*, April 18, May 1, 2, 1846, Aug. 12, 15, 1848; *Illustrirte Zeitung* (Leipzig), Nov. 3, 1849; *San Francisco Journal*, April 13, 1855. The Germans who immigrated during the colonial period came from an earlier German cultural milieu and their festive traditions will not be considered here, though there were undoubtedly important links between them and the festive culture developed by the German immigration of the nineteenth century, particularly in cities like Philadelphia and Pittsburgh; cf. Susan G. Davis, *Parades and Power: Street Theatre in Nineteenth-Century Philadelphia* (Philadelphia: Temple University Press, 1986), 103–4, on the probable influence of the "Pennsylvania Germans" on Philadelphia's street theatre.

4. I shall use the terms "celebration" and "festivity" interchangeably to refer to what Robert Bocock terms "ritual occasions": "social situations defined by the people themselves as separate, 'special' set-apart occasions, set apart from the world of work and from [purely—my addition] recreational activities;" Robert Bocock, *Ritual in Industrial Society: A Sociological Analysis of Ritualism in Modern England* (London: George Allen and Unwin, 1974), 39. Note also Victor Turner's reference to celebrations as "those 'high tides,' 'peak experiences' in social life which mark an occasion or an event with ceremony, ritual, or festivity . . . in which the possibility of personal and communal creativity may arise"; "Introduction," in Victor Turner, ed., *Celebration: Studies in Festivity and Ritual* (Washington, D.C.: Smithsonian Institution Press, 1982), 11–12.

5. Adolph Wiesner, *Geist der Welt-Literatur* (New York, 1860), 303: "Die Deutschen in New-York scheinen die vergnügungssüchtigsten Menschen der Welt zu sein, wenigstens gaben sie des Jahres hindurch mehr Volksfeste, als in allen grossen Städten Europa's zusammen in zehn Jahren stattfinden. Dem guten Volke von New-York werden täglich einige Feste gegeben, bei welchen as

grossentheils zahlreich erscheint. Diese Feste dauern einen oder mehrere Tage,
ja zuweilen eine ganze Woche, und kosten viel Zeit und Geld. . . . Woher neh-
men nun die tausend und tausend Arbeiter, die diese Feste vorzugsweise be-
suchen, die Zeit, das Geld, so vielen Vergnügungen nachzujagen?"

6. *Frank Leslie's Illustrated Newspaper* (hereafter cited as FLIN) gave particular attention to German-American festivity, perhaps because it also published a German edition; *Harper's Weekly,* initially more critical of the Germans, tended to increase its favorable coverage after the Civil War.

7. For example, Robert Ernst, *Immigrant Life in New York City 1825–1863*
(New York: King's Crown Press, 1949), 130–31; John Frederick Nau, *The German People of New Orleans, 1850–1900* (Leiden: E. J. Brill, 1958), 133–28;
Conzen, *Immigrant Milwaukee,* 1, 154–91 *passim.* Carl Wittke, *Refugees of
Revolution: The German Forty-Eighters in America* (Philadelphia: University
of Pennsylvania Press, 1952), 283–86, 292–94, 311–14, 357–59, offers brief but
perceptive insights on the character and role of public festivities in German-
American communities; Hartmut Keil and Heinz Ickstadt, "Elemente einer
deutschen Arbeiterkultur in Chicago zwischen 1880 und 1890," *Geschichte und
Gesellschaft* 5 (1979), 103–24, and Carol Poore, "Whose Celebration? The
Centennial of 1876 and German-American Socialist Culture" in Frank Trommler and Joseph McVeigh, eds., *America and the Germans: An Assessment of
a Three-Hundred-Year History,* Vol. I (Philadelphia: University of Pennsylvania Press, 1985), 176–88, are pioneering examinations, drawing upon recent
studies of working-class culture in Germany, of festivity in one segment of the
German-American community.

8. John Bodnar, *The Transplanted: A History of Immigrants in Urban America* (Bloomington: Indiana University Press, 1985), 184–89; Rudolph J. Vecoli,
"Cult and Occult in Italian-American Culture: The Persistence of a Religious
Heritage," in Randall M. Miller and Thomas D. Marzik, eds., *Immigrants and
Religion in Urban America* (Philadelphia: Temple University Press, 1977), 25–
47; Robert Anthony Orsi, *The Madonna of 115th Street: Faith and Community
in Italian Harlem, 1880–1950* (New Haven: Yale University Press, 1985); Den-
nis Clark, "St. Patrick's Day Observed," in Clark, *The Irish Relations: Trials
of an Immigrant Tradition* (Rutherford, N.J.: Fairleigh Dickinson University
Press, 1982), 193–204; Timothy J. Meagher, "'Why Should We Care for a Little
Trouble or a Walk through the Mud': St. Patrick's and Columbus Day Parades
in Worcester, Massachusetts, 1845–1915,"*New England Quarterly* 58 (1985),
5–26; Jane Gladden Kelton, "New York City St. Patrick's Day Parade: Invention of Contention and Consensus," *Drama Reivew* 29 (1985), 93–105. I have
borrowed the term "festive culture" from Klaus Tenfelde, "Mining Festivals
in the Nineteenth Century," *Journal of Contemporary History* 13 (1978), 377,
and am using it to refer to occasions and rituals of public celebration within
the immigrant community.

9. Sean Wilentz, "Artisan Republican Festivals and the Rise of Class Conflict in New York City, 1788–1837," in Michael H. Frisch and Daniel J. Wal-

kowitz, eds., *Working-Class America: Essays on Labor, Community, and American Society* (Urbana: University of Illinois Press, 1983), 37–77; Roy Rosenzweig, *Eight Hours for What We Will: Workers and Leisure in an Industrial City, 1870–1920* (Cambridge: Cambridge University Press, 1983); Davis, *Parades and Power,*; David Glassberg, "Public Ritual and Cultural Hierarchy: Philadelphia's Civic Celebrations at the Turn of the Twentieth Century," *Pennsylvania Magazine of History and Biography* 107 (1983), 421–48.

10. Bocock, *Ritual in Industrial Society*, 37.

11. Raymond Firth, *Symbols: Public and Private* (Ithaca: Cornell University Press, 1973), 76–90; Anthony F. C. Wallace, *Religion: An Anthropological View* (New York: Random House, 1966), 236–39.

12. Victor Turner, *The Ritual Process: Structure and Anti-Structure* (Ithaca: Cornell University Press, 1969), 42–43, 93–97; quotation 93.

13. Turner, "Introduction," 29.

14. Turner, *Ritual Process,* 127, 131, 126, 129, 185, 201.

15. Wallace, *Religion,* 106–66, quotation 106; Bocock, *Ritual in Industrial Society,* 37–59, quotation 50.

16. W. Lloyd Warner, *The Living and the Dead: A Study of the Symbolic Life of Americans* (New Haven: Yale University Press, 1959); Bocock, *Ritual in Industrial Society*; Joseph R. Gusfield and Jerzy Michalowicz, "Secular Symbolism: Studies of Ritual, Ceremony, and the Symbolic Order in Modern Life," *Annual Review of Sociology* 10 (1984), 417–35; Eric Hobsbawm and Terence Ranger, eds., *The Invention of Tradition* (Cambridge: Cambridge University Press, 1983); David Cannadine, "The Transformation of Civic Ritual in Modern Britain: The Colchester Oyster Feast," *Past and Present* 94 (1982), 107–30; Charles Rearick, "Festivals in Modern France: The Experience of the Third Republic," *Journal of Contemporary History* 12 (1977), 435–60; Harry C. Payne, "The Ritual Question and Modernizing Society, 1800–1945—A Schema for a History," *Historical Reflections/Réflexions Historiques* 11 (1984), 403–32.

17. J. Milton Yinger, "Ethnicity," *Annual Review of Sociology* 11 (1985), 151–80; William L. Yancey, Eugene P. Ericksen, and Richard N. Juliani, "Emergent Ethnicity: A Review and Reformulation," *American Sociological Review* 41 (1976), 391–403.

18. Kathleen Neils Conzen, "Germans," in Stephan Thernstrom, Ann Orlov, and Oscar Handlin, eds., *Harvard Encyclopedia of American Ethnic Groups* (Cambridge, Mass.: Harvard University Press, 1980), 405–25; and "Patterns of German-American History," in Randall M. Miller, ed., *Germans in America: Retrospect and Prospect* (Philadelphia: German Society of Pennsylvania, 1984), 14–36.

19. Thomas Nipperdey, "Verein als soziale Struktur in Deutschland im späten 18. und frühen 19. Jahrhundert: Eine Fallstudie zur Modernisierung I," in Nipperday, *Gesellschaft, Kultur, Theorie: Gesammelte Aufsätze zur neueren Geschichte* (Göttingen: Vandenhoeck & Ruprecht, 1976), 174–205; Otto Dann,

"Gruppenbildung und gesellschaftliche Organisierung in der Epoche der deutschen Romantik," in Richard Brinkmann, ed., *Romantik in Deutschland: Ein interdisziplinäres Symposion* (Stuttgart: J. B. Metzlersche Verlagsbuchhandlung, 1978), 115–31; Wolfgang Köllmann, *Sozialgeschichte der Stadt Barmen im 19. Jahrhundert* (Tübingen: J. C. B. Mohr, 1960), 102–30; Heinz Schmitt, *Das Vereinsleben der Stadt Weinheim an der Bergstrasse* (Weinheim a. d. B.: Weinheimer Geschichtsblatt Nr. 25, 1963), 7–32; Herbert Freudenthal, *Vereine in Hamburg: Ein Beitrag zur Geschichte und Volkskunde der Geselligkeit* (Hamburg: Museum für Hamburgische Geschichte, 1968), esp. 483–513; Dieter Dowe, "The Workingmen's Choral Movement in Germany before the First World War," *Journal of Contemporary History* 13 (1978), 269–96; Tenfelde, "Mining Festivals."

20. Dann, "Gruppenbildung und gesellschaftliche Organisierung;" Rainer Noltenius, *Dichterfeiern in Deutschland: Rezeptionsgeschichte als Sozialgeschichte am Beispiel der Schiller- und Freiligrath-Feiern* (München: Wilhelm Fink Verlag, 1984), 51–53.

21. Robert Reinhold Ergang, *Herder and the Foundations of German Nationalism* (New York: Columbia University Press, 1931); Dieter Narr, "Fest und Feier im Kulturprogramm der Aufklärung," *Zeitschrift für Volkskunde* 62 (1966), 184–203; Dann, "Gruppenbildung und gesellschaftliche Organisierung," 119–20, 124: Heidemarie Gruppe-Kelpanides, "Das Frankfurter Bundesschiessen von 1862—ein 'nationales Verbrüderungsfest': Eine Untersuchung zu deutschen Nationalfesten zwischen 1859 und 1866," in Andreas C. Bimmer and Heidemarie Gruppe-Kelpanides, eds., *Feste in Hessen*, vol. 4., Hessische Blätter für Volks- und Kulturforschung (Giessen: Wilhelm Schmitz Verlag, 1977), 19; George Mosse, *The Nationalization of the Masses* (New York, 1973), 74–97; the quotation, *ibid.*, 128.

22. Eric Hobsbawm, "Introduction: Inventing Traditions," in Hobsbawm and Ranger, eds., *Invention of Tradition*, 1–14; Mosse, *Nationalization of the Masses*; Noltenius, *Dichterfeiern*, 85–87; Gisela Jaacks, *Das Ljauubecker Volks- und Erinnerungsfest (Allgemeines Scheibenschiessen): Untersuchungen zur Entstehung und Entwicklung eines Grossstadt-Volksfestes*, Volkskundliche Studien, vol. V (Hamburg: Museum für Hamburgische Geschichte, 1971), 15–46; Gruppe-Kelpanides, "Frankfurter Bundesschiessen," 19–37; Wolfgang Hartmann, *Der historische Festzug: Seine Entstehung und Entwicklung im 19. und 20. Jahrhundert* (München: Prestel-Verlag, 1976); I am indebted to George Mosse, "Mass Politics and the Political Liturgy of Nationalism," in Eugene Kamenka, ed., *Nationalism: The Nature and Evolution of an Idea* (Canberra: Australian National University Press, 1973), 38–54, for his insight into the liturgical and sacramental character of the German national fests.

23. See Heinz Kloss, *Um die Einigung des Deutschamerikanertums: Die Geschichte einer unvollendeten Volksgruppe* (Berlin: Volk und Reich Verlag, 1937), 50–60.

24. Franz Löher, *Geschichte und Zustände der Deutschen in Amerika* (Cin-

cinnati: Eggers & Wulkop, 1847); C. L. Bernays, "Der deutsche Sonntag in Amerika," *Deutsch-Amerikanische Monatshefte* 3 (June 1866), 509–10; Friedrich Kapp, *Geschichte der Deutschen im Staate New York,* 3rd ed. (New York: E. Steiger, 1869), i–xiii; "Amerikanisirung," *Der deutsche Pioneer* 13 (June 1881), 201–2.

25. St—o [probably J. B. Stallo], in *Cincinnati Volksfreund,* Nov. 13, 1848: "Es ist hierlande um uns Deutsche eine eigene Sache, wir suchen und finden hier äussere Unabhängigkeit, ein freies, bürgerliches Leben, unbeschränkten industriellen Verkehr, kurz politische Freiheit; insofern sind wir Amerikaner. Aber wir sind Amerikaner, Deutsche. Wir bauen uns amerikanische Häuser; aber drinnen glimmt ein deutsches heerd. Wir tragen einen amerikanisches Hut; aber drunter weg schauen deutsche Augen aus einem deutschen Gesicht. Wir lieben unsere Frauen mit deutscher Treue . . . ; der liebe Gott hält sich für unsern Kirchengebrauch ein ein deutsches Privatohr; der amerikanische Catawba übersetzt sich in unserm Hirn in deutsche Träume, und fliesst von der lallenden Zunge in gemütlich deutschen Tonen. Wir leben nach amerikanischen Sitten, aber wir halten uns an deutsche Sitte. Wir rednen Englisch, aber wir denken und fühlen Deutsch. Unser Verstand spricht mit den Worten der Anglo Amerikaner, aber unser Herz versteht nur die Muttersprache. Während unser Blick über einen amerikanischen Horizont schwebt, wolbe sich in unserer Seele noch der alte deutsche Himmel. Unser ganzes Gemüthsleben ist mit einem Worte deutsch, und was immer die Bedürfnisse des Gemüths befriedigen soll, muss ihm erscheinen in deutschem Gewande."

26. Samuel Ludvigh, 8 ["Zwischen Markt und Kirche bewegt sich das Leben der Amerikaner, Geschäfte machen und beten sind die höchsten Momente der modernen Republikaner"], 26 ["die eigentliche Festtage der Republikaner"]; *Meyers Monats-Hefte* 1 (August 1853), 231 ["Immer wieder die alte Leier, die vieluniformige Miliz, dazwischen die schwarzen Fracks der Beamten in Wagen, das war der Kern des Festzuges, der sich von dem bei dem Leichenbegängnisse Henry Clay's nur dadurch unterschied, dass der Leichenwagen diesmal durch die Person des Präsidenten ersetz war"]; Ed. Grien, *Bunte Skizzen aus den Vereinigten Staaten von Amerika* (Leipzig: Gustav Weigel, 1882), 181 ["ideales und künstlerisches Gepräge"]; Ludwig C. W. von Baumbach, *Neue Briefe aus den Vereinigten Staaten von Nordamerika in die Heimath* (Cassel: Theodor Fischer, 1856), 184, 185; Christian Esselen, "Westliche Briefe," *Atlantis* 4 (1856), 382 ["Alles wird hier profan und gewöhnlich . . . "], "Aus den Papieren eines Misanthropen," *Atlantis* 7 (1857), 399 [" . . . dem amerikanischen Volke geht die Natürlichkeit, naivität und der Humor ab, und in einem Lande eines freien öffentlichen Lebens, wo jede Thätigkeit, jedes Bestreben, jede Ansicht sich ungehindert geltend machen kann, finden wir kein eigentliches Volksleben . . . "], "Am 4. Juli," *Atlantis* 3 (1855), 38 ["Der Amerikaner kann sich nicht begeistern; er kann sich nicht einmal freuen, davon ist der 4. Juli ein regelmässig wiederkehrender Beweis. . . . ist dieses Volk seines Ehrentages nicht mehr wert."]; for a particularly caustic look at Amer-

ican holidays, see Theodor Griesinger, *Land und Leute in Amerika: Skizzen aus dem amerikanischen Lebe,* vol. 2 (Stuttgart: A. Kröner, 1863), 819–39.

27. My examples are taken from the pages of the St. Cloud [Minnesota] *Journal,* 1865–71.

28. Bruce Laurie, *Working People of Philadelphia, 1800–1850* (Philadelphia: Temple University Press, 1980), 53–66; Susan G. Davis, "'Making Night Hideous': Christmas Revelry and Public Order in Nineteenth-Century Philadelphia," *American Quarterly* 34 (1982), 185–99; Rosenzweig, *Eight Hours,* 35–90; Steven J. Ross, *Workers on the Edge: Work, Leisure, and Politics in Industrializing Cincinnati, 1788–1890* (New York: Columbia University Press, 1985), 18–24, 164–79; Francis G. Couvares, *The Remaking of Pittsburgh: Class and Culture in an Industrializing City, 1877–1919* (Albany: State University of New York Press, 1984), 31–50.

29. Davis, *Parades and Power;* "Holidays," *North American Review* No. 175 (April 1857), 334–63. To German eyes at least, Irish-Americans shared the polarized and "unaesthetic" American celebratory tradition; one of Milwaukee's German press, for example, reported in 1859 that the city's Irish celebrated St. Patrick's Day "in customary fashion [herkömmlicher Weise]" with a militia parade, Mass, and evening banquet; *Banner und Volksfreund,* March 12, 1859.

30. The banquet was also criticized for being expensive and "exclusive"; *Illustrirte Welt,* Nov. 19, 1859; "Germany in New York," *Atlantic Monthly* 19 (May 1867), 555–64; *Illustrirte Welt,* Oct. 20, 1860. The 1859 May Festival parade in New Orleans included a May Queen and her maids of honor in carriages, accompanied by "an immense car, covered with wreaths of evergreen, filled with little children dressed in white and smothered in flowers;" FLIN, May 28, 1859, 408.

31. Dr. A. Kirsten, *Skizzen aus den Vereinigten Staaten von Nord-Amerika* (Leipzig: F. A. Brockhaus, 1854), 315–17; *Illustrirte Welt* (New York), Nov. 26, 1859; B., "Das Bier und der Sabbath," *Atlantische Studien* 3 (1853), 141–57; "Plaudereien aus Boston," *Meyer's Monats-Hefte* 5 (Feb. 1855), 144–49; Bernays, "Der deutsche Sonntag," 509–19.

32. Julius Fröbel was one of the most significant dissenters from the common German-American criticism of American culture. He recognized in the tenor of American life a true "folk culture" based upon the realities of class equality, and argued that importing German popular culture meant importing the culture of one particular class in Germany and destroying the cultural uniformity on which American politics rested: "In so far as from the nation as a whole, from the *Volk* in a political sense, they single out a *Volk* in a social sense—that which the monarchical states of Europe are accustomed to calling the *Volk*—they are creating out of its midst at the same time both a proletariat and over it an aristocracy;" Julius Fröbel, *Aus Amerika: Erfahrungen, Reisen und Studien* (Leipzig: J. J. Weber, 1857), 510. But few German-American apologists had his hard-headed appreciation for the realities underlying their cultural rhetoric, and failed to see anything approaching a true *Volkfest* tradition in America.

33. *Banner und Volksfreund* (Milwaukee), July 21, 1858 ["wie . . . in der alten Heimath"]; *Atlantis,* July 20, 1853, 218 ["Es war ein Fest nach echter deutscher Weise, und man schmechte keinen Tropfen von dem Salzwasser hindurch, welches uns von dem alten Vaterlande trennt"]; *Banner und Volksfreund,* Feb. 18, 1858 ["kurz Alles wirkte zusammen, um sich in Gedanken auf einen jener glänzenden Maskenballe in der alten Heimath versetzt zu wähnen, deren Veranstaltung man bis jetzt in Amerika, und namentlich im 'fernen Westen', für eine Unmöglichkeit gehalten hatte"]; *Leipziger Illustrirte Zeitung* Aug. 25, 1855, 142 ["Der Deutsche fühlte sich neu gestärkt und gehoben; er hatte einige Tage in den schönsten Erinnerungen an vergangene glückliche Tage schwelgen können . . . er hatte Gram und Kummer vergessen und sich ganz den versöhnenden Einflüssen des edlen Gesanges überlassen"].

34. Ibid. ["er konnte ver seinen amerikanischen Mitbürgern eine der schönsten Seiten des deutschen Nationallebens entfalten; er konn die tiefe Poesie, die innige Harmonie, welche die Grundelemente des deutschen Charakters bilden, offenbaren"].

35. For documentation and fuller development of the argument here and in the following paragraphs, see Kathleen Neils Conzen, "German-Americans and the Invention of Ethnicity," in Trommler and McVeigh, *America and the Germans,* Vol, I, 131–47.

36. Julius Fröbel in *San Francisco Journal,* April 27, 1855 ["der isolirte Stellung der Fremden in diesem Lande;" "das Bedürfniss nach Einigung;" "gerade die Maifeste sind es, in deren Feier jenem Bedürfniss einige Befriedigung geboten wird;" "eine erwünschte Gelegenheit bieten, sich mit ihren Landsleuten nach altvaterländischer Weise zu vergnügen, and dadurch anzuerkennen, dass nationale Gebräuche, sofern ihnen eine moralische Bedeutung zu Grunde liegt, auch in der weitesten Entfernung von ihrem Ursprungsort haltbar sind"]; W. R., Philadelphia, in *Meyer's Monats-Hefte* 2 (Dec. 1853), 155 ["sie gibt dem deutschen Elemente Gelegenheit, sich dem Amerikanerthum von seiner schönsten Seite darzustellen; deutsche Kraft, deutsche Bildung und Freude sollen wie versöhnende Gestalten mitten auf den lauten Markt des amerikanischen Geschäfts- und Staatslebens treten und auch diesem durch ihren veredelnden Einfluss nach und nach eine höhere Weihe geben"]; G. B., *Ibid.* 1 (Aug. 1853), 232 ["deren eigentliche Bedeutung, deren wahres Wesen, deren reallen Inhalt und wichtigsten Einfluss"].

37. Mosse, *Nationalization of the Masses,* 87–89; Noltenius, *Dichterfeiern,* 10–11, 71–87; *New York Times,* Dec. 9, 1859 (hereafter cited as NYT).

38. Friedrich Kapp, "Die Achtundvierziger in den Vereinigten Staaten (1861)," in Kapp, *Aus und über Amerika: Thatsachen und Erlebnisse,* I (1876), 329; *Illustrirte Zeitung* (Leipzig), Jan. 14, 1860, 23–25; FLIN, Nov. 26, 1859; *Chicago Press and Tribune,* Nov. 9, 1859; *Illustrirte Welt* (New York), Nov. 19, 1859; Wittke, *Refugees of Revolution,* 311–13.

39. Kapp, "Achtundvierziger," 329; Kapp saw in these "earnest, elevating" festivities the "highpoint" of German "development and intellectual significance" in America.

40. See the essays and poems collected in *Schiller-Album*, especially Peter August Moelling (Galveston), "Schiller's Ideale," 86–88 (melancholy memories); Philemon (Philadelphia), "Schiller und Goethe," 92–93 (brotherhood); "Dedication," v–vii (Germany not the soil, but spiritual treasures); Th. Schuckhart (Brooklyn), "Einer deutschen Auswandererschaar," 76–77 (remain German); Marie Westland (Philadelphia), "Huldigung," 46–50 ("Es ruht sich gut im Schatten seines Ruhms!"); Dr. Carl Friedrich Neidhard, "Der Herold der Freiheit," 83–84 (preserve American institutions). Dr. [Wilhelm?] Löwe's New York speech is quoted in *Illustrirte Zeitung* (Leipzig), Jan. 14, 1860, 23.

41. For a similar, more systematic typology of private and public German festive occasions, see Andreas C. Bimmer, "Zur Typisierung gegenwärtiger Feste," in Bimmer and Gruppe-Kelpanides, *Feste in Hessen*, 38–48.

42. *San Francisco Journal*, April 13, May 1, May 8, 1853.

43. Rudolph Koss, *Milwaukee* (Milwaukee: Herold, 1871), 164; *Banner und Volksfreund* (Milwaukee), Nov. 12, 1859.

44. *New Yorker-Criminal-Zeitung und Belletristisches Journal* (hereafter cited as NYBJ), June 1, 1860 ("Es fehlt die Theilnahme der *ganzen* Bevölkerung. . . . Soll man sich recht festlich fühlen, so muss, wie in Deutschland, Alles das Festkleid tragen, Alles in den Jubel einstimmen. Das Auge darf nicht durch das geschäftige Alltagstreiben, das Gemüth nicht durch den Gedanken gestört werden, dass man eigentlich von der Arbeit, welcher der Tag von Rechtswegen gehört, eskappirt ist").

45. German-Americans would have found congenial the logic of a late nineteenth-century German commentator: "If a festival, a great folk festival that is to move all hearts, is to be celebrated, it is not enough just for individual deputations to make their way to the palace, or for leading officials to drink toasts at a private dinner. The entire Volk wants to pay homage. . . . But that only occurs with a great public procession . . . a meaningful parade, which moves slowly through the festively decorated streets of a large city to the sound of music, can be seen, wondered over, and understood by thousands upon thousands. It passes rich and poor at the same time . . . all classes, all circles of the population can and should participate . . . each and all will find representation." Quoted in Hartmann, *Der historische Festzug*, 133–34.

46. FLIN, Sept. 12, 1857; for the busy world of local *Verein* celebrations, see, for example, NYBJ, June 22, 1860; this issue alone announced more than a dozen anniversary celebrations and excursions in the New York area.

47. FLIN, Aug. 5, 313, 316; Sept. 16, 1865, 413; Aug. 3, 1867, 316; for other examples, see FLIN, July 11, 1868, 268; July 18, 1868, 283; Aug. 26, 1871, 405; July 6, 1872, 267; Aug. 3, 1872, 333.

48. *Atlantis* [Dessau] 1 1853, 246–48; *Wisconsin Banner* (Milwaukee), June 21, July 5, 1845; *Banner und Volksfreund* (Milwaukee), June 14, 21, July 2, 1858; June 29, July 6, 1859; June 14, 1860; Joseph Eiboeck, *Die Deutschen von Iowa und deren Errungenschaften* (Des Moines: Iowa Staats-Anzeiger, 1900), 755–57: Klauprecht, *Deutsche Chronik*, 192–96; "Aus Pittsburg," *Steiger's*

Literarischer Monatsbericht 1 (Dec. 1869), 24; Heinrich Börnstein, *Fünfund-siebzig Jahre in der Alten und Neuen Welt: Memoiren eines Unbedeutenden* (Leipzig, 1881), II: 120–23.

49. Conzen, *Immigrant Milwaukee*, 167–91; Wittke, *Refugees of Revolution*, 280–99.

50. For patterns of working-class celebration, see Hartmut Keil, John B. Jentz, et al., eds., *Deutsche Arbeiterkultur in Chicago von 1850 bis zum Ersten Weltkrieg: Eine Anthologie* (Ostfildern: Scripta Mercaturae Verlag, 1984), 226–300; for examples of one kind of German church-oriented culture, see Jay P. Dolan, *The Immigrant Church: New York's Irish and German Catholics, 1815–1865* (Baltimore: Johns Hopkins University Press, 1975), 68–86.

51. For an excellent contemporary discussion of the consequences of growing social differentiation for German-American community life and festivity, see Wilhelm Hense-Jensen and Ernest Bruncken, *Wisconsin's Deutsch-Amerikaner bis zum Schluss des neunzehnten Jahrhunderts,* Vol. 2 (Milwaukee: Im Verlage der Deutschen Gesellschaft, 1902), 205–15.

52. Benno Haberland, *Das deutsche Element in den Vereinigten Staaten von Nord-Amerika* (Leipzig: H. Matthes, 1866), 53–55, 84–87; Daniel Hertle, *Die Deutschen in Nordamerika und der Freiheitskampf in Missouri* (Chicago: Druck der 'Illinois Staatszeitung', 1865), 24–35, 112; *Steiger's Literarisches Magazin* 1 (1869), 33.

53. Best known, perhaps, is the story of the 300 German singers who gathered to sing at the bier of President Lincoln when his body lay in state in Chicago on May 1 and 2, 1865; Max Stern and Fred Kressmann, eds., *Chicago's Deutsche Maenner: Erinnerungs-Blätter an Chicago's Fünfzigjähriges Jubiläum* (Chicago: Max Stern & Co., 1885), 61–62. It is typical of the German attitude toward public ceremonial that German newspapers deplored the lack of national commemoration of the first anniversary of Lincoln's assassination; *Deutsch-Amerikanische Monatshefte* 3 (1866), 495.

54. Landscape Research, *Built in Milwaukee: An Architectural View of the City* (Milwaukee: City of Milwaukee, 1981), 9, 112–14; Daniel Hurley, *Cincinnati: The Queen City* (Cincinnati: Cincinnati Historical Society, 1982), 67–70.

55. NYBJ, May 20, 1869.

56. *New-Yorker Criminal-Zeitung und Belletristisches Journal,* July 27, 1860.

57. Roger Kennedy, *Minnesota Houses: An Architectural and Historical View* (Minneapolis: Dillon Press, 1967), 61–77; Landscape Research, *Built in Milwaukee,* 141–42, 165, 168.

58. Kirsten, 1851, pp. 62–64; FLIN, Sept. 27, 1856, p. 247; May 19, 1860, p. 394; June Hargrove, "A Social History of the Public Monument in Ohio," in Marianne Doezema and June Hargrove, *The Public Monument and Its Audience* (Cleveland: Cleveland Museum of Art, 1977), 23–27; FLIN, June 18, 1870, pp. 220, 222; Aug. 16, 1884, p. 413; Aug. 28, 1886, p. 28; *New York Monthly* [German] 10 (June 1899), 11–13; (July 1899), 1–2, 11; Thomas Nipperdey, "Nationalidee und Nationaldenkmal in Deutschland im 19. Jahrhun-

dert," in Nipperdey, (1976), 133–73; Mosse, *Nationalization*, 47–71; Conzen, "Invention of Ethnicity," 142–43.

59. Angela Redinger, *Der "Schwabenverein" in Chicago: Organisation, Funktion und Wandel eines deutsch-amerikanischen Vereins von 1880–1920.* Hausarbeit zur Erlangung des Magistergrades der Ludwig-Maximilians-Universität München im Fachbereich Sozialwissenschaften, 1983; *New York Monthly* 10 (July 1899), 13–14. For similar festivals elsewhere see FLIN, Oct. 17, 1868, p. 67; Sept. 20, 1884, p. 71.

60. *Banner und Volksfreund* (Milwaukee), March 4, 1857, Jan. 30, Feb. 10, 1858, Feb. 22, 1860; FLIN, Feb. 25, 1860, p. 199; March 9, 1861, pp. 244, 253; March 7, 1868, p. 393; March 5, 1870, 420; March 4, 1871, p. 415; Feb. 24, 1872, pp. 373–74; March 2, 1872, pp. 396–97; Feb. 21, 1895, p. 124; FLIZ, March 13, 1875; Georg von Skal, "Die wahre Bedeutung des Carnevals in Amerika," *New York Echo* 1 (Dec. 20, 1902), 2

61. *Banner und Volksfreund* (Milwaukee), March 4, 1857; see also *ibid.,* Jan. 30, Feb. 8, Feb. 12, Feb. 15, Feb. 16, 1858, Feb. 5, Feb. 14, Feb. 22, 1860. The last cited issue reported that the 1860 parade include caricatures of a current scandal involving county orders, and of "music of the future;" workers participated with their own carnival association, and six collectors accompanied the parade soliciting money from spectators for the workers' soup kitchen. On German carnival traditions, see Joseph Klersch, *Die Kölnische Fastnacht von ihren Anfängen bis zur Gegenwart* (Köln: J. P. Bachem, 1961), 84–146: Anton M. Keim, *11 Mal politischer Karneval: Weltgeschichte aus der Bütt* (Mainz: v. Hase & Koehler Verlag, 1966), 37–101; the role in America of the German carnival tradition is sufficiently complex to merit a study of its own.

62. von Skal, "Die wahre Bedeutung des Carnevals," 2.

63. *N.Y. Staats-Zeitung,* Sept. 15, 1869; NYT, Sept. 14, Sept. 15, 1869; Kloss, *Um die Einigung,* 230–31.

64. Stern and Kressmann, eds., *Chicago's Deutsche Männer,* 65–66.

65. FLIN, April 29, 1871, p. 107; for similarly elaborate celebrations in other cities, see FLIN, June 17, 1871, p. 221.

66. NYT, Oct. 8, 9, 1883; *Chicago Tribune,* Oct. 7, 8, 9, 10, 1883; "Aufruf an die Deutschen in Amerika," *Der deutsche Pionier* 15 (June 1883), 212–13; H. Neelmeyer-Vukassowitsch, *Die Vereinigten Staaten von Amerika* (Leipzig: Franz Duncker, 1884), 262–64.

67. *New York Monthly* [German] 8 (May 1897), 3, 13; 9 (March 1898), 12n13; 10 (July 1899), 13–14; (October 1899), 11; *New York Echo* [German], Aug. 23, 1902, p. 6; Aug. 30, 1902, p. 6; Nov. 15, 1902, p. 14; Dec. 20, 1902, p. 2; Kloss, *Um die Einigung,* 251–53.

68. Contemporaries judged the very elaborate parade, speeches, and bonfire with which Milwaukee's 1890 German Day was celebrated "successful in every way," largely, it seems, because of the "deep impression it made on fellow citizens of other nationalities;" Hense-Jensen and Bruncken, *Wisconsin's Deutsch-Amerikaner,* Vol. 2, p. 214.

69. Frederick C. Luebke, *Bonds of Loyalty: German Americans and World*

War I (DeKalb: Northern Illinois University Press, 1974); David W. Detjen, *The Germans in Missouri, 1900–1918: Prohibition, Neutrality, and Assimilation* (Columbia: University of Missouri Press, 1985); Melvin G. Holli, "The Great War Sinks Chicago's German *Kultur*," in Holli and Peter d'A. Jones, eds., *Ethnic Chicago* (Grand Rapids, Mich.: William B. Eerdmans Publishing Co., rev. ed., 1984), 460–512; Bayrd Still, *Milwaukee: The History of a City* (Madison: State Historical Society of Wisconsin, 1948), 261–67; Conzen, "Invention of Ethnicity." For a telling discussion of change and cultural ossification within one German-American sub-group, see Klaus Ensslen and Heinz Ickstadt, "German Working-Class Culture in Chicago: Continuity and Change in the Decade from 1900 to 1910," in Hartmut Keil and John B. Jentz, eds., *German Workers in Industrial Chicago, 1850–1910: A Comparative Perspective* (DeKalb: Northern Illinois University Press, 1983), 236–52.

70. *Die Fackel* 8 (June 1855), 25; "Das Gesangfest zu Milwaukee," *Atlantis* 5 (1856), 28 ("die herzliche Geselligkeit, die Eintracht und Einmüthigkeit, Alles das, was wir mit dem so oft verspotteten Namen der deutschen Gemüthlichkeit bezeichnen, gab diesem Feste einen eigenthümlichen Reiz"); Friedrich Kapp, "Rede," *Deutsch-Amerikanische Monatshefte* 2 (1865), 184 ("um wenigstems für Augenblicke die Arbeit des Tages zu vergessen, um Mensch unter Mensch zu sein;" "in der Oede des hiesigen öffentlichen Lebens;" "so sind Musik und Gesang das reinigende Bad"); NYBJ, July 23, 1869 ("während eines Sängerfestes fliegen die Stunden und die Tage laufen mit Siebenmeilenstiefeln davon").

71. Significantly, Kloss (*Um die Einigung*, 252) notes that many German Catholics felt uncomfortable with the ethnic definition communicated in turn-of-the-century German Day celebrations, and after 1910 promoted their own Catholic equivalent, a celebration of St. Boniface Day. For an excellent discussion of the intertwining of class and ethnic identities, see Keil and Ickstadt, "Elemente einer deutschen Arbeiterkultur."

72. "Die Humboldt-Jubelfeier und ihre praktischen Resultate," *Steiger's Literarischer Monatsbericht* 1 (Nov. 1869), 22–25; Frederick C. Luebke, "German Immigrants and American Politics: Problems of Leadership, Parties, and Issues," Miller, *Germans in America*, 57–74, and his *Bonds of Loyalty*, 27–81; Kloss, *Um die Einigung*, 248–85.

73. *Illustrirte Welt*, June 18, 1859; *Harper's Weekly*, July 4, 1857, 425; FLIN, Oct. 11, 1856, 278, 281; Aug. 31, 1867, 376; Jan. 6, 1872, 268–70.

74. *Steiger's Literarische Monatshefte* 1 (Aug. 1869), 32; on this point, see Wittke, *Refugees of Revolution*, 294–95, who also quotes Karl Heinzen referring to the New York Humboldt Parade as "conceived in beer and buried in beer" (314). An 1859 cartoon satirized the planning committee for a German national fest that was trying to decide whether the German national honor should be tippled ["kneipen"] in beer or champagne: "One of the members proposes an amendment to celebrate with beer, and the proposal is unanimously accepted in this form. The honor of the German nation in both hemispheres is rescued;" *Illustrirte Welt*, Nov. 5, 1859.

75. NYT, Oct. 9, 1883.

76. FLIN, Sept. 12, 1857; see also, for example, *Cincinnati Gazette*, 1849, cited in Faust, II, 382; *Chicago Daily Tribune*, June 6, 1857; *Chicago Press and Tribune*, Nov. 5, 1859; for a contemporary American criticism of the inadequacies of American festive culture, see "Holidays," *North American Review* No. 175 (April 1857), 334–63.

77. NYT, Sept. 15, 1869, Oct. 9, 1883.

78. Walter Nugent, "The American People and the Centennial of 1876," *Indiana Magazine of History* 75 (1979), 53–69; George William Douglas, *The American Book of Days* (New York: H. W. Wilson Co., 1937), 7, 481, 9; Leonard V. Huber, *Mardi Gras: A Pictorial History of Carnival in New Orleans* (Gretna, La.: Pelican Publishing Company, 1977); Jean A. Spraker, "The Rollicking Realm of Boreas: A Century of Carnivals in St. Paul," *Minnesota History* 49 (1985), 322–31; Constance Cary Harrison, "American Rural Festivals," *The Century Magazine* 50 (July 1895), 323–33.

79. Davis, *Parades and Power*, 165–73; Couvares, *Remaking of Pittsburgh*, 108–11; Rosenzweig, *Eight Hours*, 153–68.

80. Meagher, "Why Should We Care;" Rowland Berthoff, "Under the Kilt: Variations on the Scottish-American Ground," *Journal of American Ethnic History* 1 (1982), 5–34.

81. FLIN, March 31, 1860, 282; July 20, 1867, 285; Sept. 2, 1871, 421; Philadelphia and St. Louis both had a German carnival tradition, and both had been the sites of major German-American conventions, as well as the Peace celebration, in the years preceding the Mummers and Veiled Prophet parades; FLIN 36 (March 13, 1875), 174. By the late 1860s, cities were routinely suspending enforcement of their Sunday ordinances during national German conventions, and state and city officials were not only reviewing the parades, but actually riding in them. NYBJ, May 20, July 23, 1869.

82. Lewis A. Erenberg, *Steppin' Out: New York Nightlife and the Transformation of American Culture, 1890–1930* (Westport, Conn.: Greenwood Press, 1981); Francis G. Couvares, "The Triumph of Commerce: Class Culture and Mass Culture in Pittsburgh," in Frisch and Walkowitz, eds., *Working-Class America*, 123–52: Rosenzweig, *Eight Hours*, 171–228; John F. Kasson, *Amusing the Million: Coney Island at the Turn of the Century* (New York: Hill & Wang, 1978).

83. *New Yorker Criminal-Zeitung*, June 9, 1854, 201; *Arbeiter-Union*, quoted in *Steiger's Literarische Monatshefte* 1 (Aug. 1869), 32; *Der deutsche Pionier* 7 (Aug. 1875), 221–22; ibid. 8 (April 1876), 154; ibid. 13, June 1881, 201–2; Emil Rothe, "Das deutsche Element in Amerika," in Armin Tenner, ed., *Amerika: Der heutige Standpunkt der Kultur in den Vereinigten Staaten* (New York: Westermann & Co., 1884), 198–99.

84. Albert B. Faust, *The German Element in the United States*, vol. 2 (Boston: Houghton Mifflin, 1909); quotation, 383.

85. Ibid., 383.

86. For a perceptive evocation of this change in one community, see Georg

Mann, "The Furor Teutonicus: Upper Mississippi Abteilung," *Yale Review* 60 (1971), 306–20.

87. On these distinctions, see Werner Sollors, *Beyond Ethnicity: Consent and Descent in American Culture* (New York: Oxford University Press, 1986), 20–39; Yinger, "Ethnicity;" Barbara Ballis Lal, "Perspectives on Ethnicity: Old Wine in New Bottles," *Ethnic and Racial Studies* 6 (1983), 154–73; Herbert J. Gans, "Symbolic Ethnicity: The Future of Ethnic Groups and Cultures in America," *Ethnic and Racial Studies* 2 (1979), 1–20.

88. John Plamenatz, "Two Types of Nationalism," in Kamenka, ed., *Nationalism*, 22–36.

89. The Scots may offer one of the best comparisons with the German experience. Like the Germans, they too turned invented homeland rituals and symbols of nationalism to ethnic purposes in America. Unlike the Germans, however, their cultural difference from native-born Americans was slight and they had few if any defensive concerns. Their turn to ethnic ritual was almost purely a search for communitas to leaven the individualism of the liberal society in which they had prospered (many who participated were generations removed from immigration), and suggests what might have happened to German ethnic ritual and group membership had not two world wars destroyed its laboriously constructed positive image; see Hugh Trevor-Roper, "The Invention of Tradition: The Highland Tradition of Scotland," in Hobsbawm and Ranger, *Invention of Tradition*, 15–42; Berthoff, "Under the Kilt."

Defining the Race, 1890–1930

1. "Prejudice not Natural" (June 8, 1848), in Howard Brotz, ed., *Negro Social and Political Thought, 1850–1920* (New York, 1966), 213.

2. "An Address to the Colored People of the United States" (Sept. 29, 1848) ibid., 210.

3. Cited in William Ivy Nair, *Bourbonism and Agrarian Protest: Louisiana Politics, 1877–1900* (Baton Rouge, 1969), 173.

4. Cited in Theodore Draper, *American Communism and Soviet Russia* (New York, 1960), 324. Briggs's ideas were embodied in the African Blood Brotherhood, a short-lived organization he helped to create during World War I. He joined the Communist party in the early 1920s.

5. "Open Letter" Key West, Fla., Jan 18, 1919, copy in C-319, National Association for the Advancement of Colored People Papers, Library of Congress.

6. L. A. Gabriel to James W. Johnson, Jan. 26, 1919, ibid.

7. John Higham, "Integrating America: The Problem of Assimilation in the Nineteenth Century," *Journal of American Ethnic History* 1 (Fall 1981), 7–22.

8. Hair, *Bourbonism and Agrarian Protest*, pp. 170–97.

9. C. Vann Woodward, *The Origins of the New South, 1877–1913* (Baton Rouge, 1951), 321–95; J. Morgan Kousser, *The Shaping of Southern Politics:*

Suffrage Restriction and the Establishment of the One-Party South, 1880–1910 (New Haven, 1974), esp. 250–57; David Gerber, *Black Ohio and the Color Line, 1860–1915* (Urbana, 1976), 247–70.

10. Cited in Kousser, *Shaping of Southern Politics, 252.*

11. *Nation,* April 9, 1874: John Bukowczyk, "The Transformation of Working-Class Ethnicity: Corporate Control, Americanization, and the Polish Immigrant Middle Class in Bayonne, New Jersey, 1915–1925," *Labor History* 25 (Winter, 1984), 69.

12. For a good discussion of differences between elitist and popular notions of reform, see Melvin G. Holli, *Reform in Detroit: Hazen S. Pingree and Urban Politics* (New York, 1969), esp. 157–81.

13. See George Fredrickson, *The Black Image in the White Mind* (New York, 1971) and Kousser, *Shaping of Southern Politics.* The best theoretical statement of the problem is Barbara J. Fields, "Race and Ideology in American History," in J. Morgan Kousser and James M. McPherson, eds., *Region, Race, and Reconstruction: Essays in Honor of C. Vann Woodward* (New York, 1982), 143–77.

14. Cited in Gerber, *Black Ohio,* 182.

15. Ibid., 111–36, 320–70; David M. Katzman, *Before the Ghetto: Black Detroit in the Nineteenth Century* (Urbana, 1973), 135–206.

16. Owen Charles Mathurin, *Henry Sylvester Williams and the Origins of the Pan-African Movement, 1869–1911* (Westport, Conn., 1976), esp. 49, 63, 68, for context.

17. W. E. B. Du Bois, "The Conservation of Races," in *Negro Social and Political Thought,* 487–88; Mathurin, *Henry Sylvester Williams,* 60–85.

18. Cited in Robert W. July, *The Origins of Modern African Thought* (New York, 1967), 211, 221.

19. Ibid., 186–90; Hollis Lynch, *Edward Blyden: Pan-Negro Patriot* (New York, 1967), 198–201.

20. E. J. Hobsbawm, *The Age of Capital, 1848–1875* (New York, 1975), 89.

21. Lynch, *Blyden,* 242–43.

22. Du Bois, "The Conservation of Races," 485, 483. For a detailed discussion of cultural pluralism see Werner Sollors, *Beyond Ethnicity: Consent and Descent in American Culture* (New York, 1986), esp. 181–95.

23. Ibid., 490.

24. Arnold Rampersad, *The Art and Imagination of W. E. B. Du Bois* (Cambridge, 1976), 88.

25. Like much of the black middle class, Du Bois looked askance at popular urban music—jazz and the blues. In *Dusk of Dawn: An Essay toward an Autobiography of a Race Concept* (New York, 1940), 202–3, he identifies jazz with caricature and implicitly argues that its flourishing reflects the white demand for amusement, not art, from blacks.

26. His fiction has been so pervasive that it has been accepted by astute scholars. Thus, Rampersad writes, "Du Bois *admitted* that 'death, disease and

crime' were the rule of black life" (emphasis added). *Art and Imagination of W. E. B. Du Bois*, 81.

27. Du Bois, "The Talented Tenth," in Booker T. Washington et al., *The Negro Problem* (New York, 1903), 31–75.

28. Du Bois to Streator, April 17, 1935. In 1946, Du Bois advised against creating organizations of young rural blacks. "Negro youth in the rural districts are too ignorant to form an intelligent organization." By 1958, he modified somewhat his faith in the black middle class. Du Bois to Cleo Hamilton, Sept. 10, 1946; Du Bois, speech at Charles University, Prague, Oct. 23, 1958, W. E. B. Du Bois Papers.

29. Theodore Rosengarten, *All God's Dangers: The Life of Nate Shaw* (New York, 1974), 108.

30. Cited in Eric Foner, *Nothing but Freedom: Emancipation and Its Legacy* (Baton Rouge, 1983), 71–72.

31. *All God's Dangers*, 250.

32. Ibid., 262–63, 390.

33. Judith Stein, *The World of Marcus Garvey: Race and Class in Modern Society* (Baton Route, 1986), 24–29.

34. Garvey, "Universal Negro Improvement Association: Address Delivered by the President at the Annual Meeting," Kingston *Daily Gleaner*, Aug. 26, 1915.

35. Stein, *World of Marcus Garvey*, 30–36.

36. Ibid., 37.

37. Katzman, *Before the Ghetto*, 78.

38. Gerber, *Black Ohio*, 271–96, 371–467; August Meier, *Negro Thought in America, 1880–1915* (Ann Arbor, 1963), 121–70.

39. Garvey to Nicholas Murray Butler, Feb. 5, 1918, in Robert A. Hill, ed., *The Marcus Garvey and Universal Negro Improvement Papers (Berkeley, 1983–)*, 1:250.

40. "Open Letter" (Jan. 18, 1919), C-304, NAACP Papers; John Riley to R. R. Moton, Oct. 21, 1918, R. R. Moton Papers, Tuskegee Institute.

41. Although Du Bois did not join the league, his thinking on African self-determination was very similar. See his, "Memorandum on the Future of Africa" (n.d. [1918]), C-385, NAACP Papers.

42. Cited in Stein, *World of Marcus Garvey*, 50.

43. *Negro World*, Oct. 11, 1919.

44. Garvey, speech, New York, Oct. 30, 1919, in Hill, ed., *Marcus Garvey Papers*, 2:128.

45. Gilbert Osofsky, *Harlem: The Making of a Ghetto: Negro New York, 1890–1930* (New York, 1963), 170.

46. *Negro World*, Feb 1, 1919.

47. Stein, *World of Marcus Garvey*, 65–66.

48. *Negro World*, June 7, Aug. 2, 1919.

49. Stein, *World of Marcus Garvey*, 71.

50. *Negro World*, Aug. 2, 1919.

51. William Ferris, *African Abroad; or, His Evolution in Western Civilization, Tracing His Development under Caucasian Milieu*, 2 vols. (New Haven, 1913), 1:268, 407.

52. *Negro World*, March 20, 1920.

53. W. E. B. Du Bois, *Crisis* 21 (Dec. 1920), 58–60; 24 (Sept. 1922), 210.

54. Stein, *World of Marcus Garvey*, 92, 223–29.

55. Ibid., 141–43

56. Ibid., chap. 12.

57. William V. Kelley to George Haynes, Aug. 25, 1919; Haynes to Kelley, Sept. 11, 1919, RG 174, Records of the Department of Labor, National Archives; Joe William Trotter, J., *Black Milwaukee: The Making of an Industrial Proletariat, 1915–1945* (Urbana, 1985), 127.

58. David Levering Lewis, "Parallels and Divergences: Assimilationist Strategies of Afro-American and Jewish Elites from 1910 to the Early 1930s," *Journal of American History* 71 (Dec. 1984), 564.

59. Ralph J. Bunche, "Extended Memorandum of the Programs, Ideologies, Tactics, and Achievements of Negro Betterment Interracial Organizations: A Research Memorandum" (June 7, 1940), p. 144, Carnegie-Myrdal Study: The Negro in America, Schomburg Center, New York Public Library.

60. Roy Wilkins, *Standing Fast: The Autobiography of Roy Wilkins* (New York, 1982), 174.

61. Stein, *World of Marcus Garvey*, 140–52.

62. Jesse Jackson's 1984 campaign drew on similar strengths and weaknesses. Reflecting the absence of clear objectives and targets in post–civil rights politics, his tactic was to unite blacks through his person. His argument that the Democratic party's recognition of him was equivalent to respect for all black people was a surrogate for a political program. This rationale echoed Garvey's efforts to identify his success with the success of all blacks. Indeed, because whites often assume the organicism of the black community, Jackson's preeminence was instantly accepted by the media and politicians, normally requiring more substantial tests. See Adolph L. Reed, Jr., *The Jesse Jackson Phenomenon* (New Haven, 1986), esp. 61–78, 106–22.

63. Stein, *World of Marcus Garvey*, 223–47.

64. Charles Hall, "Industrial Trends" (n.d. [1930]), Oxley-Phillips file, in RG 174, Records of the Department of Labor; James Weldon Johnson, *Black Manhattan* (New York, 1930), 159.

65. Johnson, *Black Manhattan*, 166, 281.

66. In contrast, the "new immigrant" working class was more homogeneous. It came at approximately the same economic stage, 1890–1914, when American industry was being transformed by mass production.

67. F. Alden Wilson, "Occupational Structure of the Negro in the Iron and Steel Industry: Pittsburgh and Environs" (March–May 1934), 29, 42, Pittsburgh Urban League Papers, Hillman Library, University of Pittsburgh.

68. A common explanation is that white bosses preferred white labor. This

rests on several false assumptions. First, the foreigners did not enter the white race until after World War II. Often, white elites thought blacks' behavior was superior to that of foreigners. In 1905, the leading Pittsburgh newspaper claimed the Italian section was filled with "throngs of greasy, unkempt Italians standing around in front of crazy little grocery stores, jabbering or smoking, while slovenly women with filthy youngsters sit on steps or parade up and down in the street strewn with old vegetables, filthy water, and rubbish of all kinds." The newspaper applauded the black neighborhood, Hayti, composed of "good negroes . . . although the moral tone of the ward is not above reproach." Cited in John Bodnar, Roger Simon, and Michael P. Weber, *Lives of Their Own: Blacks, Italians, and Poles in Pittsburgh, 1900–1960* (Urbana, 1982), 70. The hiring of cheap labor was not determined by racial likes and dislikes. Foreigners had many qualities which made them desirable workers, if not desirable neighbors. Their expectations were generally lower than those of American whites and blacks. They lacked the citizenship that could provide the justification for equal rights. A Chicago clothing contractor summed up their virtues: "[T]hese greenhorns, Italian people, Jewish people, all nationalities, they cannot speak English and they don't know where to go and they just came from the old country and I let them work hard, like the devil, and these I get for less wages." Cited in Daniel T. Rodgers, "Tradition, Modernity, and the American Industrial Worker: Reflections and Critique," in Theodore K. Rabb and Robert I. Rotberg, eds., *Industrialization and Urbanization: Studies in Interdisciplinary History* (Princeton, 1981), 229.

69. See Gavin Wright, *Old South, New South: Revolutions in the Southern Economy since the Civil War* (New York, 1986).

70. Ronald L. Lewis, "Job Control and Race Relations in Coal Fields, 1870–1920," *Journal of Ethnic Studies* 12 (Winter 1985), 36

71. Ibid., 7, 29–38, 91–94; Gerber, *Black Ohio,* 282–83; Lawrence Levine, *Black Culture, Black Consciousness: Afro-American Folk Thought from Slavery to Freedom* (New York, 1977), 223–24; see also LeRoi Jones, *Blues People: Negro Music in White America* (New York, 1966).

72. Peter Gottlieb, "Migration and Jobs: The New Black Workers in Pittsburgh, 1916–1930," *Western Pennsylvania Historical Magazine* 61 (Jan. 1978), 1–16.

73. See, for example, James Borchert, *Alley Life in Washington: Family, Community, Religion, and Folklife in the City, 1850–1970* (Urbana, 1980). Borchert sometimes exaggerates the harmony of the lives of the poor, so intent is he on disproving the theory of social disorganization.

74. Alexander Keyssar, *Out of Work: The First Century of Unemployment in Massachusetts* (Cambridge, 1986).

75. "Study of the Relation between Trade Unionism and Colored Workers in Warren, Ohio" (Oct. 1925), p. 2, Labor Union Survey, Box 89, National Urban League Papers, Library of Congress.

76. Cited in Horace R. Cayton and George S. Mitchell, *Black Workers and the New Unions* (Chapel Hill, 1939), 202.

77. George Schuyler, "Reflections on Negro Leadership," *Crisis* 64 (Nov. 1937), 328.

78. The best example of this tendency is Thomas Sowell's *Ethnic America* (New York, 1981). However, scholars with less of an ideological bent also miss broader forces when they study one group, homogenize all others, and treat national changes as background only.

79. Claude McKay to James Weldon Johnson, May 16, 1935, NAACP Papers.

80. Roosevelt used populist ideology to weld the New Deal coalition. During this period, the multi-racial character of much of the new politics was usually stressed by the Left.

81. Cited in Nancy J. Weiss, *Farewell to the Party of Lincoln: Black Politics in the Age of FDR* (Princeton, 1983), 216.

82. Conversely, the paradigms of Afro-American thought have been more closely associated with national culture than those of any other group, except perhaps the earliest English settlers. In contrast, the new immigrant groups, who came to the United States in 1890–1914, were relatively isolated from national thought. They were significant only on the local level. Unlike blacks, specific groups interacted with American culture, if at all, on the plane of local politics, at once a much more isolated and hospitable environment. Immigration was a national issue, but there was no national Polish or Slavic problem. At the national level, specific groups had few defenders but generally racial attacks were on foreigners, not specific nationalities. Their leaders were not integrated in the national or international racial dialogues. Thus, at the Universal Race Congress in London in 1911, W. E. B. Du Bois spoke for blacks, but W. Jeff Lauck, a white Southerner, spoke for immigrants. It is not surprising, therefore, that there was more Afro-American theorizing, by members of the group and others, than for most of the foreign-born groups, although the discussions on immigrations in general was enormous. In the international arena, Jews were closer to blacks than to other immigrants; Israel Zangwill spoke for Jews at the race congress. The sizable number of culturally-assimilated Jewish and Afro-American intellectuals may be one source of both groups' acute self-consciousness in this era of racialist thinking. Both groups, earlier than others, collided with Anglo-Saxon cultural institutions, like universities, in the 1920s. The timing of the emergence of a sizable intelligentsia is an important source of ethnic tradition. Thus, the portrait of the various groups during the 1960s and the 1970s, among other things, reflected the era's official cultural pluralism and politics as much as the history of the group. Ethnicity looked very different to outsiders and insiders during the 1920s. In both cases, the character of the group reflected the larger culture as much as the particularity of the group.

83. For an analysis of these tendencies, with specific reference to sexuality, see Robert A. Padgug, "Sexual Matters: On Conceptualizing Sexuality in History," *Radical History Review* 20 (Spring/Summer, 1979), 3–23.

Anzia Yezierska and the Making of an Ethnic American Self

1. For a discussion of Hawthorne's footprint, see Werner Sollors, "Literature and Ethnicity," in Stephan Thernstrom, Ann Orlov, and Oscar Handlin, eds., *Harvard Encyclopedia of American Ethnic Groups* (Cambridge: Harvard Univ. Press, 1980), 647–65.

2. Anzia Yezierska, *Bread Givers* (1925; New York: Persea Books, 1975), 18. Further references will be made parenthetically to *BG* in the text.

3. Alice Kessler-Harris has been instrumental in the Yezierska revival, providing introductions to *Bread Givers* and *The Open Cage: An Anzia Yezierska Collection* (New York: Persea Books, 1979). Critical works include the following: Babette Inglehart, "Daughters of Loneliness: Anzia Yezierska and the Immigrant Woman Writer," *Studies in American Jewish Literature* 1 (Winter 1975), 1–10; *Studies in American Jewish Literature* 3 (1983), which has articles by Rose Kamel, Ellen Golub, and Susan Hersh Sachs on Yezierska; Sam Girgus's chaper, "'Blut-und-Eisen': Anzia Yezierska and the New Self-made Woman," in his *The New Covenant: Jewish Writers and the American Idea* (Chapel Hill: Univ. of North Carolina Press, 1984), 108–17; and Blanche Gelfant, "Sister to Faust: The City's 'Hungry Woman' as Heroine," *Novel* 15 (1981), 23–38.

4. See my discussion of Yezierska in *Pocahontas's Daughters: Gender and Ethnicity in American Culture* (New York: Oxford Univ. Press, 1986).

5. The best sources for Yezierska's life are Alice Kessler-Harris's two introductions to recent reprints; an afterword by Louise Levitas Henriksen, Yezierska's daughter, to *The Open Cage,* 253–62; Jules Chametzky's entry in *Notable American Women: The Modern Period* (Cambridge, Harvard Univ. Press, 1980), 753–54; and Carol B. Schoen's *Anzia Yezierska* (Boston: Twayne, 1982). A rich but often inaccurate source is Ralda M. Sullivan, "Anzia Yezierska, an American Writer" (Ph.D. diss., Univ. of California, Berkeley, 1975).

6. For discussions of Jewish immigrant fathers and daughters and the patriarchal dimensions of Judaism, see, for instance, Charlotte Baum, Paula Hyman, and Sonya Michel, *The Jewish Woman in America* (New York: Dial Press, 1976); Carolyn Heilbrun, *Reinventing Womanhood* (New York: Norton, 1979); and Norma Fain Pratt, "Jewish American Women through the 1930s," *American Quarterly* 30 (Winter 1978), 681–702.

7. Sonya Michel, "Mothers and Daughters in American Jewish Literature: The Rotted Cord," in Elizabeth Koltun, ed., *The Jewish Woman: New Perspectives* (New York: Schocken, 1976), 272–82.

8. Mary Antin, *The Promised Land* (Boston: Houghton Mifflin, 1912), 163.

9. Yezierska's great-niece, Shana Alexander, makes this point in *Anyone's Daughter* (New York: Viking, 1979), 268–69. Alexander has some interesting personal recollections about Yezierska in this passage.

10. Yezierska, *Children of Loneliness* (New York: Funk and Wagnalls, 1923), 38.

11. Quoted in Sullivan, "Anzia Yezierska," 42. These remarks were made in an interview by Sullivan of Yezierska in 1969. See Clara de Hirsch Home for Immigrant Girls, *Report of Officers* (New York: Press of Philip Cowen, 1901), 53, which describes one resident as "having received through the Educational Alliance a scholarship to the Domestic Science Department of the Teachers College, which will enable her to become a teacher of cooking," and the [*Educational*] *Alliance Review* 1 (Sept. 1901), 183, which describes a cooking class organized by "Miss Hattie Mayer, who is a member of the Clara de Hirsch home."

12. Louise Levitas Henriksen, "Afterword," *The Open Cage*, 258.

13. Rodman was a friend of John Reed and other radicals, a leader of the Liberal Club, and a feminist activist who crusaded for the rights of teachers. She was the model for Floyd Dell's Egeria in *Love in Greenwich Village*. See Sullivan, "Anzia Yezierska," 53–55. On Rodman's life, see, for example, June Sochen, *Movers and Shakers: American Women Thinkers and Activities, 1900–1970* (New York: Quadrangle, 1973).

14. Quoted in Sullivan, "Anzia Yezierska," 64–65. Newspaper accounts of Yezierska's companionate marriage appear in the *New York American* of May 23 and 25, 1911. A letter to *Survey* 30 (April 26, 1913), 150–51, signed Mrs. A. Levitas, describes a plan Yezierska proposed for what sounds like a modern day-care center for the children of "intelligent self-supporting mothers, such as schoolteachers and journalists."

15. William Schack, *Art and Argyrol; The Life and Career of Dr. Albert Barnes* (New York: A. S. Barnes, 1960), 102–3.

16. Yezierska, *Salome of the Tenements* (New York: Boni and Liveright, 1923), 51.

17. Quoted in Jo Ann Boydston, "Introduction," *The Poems of John Dewey*, ed. Jo Ann Boydston (Carbondale: Southern Illinois Univ. Press, 1977), xxxii. Boydston's introduction, ix–lxvii, contains a valuable discussion of the Dewey/Yezierska relationship. Copyright © 1977 by Southern Illinois University Press. Reprinted by permission of the publisher.

18. Yezierska, *Red Ribbon on a White Horse* (1950; New York: Persea Books, 1978), 116. Further references will be made parenthetically to *RR* in the text.

19. Quoted in Sullivan, "Anzia Yezierska," 73, from the 1969 interview.

20. Yezierska, "America and I," in *The Open Cage*, 33.

21. Alice Kessler-Harris, "Introduction," *Bread Givers*, viii.

22. Yezierska, "Children of Loneliness," in *The Open Cage*, 162.

23. Quoted in Sullivan, "Anzia Yezierska," 102, from the 1969 interview.

24. Henriksen, "Afterword," *The Open Cage*, 254.

25. See discussion of reviews in Inglehart, "Daughters of Loneliness," 1–10, and Schoen, *Anzia Yezierska*.

26. From Fisher's notes on the Fisher/Yezierska letters in the Fisher Collec-

tion at the Univ. of Vermont Bailey/Howe Library. All Yezierska/Fisher correspondence quoted is from this collection.

27. Yezierska to Charles Olson, April 1, 1953, Charles Olson Papers, Univ. Library, Univ. of Connecticut.

28. Henriksen, "Afterword," *The Open Cage*, 255–56.

29. Yezierska, "The Immigrant Speaks," *Good Housekeeping*, June 1920, 20–21.

30. Yezierska, "Prophets of Democracy," *The Bookman* 52 (1921), 496–99.

31. Henriksen, "Preface, *Hungry Hearts*, x.

32. Yezierska, "The Love Cheat," *Metropolitan*, July 1923, 54–56, 92–94.

33. Yezierska to Dorothy Canfield Fisher, April 7, 1931.

34. Yezierska to Dorothy Canfield Fisher, April 7, 1932.

35. Yezierska to Mary Austin, December 18, [1922?], Henry E. Huntington Library and Art Gallery.

36. Yezierska to Malcolm Cowley, Aug. 8, 1950, Malcolm Cowley Papers, The Newberry Library.

37. Quoted in Sullivan, "Anzia Yezierska," 55–56.

38. Anna Marcet Haldeman-Julius to Alice Haldeman-Julius, March 28, 1925. Deposited in the Haldeman-Julius Collection, Leonard H. Axe Library, Pittsburg (Kansas) State Univ.

39. "We Can Change Our Noses But Not Our Moses" is in the Anzia Yezierska Collection at the Mugar Memorial Library of Boston Univ.; it is listed as part of the manuscript of *Red Ribbon on a White Horse*. "You Can't Be an Immigrant Twice," an interview of Yezierska by Richard Duffy, appears in *Children of Loneliness*.

40. For the rise of advertising, see, for example, Stuart and Elizabeth Ewen, *Channels of Desire: Mass Images and the Shaping of American Consciousness* (New York: McGraw-Hill, 1982); T. J. Jackson Lears, "From Salvation to Self-Realization: Advertising and the Therapeutic Roots of the Consumer Culture," in Richard Wightman Fox and T. J. Jackson Lears, eds., *The Culture of Consumption: Critical Essays in American History, 1880–1980* (New York: Pantheon, 1983); and Daniel Pope, *The Making of Modern Advertising* (New York: Basic, 1983). Marion Marzolf, "Americanizing the Melting Pot: The Media as Megaphone for the Restrictionists," in Catherine L. Covert and John D. Stevens, eds., *Mass Media between the Wars: Perceptions of Cultural Tension* (Syracuse: Syracuse Univ. Press, 1984), 107–25, analyzes the response of the press and the role of public relations as elements in the move for immigration restriction.

41. Philip Lesly et al., *Public Relations Handbook* (New York: Prentice-Hall, 1950), 4.

42. See Edward L. Bernays, *Public Relations* (Norman: Univ. of Oklahoma Press, 1952).

43. Quoted ibid., 93.

44. Frank Crane, "A Voice from the East Side," *New York Journal American*, Dec. 12, 1920.

45. Carol Easton, *The Search for Sam Goldwyn: A Biography* (New York: William Morrow, 1976), 51.

46. Arthur Marx, *Goldwyn: A Biography of the Man behind the Myth* (New York: Norton, 1976), 98.

47. Edward L. Bernays, *Biography of an Idea: Memoirs of Public Relations Counsel Edward L. Bernays* (New York: Simon and Schuster, 1965), 149–50.

48. Goldwyn did not change his name to disguise his background; his association with a partner, Edgar Selwyn, led others and then himself to conflate their two names. See Marx, Easton, and Philip French, *The Movie Moguls: An Informal History of the Hollywood Tycoons* (Chicago: Henry Regnery, 1969).

49. Quoted in Lary L. May and Elaine Tyler May, "Why Jewish Movie Moguls: An Exploration in American Culture," *American Jewish History* 72 (Sept. 1982), 12. For Jews in Hollywood, see Lary L. May, *Screening Out the Past: The Birth of Mass Culture and the Motion Picture Industry* (New York: Oxford Univ. Press, 1980); Patricia Erens, *The Jew in American Cinema* (Bloomington: Indiana Univ. Press, 1984); Sarah Blacher Cohen, ed., *From Hester Street to Hollywood: The Jewish-American Stage and Screen* (Bloomington: Indiana Univ. Press, 1983); and Lester D. Friedman, *Hollywood's Image of the Jew* (New York: Frederick Ungar, 1982).

50. Mary Roberts Rinehart, *My Story* (New York: Farrar and Rinehart, 1931), 294. Gertrude Atherton, *Adventures of a Novelist* (New York: Liveright, 1932).

51. Yezierska, "This Is What $10,000 Did for Me," *Hearst's International-Companion*, Oct. 1925, 41, 154–56.

52. W. Adolphe Roberts, "Hungry Souls" [review of *Salome of the Tenements*], *New York Tribune*, Dec. 17, 1922.

53. Burton Rascoe, "A Bookman's Day Book," *New York Tribune*, Dec. 31, 1922.

54. Yezierska to Dorothy Canfield Fisher, Aug. 28, 1950.

55. Henriksen, "Afterword," *The Open Cage*, 254–55.

Deviant Girls and Dissatisfied Women

I wish to thank Werner Sollors and Steven Marcus for help, suggestions, and encouragement.

1. William Isaac Thomas, "Life History," ed. Paul Baker, *American Journal of Sociology* 79 (Sept. 1973), 246, my emphasis.

2. W. I. Thomas was born in rural Virginia in 1863 to Sarah Price and Thaddeus Peter Thomas, preacher by vocation and farmer by need. After completing a Ph.D. in classical and modern languages at the University of Tennessee,

Thomas remained at that institution to teach Greek, Latin, French, German, and English for four years. Like many other Americans of his time, he then decided to go to Germany to further his studies. In Berlin and Göttingen he continued to study philology while discovering the new disciplines of ethnology and folk psychology. Upon returning to the United States, he obtained a position at Oberlin College, where his approach began to shift toward comparative literature and where he also read for the first time Herbert Spencer's *Principles of Sociology*. He remained at Oberlin until 1893 when, in a bold decision, he moved to Chicago and enrolled as one of the first graduate students in the newly organized Department of Sociology at the University of Chicago. After completing his doctorate in 1896, Thomas became a professor there. His appointment was abruptly terminated in 1918 when, despite his prominence and seniority, a scandal over his "moral" conduct exiled him from the University of Chicago and relegated him to the margins of sociological research and teaching for the rest of his life. Since this is most of what is known about Thomas's life, it would be euphemism to say that it is scant. Fragments of information may be gathered from a short autobiographical statement that Thomas wrote in 1928, upon Luther L. Bernard's request, as a contribution to a never published "History of Sociology in the United States" (see n. 1). Scarcely more will be found in Morris Janowitz, "Introduction" to W. I. Thomas, *On Social Organization and Social Personality* (Chicago: Univ. of Chicago Press, 1966), ix–xviii, and in "Biographical Note," in Edmund H. Volkart, ed., *Social Behavior and Personality: Contributions of W. I. Thomas to Theory and Social Research* (New York: Social Science Research Council, 1951), 323–24.

3. W. I. Thomas and Florian Znaniecki, *The Polish Peasant in Europe and America*, 5 vols. (Boston: Badger, 1918–20).

4. Robert E. Faris, *Chicago Sociology, 1920–1932* (San Francisco: Chandler, 1967), 17.

5. For an interesting and useful discussion of Chicago urban sociology, see Ulf Hannerz, *Exploring the City: Inquiries toward an Urban Anthropology* (New York: Columbia Univ. Press, 1980), esp. chap. 2. Further secondary references can be found in Lester R. Kurtz, *Evaluating Chicago Sociology: A Guide to the Literature with an Annotated Bibliography* (Chicago: Univ. of Chicago Press, 1984). Two recent publications provide useful discussions and overviews of Chicago literature: Clarence A. Andrews, *Chicago in Story: A Literary History* (Iowa City: Midwest Heritage Publishing Co., 1982), and Carl S. Smith, *Chicago and the American Literary Imagination, 1880–1920* (Chicago: Univ. of Chicago Press, 1984).

6. William Isaac Thomas, *The Unadjusted Girl: With Cases and Standpoint for Behavior Analysis* (Boston: Little, Brown, 1923). All page references are to this edition and, hereafter, are noted in parentheses. At the time when *The Unadjusted Girl* was published, social reform, academic research, and private philanthropy often overlapped. Thomas's study was commissioned and funded

by Mrs. Ethel Dummer, the wife, daughter, and granddaughter of three Chicago bankers. Closely linked with Hull House and many other associations of urban reformers, she was a model of early-twentieth-century liberal philanthropy. Janowitz, "Introduction," xvi. *New York Times*, Feb. 27, 1954.

7. The words are by Michael Parenti, in his insightful "Introduction" to *The Unadjusted Girl*, by William Isaac Thomas, rev. ed. (New York: Harper Torchbooks, 1967).

8. A number of recent discussions have converged to make this project possible. On the one hand there has been a debate over the manufactured and un-"natural" nature of ethnicity and of related concepts. For example, Werner Sollors, in his *Beyond Ethnicity: Consent and Descent in American Culture*, has analyzed two of the most deep-rooted ideas of Western culture—consent and descent—and traced their peregrinations through American culture. By showing that some of the most cherished essences of our culture—love, kinship, ethnicity—are empirically no more tangible than the Ptolemaic system was, Sollors has made those ideas available for rhetorical and symbolic analysis, has shown how they shape people's identities, and has asked that we rethink their cultural and historical nature as they give form to our lives and our representations. Most important for us here, he has gone well outside the boundaries of strictly defined literature in order to discover that historians and sociologists—no less than writers of "fiction"—participate and contribute to the endeavor of imagining and representing both the "ethnic" and the "American" identity. Steven Marcus was one of the first who engaged in the systematic dismantling of the wall that separates different disciplines and forms of writing. With his studies of Victorian sexual culture and, later, of Engels and Freud, Marcus has brought literary analysis closer to cultural studies and has put new written texts under the light of literary criticism, showing the way to scholars who wish to set literary analysis more firmly on historical, social, and cultural grounds. Crucial to the present discussion was also the discovery that within the social and the natural sciences a concerted effort is under way to examine the cultural and literary nature of these disciplines and of their writings. This collective task includes the work of Richard Brown, Robert Nisbet, and Susan Krieger in sociology, of James Clifford and George Marcus in anthropology, of Lawrence Stone, Paul Hernandi, and Hayden White in historiography, and of Nancy Stepan, Sander Gilman, and Donna Haraway in the natural sciences.

See Werner Sollors, *Beyond Ethnicity: Consent and Descent in American Literature* (New York: Oxford Univ. Press, 1986); Steven Marcus, *The Other Victorians: A Study of Sexuality and Pornography in Mid-Nineteenth Century England* (New York: Basic, 1966), *Engels, Manchester and the Working Class* (New York: Random House, 1974), and *Freud and the Culture of Psychoanalysis: Studies in the Transition from Victorian Humanism to Modernity* (Boston: G. Allen and Unwin, 1984); Richard H. Brown, *A Poetic for Sociol-*

ogy: Toward a Logic of Discovery for the Human Sciences (New York: Cambridge Univ. Press, 1977); Robert Nisbet, *Sociology as an Art Form* (New York: Oxford Univ. Press, 1976); Susan Krieger, "Fiction and Social Science," in *The Mirror Dance: Identity in a Women's Community* (Philadelphia: Temple Univ. Press, 1983), 173–97; James Clifford, "On Ethnographic Surrealism," *Comparative Study of Society and History* 23 (1981), 539–64, and "On Ethnographic Authority," *Representations* 1 (1983), 120–43; George E. Marcus and Dick Cushman, "Ethnographies as Texts," *Annual Review of Anthropology* 11 (1982), 25–69; Paul Hernandi, "Re-Presenting the Past: A Note on Narrative Historiography and Historical Drama," *History and Theory* 15 (1976), 45–51; Lawrence Stone, "The Revival of Narrative: Reflections on a New Old History," *Past and Present*, no. 85 (1979), 3–24; Hayden White, *Tropics of Discourse* (Baltimore: Johns Hopkins Univ. Press, 1978); Sander Gilman, *Difference and Pathology: Stereotypes of Sexuality, Race and Madness* (Ithaca: Cornell Univ. Press, 1985); Donna Haraway, "Teddy Bear Patriarchy: Taxidermy in the Garden of Eden, New York City, 1908–1936," *Social Texts* (1985), 20–64; Nancy L. Stepan, "Race and Gender: The Role of Analogy in Science," *Isis* 77 (1986), 261–77.

9. On the origins and development of Thomas's theory of the wishes and of the situation see Kimball Young, "Contributions of William Isaac Thomas to Sociology," *Sociology and Social Research* 47, 4 installments (Oct. 1962, Jan., April, July 1963); Volkart, *Social Behavior*; Janowitz, "Introduction." See also Herbert Blumer, *An Appraisal of Thomas and Znaniecki's "The Polish Peasant in Europe and America"* (New York: Social Science Research Council, 1939).

10. Several human types are determined by this wish. They include not only "the craftsman, the artist, the scientist, the professional man and to some extent the business man" (11) but also the vagabond, the criminal, the thief, the prostitute, the vamp, the charity girl, and the bohemian: in all of these types the desire for new experience is preponderant.

11. The "philistine" and the "miser" exemplify the wish for security.

12. Parental love and sexual love—in the form of courtship, mating, marriage, jealousy, flirting—as well as the love of the woman who is promiscuous but nevertheless not a prostitute all originate in the wish for response.

13. In fictional form, the episode in Richard Wright's autobiography describing his joining the church against his own will, reproduces this same model. Carla Cappetti, "Sociology of an Existence: Richard Wright and the Chicago School," *MELUS* 12. 2 (Summer 1985): 25–43.

14. See Sollors, *Beyond Ethnicity,* esp. 149–73, for a discussion of symbolic kinship and of how romantic love can mediate or polarize ethnic and American identities.

15. Overall, Thomas's representation of the old world is markedly antipastoral. His old world, in fact, finds its closest complement in the work of three

of the most skillful critics of small-town America: Edgar Lee Masters, Sherwood Anderson, and Sinclair Lewis, the writers who most contributed to demythologizing the image of an idyllic preurban America.

16. See Warren Susman's "Culture and Civilization: the Nineteen-twenties," in his *Culture as History* (New York: Pantheon, 1984), 105–21, an essay that provides a useful framework for many of the themes discussed here.

17. A version of this same story appears in *The Rise of David Levinsky* (1917; New York: Harper & Row, 1976), whose author, Abraham Cahan, was the editor of "*Bintl Brief*"—the letters column of the New York Jewish daily *Forward,* from which Thomas drew many of his documents. In a few of Cahan's short stories one can find some of the same concerns that occupy Thomas. The conflict between and the interpenetration of tradition and modernity find a remarkable expression in Cahan's short story "Yekl" (1986).

18. Written by the short-story writer Hutchins Hapgood and quoted as "At Christine's, (Manuscript)."

19. Written at a time when Thomas's work was a typical mixture of biologism, evolutionism, suffragism, and radicalism, "The Mind of Woman" was actually an article published in 1908 in the widely circulated *American Magazine*. That essay and "The Psychology of Woman's Dress," "The Older and Newer Ideals of Marriage," "Votes for Women," and "Women and the Occupations" represent Thomas's early attempts to uncover some of the social and cultural components of women's oppression.

20. Mary J. Deegan and John S. Burger, "W. I. Thomas and Social Reform: His Work and Writings," *Journal of the History of the Behavioral Sciences,* V. 17 (1981), p. 115.

21. Janowitz, "Introduction," xv.

22. Deegan, 115; Janowitz, "Introduction," x, xviii.

23. *New York Times,* April 22, 1918.

24. Janowitz, "Introduction," xiv.

25. Deegan, 118.

26. Janowitz, "Introduction," ix. In his foreword to Volkart's volume, Donald Young has appropriately noted that "the man who established the personal document and the life history as basic sources in social sciences has left no such materials about himself."

27. *New York Times,* April 13, 1918.

28. See J. Edward Chamberlin and Sander L. Gilman, eds., *Degeneration: The Dark Side of Progress* (New York: Columbia Univ. Press, 1985), esp. Robert Nye, "Sociology and Degeneration: The Irony of Progress," 49–71, and Nancy Stepan, "Biology and Degeneration: Races and Proper Places," 97–120.

29. See Stuart Ewen, *Captains of Consciousness: Advertising and the Social Roots of Consumer Culture* (New York: McGraw-Hill, 1976); also Stuart and Elizabeth Ewen, *Channels of Desire: Mass Images and the Shaping of American Consciousness* (New York: McGraw-Hill, 1982).

30. Thomas, "Life History," 250.

31. The German philosopher and literary critic Walter Benjamin was, in a different context but in more or less the same years, also confronting urban modernity. Both were flaneurs of the city. Walter Benjamin strolled the arcades of Paris, the harbor of Marseilles, the courtyards of Naples; Thomas strolled the back alleys of Chicago.

32. Ernest W. Burgess, "William I. Thomas as a Teacher," *Sociology and Social Research* 33 (1918), 760–67.

33. *Bookman*, Oct. 1923, 214.

34. Michel Foucault, "The Life of Infamous Men," in Meaghan Morris and Paul Patton, eds., *Michel Foucault: Power, Truth, Strategy* (Sydney: Feral Publications, 1979), 76.

35. I am referring on the one hand to Julia and Herman Schwendinger, "Sociology's Founding Fathers: Sexist to a Man," *Journal of Marriage and the Family* 33 (Nov. 1971), 783–99, and to Carol Smart, *Women, Crime and Criminology: A Feminist Critique* (London: Routledge & Kegan Paul, 1976), 37–46; on the other to Mary Joe Deegan and John Burger, "William Isaac Thomas and Social Reform: His Work and Writings," *Journal of the History of the Behavioral Sciences* 17 (1981), 114–25, and to Rosalind Rosenberg, *Beyond Separate Spheres: Intellectual Roots of Modern Feminism* (New Haven: Yale Univ. Press, 1982). In these four discussions of Thomas are contained two antithetical positions, both within the framework of a feminist analysis. It may be that if read chronologically the four assessments reflect some aspect of how feminist theory and analysis has evolved since the early seventies.

Ethnic Trilogies

1. The trilogy editions I will rely on here are the following: John Cournos, *The Mask* (London: Methuen, 1919), *The Wall* (London: Methuen, 1921), *Babel* (New York: Boni and Liveright, 1922); Ole Rølvaag, *Giants in the Earth* (New York: Harper, Perennial Library, 1927), first published in Norwegian in 1924 and 1925, *Peder Victorious* (New York: Harper, 1929), *Their Fathers' God* (New York: Harper, 1931); Sophus Keith Winther, *Take All to Nebraska* (New York: Macmillan, 1936), *Mortgage Your Heart* (New York: Macmillan, 1937), *The Passion Never Dies* (New York: Macmillan, 1938); James T. Farrell, *Young Lonigan* (1932), *The Young Manhood of Studs Lonigan* (1934), *Judgment Day* (1935), collected in James T. Farrell, *Studs Lonigan* (New York: New American Library, 1965); Daniel Fuchs, *Three Novels* (New York: Basic, 1961), which includes *Summer in Williamsburg* (1934), *Homage to Blenholt* (1936), *Low Company* (1937); John Dos Passos, *U.S.A.* (New York: Modern

Library, 1938), which contains *The 42nd Parallel* (1930), *1919* (1932), and *The Big Money* (1936); August Derleth whose long series of novels set in "Sac Prairie" includes, among others, *Wind Over Wisconsin* (New York: Scribner's 1938), *Restless Is the River* (New York: Scribner's, 1939), *Shadow of Night* (New York: Scribner's, 1943); William Carlos Williams, *White Mule* (New York: New Directions, 1967; originally pub. 1937), *In the Money* (Harmondsworth: Penguin Books, 1972; originally pub. 1940), *The Build-Up* (New York: New Directions, 1952); Pietro Di Donato, *Christ in Concrete* (Indianapolis and New York: Bobbs-Merrill, 1939), *This Woman* (New York: Ballantine Books, 1958), *Three Circles of Light* (New York: Ballantine Books, 1960); Vilhelm Moberg, *The Emigrants*, trans. Gustaf Lannestock (New York: Popular Library, 1951), originally published in Swedish in 1949; *Unto a Good Land* (New York: Popular Library, 1954), in Swedish in 1952; *The Settlers* (New York: Popular Library, 1961), in Swedish in 1956; *Last Letter Home* (New York: Popular Library, 1961), in Swedish in 1959. This list of trilogies is by no means complete. For example, Dos Passos, Farrell, and even Derleth went on to write other trilogies or sagas.

2. T. S. Eliot, "The Waste Land," in *Selected Poems* (New York: Harbrace Paperbound Library, 1964).

3. For a general reference on modernism, I refer the reader to *Modernism*, ed. Malcolm Bradbury and James McFarlane (Harmondsworth: Penguin Books, 1976); Jürgen Schramke, *Teoria del romanzo contemporaneo*, trans. Cinzia Romani [original title *Zur Theorie des modernen Romans*, 1974] (Naples: Liguori Editore, 1980); Georg Lukács, *Realism in Our Time*, trans. J. and N. Mander (New York: Harper Torchbooks, 1971).

4. See Georg Lukács, "The Ideology of Modernism," *Realism in Our Time*, 34; Austin M. Wright, *The Formal Principle in the Novel* (Ithaca: Cornell Univ. Press, 1982), esp. chap. 5; Patricia D. Tobin, *Time and the Novel* (Princeton: Princeton Univ. Press, 1978), esp. the introd. I am particularly indebted to the last two for key ideas in my essay.

5. By "isotopy" is meant a semantic unity (a homogeneous level of meaning) that organizes one's interpretative journey in a text; it defines a level of coherence. See Jonathan Culler, *Structural Poetics* (Ithaca: Cornell Univ. Press, 1977), 79–83.

6. This phrase alludes to the title of Irving Howe's *World of Our Fathers* (New York: Simon and Schuster, 1976).

7. For the consequences of this metacultural dynamic, see my essay "The Brave New World of Immigrant Autobiography," in Marc Chenetier and Rob Kroes, eds., *Impressions of a Gilded Age: The American Fin de Siècle* (Amsterdam: Amerika Instituut, Universiteit van Amsterdam, 1983).

8. Henry Adams, *The Education of Henry Adams* (Boston: Houghton Mifflin, 1974), 238.

9. *The Build-Up*, 333, 308, respectively.

10. Quoted in Kenneth Silverman, *The Life and Times of Cotton Mather* (New York: Columbia Univ. Press, Morningside Books, 1985), 420.

11. *The Build-Up*, 244.

12. For a further discussion of the type of "procedural approach" I am suggesting here, see Robert de Beaugrande and Wolfgang Dressler, eds., *Introduction to Text Linguistics* (London: Longmans, 1981), chap. 3.

13. By "paradigmatic level" I am referring to the virtual, formal, and semantic similarities that exist among ethnic trilogies and that allow one to speak of these texts as a semiotic unity superior to any single trilogy manifestation. One should not look for an exact correspondence between the three narrative paradigms that define the objective possibilities of ethnic-trilogy poetics and the three volumes of a trilogy. The paradigms are metatextual. But it is only at the level of the fully elaborated ethnic-trilogy program that one can properly evaluate the extent to which individual works (whether a single text, a tetralogy, or even a longer narrative series) have invested—in both intensional and extensional terms—in what for procedural reasons I have called an ethnic-trilogy poetics.

14. The phrase "actantial roles" refers to the set of actions or narrative predicates that characters have in common: a "chronotopy" is, in the Bachtinian sense, a single controlling time/space nexus that unites form and content into a single narrative regime. See Michail Bachtin, *Estetica e romanzo,* translated from the Russian by Clara Strada Janovic (Turin: Einaudi, 1980), 231ff.

15. For a theory of modal analysis, see A. J. Greimas, *Du Sens II* (Paris: Éditions du Seuil, 1983), 67–102. By "modalization" is meant "a modification of the predicate by the subject." The identification of a dominant modality refers to the hierarchy of modes and not to their mutual exclusion. Thus, other modalities (*devoir, savoir, pouvoir,* and so on) can still operate while being subordinate to a dominant one.

16. *Giants in the Earth*, 32.

17. *Christ in Concrete*, 15.

18. *The Settlers*, 9.

19. *The Mask*, 102–3.

20. *Take All to Nebraska*, 279.

21. See Boelhower, "The Immigrant Novel as Genre," *MELUS* 8, no. 1 (Spring 1981), 3–13.

22. *Homage to Blenholt*, 205.

23. *Summer in Williamsburg*, 59.

24. *Mortgage Your Heart*, 28.

25. *The Wall*, 32.

26. Ibid., 52.

27. *Summer in Williamsburg*, 13.

28. *This Passion Never Dies*, 276–77.

29. *The Wall*, 256.

30. *The Mask*, 1, 5–6.

31. I am referring to the philosophical position that has its roots in the thought of Heidegger and Nietzsche; see Gianni Vattimo and Pier Aldo Rovatti, eds., *Il pensiero debole* (Milan: Feltrinelli, 1983).

32. See Yosef Hayim Yerushalmi, *Zakhor* (Parma: Pratiche Editrice, 1983).

33. *Summer in Williamsburg*, 51.

34. *Babel*, 385.

35. *The Mask*, 31.

36. *Summer in Williamsburg*, 247.

37. *Their Fathers' God*, 338.

38. Ibid., 207.

39. Ibid., 210.

Blood in the Marketplace

1. It is not unreasonabale to assume that Puzo derived his emphasis on the familial aspect of the Mafia from the reports of Joseph Valachi, whose Senate hearings were in 1963 and whose book came out in 1967. In *The Italians,* itself a nonfiction leading seller of 1964, Luigi Barzini summarized how Valachi's testimony reshaped common American ideas about organized crime:

> The convicted American gangster, Joseph Valachi . . . explained the facts of life of the Sicilian village, probably as old as Mediterranean civilization, the principles guiding Homeric kings and heroes in their decisions, to a Senate committee and an awestruck twentieth-century television audience. He patiently pointed out that an isolated man was a dead duck in the American underworld; that he had to belong to a family, his own, or one which accepted him; that families were gathered in alliances, and the alliances in a loose federation called *Cosa Nostra,* governed by an unwritten code.

Luigi Barzini, *The Italians* (New York: Bantam, 1965), 284.

Puzo may have derived his view of the Mafia, then, not only from his Hell's Kitchen experience but from Valachi, either directly or through Barzini's explication (Don Corleone's biggest competitor is named Barzini). But if Valachi first introduced the notion of family crime, and Barzini explicated it, it was Puzo who made the symbol ubiquitous.

2. The preceding two quotations are from John G. Cawelti, *Adventure, Mystery, Romance: Formula Stories as Art and Popular Culture* (Chicago: Univ. of Chicago Press, 1976), 78. The tandem reappears in John Sutherland's *Bestsellers* and in essays by Fredric Jameson and Eric Hobsbawm. E. J. Hobsbawm, "Robin Hoodo: A Review of Mario Puzo's *The Sicilian,*" *New York Review of Books,* Feb. 14, 1985, 12–17; Fredric Jameson, "Reification and Utopia in Mass Culture," *Social Text* 1 (1979), 130–48; John Sutherland, *Bestsellers: Popular Fiction of the 1970s* (London: Routledge & Kegan Paul, 1981), chap. 3.

3. Jameson, "Reification and Utopia," 146.

4. Puzo's own, scattered comments on the social realities behind *The Godfather* reveal little. In an interview, he emphasizes that the novel was meant to be not realistic but romantic: "To me *The Godfather* isn't an exposé; it's a romantic novel." As quoted by Tom Buckley, "The Mafia Tries a New Tune," *Harper's,* Aug. 1971, 54. In *The Godfather Papers,* Puzo claims to have written the novel "entirely from research," then testifies that actual mafiosi found his fictional depictions very true to life. Mario Puzo, *The Godfather Papers and Other Confessions* (New York: Putman, 1972), 35.

5. Puzo's autobiographical novel, *The Fortunate Pilgrim* (1964), seems on its surface to exemplify the long-standing tradition of interpreting Italian-American familialism as a barrier to mobility. One reviewer wrote, "The writer renders with fidelity the life-style of an Italian-American community in which Old Country values of propriety, order and obedience to established authority collide with New World ambition, initiative, and disdain for tradition." Sheldon Grebstein, "Mama Remembered the Old Country," *Saturday Review,* Jan. 23, 1965, 44. Yet, I would argue, the novel harbors a countervailing analysis, demonstrating how the Puzo family used traditional values to ensure a steadily progressive mobility, culminating in Mario's freedom to become a writer.

6. Herbert J. Gans, *Urban Villagers: Group and Class in the Life of Italian-Americans* (New York: Free Press, 1962); Virginia Yans-McLaughlin, *Family and Community: Italian Immigrants in Buffalo, 1880–1930* (Ithaca: Cornell Univ. Press, 1977); Thomas Kessner, *The Golden Door: Italian and Jewish Immigrant Mobility in New York City, 1880–1915* (New York: Oxford Univ. Press, 1977); Thomas Sowell, *Ethnic America* (New York: Basic, 1981).

Most Italian immigrants to the United States originated from the *Mezzogiorno,* the regions of Italy south and east of Naples, including Sicily. The traditional view of Italian-American ethnicity is extrapolated from several very well known, mid- to late-twentieth-century studies of southern Italy: Phyllis H. Williams, *South Italian Folkways in Europe and America: A Handbook for Social Workers, Visiting Nurses, Schoolteachers, and Physicians* (New Haven: Yale Univ. Press, 1938); Carlo Levi, *Christ Stopped at Eboli,* trans. Frances Frenaye (New York: Farrar, Straus & Giroux, 1947); Edward Banfield, *Moral Basis of a Backward Society* (New York: Free Press, 1958); and Ann Cornelisen, *Women of the Shadows* (New York: Dell, 1976). These essays prompted American social workers like Leonard Covello and scholars like Herbert Gans, Rudolph Vecoli, Thomas Sowell, Thomas Kessner, and Virginia Yans-McLaughlin to adopt a variant on the "culture of poverty" argument for blue-collar Italian Americans, although Cornelisen, for one, warns against approaches based on "residual vestiges of peasant mentality." Cornelisen, *Women of the Shadows,* 220.

For an overview of traditional scholarship on Italian-Americans, including an analysis of its limitations, see Micaela di Leonardo, *The Varities of Ethnic Experience: Kinship, Class, and Gender among California Italian-Americans* (Ithaca: Cornell Univ. Press, 1984), 17–25, 96–108.

7. Leonard Covello, "The Influence of Southern Italian Family Mores upon the School Situation in America," in Francesco Cordasco and Eugene Bucchioni, eds., *The Italians: Social Backgrounds of an American Group* (Clifton, N.J.: Kelley, 1974), 516. Covello's extremely influential essay was originally written as a dissertation in 1944 and finally published as *The Social Background of the Italo-American School Child: A Study of the Southern Italian Family Mores and Their Effect on the School Situation in Italy and America* (Totowa, N.J.: Rowman & Littlefield, 1972).

8. Francis A. J. Ianni, with Elizabeth Reuss-Ianni, *A Family Business: Kinship and Social Control in Organized Crime* (New York: Russell Sage Foundation, 1972), 55. Ianni notes that "the acculturation process works in crime as elsewhere" (61), but nonetheless traces the familial structure of the Luppollo syndicate back to Italy: "The origins of this familialism are Italian and not American" (155).

The urgency to place the Mafia along an Old World–New World continuum resurfaces in the work of the historian Humbert S. Nelli, who adopts the opposite position from Ianni's. Nelli concedes the "group unity" and "cooperative effort" of Italian-American mobs, but stresses almost entirely the individualism and "American way of life" of the gang leaders. See Humbert S. Nelli, *The Business of Crime: Italians and Syndicate Crime in the United States* (Chicago: Univ. of Chicago Press, 1976), 255–57.

Scholars of the Mafia in southern Italy also insist on the evolving interdependence of familial and/or fraternal organization and capitalist enterprise. The Italian Mafia in recent years is thought to have been restructured in imitation of the Italian-American Mafia. See Pino Arlacchi, *Mafia Business: The Mafia Ethic and the Spirit of Capitalism*, trans. Martin Ryle (New York: Schocken, 1986); Anton Blok, *The Mafia of a Sicilian Village, 1860–1960: A Study of Violent Peasant Entrepreneurs*, with a foreword by Charles Tilly (New York: Harper & Row, 1975); and E. J. Hobsbawm, *Primitive Rebels: Studies in Archaic Forms of Social Movement in the 19th and 20th Centuries*, 2d ed. (New York: Praeger, 1963), chap. 3.

9. Eli Zaretsky, *Capitalism, the Family, and Personal Life* (New York: Harper & Row, 1976). Zaretsky's small book, little known, is an extraordinarily lucid reappraisal, spanning several centuries, of the relation between Western family structure and capitalism.

10. For a review essay on what I am calling the new ethnic theory, consult Werner Sollors, "Theory of American Ethnicity, or: "? S ETHNIC?/TI AND AMERICAN/TI, DE OR UNITED (W) STATES S S1 AND THEOR?" *American Quarterly* 33 (Bibliography, 1981), 257–83. I am myself indebted to this article for bringing Abner Cohen, among others, to my attention.

The rise of the new ethnicity, as represented in the work of Michael Novak, Peter Schrag, Richard Gambino, even Glazer and Moynihan, has prompted severely critical responses, primarily from the political Left. Typically, the work of the ethnic demythologizers challenges the romance of ethnicity either by dismissing ethnic cultural difference altogether or by reducing difference to a variable entirely dependent upon *class*. In Stephen Steinberg's *The Ethnic Myth*, ethnicity is, for all explanatory purposes, entirely discounted. In Herbert Gans's very influential work, family values are interpreted as the product of working-class status and are hence "pan-ethnic," shared by blue-collar folk of all backgrounds, whereas the ethnicity of the middle class is what Gans calls "symbolic," meaning that it is private, a matter of individual identity and friendship without socioeconomic significance. Tellingly, Gans says middle-class ethnicity is "cost-free" without inquiring into its profitability; the middle-class family is implicated in capitalism, once again, only as a buffer or safety valve for the system. See Steinberg, *The Ethnic Myth: Race, Ethnicity, and Class in America* (New York: Atheneum, 1981); Gans, "Symbolic Ethnicity: The Future of Ethnic Groups and Cultures in America," in Herbert J. Gans et al., eds., *On the Making of Americans: Essays in Honor of David Riesman* (Philadelphia: Univ. of Pennsylvania Press, 1979); Gans, foreword to Neil C. Sandberg, *Ethnic Identity and Assimilation* (New York: Praeger, 1974).

11. The quote is from Abner Cohen, *Two-Dimensional Man: An Essay on the Anthropology of Power and Symbolism in Complex Society* (Berkeley: Univ. of California Press, 1974), 99. See also Abner Cohen, "Introduction" to *Urban Ethnicity*, ed. A. Cohen (London: Tavistock, 1974), ix–xxiv.

Major critical efforts to reconceive ethnic literature in the light of new ideas about ethnicity include William Boelhower, *Through a Glass Darkly: Ethnic Semiosis in American Literature* (Venice: Edizioni Helvetia, 1984); Jules Chametzky, *Our Decentralized Literature: Cultural Mediations in Selected Jewish and Southern Writers* (Amherst: Univ. of Massachusetts Press, 1986); Mary V. Dearborn, *Pocahontas's Daughters: Gender and Ethnicity in American Culture* (New York: Oxford Univ. Press, 1986); and Werner Sollors, *Beyond Ethnicity: Consent and Descent in American Culture* (New York: Oxford Univ. Press, 1986).

12. Rose Basile Green, *The Italian-American Novel: A Document of the Interaction of Two Cultures* (Rutherford, N.J.: Fairleigh Dickinson Univ. Press, 1974), 355, 357, 364.

For a brief yet elegant discussion of *The Godfather*, in the context of an overview of Italian-American literature, see Robert Viscusi, "*De Vulgari Eloquentia*: An Approach to the Language of Italian American Fiction," *Yale Italian Studies* 1 (Winter 1981), 21–38. Implicitly challenging traditional accounts of ethnic literature, Viscusi acknowledges the inventive role of the imagination in the creation of a post-European ethnic culture. His language-oriented approach is itself calculated to invent terms in which we might appreciate a previously ignored literature. By emphasizing the linguistic savvy of Italian-American writing, Viscusi means to present this literature in the strongest possible light, given the bias toward language of the journal sponsoring his essay and, more important, of the critical community it represents. Whereas Viscusi's highly "literary" approach seems to have nothing whatsoever to do with business, is it a coincidence that the most important property he attributes to Italian-American literature is its ability to "be *diplomatic,* to *negotiate* the terms on which Italian America can exist" (emphasis mine)?

13. Mario Puzo, *The Godfather* (New York: Putnam, 1969), 216. Further references to this edition are given in parentheses in the text.

14. Cohen, "Introduction," xvii.

15. Peter Dobkin Hall, "Marital Selection and Business in Massachusetts Merchant Families, 1700–1900," in Michael Gordon, ed., *The American Family in Social-Historical Perspective,* 2d ed. (New York: St. Martin's, 1978), 101–14.

For other discussions of ethnicity, economics, and ethnic businesses, see Ivan H. Light, *Ethnic Enterprise in America: Business and Welfare among Chinese, Japanese, and Blacks* (Berkeley: Univ. of California Press, 1972); John Bodnar, Roger Simon, and Michael P. Weber, *Lives of Their Own: Blacks, Italians, and Poles in Pittsburgh, 1900–1960*; Thomas Sowell, *Race and Economics* (New York: McKay, 1975).

16. Ianni, *A Family Business,* 157.

17. Ibid., 64–65, 92, 116–18.

18. The don reminds Tom of his real background, less to take away from the meaning of Tom's initiation into the don's nuclear family than to highlight, by contrast, that meaning. Tom's marriage to an Italian-American, like his adoption by Don Corleone, constitutes a rebirth as an Italian-American on his wedding day.

19. There is much excess baggage in this sprawling, desperately populist novel: great detail on postures of war between the families, which Sutherland deviously and persuasively attributes to Puzo's reaction to World War II (*Bestsellers,* 45); well-stroked portrayals of the making of the Corleone soldiers, including Rocco Lampone, Luca Brasi, and the ex-cop Albert Neri; speculations in the *National Enquirer* vein into the activities, both private and public, of Frank Sinatra and friends; painfully unnecessary excursions into the sexual lives of Sonny, his mistress Lucy Mancini, and Dr. Jules Segal. In my experience teaching the novel, the reactions to these tangents vary. Sinatra merits a passing interest, the sex lives of Sonny and the doctor hardly any at all. The passages that chronicle the making of McCluskey the bad cop and Neri the enforcer are avidly read; similar chronicles become hallmarks of the Mafia genre subsequently. In *The Godfather,* the tangents do not so much detract from the main narrative as fill it out during its middle stretches, sustaining interest while holding final revelations in abeyance.

20. "The visual scheme is based on the most obvious life-and-death contrasts; the men meet and conduct their business in deep-toned, shuttered rooms, lighted by lamps even in the daytime, and the story moves back and forth between the hidden, nocturnal world and the sunshine that they share with the women and children." Pauline Kael, "Alchemy: A Review of Francis Ford Coppola's *The Godfather,*" *New Yorker,* March 18, 1972, 132.

21. "The novel is a tale of family succession, showing the rise of the true son and heir and reaching a climax with his acceptance of the power and responsibilities of Godfather. It tells how Michael Corleone comes to understand his father's character and destiny and then allows himself to be shaped by that same destiny." Cawelti, *Adventure, Mystery, Romance* 52–53.

In his review of the first *Godfather* film for *Commentary,* William S. Pechter was perhaps the first critic to emphasize that while the icon of "the Godfather" meant Don Vito Corleone, the narrative belonged to Michael:

> What is the family whose claims override all others in *The Godfather*? It is, for one thing, a patriarchy, and the story the film has to tell is basically not Don Corleone's but Michael's: a story of his initiation into the family by an act of murder, of the succession of the youngest, most assimilated son to the patriarchal powers and responsibilities and the ethnic mystique of his father.

Pechter, "Keeping Up with the Corleones," *Commentary* 54 (July 1972), 89.

22. "[The southern Italian peasant] despised as a *scomunicato* (pariah) anyone in any family who broke the ordine della famiglia or otherwise violated the *onore* (honor, solidarity, tradition, 'face') of the family." Richard Gambino, *Blood of My Blood: The Dilemma of the Italian-Americans* (Garden City, N.Y.: Doubleday, 1974), 4.

23. Mary Antin wrote in 1912, "I was born, I have lived, and I have been made over. . . . Did I not become the parent and they [her parents] the children, in those relations of teacher and learner?" Antin, *The Promised Land* (Boston: Houghton Mifflin, 1912), xii. In 1981, Richard Rodriguez echoed Antin's Emersonian image of self-birth, in an aside to "my parents—who are no longer my parents, in a cultural sense." Rodriguez, *Hunger of Memory: The Education of Richard Rodriguez* (Boston: Godine, 1981), 4.

24. Claude Brown reports that "godfather" ranks among the most popular handles, or nicknames, of black inner-city America. *New York Times Magazine,* Sept. 16, 1984, 38. I have a suspicion that *The Godfather* is also a secret vice for very different segments of American society. More than one professor of English has confessed that Puzo may, after all, have some considerable gifts. A black woman, also an English professor, told me she had read the novel five times and once saw the film at a theater three days in a row! I hope, by explaining my own fascination with the text, I do not deprive others of the mystique of a favorite vice.

It is also a wonderful fact, without being a coincidence, that Puzo's major project after *The Godfather* screenplays was scripting *Superman: The Movie* and *Superman II.* For what is the story of Superman if not a meta-narrative of immigration, about a refugee whose power derives from his dislocation, whose secret identity is hidden under a disabling Anglo-conformity (as Clark Kent), but whose true promise is revealed in his fight "for truth, justice, and the American way"? And who, conversely, is Don Corleone if not the latest in a

continuing series of ethnic supermen? For a discussion of superman imagery in the context of American ethnicity, consult Sollors, *Beyond Ethnicity,*
chap. 3.

25. "The Making of *The Godfather,*" *Time,* March 13, 1972, 61. By 1980,
reports John Sutherland, *The Godfather*'s publishers were claiming worldwide
sales of fifteen million. The title Sutherland gives the novel, "the bestseller of
bestsellers," echoes nicely the Sicilian phrase for the boss of bosses, *capo di
tutti capi.* Certainly, no other contemporary work has sold as well. How one
compares a present-day popular novel with, say, *Gone with the Wind* or *Uncle
Tom's Cabin* is no easy matter. Sutherland, *Bestsellers,* 38, 46.

26. For a review of the Mafia literature from 1969 to 1975, see Dwight C.
Smith, Jr., "Sons of the Godfather: 'Mafia' in Contemporary Fiction," *Italian
Americana* 2 (Spring 1976), 191–207; the statistical reference is from p. 192. A
shorter bibliography appears in Cawelti, *Adventure, Mystery, Romance,* 304n.

27. In Jameson's view ("Reification and Utopia," 145), the butchery of the
Corleones symbolizes the "wanton ecocidal and genocidal violence" of capitalism in America. Cawelti adds (*Adventure, Mystery, Romance,* 78), "I suspect there is a definite relation between the fascination with limitless criminal
power . . . and the public's reluctant awareness of the uncontrollable power of
violence in the hands of the government."

28. Jameson, "Reification and Utopia," 146; Cawelti, *Adventure, Mystery,
Romance,* 78.

29. "At a time when the disintegration of the dominant communities is persistently 'explained' in the (profoundly ideological) terms of the deterioration
of the family, the growth of permissiveness and the loss of authority of the
father, the ethnic group can seem to project an image of social reintegration by
way of the patriarchal and authoritarian family of the past." Jameson, "Reification and Utopia," 146–47.

30. Well into the seventies, even after the rise of the new ethnicity, it was
conventional to attribute the poor performance of Italian-Americans in the
professions, the arts, the American Catholic church, politics, and big business
to the tenacity of familial values and southern Italian culture. In the last few
years, however, the conspicuous rise of Italian-Americans has reversed the
age-old formula. Stephen S. Hall wrote in a 1983 cover story for the Sunday
New York Times Magazine:

> Is there a single thread that runs through all these [stories of suc-
> cessful Italian-Americans]? If anything, it is the unusual propen-
> sity to merge, rather than separate, the professional and the per-
> sonal. Borrowing from a culture in which the extended family can
> easily include 30 to 40 "close" relatives, Italians thrive on com-
> munity. They are accustomed to large numbers of people, and they
> seem to have developed an emotional facility in dealing with them.

Even in large companies, they have a knack for keeping things on a human scale. "The professional community," explains one Italian-American psychotherapist, "becomes the next family."

Hall, "Italian-Americans: Coming Into Their Own," *New York Times Magazine*, May 15, 1983, 29.

31. It is amusing to speculate how Puzo's usage of ethnicity in his career as a writer parallels, broadly speaking, the usage of ethnicity depicted in his novels. Puzo began his career in the now venerable fashion of aspiring American literati, with a novelistic account of his years as an expatriate (in postwar Germany), *The Dark Arena* (1955). Only subsequently did he specialize in ethnic narrative and become known as a specifically Italian-American writer. With *The Fortunate Pilgrim* (1964), Puzo was able to promote himself as an earnest realist, little known but "serious," as if Italian-American writers toiled honestly on the margins of the American literary community just as their characters worked on the margins of the American economy. With *The Godfather* (1969) and its offspring, Puzo launched himself on a career as both a popular novelist and a Hollywood screenwriter, exploiting ethnic materials for power and profit, as if in faint imitation of the exploitation of family and ethnicity by his Mafia characters.

32. Jameson, "Reification and Utopia," 145.

33. Pauline Kael, "Fathers and Sons," *New Yorker*, Dec. 23, 1974, 64.

34. Francis Coppola, as quoted by William S. Pechter, "Godfather II," *Commentary* 59 (March 1975), 79.

35. "Many people who saw 'The Godfather' developed a romantic identification with the Corleones; they longed for the feeling of protection that Don Vito conferred on his loving family. Now that the full story has been told, you'd have to have an insensitivity bordering on moral idiocy to think that the Corleones have a wonderful life, which you'd like to be part of." Pauline Kael, "Fathers and Sons," 64. See also her review of the first film: Kael, "Alchemy," 132–44.

36. Jameson, "Reification and Utopia," 147.

37. Isaac Rosenfeld, "David Levinsky: The Jew as American Millionaire," in Abraham Chapman, ed., *Jewish-American Literature: An Anthology* (New York: New American Library, 1974), 619.

38. Pechter, "Godfather II," 79.

39. Stanley Kauffmann, "On Films," *New Republic*, April 1, 1972, 26.

40. Pechter, "Godfather II," 80. Pechter, furthermore, is the only critic I know who prefers the first film to the second, and the only one to recognize the retrospective romanticization of *Godfather II*. He emphasizes how "the schematic ironies of Part II—that Michael's fall should parallel his father's rise—dictate that the young Vito Corleone be glorified (as a pre-organization-man gallant bandit) far beyond any such romanticization in part one." I would stress less the explicit romance of Vito as bandit than the implicit romance of

the more mature Vito's family. The precondition to Michael's fall is a state of grace, represented not by young Vito but by the Corleone family of his youth.

41. Richard Condon, *Prizzi's Honor* (New York: Coward, McCann & Geoghegan, 1982), 11–12. Further references to this edition are given in parentheses in the text.

42. [Puzo uses the term *consigliori,* with an "o" and an "i," throughout *The Godfather*; Condon spells it *"consigliere,"* with the "e"s, in the Italian fashion. Condon's spelling seems to be much the more common usage.] Both authors liberally spray italicized words throughout their novels, in a long-standing tradition of ethnic representation. Condon uses even more Italian terms than Puzo (Charley is always cooking up something) and takes care to spell correctly in (western) Sicilian dialect. This is another instance of Condon's fine-tuning of Puzo's detail.

43. Don Corrado, Angelo Partanna, and Vincent Prizzi are all widowers (exceedingly strange, in a world in which men kill men, that these three have outlived their womenfolk). Eduardo takes mistresses but does not marry. And Charley, who lost his mother as a child, is a bachelor pressing fifty. These men "mother" each other, incorporating the female realm into the male, the personal into the professional. "[Angelo] swore to God he didn't know how Charley did it. 'I'm telling you, Charley, I close my eyes and and I think your mother cooked this.'" Appropriately enough, the one significant Prizzi female, Maerose (the only Prizzi who cooks better than Charley), is an outcast. Exiled, Maerose spends the course of the novel conniving to be forgiven for her sins and readmitted to the family.

44. I am quoting the blurb from the 1985 movie tie-in paperback edition: Richard Condon, *Prizzi's Honor* (New York: Bantam, 1986).

45. It is preposterous that Irene could keep the money from the Las Vegas scam, not to mention her life. It is also preposterous that Charley would not imagine Irene's participation, especially after learning the nature of her profession. The novel assumes that Charley is willing to cover for Irene; the film supposes that Irene lies to Charley and that Charley is so in love that he is willing to take her word.

46. Operating within the mob's sphere of influence, never mind subcontracts, is tricky business. As Barzini paraphrases Valachi, "An isolated man was a dead duck in the American underworld; . . . he had to belong to a family, his own, or one which accepted him." Barzini, *The Italians,* 284. Henry Hill's autobiography, written with Nicholas Pileggi and entitled *Wiseguy,* could restore the image of the mob outlaw to respectability.

List of Contributors

Editor

WERNER SOLLORS is a Professor of American Literature and Language and of Afro-American Studies at Harvard University. Among his publications are the books *Amiri Baraka/LeRoi Jones: The Quest for a "Populist Modernism"* (1978) and *Beyond Ethnicity: Consent and Descent in American Culture* (1986) as well as contributions to the *Harvard Encyclopedia of American Ethnic Groups, Reconstructing American Literary History,* and the *Columbia Literary History of the United States* and to such periodicals as *Prospects, In Their Own Words, Massachusetts Review,* and *American Quarterly.* He has edited the two-volume *Bibliographic Guide to Afro-American Studies* and coedited (with Thomas A. Underwood and Caldwell Titcomb) *Varieties of Black Experience at Harvard* (1986). He is currently at work on a study entitled "Intermarriage and the Mulatto in Western Culture," to be published by Oxford University Press.

Contributors

WILLIAM BOELHOWER teaches at the University of Trieste; his scholarly work includes translations of the writings of Antonio Gramsci and Lucien Goldman as well as the books *Immigrant Autobiography in the United States* (1982) and *Through a Glass Darkly: Ethnic Semiosis in American Literature* (1987). He is editor of the European journal of American ethnic studies, *In Their Own Words.*

ALIDE CAGIDEMETRIO is a member of the faculty of the Anglo-American Literature Department at the University of Venice and has published the books *Una strada nel bosco: Scrittura e coscienza in Djuna Barnes* (1980) and *Verso il West: L'autobiografia dei pionieri americani* (1983) as well as studies of James Fenimore Cooper, Louisa May Alcott, Henry James, Gertrude Stein, James Purdy, and Robert Coover.

BOB CALLAHAN is a poet and publisher. His column, "Shelf Life," appears in the San Francisco *Examiner.* He is the editor of *Callahan's Irish Quarterly* and of *Spunk: The Selected Short Stories of Zora Neale Hurston* (1985).

CARLA CAPPETTI is an Assistant Professor of English at the City College of the City University of New York and has published on Richard Wright and the Federal Writers' Project. Her essay is part of her Columbia University dissertation, "Urbanism as a Way of Writing."

KATHLEEN NEILS CONZEN is a member of the history faculty at the University of Chicago, where she teaches American urban and social history. She is the author of *Immigrant Milwaukee, 1836–1860* (1976) and various articles on urban and ethnic history. She is currently completing a book-length study of German peasant communities in frontier Minnesota.

MARY V. DEARBORN is currently a Mellon Fellow in the Humanities at Columbia University. She is the author of *Pocahontas's Daughters: Gender and Ethnicity in American Culture* (1986).

THOMAS J. FERRARO, an Assistant Professor in the English Department at Duke University, formerly taught American literature at the University of Geneva. "Blood in the Marketplace" is excerpted from his Yale University dissertation, "Ethnic Passages: Studies in Twentieth-Century American Narrative."

ANDREW HOPE is a Tlingit Big Man and a poet. He is the director of the Sitka Community Association. He is also the editor of the *Raven's Bones Journal.*

ALBERT MURRAY, a Tuskegee graduate and retired Air Force major, is the author of the novel *Train Whistle Guitar* and the books *South to a Very Old Place, The Omni-Americans, The Hero and the Blues, Stomping the Blues,* and, most recently, *Good Morning Blues: The Autobiography of Count Basie.* He is currently at work on a new novel.

ISHMAEL REED is the author of two books of essays, four books of poetry, and the seven novels *The Free-Lance Pallbearers, Yellow Back Radio Broke-Down, Mumbo Jumbo, The Last Days of Louisiana Red, Flight to Canada, The Terrible Twos*, and, most recently, *Reckless Eyeballing*. He is also the director of I. Reed Books and copublisher of *Quilt* magazine.

RICHARD RODRIGUEZ is a writer and journalist living in San Francisco. In 1982, he published *Hunger of Memory*—a description of a life experienced through language. His second book is about the memory of Mexico in California.

JUDITH STEIN is Professor of History at the City College of the City University of New York. She is the author of *The World of Marcus Garvey: Race and Class in Modern Society* (1986) and is working on a book on class and race relations in the twentieth century.

SHAWN WONG teaches at the University of Washington at Seattle. His novel *Homebase*, published by I. Reed Books, was the first novel by a Chinese-American male to be published in the United States.

Index